"Evangelism, for certain, is an exercise of the mind. You have to know the gospel to share the gospel. But, even more, evangelism is an exercise of the heart. Few people know the world of evangelism like Tim Beougher. Few people have the heart of evangelism like Tim Beougher. Such are the reasons *Invitation to Evangelism: Sharing the Gospel with Compassion and Conviction* will become one of my most recommended books on the incredible topic of evangelism."

—Thom S. Rainer
Founder and CEO of Church Answers
Author of *The Post Quarantine Church*

"In *Invitation to Evangelism*, Tim Beougher grants readers a solid biblical foundation for evangelism while at the same time equipping them to put their convictions regarding the gospel and making disciples into practice. He writes from the experience of an academician who is a serious student of evangelism and a pastor who lives out the Great Commission in his ministry. This book offers a well-rounded introduction to evangelism for students, pastors, and church members. I will be using it as my primary textbook in my evangelism classes at Anderson University. It's that good!"

—Tim McKnight
Associate Professor of Youth Ministry and Missions
Director of the Global Center for Youth Ministry
College of Christian Studies, Anderson University

"Tim Beougher has taught more students in courses related to the theology and practice of evangelism than any other professor in the 160-year-plus history of The Southern Baptist Theological Seminary. Now with the publication of his latest book *Invitation to Evangelism*, anyone anywhere can benefit from the same biblically faithful, personally focused approach to sharing the good news of Jesus Christ with those who have yet to believe. I cannot recommend this work highly enough."

—Adam W. Greenway
President, Southwestern Baptist Theological Seminary

"*Invitation to Evangelism* is a comprehensive guide. It covers evangelism from every possible angle—biblical, historical, practical, and pastoral. Beougher's solid academic approach combines with his genuine pastoral concern to produce a practitioner's handbook. Readers will be encouraged to believe the gospel and share it!"

—Jimmy Scroggins
Lead Pastor, Family Church, West Palm Beach, Florida
Author of *3 Circles*

"I cannot recommend highly enough Dr. Tim Beougher's *Invitation to Evangelism*. As I read this thorough treatise on the wonderful subject of evangelism, I thought about two words: anointing and favor. God has given us an anointed and helpful resource from the gifted mind and pen of Dr. Beougher. But that is not all. This book has the favor of God upon it, and I predict it will become the standard textbook for classes in evangelism at both the college and seminary levels. I recommend it to every pastor and student of the Word of God. You will be blessed, motivated, and challenged. I absolutely loved reading it!"

—Danny Forshee
Lead Pastor, Great Hills Baptist Church, Austin, Texas

"This is a time the church has thankfully become alert to the different aspects of the mission of God. A side effect of this could be not giving sufficient attention to the evangelistic mandate. Behind this mandate are hard countercultural realities which, if not constantly kept before the church, she can (to her peril) begin to ignore. In an eminently readable style, this book does a great service by alerting the church to what lies behind the call to evangelism and how we can be faithful to it today."

—Ajith Fernando
Teaching Director, Youth for Christ, Sri Lanka
Author of *Discipling in a Multicultural World*

"*Invitation to Evangelism: Sharing the Gospel with Compassion and Conviction* is filled with practical insight, personal testimony, and profound theology—an ideal introduction to a life-and-death topic."

—David A. Currie
Dean of the Doctor of Ministry Program
Vice-President of Cohort-Based Education
Professor of Pastoral Theology, Gordon-Conwell Theological Seminary

"My wife and I are blessed with a fascinating circle of not-yet-Christian friends, some profoundly secular, some from traditional religions, and some from a postmodern 'spirituality' that is ambiguous at best. Yet, most of these dear ones are open to spiritual conversations. So, we often grapple with, 'How can we make the gospel *clear*, and how might we, by the power of the Spirit, offer a loving, compelling *call* to follow Christ as Lord?' Tim Beougher's *Invitation to Evangelism* offers us biblically grounded, practical, and varied answers to both of these questions— plus so much more!"

—George Guthrie
Professor of New Testament
Regent College

"My understanding of evangelism was deepened more than two decades ago when I sat under the teaching of Tim Beougher as one of his Ph.D. students. His biblical exposition, clarity of thought, and personal example helped shape and strengthen my personal convictions. In *Invitation to Evangelism: Sharing the Gospel with Compassion and Conviction,* those lessons are now available to everyone, with no matriculation requirements. This book is a gift to the church and, prayerfully, will result in the gift of the gospel being offered to the lost."

—Paul Chitwood
President, International Mission Board of the Southern Baptist Convention

"The litmus test for any book on evangelism is that it encourages the believer to go out and share with compassion, zeal, and urgency the good news of the gospel. Tim Beougher's *Invitation to Evangelism,* comprehensively meets that test. Tim's book is theologically rich, equips the believer to share the gospel, and fosters a deep compassion for the lost. It is comprehensive but easy to read, and full of personal and practical illustrations that both inspire and challenge the believer towards active evangelism. This book will be a huge blessing to the church and will stir believers to take seriously the Great Commission given to us by the Lord Jesus Christ. I will be encouraging my network of churches to read this book."

—Andy Constable
Co-pastor, Niddrie Community Church,
Edinburgh, Scotland
Director, 20 Schemes

"When Jesus commissioned his followers to proclaim the gospel, beginning in Jerusalem and then to all nations, he was sending them first to the very people who had crucified him. The Roman soldiers who had spat upon Jesus, scourged and mocked him, driven nails through his hands and feet, were to hear of God's love and Jesus's atoning death. The scornful, self-righteous Scribes and Pharisees were to be presented with their need to repent and believe. Religious people who had bayed for Jesus to be crucified were to be told of forgiveness and the promise of eternal life. The ordinary people who had called out 'Hosannah' to the King of Kings were to understand that the risen, living Jesus could be their Lord and Savior. And sinners—every creature—in all nations should each know the most wonderful yet urgent message that Jesus saves. Tim Beougher has gifted to the church a 'more-than-a-manual', but a practical, down-to-earth primer on evangelism that will equip Christians in ensuring that every person, in every nation, in each succeeding generation hears the news that Christ can save. *Invitation to Evangelism* will stir and encourage any Christian in making Jesus known to all."

—Roger Carswell, Evangelist
Author of *Evangelistic Living*

"The textbook that you need is from the learned man who practices what he teaches. Dr. Beougher offers the reader years of wisdom, understanding of evangelistic principles, and the practical application that you will you need when leaving the textbook. He is one of God's gifts to us in this generation."

—David Evans
Senior Pastor, Springfield Baptist Church, Springfield, Tennessee

"Some may say, 'We do not need another book on evangelism.' I would say we do not need just another book on evangelism, but we do need this one. Dr. Tim Beougher's *Invitation to Evangelism* is comprehensive, convictional, and consistently biblical. The reader is receiving in one volume the content of seminary level evangelistic training and yet written in a winsome way that will not feel overly academic. I encourage you to read and implement its clear and compelling directives. The chapter on witnessing to children is worth the price of the book all by itself. My prayer is that God will use this book, and its author, to the end that lost people will be saved and saved people will become more evangelistic."

—Todd Gray
Executive Director-Treasurer
The Kentucky Baptist Convention

"Tim Beougher is 'Professor Evangelist'—and not just the Billy Graham Professor of Evangelism at Southern Seminary. Since he began teaching at The Southern Baptist Theological Seminary twenty-five years ago, Dr. Beougher has faithfully instructed countless students in the stewardship of evangelism. This book is the outpouring of Dr. Beougher's sustained dedication and conviction. *All* Christians will greatly benefit from this vital book—a book full of gospel wisdom and practical help to overcome barriers to evangelism. I am proud to have Dr. Beougher on the faculty and I am proud to know him as friend and colleague. This timely volume will encourage Christians everywhere to engage in the task of evangelism with clarity and boldness."

—R. Albert Mohler, Jr.
President, The Southern Baptist Theological Seminary

"As one of the leading, most respected, and well-loved professors of evangelism, it is no surprise that Dr. Tim Beougher has produced a thorough and needed reference manual for every pastor's toolbox. *Invitation to Evangelism* is excellent and a must read for pastors, church leaders and students."

—Jaye Martin
Jaye Martin Ministries

"I have known Tim Beougher over the years in many capacities: as my professor, as one of my doctoral supervisors, and then as a colleague in the Billy Graham School at Southern Seminary. Dr. Beougher is the quintessential example of a scholar-practitioner in evangelism. He set the standard for teaching young theologues the practical art and the passion for evangelism. Personally, he not only teaches how to evangelize; he puts his words to action. This book is a necessary addition to anyone's library who desires to learn, teach, and inspire others to be consistent and obedient in leading people to Christ."

—Bill Henard
Senior Pastor, First Baptist Church, Athens, Tennessee

"I have found in this work what I've been seeking a number of years: a theologically strong and practically relevant toolbox for doing evangelism. Too many books on evangelism assume a knowledge of the biblical basis for evangelism, but this one starts there. Some neglect the personal walk of the one evangelizing, but not so with this book. Several offer only one or two ways for doing evangelism, but this book provides multiple strategies for proclaiming the gospel to nonbelievers. Others give little attention to the process of preserving evangelistic results, but this work ends there. Because I know Tim Beougher—a man whose heart beats with evangelism—and because I see this book as incredibly valuable, I will encourage its use in the classroom and in the local church. And, I will return to it often as a primary resource for my own evangelistic efforts."

—Chuck Lawless
Professor of Evangelism and Missions; Dean of Doctoral Studies
Vice President for Spiritual Formation and Ministry Centers
Southeastern Baptist Theological Seminary

"For over three decades, Tim Beougher has taught and modeled for thousands of students how to faithfully share the gospel of Jesus Christ. On this urgent topic, Beougher's character, wisdom, and experience are unrivaled. In this book, he provides students, pastors, and Christians with a biblically based practical guide on how to effectively communicate the good news of the gospel. This is a book that will bear fruit now and for eternity!"

—Paul Akin
Dean, Billy Graham School, The Southern Baptist Theological Seminary

"Dr. Beougher has been a student, practitioner, and professor of evangelism for many years. This book is the compilation of that knowledge and experience. It's not only a resource for students in Bible college or seminary, but also helps pastors and churches get involved in sharing the gospel in their everyday contexts. Readers will grow in their own affections to engage the lost in evangelism."

—Erik Reed,
Pastor, The Journey Church, Lebanon, Tennessee
Founder, Knowing Jesus Ministries.

Invitation to Biblical Hebrew: A Beginning Grammar
Russell T. Fuller & Kyoungwon Choi

Invitation to Biblical Hebrew: A Beginning Grammar (DVDs)
Russell T. Fuller & Kyoungwon Choi

Invitation to Biblical Hebrew: A Beginning Grammar (Workbook)
Russell T. Fuller & Kyoungwon Choi

Invitation to Biblical Hebrew Syntax: An Intermediate Grammar
Russell T. Fuller & Kyoungwon Choi

*Invitation to Biblical Interpretation 2nd Edition: Exploring the Hermeneutical Triad of History,
Literature, and Theology*
Andreas J. Köstenberger with Richard D. Patterson

Invitation to Biblical Preaching: Proclaiming Truth with Clarity and Relevance
Donald R. Sunukjian

Invitation to Biblical Theology: Exploring the Shape, Storyline, and Themes of Scripture
Jeremy M. Kimble & Ched Spellman

Invitation to Christian Ethics: Moral Reasoning and Contemporary Issues
Ken Magnuson

Invitation to Church History: American
John D. Hannah

Invitation to Church History: World
John D. Hannah

Invitation to Educational Ministry: Foundations of Transformative Christian Education
George M. Hillman Jr. & Sue G. Edwards

Invitation to Evangelism: Sharing the Gospel with Compassion and Conviction
Timothy K. Beougher

Invitation to World Missions: A Trinitarian Missiology for the Twenty-first Century
Timothy C. Tennent

INVITATION TO THEOLOGICAL STUDIES SERIES

INVITATION TO
EVANGELISM

*Sharing the Gospel with
Compassion and Conviction*

TIMOTHY K. BEOUGHER

KREGEL
ACADEMIC

To my grandchildren, Marshall, Savannah, Trenton, Brandon, Aaleigha, Abigail, Andrew, Emma, Evelyn, and James Timothy (and all my future grandchildren):

May you come to know and love the gospel, and may your lives reflect sharing the gospel with compassion and conviction.

CONTENTS

FOREWORD

A COLLEGE FRESHMAN WAS WEARING a large lapel button that had printed on it the letters BAIK. When asked by a friend what that meant, he replied, "Boy Am I Konfused." The friend reminded him, "Don't you know, 'confused' is not spelled with a K?" "Man," he exclaimed, "You don't know how confused I am."

The young man's predicament is not unlike that of many people in the church today. Few subjects, I suspect, are connected with more misunderstanding than Christ's last command to his followers: "Go . . . preach the gospel" (Mark 16:15) and "make disciples of all nations" (Matt. 28:19).

Evangelism is our watchword—the astounding news that "God so loved the world, that he gave his only Son that whoever believes on him shall not perish but have eternal life" (John 3:16). Making known this gospel brings the church into existence. Apart from its continual practice of evangelism by word and deed, the church would soon become extinct.

This is why the teaching of this book is so refreshing to mind and soul. Like the sun, it breaks through the fog and penetrates the heart of the gospel mandate. Not only does the author clarify biblical and doctrinal foundations of evangelism, he goes on to explain that what we believe finds practical expression in the way we live, both individually and together as the body of Christ. The book is remarkably comprehensive, and Dr. Beougher unwraps multiple facets of evangelism. Flowing through it all and giving direction to the whole book is the call to an ongoing lifestyle of the Great Commission.

I have known Dr. Beougher for many years. He is an unpretentious, authentic man of God. He is a gifted teacher and earnest scholar, but more significant, he is the same at home as he is in the pulpit and classroom. It is both a joy and honor to commend this book to you.

—Robert E. Coleman
Wilmore, Kentucky

ACKNOWLEDGEMENTS

I OWE A DEBT OF GRATITUDE to many people for this book. Dr. Roy Fish and Dr. Robert Coleman must be mentioned first because they taught and modeled the principles I share in these pages. I have tried to give credit to their contributions, but these two men so shaped me I am sure I have missed some attributions. As someone once said about the great theologian Augustine, "All theology since the fifth century is simply a footnote to Augustine," my practice of evangelism is a long footnote to Roy Fish and Robert Coleman. While not a professor, Dr. Billie Hanks Jr. has modeled evangelism for me for four decades. I know of no more consistent personal witness than Dr. Hanks.

Other professors shaping me in key areas were Dr. F. B. Huey, Dr. Murray Harris, Dr. James Leo Garrett, Dr. Harold O. J. Brown, Dr. Kenneth Kantzer, Dr. J. I. Packer, Dr. John Woodbridge, and Dr. Joel Gregory. A discerning reader will readily see their influence on my understanding of biblical, theological, historical, and practical topics.

In my own spiritual development, I must mention five men I fellowshipped with while a student at Kansas State University: Bob Anderson, Daryl Edmonds, Carl Herrington, Dick Jaques, and Lynn Rundle. They have remained friends and accountability partners for four decades. Other friends who have encouraged me in my spiritual journey are Nate Adams, Rick Barton, Ted Cabal, Ron Clement, David Currie, Lyle Dorsett, Steve Drake, Todd Gray, Glenn Hodge, Dave Hume, Al Jackson, Rob Jackson, Ken Magnuson, Dave Martin, George Martin, Larry Purcell, Dennis Reed,

Mike Sabo, David Shanks, Ed Stucky, and William Taylor. Thank you all for being "a friend who sticks closer than a brother."

I have learned from many other men who have taught evangelism. Thank you to Thom Rainer, Chuck Lawless, Mark Terry, Don Cox, Zane Pratt, Adam Greenway, J. D. Payne, Thomas Johnston, Tim McKnight, Ken Hemphill, Preston Nix, Matt Queen, Carl Bradford, Bo Rice, Scott Hildreth, Larry McDonald, Robin Jumper, Bill Henard, Paul Chitwood, Travis Kerns, Eddie Pate, David Wheeler, Jake Roudkovski, Brad Waggoner, Malcolm McDow, and George Robinson.

I have had the privilege to work alongside and get to know key individuals in the Billy Graham Evangelistic Association: Sterling Houston, John Akers, T. W. Wilson, David Bruce, Bill Conard, Leighton Ford, Tom Phillips, and Billy Graham himself. Serving as the Billy Graham Chair of Evangelism at The Southern Baptist Theological Seminary remains a privilege I reflect on daily, and I beg God's help to fulfill this role faithfully.

I am grateful to my seminary president, Dr. R. Albert Mohler, for his confidence in hiring a young professor to teach evangelism at The Southern Baptist Theological Seminary in 1996. I am thankful his vision for the recovery of the seminary included not only correct theology but also faithful practice.

I have learned so much from so many, and their insights are found in the pages of this book, oftentimes attributed to them, yet at other times so much a part of my life I cannot remember where I first learned it. I have been privileged to teach evangelism to thousands of students over the past thirty-five years in classrooms at Trinity College, Trinity Evangelical Divinity School, Wheaton College, Gordon-Conwell Theological Seminary, and The Southern Baptist Theological Seminary. These students' questions and comments have sharpened my views along the way.

I also am grateful to those who reviewed the book in draft form and made helpful comments: Sharon Beougher and Colin McCulloch. Nick Clark helped compile the bibliography and contributed significant content for the chapter on evangelism and apologetics. Paul Worcester gave permission to include his material on "Gospel Appointments," and Steven Kunkel contributed helpful content on "Evangelism and the Internet/Social Media." David Closson compiled the Index.

I am thankful for my family. My parents, Ken and Barbara Beougher, instilled many of these principles in me. My wife, Sharon, God's greatest gift to me after my salvation, loves me well and encourages me constantly. She not only painstakingly worked through each page of the book, but she consistently lives out these principles in her daily life. Our five children, their spouses, and our ten grandchildren are blessings far beyond what I deserve.

I have been privileged to serve fourteen churches as pastor or interim pastor, and I am thankful for all of them. Currently I serve as pastor of West Broadway Baptist Church in Louisville, Kentucky. This congregation of believers has truly become our spiritual family. They graciously provided me with a three-month sabbatical leave to finish this book. I am grateful.

As most acknowledgements end with a disclaimer, so must this one—many of the good things in this book have come from others, and any mistakes and limitations are all mine.

PREFACE

AS AN INTRODUCTORY TEXTBOOK ON EVANGELISM, this work is written for "students of evangelism" at Christian Bible colleges, universities, and seminaries. But I am confident it will also encourage Christians who are not engaged in formal theological training.

An introductory work requires inclusion of some topics and omission of others that would be included in a larger work. The goal involves "introducing" topics, not seeking to have the final word on them. I have included topics some might leave out of a work of this nature, and I am sure I have left out topics others would want to see included. In addition, some may think I have gone too deep in some chapters of this introductory book, while others might argue I have not gone deep enough in some chapters. I am reminded of the applicability of one of my axioms of life: "If you have two people who agree on everything, there's no need for one of them."

The material in this book consists of three main sections.

Preparing for Evangelism. This section sets forth a biblical, theological, and historical foundation for the practice of evangelism. It includes chapters on the gospel message, motivations for evangelism, and prayer and evangelism. This section concludes with a chapter titled "Concentric Circles of Concern," where the reader can identify persons already in his/her sphere of influence who need the gospel message.

Practicing Evangelism. This section begins with an overview on maintaining a lifestyle of evangelism and then proceeds to present several practical ways to communicate the gospel, including specific helps in presenting the gospel to various groups.

Preserving Evangelism. This section amplifies the reality that the Great Commission mandate involves making disciples, not decisions.

An afterword gives a closing challenge that will encourage the reader to a life of faithfulness in evangelism.

I have been privileged to teach evangelism at the college or seminary level for the past thirty-five years. Ultimately, however, one cannot learn how to do evangelism in a classroom setting. Similar to learning how to swim, one can learn some basic principles from a book or in a classroom setting, but the only way to learn how to swim is to get in the water and start swimming! The truths in this book will "come alive" for the reader as he or she puts them into practice in the real world.

Another axiom about evangelism advocates that it is "more caught than taught," and that axiom proves true. But part of "catching on" to the practice of effective witnessing requires understanding key principles. You can learn key principles through a book or in a classroom. And you can learn from models, both biblical and historical. But ultimately to learn evangelism you have to "get in the water."

A college student sold books during the summer to make money. He approached an elderly farmer with a book on the latest and greatest farming methods and said, "Sir, if you will buy this book, I guarantee you that by this time next year you'll be farming twice as good as you are right now or you get a full refund." The old farmer looked at this young college student and said, "Sonny, I don't need to buy that book. I ain't farming half as good as I know how to right now!" I think we could say something similar as we begin reading a book on evangelism. "Why should I learn more? I'm not witnessing half as well as I know how to right now!" The key is not to stop learning but to begin *applying* what we are learning. As you read through this book, some of this material may be review for you. The question I want you to ask as you read is not, "Have I heard this before?" or "Do I know this truth intellectually?" but "Does my life reflect this reality right now?" If it is not a part of your life right now, then do you *really* know it? My ultimate goal for this book is not merely to increase your knowledge of evangelism but to increase your application of evangelism.

The principles I share in this book have guided my own evangelistic practice, and I am confident they will benefit you as well. If there are parts of this book with which you disagree, that is okay. My own views on evangelism have changed over the years, so I do not always agree with myself! Leighton Ford notes D. L. Moody's classic reply to a critic who disapproved of his methods. "I don't like them too much, myself," he admitted. "What methods do you use?" When the critic replied that he used none, Moody retorted, "Well, I think I like the way I do it better than the way you don't!"[1]

Jesus's command to his early disciples "you shall be my witnesses" remains the clarion call for all Christ-followers today. I pray this book helps you to that end. It has been noted that evangelism is a banner that many people *wave* but few people *carry*. Let's do more than learn about evangelism; let's practice it, for our neighbor's eternal good and for God's eternal glory.

---

1. Leighton Ford, *The Christian Persuader* (New York: Harper & Row Publishers, 1966), 68.

PART 1

PREPARING
FOR EVANGELISM

CHAPTER 1

What Is Evangelism?

EVANGELISM PRESENTS AN OFFENSIVE PICTURE to people both inside and outside the church. When some hear the word *evangelism*, they equate it with hardline psychological pressure, yelling through a bullhorn, or proselytizing people against their will. Yet those negative connotations express poor stereotypes of an activity that by its very nature means the communication of "good news." And indeed, if you have good news, life-saving news—even eternal life-saving news—how can you not desire to share that message with others?

In this opening chapter we first will examine biblical terminology employed for the practice of evangelism and then observe various definitions of evangelism. I trust this overview will remind believers not only of the great responsibility of evangelism, but also of the unbelievable privilege that is ours of testifying to the good news of what God has done for us in Christ.

Biblical Terminology

Our word *evangelism* is taken from the Greek word *euangelion*, translated "the gospel." Within the word *evangelism* we see the word *evangel*, meaning "good news." The evangel which lies at the heart of the Christian faith is the good news about who God is and how he has provided reconciliation for sinful humanity.

So evangelism is to announce the *euangelion*, the good news. The noun form appears over seventy times in the New Testament, while the verb form *euangelizō* appears over thirty times. We find both the noun and the verb forms in Romans 1:15, "So, for my part, I am eager to preach the gospel to you also who are in Rome."

The term *kerygma*, meaning "to proclaim," highlights the proclamation of the gospel. The verb form appears more than sixty times in the New Testament, and while not always referencing the proclamation of the gospel, it is often used in that context—for example, in 1 Corinthians 1:21: "God was well-pleased through the foolishness of the message preached [*kerygma*] to save those who believe." In Romans 10:14–15, the terms *kērussō* and *euangelizomai* are used synonymously.

Another biblical term that relates to evangelism is *martyreō*, meaning "bearing witness." A witness is someone who brings firsthand testimony of what he or she has seen or heard or experienced. This term is used in Jesus's declaration to the disciples found in Acts 1:8, "You shall be my witnesses."[1]

Defining Evangelism

Humpty Dumpty's assertion in the fictional work *Through the Looking Glass* highlights the problem we face when it comes to definitions: "When I use a word, it means just what I choose it to mean—neither more nor less."[2] You could place one hundred people in a room, ask them to define evangelism, and probably come up with two hundred different definitions.[3]

Sometimes the best way to define a term is first to define what it is not. Many things that fly under the banner of evangelism do not constitute true evangelism when viewed from a biblical perspective. While numerous examples could be listed of what evangelism is not, I have found that two particular misconceptions about evangelism often confuse people.

---

1. Tom Johnston, a dear friend and professor of evangelism at Midwestern Baptist Theological Seminary in Kansas City, has done extensive work on these biblical terms and how they are translated in various historical translations of the Scriptures. For an in-depth discussion, see Thomas P. Johnston, *Evangelizology, Vol. 1: Motivation and Definition* (Liberty, MO: Evangelism Unlimited, 2011), 209.
2. Lewis Carroll, *Through the Looking-Glass and What Alice Found There* (Chicago: Rand McNally, 1917), 99.
3. David B. Barrett, *Evangelize: A Historical Survey of the Concept* (Birmingham, AL: New Hope, 1987) lists seventy-five different definitions.

Evangelism: What It Is Not

First, evangelism is not "mere presence." We hear that perspective expressed often today. Some people declare, "I'm just going to witness with my life. I'm going to let my life do the talking." Some even misquote St. Francis of Assisi (1181/1182–1226), claiming he opined, "Preach the gospel at all times; use words if necessary." Scholars of St. Francis assert he never said those words, but I maintain even if he had said them, they still would be wrong! This is like saying, "Feed the hungry at all times; use food if necessary."

Your life is not the gospel. The good news of what God has done for us in Jesus Christ must be shared verbally. Evangelism is more than mere presence. If you live a committed Christian life in front of people but never share the reason for the hope within you, they are going to assume one of two things about you.

First, they might assume you are a good person. And by human standards you might fall into the overall category of "good" instead of "bad." But your life is not the gospel. Do good works save? No—they emphatically do not. We are saved by grace through faith in Christ, not because of our works.

Second, others might assume you are a religious person. After all, they see you going to church each Sunday, and sometimes other times as well. Does religion save? No—religion does not save; only a relationship with the Lord Jesus Christ saves.

I heard Bill Bright, founder of Campus Crusade for Christ (now Cru), tell of a Christian businessman who worked for years in the same office and had never opened his mouth to testify about Christ. He sought to live a life of integrity and model compassion among his fellow workers. Finally, after several years, a man came to his office and asked if he had a few minutes to answer a personal question. This Christian businessman said "sure," confident he was about to be asked the reason for the hope within him. The coworker began by noting he had witnessed a difference between this man and the other workers in the office, filling the Christian man's heart with excitement for the inevitable question about Christianity. But instead, the coworker asked him, "Are you a Buddhist?" Bright noted the Christian businessman had convinced this coworker he was different, but apart from any verbal sharing of the gospel, the coworker mistakenly assumed he was a follower of a different religion.

LeRoy Eims shares a similar story:

> A Christian businessman in Seattle confessed how he had unknow-
> ingly discouraged a business associate from coming to Christ for years.
> One day the friend told the Christian businessman he had met the
> Lord the night before at a Billy Graham meeting. The longtime Chris-
> tian was elated and said so, but the new Christian replied, "Friend,
> you're the reason I have resisted becoming a Christian all these years.
> I figured if a person could live a good life as you do and not be a Chris-
> tian, there was no need to become one![4]

As Eims points out, this Christian businessman had sought to live an exem-
plary life, but he had not communicated his source of strength for doing so.

How will people know where our hope is found if we do not tell them?
We may think that our life is bearing testimony, but without an accompa-
nying verbal witness, the gospel has not been communicated. Evangelism
is not "mere presence." We might recast the mistakenly attributed quote
of St. Francis of Assisi in this way: "Share the gospel at all times, and use
words, because they are necessary."

A second thing that evangelism is not is "spiritual mugging." Some
people seem to think that unless you are browbeating someone with the
truth, you are not truly witnessing. One of my college friends was accosted
by well-meaning but overly zealous "witnesses" in the laundry room of
his dormitory. As he was folding his clothes, four fellow students backed
him into a corner and told him he needed to pray the sinner's prayer. He
told them he wasn't interested, but they weren't taking "no" for an answer.
They kept insisting that he "pray the prayer," and he realized they were
not going to leave until he did, so he went through the motions. These
four men left rejoicing over their new convert, but he was as lost after the
encounter as he was before.

Evangelism is not spiritual mugging. Jesus was willing to let people
walk away (see the account of the rich young ruler in Matthew 19:16–30).
Only God can change hearts. You cannot browbeat someone into the
kingdom of God. You can browbeat them into praying a prayer or doing

---

4. Leroy Eims, *One-to-One Evangelism: Winning Ways in Personal Witnessing*
   (Wheaton, IL: Victor, 1990), 39.

some other type of religious activity, but you cannot "mug" them into genuine conversion. We must avoid the ditches of "mere presence" and "spiritual mugging" in our evangelism. If those two approaches show us what evangelism is not, then what is evangelism? The following section will seek to clarify what evangelism is through the use of various definitions.

What Evangelism Is: Various Definitions

1918 Anglican Definition

A special committee was appointed in 1918 by the Archbishop of Canterbury, William Temple, to bring clarity to the task of evangelism. The appointed group of Anglican bishops produced this definition: "To evangelise is so to present Christ Jesus in the power of the Holy Spirit, that men shall come to put their trust in God through him, to accept him as their Saviour, and serve him as their King in the fellowship of his church."[5] This definition has numerous strengths. It reminds us that evangelism is good news about Jesus Christ. It reinforces the reality that evangelism depends completely on its effectiveness from the power of the Holy Spirit. It highlights that while people come to faith individually, faithful evangelism leads to incorporation into the church. It points out that true evangelism calls for a response to the message. The gospel is a message that demands a response, a "yes" or "no" to Christ's offer of forgiveness. The definition also reminds us that evangelism should result in discipleship. A disciple is a learner or follower of Christ. Response to the gospel involves a change from going my own way to following Christ's way.

Yet in spite of these strengths, J. I. Packer, himself an Anglican, offers a critique of the definition, particularly of the phrase "*that* men shall come to put their trust in God through Him." Packer believes that phrase defines evangelism in terms of its results and comments, "This is to define evangelism in terms of an effect achieved in the lives of others; which amounts to saying that the essence of evangelizing is producing converts."[6] Regarding this same clause in the definition, John R. W. Stott asserts, "Evangelism must not be defined in terms of its results. . . . To 'evangelize' in the biblical

---

5. Bryan Green, *Practice of Evangelism* (New York: Charles Scribner's Sons, 1951), 6.
6. J. I. Packer, *Evangelism and the Sovereignty of God* (Downers Grove, IL: IVP, 1961), 40.

usage does not mean to win converts (as it usually does when we use the word) but simply to share the good news, irrespective of the results."[7] This point rings true. Evangelism must be defined in terms of the message proclaimed, not the results achieved.

D. T. Niles

D. T. Niles, a theologian from Ceylon (now Sri Lanka), offered this memorable definition: "Evangelism is witness. It is one beggar telling another beggar where to get food."[8] Reminiscent of the four starving men in 2 Kings 7:1–9 who stumbled upon an abundance of food, this definition reminds us that we have come to faith due to God's mercy and grace. The difference between the two classes of beggars in Niles's definition is that one has discovered the bread of life, and the other needs to know that truth.

This definition reminds us of the importance of humility in our witness. If our salvation were something we could earn by our own efforts or good works, then we would have grounds for boasting. But the Scriptures constantly remind us that salvation is a gift from God that is completely undeserved on our part (Eph. 2:8–9). The ground is indeed level at the foot of the cross. This humility is crucial in our witness because a major reason unbelievers are turned off by Christianity is they perceive Christians as somehow claiming they are better than everyone else. If we understand grace, we will be humble. Christians should be the most humble people in the world. We can share the gospel with deep conviction but also with genuine humility. We truly are "one beggar telling other beggars where to find food."

Bill Bright (Campus Crusade for Christ)

Bill Bright shared his perspective on evangelism with this statement: "Success in witnessing is simply taking the initiative to share Christ in the power of the Holy Spirit, and leaving the results to God."[9] This definition reminds us that real "success" in evangelism is based on our sharing the good news, not on the person's response. It also highlights the necessity of the work of the Holy Spirit in the gospel conversation.

---

7. John Stott, "The Biblical Basis of Evangelism," in *Let the Earth Hear His Voice*, ed. J. D. Douglas (Minneapolis: World Wide Publications, 1975), 69.
8. D. T. Niles, *That They May Have Life* (New York: Harper, 1951), 96.
9. Bill Bright, *Witnessing without Fear: How to Share Your Faith with Confidence* (San Bernardino, CA: Here's Life, 1987), 69.

1974 Lausanne Covenant

In 1974, Christian leaders from all over the world met at the International Congress on World Evangelization in Lausanne, Switzerland. One of the results of that meeting was a fresh definition of evangelism: "To evangelize is to spread the good news that Jesus Christ died for our sins and was raised from the dead according to the Scriptures, and that as the reigning Lord he now offers the forgiveness of sins and the liberating gift of the Spirit to all who repent and believe."[10] I have read scores of books on evangelism since 1975, and my unscientific survey concludes this definition is the most-quoted definition on evangelism in recent decades.

This definition reminds us that evangelism involves communicating the good news of the gospel, which is set forth in 1 Corinthians 15, and includes an emphasis on the resurrection. Many "gospel presentations" used today focus on the cross (and rightly so!) but neglect any reference to the resurrection. The definition also highlights key benefits of salvation (forgiveness of sins and the liberating gift of the Spirit) as well as the necessary response of repentance and faith. Obviously, the longer the definition, the more that can be included.

MY DEFINITION

As I have practiced evangelism for more than four decades and taught evangelism for more than three decades, I have settled on this definition of evangelism: it is *the compassionate sharing of the good news of Jesus Christ with lost people, in the power of the Holy Spirit, for the purpose of bringing them to Christ as Savior and Lord, that they in turn might share him with others.* In order to unpack that definition, I would like to break it down into key phrases, each with an important emphasis.

The Spirit of Evangelism: Compassion

Douglas Stewart has argued the single greatest reason we fail to witness is that we do not possess the compassion of Christ.[11] I begin my definition of evangelism with compassion because of the example of Christ. Matthew 9:36 reminds us that when Jesus saw the multitudes, he "felt

---

10. "The Nature of Evangelism," Lausanne Covenant 4, in *Let the Earth Hear His Voice*, 4.
11. Douglas Stewart, "Evangelism," *Expository Times* 67, no. 10 (July 1956): 312.

compassion for them." How do we respond when we encounter sinful multitudes? What is our response when we are confronted with sinful humanity? I fear too often our response is not of one of compassion but one of coldness, callousness, criticism, or condemnation.

When our daughter Karisa turned seventeen years old, I took her to get her ears double-pierced. Since she was not yet eighteen, a parent had to go and sign a permission form before the procedure. My daughter wanted to go to a store on Bardstown Road in Louisville, a section of town where tattoos and piercings are common. As we were waiting in line, a woman joined the line behind us. She not only had her ears pierced multiple times, but she also had her nose, eyebrows, lips, and tongue pierced multiple times. My first reaction was one of amazement, then analysis, and finally criticism: *Why would she do that to her body?* I was not feeling compassion for this woman but instead criticism and condemnation.

The silence of my thoughts was broken by my daughter's voice as she asked this woman if she knew God. "No," the woman replied. "I don't know God. What would God want with someone like me?" As we waited in this very long line, my daughter Karisa shared with this woman about how God so loved the world that he gave his one and only Son, that *whoever* believes in him shall not perish but have everlasting life.

I experienced a conflict of emotions in my heart. I felt incredible fatherly pride in my daughter. Karisa was not old enough to get her ears pierced by herself, but she had compassion for this woman and was seeking to point her to the Savior. But I also had the contrasting emotion of incredible disappointment in myself. How could my heart so quickly fill with criticism instead of compassion? When Jesus saw the multitudes, he had compassion on them. They were wandering aimlessly like sheep without a shepherd. Why is it that so many of us who claim to follow the Compassionate One are sometimes lacking in compassion?

Christians can develop a cold heart toward the unsaved, which can lead to a calloused, hard heart. From time to time we may need to get on our faces before God and cry out for a heart of compassion for the lost. It was said of D. L. Moody that he never spoke about lost souls without tears in his eyes. John Henry Jowett emphasizes the importance of compassion by saying, "The gospel of a broken heart demands the ministry of bleeding hearts. As soon as we cease to bleed, we cease to bless. . . . Tearless hearts can never be the heralds of the Passion."[12] Compassion undergirds the spirit of evangelism.

The Method of Evangelism: Sharing

I utilize the word *sharing* very deliberately. Sharing involves both our verbal and nonverbal communication; it involves both talking and listening, and it is both an act and a process. In Acts 8:35, as Philip dialogued with the Ethiopian eunuch, the Scriptures record, "Philip shared Jesus with him." Sharing involves communication—both talking and listening. Much of our evangelism training focuses on us learning how to talk, and rightly so. As we have already argued, "mere presence" without verbal communication is not evangelism. But good evangelism is a dialogue, not a monologue. And we do not receive much training in how to listen. My wife Sharon is one of the best personal witnesses I know, and it is in no small part due to her listening skills. We must listen with alertness and sensitivity in order to understand what the other person believes and where he or she is coming from. Listening is hard for us because in a dialogue, when the other person is talking, our mind usually begins formulating what we will say next. Several verses in Proverbs 18 remind us of the importance of active listening: "A fool does not delight in understanding, but only in revealing his own mind" (v. 2); "He who gives an answer before he hears, it is folly and shame to him" (v. 13); and "The mind of the prudent acquires knowledge, and the ear of the wise seeks knowledge" (v. 15).

If you will learn to ask good questions and then listen, most people will open up and talk about their life and their beliefs. They will often self-diagnose themselves in terms of what they are trusting in and where their hope is found. In later chapters we will discuss how to communicate the gospel message and focus on helpful ways to begin spiritual conversations, but underlying it all we have to learn to listen to what the person is saying in response. Evangelism involves both talking and listening.

The Content of Evangelism: The Good News of Jesus Christ

In announcing the birth of Christ in Luke 2:10, the angels testified of "good news of great joy!" The content of evangelism is good news! Some-times our attitude seems to convey that what we are sharing is somehow

---

12. John Henry Jowett, *The Passion for Souls* (New York: Revell, 1905), 30, 34.

less than good news to this person. We drag our heels and often seem re-luctant to open our mouths. Why do we act like that at times? The gospel is the greatest news this world has ever known! It is the greatest news any person could ever hear! We will unpack the gospel message more fully in a later chapter, but for now remember that it is *good news!* The content of evangelism is the good news of Jesus Christ: who he is and what he has done for sinners.

The Recipients of Evangelism: Lost People

In Luke 19:10, Jesus reminded us that his mission was to "seek and to save that which was lost." Part of making his mission our mission in-volves understanding that people are lost. When you are lost you do not know the way. My current hometown of Louisville, Kentucky, has been described as the location where "the Bible belt buckles," but in my more than two decades of living here, the vast majority of people I witness to do not know the gospel message. We mistakenly assume that in a place like Louisville people must have heard the gospel at least a hundred times and just continue to refuse to bow their knees before Christ. And yes, there are people in Louisville who have heard and understood the gospel and yet reject it. And yet most people I talk with are not only lost in sin—they are lost in sin with no clue as to the road map pointing them to the narrow road that leads them out of their predicament.

That means that not all evangelism can be done inside the church building. Most lost persons will never come to church—because they are lost! Some churches have subtly reversed the Great Commission; instead of "go and tell," it has become "come and hear." I am not against doing evangelism inside the church building. Every time I preach, I seek to com-municate the gospel message, as I never assume that everyone who attends that day already knows Christ personally. But we cannot rely on a "come and hear" strategy when so many people will never come and hear. The only way they will know the gospel is if we "go and tell." People are lost, and that means we must go to them with the gospel and initiate those spiritual conversations. The recipients of evangelism are lost people.

The Power for Evangelism: The Holy Spirit

In Acts 1:8, Jesus encouraged a rather discouraged band of disciples with the words, "But you will receive power when the Holy Spirit has come upon you; and you shall be My witnesses both in Jerusalem, and in all Judea and Samaria, and even to the remotest part of the earth." Often when I hear someone reference Acts 1:8 they focus on the strategy for evangelism contained within that verse. This strategy reflects concentric circles, beginning where you are (your Jerusalem) and continuing outwardly to "the uttermost parts of the earth." Certainly that strategy is found there, and we see it enacted throughout the remainder of the book of Acts. But too often we focus on the strategy and forget the power. Jesus didn't tell the disciples, "Here is your strategy, now do the best you can in your own strength." No, the strategy is impotent without the power! Jesus told them to tarry until they received the empowerment of the Holy Spirit because their ministry (and ours as well) would be worthless without the power.

I have adopted 2 Corinthians 4:7 as my life verse (my translation): "We have this treasure in earthen vessels, that the surpassing greatness of the power might be from God and not from we ourselves." Periodically I'll have someone say to me, "I just don't feel adequate to do evangelism." Do you know how I reply? I grab their shoulders and exclaim, "That's great! That's wonderful! You are exactly where God wants you to be! God doesn't work through people who feel they are adequate, but through those who acknowledge their weakness and need for God's empowering strength." If you feel inadequate to do evangelism, then you are a perfect candidate for God's power.

Reflect on what the apostle Paul wrote in 1 Corinthians 2. He reminisced about his first visit there and recalled that he was with them "in weakness and fear and much trembling." Think about who wrote those words! Not a brand-new believer or a backslidden Christian, but the apostle Paul! Paul affirms that when he was in Corinth, he was shaking in his sandals with fear, but he goes on to testify that his ministry among them was a demonstration of the Spirit in power. Even the great apostle Paul had to learn the lesson that he could not do ministry in his own strength but only in the Spirit's empowering.

We see a similar lesson learned by the apostle Peter. In Matthew 26 when Jesus told the disciples they would fall away due to persecution, Peter protested Jesus's words: "Peter said to Him, 'Even if I have to die with You, I will not deny You'" (v. 35). But if we fast-forward to Jesus's trial, we see Peter identified by a servant girl as one of Jesus's followers. How does Peter respond to this accusation? He told her, "I do not even know the man." Luke tells us at that moment Jesus turned around and looked right into Peter's eyes. What was Peter's response? He went out and "wept bitterly." Those tears were bitter because he had denied his Lord and Master, even after vowing he would do no such thing.

But now let's fast-forward to Acts chapter 4. Peter is not being questioned by a servant girl; now he's standing before the top civic and religious authorities of the land. They ordered him to stop talking about Jesus, and how does Peter reply? "Whether it is right in the sight of God to give heed to you rather than to God, you be the judge; for we cannot stop speaking about what we have seen and heard" (vv. 19–20). The authorities threatened Peter and John and then let them go. After being dismissed by the authorities, Peter and John called a prayer meeting. Every time I read this account at the end of Acts 4, I feel convicted. If I had called that prayer meeting, I suspect the main request would have been different. I would have been praying for safety. I would have been asking God to build a hedge of protection around me and the other believers in Jerusalem. Yet at that prayer meeting, they were not praying for safety; they were praying for boldness. While it is not wrong for a believer to pray for safety (as in the Psalms), what strikes me is that their own personal safety wasn't what was uppermost in their minds (and in their prayers). Instead of praying for safety, they prayed for boldness.

That raises a key question. *Why* did they pray for boldness? The answer is simple yet profound. They prayed for boldness because they *needed* boldness! We don't normally pray for things we already have. We may thank God for them, but we don't ask him for them if we already have them. Why did they pray for boldness? Because they lacked it—they were scared. They didn't want to allow their fears to keep them from sharing the good news of Jesus Christ, so they prayed for boldness.

How did God choose to answer that prayer? Well, this prayer meeting witnessed phenomenal results! When they prayed, the place they were in was shaken. Wouldn't it be great if in every prayer meeting when you prayed, God would shake the building you were in as a testimony that your prayers had been heard and would be answered? I currently serve as pastor of West Broadway Baptist Church. The church building is located on the east side of Louisville, right across the road from railroad tracks. Occasionally a train rumbles by and shakes the building as we are praying during our Wednesday night prayer meetings. But in Acts 4, there was no locomotive; the place was shaken by the power of God.

God answered their prayers for boldness, and they continued to share the good news of Christ. In Acts 5 the authorities dragged Peter and John back in and said, "We gave you strict orders not to talk about Jesus and you have filled Jerusalem with your teaching" (v. 28, my translation). Reflect on that assertion for a moment: "you have filled Jerusalem with your teaching." That wasn't a report in a denominational newsletter ("we have reached our city for Christ!") but the testimony of their enemies! The authorities were basically saying, "We told you guys to shut up, but you obviously didn't because everywhere we turn, we find new followers of Christ." So this time they didn't just threaten them with words, they beat them with rods.

How did Peter and John respond to this persecution? It says they "left the presence of the council rejoicing that they have been considered worthy to suffer for Christ's name" (v. 41). Where in the world would they have gotten the idea that the way that you respond to persecution is by rejoicing? It appears in that moment they reflected back to some three years earlier when they heard Jesus utter what we know as the Beatitudes: "Blessed are you when men revile you and persecute you and utter all kinds of falsehood against you on account of me; in that day rejoice and be glad because your reward in heaven is great" (Matt. 5:11–12, my translation). So as Peter and John were limping down the street, they were rejoicing; they were celebrating.

So here is an important question for us to answer. What made the difference between Peter cowering in fear before a servant girl and Peter boldly standing up to the top authorities in the land? What made the difference between Peter's response in Matthew 26 and his response in Acts 4 and 5? The answer is simple: Acts 2! The coming of the Holy Spirit and his empowering ministry at Pentecost. The Peter who boasted he was willing to die for Jesus was Peter boasting in his own strength that "I've got this." Well, he didn't have it. The Peter in Acts chapter 4 and 5 and beyond is a Peter who is filled with the Holy Spirit. The power for evangelism is the Holy Spirit. We must be filled and empowered by the Holy Spirit as we witness.

The Purpose of Evangelism: Bringing Them to Christ as Savior and Lord (Acts 16:31)

When we share the gospel with others, what is the goal? That we bring them to a church? That they join a denomination? That they adopt a new

philosophy of life? While all those things have their place, we are bringing
them to a person—to the Lord Jesus Christ. I am convinced that many
people reject Christianity not because they have truly understood Christ's
person and work but because of the visible failure of Christians or because
they misunderstand the gospel message.

The object of saving faith is the whole and undivided person of our
Lord and Savior, Jesus Christ. We must not divide Christ up into bits and
ask people to respond to only one of the bits. He must be received as both
Savior and Lord. The purpose of evangelism is bringing lost persons to
Christ as Savior and Lord.

Perpetuation of Evangelism: They Win Others (2 Tim. 2:2)

We have already noted that evangelism should not be measured in
terms of results, but when someone does come to faith in Christ, we want
to see that person become a fruit-bearing disciple in a local church. The
perpetuation of evangelism is that the new believer will begin to reach
out in love to share the good news of salvation with others. We see this
process of spiritual multiplication in 2 Timothy 2:2: "The things which
you have heard from me in the presence of many witnesses, entrust these
to faithful men who will be able to teach others also." This verse highlights four generations: Paul, Timothy, faithful men, and then "others."
New believers have great potential in evangelism. Some of them have
large numbers of unsaved friends or family members. Helping the new
believer learn to share his/her faith from the beginning is a wise stewardship of opportunity.

CHAPTER 2

THE BIBLICAL BASIS FOR EVANGELISM (PART 1)

THIS CHAPTER SEEKS TO OFFER A BIBLICAL THEOLOGY of evangelism. It will trace the flow of the development of the good news of God's redemptive plan from the *protoevangelium* (Gen. 3:15) to the *kerygmatic* preaching of the apostles, consummating in the reality of people from every tongue and tribe and nation gathered around the throne, worshiping the Lamb. Some today unfortunately want to divorce theology and evangelism. Some theologians delve deep in the mysteries of theology but seem out of touch with lost humanity, while some evangelists dismiss theology as irrelevant and just want to "preach Jesus." Both extremes must be avoided. As the famous Scottish theologian James Denney asserted, "If our evangelists were theologians and our theologians evangelists, we would be near the ideal church."[1]

The apostle Paul provides a wonderful model for us in this regard. Was Paul a gifted theologian? Yes, perhaps the greatest theologian in history. We know the Holy Spirit inspired the book of Romans, but God chose Paul to write that book, not Peter, John, or Luke. And yet Paul wasn't only a brilliant theologian; he was also an evangelist, a missionary, and a church planter. As we examine the Scriptures, we can argue that far from

---

1. James Denney, *The Death of Christ* (New Canaan, CT: Keats Publishing, Inc., 1981), vii.

divorcing theology from evangelism, God's plan of redemption is the central theme of the Bible from the beginning to the end. Therefore, if we are to be biblical and relevant, we must not separate theology and evangelism.

In the Garden

Any treatment of evangelism in the Old Testament must begin with God's creation and His purposes for humanity (Gen. 1–2). God's saving plan is revealed as unfolding from creation to new creation and reflects salvation reaching the ends of the earth. God created the world and humanity distinct from himself and yet totally dependent on him. Genesis 3 describes the transition from innocence to guilt—the fall of mankind and the entrance of sin into the world. Man becomes a sinner, and the whole story of humankind is tragically affected by the consequences of Adam and Eve's disobedience to God. Sin cannot be ignored by a just God, since it is an affront to his holiness. Separation has occurred between God and humankind. Humanity is now dead in trespasses and sins, alienated and hostile. We do not seek, acknowledge, or honor God.

Yet even in this tragic account of sin, we see a picture of God as the pursuing evangelist (Gen. 3:8–20). We see that even when Adam and Eve were hiding, God took the initiative in making himself known (v. 8). God came to the garden to seek Adam and Eve. God the evangelist then exposes the need for redemption. In verse 9 we read, "Then the LORD God called to the man, and said to him, 'Where are you?'" Did God not know where Adam and Eve were? Of course he did! God's purpose was to expose their sin and their hiding: And God said, "Who told you that you were naked? Have you eaten from the tree of which I commanded you not to eat?" (v. 11). Again, God is not asking them this question because he does not know the answer. He is bringing them to the point of recognizing their sinfulness and need for redemption.

God the evangelist then brings a redemptive message. Genesis 3:15 sets forth the *protoevangelium*, or the prototype of the good news of redemption. In this verse we see the first glimmer of the gospel message. To the serpent God said, "And I will put enmity between you and the woman, and between your seed and her seed; He shall bruise you on the head, and you shall bruise him on the heel." In the midst of judgment there was hope, mercy, and grace! This verse captures the first announcement of the redemption to be affected in and through Christ, given figuratively to Adam and Eve in the words of God to the serpent. God brings a message of redemption in the midst of the problem of sin.

A LIGHT TO THE NATIONS

Genesis 3–11 shows the disastrous effects of the fall and the ensuing unraveling of humankind. The call of Abram (Gen. 12) and the promise of blessing to him, as well as to all the peoples of the earth, are presented against the backdrop of humanity under divine judgment. Yet judgment is not the final word. Genesis 12:1–3 is God's gracious response that gives hope amid the downward spiral of chapters 3–11. Genesis 12:1 reads, "Now the LORD said to Abram, 'Go forth from your country, and from your relatives and from your father's house, to the land which I will show you.'" As Peters notes, "Abraham did not seek God; rather, God, the God of glory, pierced the heavens and miraculously broke into history to seek Abraham. He appeared to him when the latter dwelt safely and securely in Ur of the Chaldees in a home where idolatry was practiced."[2]

God the evangelist then sets forth the purpose of the mission. Genesis 12:2–3 reads, "And I will make you a great nation, and I will bless you, and make your name great; and so you shall be a blessing; and I will bless those who bless you, and the one who curses you I will curse. And in you all the families of the earth shall be blessed." The purpose of the blessing was so that Abraham would be a blessing to many others. Not only will Abram be blessed, but he will be a source of blessing for the nations. God the evangelist also mandates the scope of the mission. In Genesis 12:2–3 we discover that Israel is to be a blessing to "all nations." Genesis 12:1–3 rightly stands as the "great commission" of the Old Testament.

I WILL BE YOUR GOD

God the evangelist then calls his people into covenant with himself. Exodus 19:3–6 says, "Thus you shall say to the house of Jacob and tell the sons of Israel: 'You yourselves have seen what I did to the Egyptians, and how I bore you on eagles' wings, and brought you to Myself. Now then, if

---

2. George Peters, *A Biblical Theology of Missions* (Chicago: Moody, 1972), 90.

you will indeed obey My voice and keep My covenant, then you shall be My own possession among all the peoples, for all the earth is Mine; and you shall be to Me a kingdom of priests and a holy nation.' These are the words that you shall speak to the sons of Israel." The phrase "if you will indeed obey My voice and keep My covenant" refers to the Mosaic covenant that God was about to give to the people. The nation of Israel was to be holy and to bless and serve the world by being distinct.

A few other Old Testament themes merit mention as well. In the Old Testament, conversion is seen through the word *shuv*, meaning "turning." *Shuv* serves as a call "to turn from evil" and "to turn to the good." Old Testament conversion is seen as a call to covenantal obedience.[3] The prophet Isaiah uses several metaphors for conversion: from blindness to sight, from deafness to hearing, and from darkness to light. The Old Testament sacrificial system underscored the need for blood sacrifice for atonement for sin. And the book of Jonah demonstrates God's concern for the nations, and his mercy to those who repent.

Another key theme in the Old Testament is Messianic expectation (2 Sam. 7; Isa. 53). Critical for an understanding of Yahweh's rule over the nations of the world and the fulfillment of his covenant promises to Abraham is the establishment of the Davidic kingship in 2 Samuel 7. In verse 13 God promises, "I will establish the throne of his kingdom forever." Ultimately Jesus of Nazareth will bring to their consummation the promises given to the house of David. Isaiah 53 provides a beautiful portrayal of the ministry, suffering, and death of the Lord Jesus Christ while bearing our sins and his ultimate victory.

God the evangelist also summons his people to a missiological obligation (Exod. 19:3–6; Ps. 67; Isa. 66:18–24). In Exodus 19:3–6, God instructs Israel to participate in God's priesthood as agents of his divine blessing. Israel is his "special possession." As his "kingly priests," the whole nation was to function on behalf of the kingdom of God in a mediatorial role in relation to the nations. As a "holy nation," they were totally God's, set apart for his service, not for their own ends. Psalm 67 shows us that God's purpose is to bless all nations. The basic thrust of the psalm is: "May God fully bless us so that the nations may look at us and say that we have been

---

3. Mark J. Boda, *Return to Me: A Biblical Theology of Repentance* (Downers Grove, IL: InterVarsity Press, 2015), 25–26.

truly blessed. Further, through the same blessing, may the rest of the nations come to know God as well." Isaiah 66:18–24 provides what Motyer calls an eschatological "vision of staggering proportions."[4] God's gracious plan for the world is marvelously presented. The Lord himself is the missionary who gathers and rescues people from "all nations," in order that they may see his glory. The ultimate goal of missions is the glory of God, that He may be known and worshipped for who He really is.[5]

I Am He

As we turn to the New Testament witness, we are called to behold our King. Jesus's life was a demonstration of the good news. His incarnation was evangelistic in intent (Matt. 1:21; Luke 2:10–11; John 1:29; Mark 10:45). Note carefully the revelation given to us about Christ's person and work in these verses:

- She will bear a Son, and you shall call His name Jesus, for He will save His people from their sins. (Matt. 1:21)

- Then the angel said to them, "Do not be afraid, for behold, I bring you good tidings of great joy which will be for all the people; for today in the city of David there has been born for you a Savior, who is Christ the Lord." (Luke 2:10–11)

- The next day [John] saw Jesus coming toward him, and said, "Behold, the Lamb of God who takes away the sin of the world!" (John 1:29)

- For even the Son of Man did not come to be served, but to serve, and to give His life a ransom for many. (Mark 10:45)

Christ's teaching was an enunciation and a clarification of the good news. Most remarkably, he claimed to be the only way to God (John 14:6).

---

4. J. Alec Motyer, *The Prophecy of Isaiah: An Introduction & Commentary* (Downers Grove, IL: InterVarsity Press, 1993), 540.
5. John Piper argues "Missions exists because worship doesn't." See John Piper, *Let the Nations Be Glad!: The Supremacy of God in Missions.* 3rd ed. (Grand Rapids: Baker Academic, 2010), 35.

In our age of pluralism and tolerance, many people want to automatically dismiss such a claim as being narrow-minded. How do we know we can trust what Jesus says? For one thing, he lived a perfect life. No other religious leader can claim that reality. First Peter 2:22 reminds us that he committed no sin, and no deceit was found in his mouth. On one occasion Jesus even challenged his enemies to point out any flaws in his life or character: "Which one of you convicts Me of sin?" (John 8:46).

If I ever claimed to be the Son of God, there are many people who could quickly disprove that claim. My wife and my children would hopefully say I'm a nice guy, but perfect? With the evidence they would present, a jury wouldn't have to deliberate more than a nanosecond to determine I was a sinner and that I couldn't possibly be the Son of God. And this would just be from the testimony of people who love me! If I ever asked all the people who didn't like me, "Which one of you convicts me of sin?" the response would be sure and swift. Jesus asked his most ardent enemies to point out even one sin in his life. And the Bible says they stood there without opening their mouths. They would have loved to have been able to point out even one fault, but they couldn't! Their silence spoke volumes. Jesus was the only person to ever lead a perfect life on this earth. Isn't that what you would expect from the Son of God? His teaching can be trusted.

His death provides the basis for the good news. The gospel is a message about Jesus Christ. His incarnate mission reaches its climax at Calvary. There in the fullness of time, Jesus bore our sins in his body on the cross, suffering in our place, "the just for the unjust, so that He might bring us to God" (1 Peter 3:18). Peter also reminds us, "And He Himself bore our sins in His body on the cross, so that we might die to sin and live to righteousness" (1 Peter 2:24). Jesus was very clear about his death. He gave his life willingly to die for the sins of those who believe in him. Scoffers cried out in derision at the cross, "He saved others; He cannot save Himself" (Mark 15:31). Those words were even truer than they could have imagined. Of course Jesus could not save himself. He had come not to save himself, but to save us. He came "to seek and to save that which was lost" (Luke 19:10).

Christ's death was not accidental. It was according to the definite plan and foreknowledge of God (Acts 2:23). It fulfilled what God had foretold through the prophets (Acts 3:18). Justice and love meet at the cross. Sin could not be overlooked if God was to remain holy and just. Yet we were hopeless to pay the penalty. In the cross we see true justice, yet sacrificial love. The cross was God's plan to deal with man's sin. God is both just, and the justi-fier (Rom. 3:26). Because he is holy, only his life was an acceptable sacrifice. He died in our place as our substitute. He died the death that we deserve. Second Corinthians 5:21 teaches us, "He made Him who knew no sin to be sin on our behalf." Galatians 3:13 tells us that Christ became a curse for us. Believers need not fear judgment day, because the one who will judge us is the one who died for us. "This is love," John writes, "not that we loved God, but that he loved us, and sent his Son as an atoning sacrifice for our sins" (1 John 4:10, NIV). No wonder he shouted, "It is finished!" just before he bowed his head and yielded his spirit. We have good news to proclaim!

Jesus Christ's life and death fulfilled the promise God had given Adam and Eve in the garden of Eden after they had sinned. God promised he would send a Savior, a Messiah, who would deliver people from the bondage of sin. Jesus came as that Savior to bring us to God. Christ's resurrection from the dead serves as validation of the good news (1 Cor. 15). I heard a story about a pastor who went on a tour of different religious sites around the world. When the tour would come to the grave of a religious leader, the tour guide would say, "Shhh—quiet. Here lies the body of so-and-so, the founder of the such-and-such religion. Let's have a moment of silence in his honor."

The tour continued in the same manner, with the tour guide asking for a moment of silence at the burial sites of various religious leaders. When they came to Jerusalem, to the tomb of Jesus, the tour guide asked the pastor if he wanted to say anything since he was a Christian. The pastor said, "This is where they laid the body of Jesus Christ after he was cruci-fied on the cross for the sins of the world. And you can shout, you can yell, you can make all the noise you want, because he isn't here!" What does the resurrection mean? It means Jesus's teaching can be trusted. No other teacher has ever risen from the dead to prove the truth of what he taught.

The Commission of the King

In this section we will examine the five different "Great Commission" passages, utilizing a key descriptor for each passage.

Matthew 28:18–20—The Authority
When I ask people to quote the Great Commission from Matthew 28, they normally begin in verse 19 (ASV): "Go ye therefore, and make

disciples of all the nations." But the Great Commission does not begin in verse 19; it begins in verse 18. One of the most foundational principles of Bible study I know is whenever you find a "therefore," find out what it is "there for." What's the "therefore" there for in verse 19? It points us back to verse 18. Why are we to go into all the world and make disciples of all the nations? Because in verse 18 Jesus says all authority has been given to him in heaven and on earth, and as a consequence of that truth, Jesus says I want you to go out and make disciples of all the nations.

We face an increasingly hostile world to the message of the gospel. When sharing the gospel with someone, they might retort, "Who gives you the right to talk to me about something so personal as my soul?" The correct answer is, "The Sovereign Lord of the universe, the creator and sustainer of all things, the one who has all authority!" If we do not comprehend verse 18, then verse 19 will never become a reality in our life. It will not take much to stop us from sharing. But when we understand we are given a commission by the King of kings, the sovereign Lord, the one to whom one day every knee will bow and every tongue will confess, that understanding radically changes our perspective.

One of my favorite figures from church history is the English Reformer Hugh Latimer. Latimer once preached before King Henry VIII and made a rather pointed application concerning sin. Henry was outraged by the boldness of Latimer's sermon and ordered him to apologize in his sermon the following Sunday. Michael Cocoris describes what happened the following Sunday after Latimer read his text to begin his sermon:

> Hugh Lattimer, dost thou know before whom thou are this day to speak? To the high and mighty monarch, the king's most excellent majesty, who can take away thy life, if thou offendest. Therefore, take heed that thou speakest not a word that may displease. But then consider well, Hugh, dost thou not know from whence thou comest—upon Whose message thou are sent? Even by the great and mighty God, Who is all-present and Who beholdeth all thy ways and Who is able to cast thy soul into hell! Therefore, take care that thou deliverest thy message faithfully.[6]

---

6. G. Michael Cocoris, *Evangelism: A Biblical Approach* (Chicago: Moody, 1984), 126.

Cocoris notes that Latimer preached the same message he had preached the week before, with even more energy!

What happened to Latimer? He was martyred, though not by Henry VIII but by his daughter, Mary, whom history knows as "Bloody Mary." I love this account about Hugh Latimer because he stood up to the King of England, the most powerful man in the world at that time, and reminded him that he answered to a higher authority than the King of England; he served the King of Kings and the Lord of Lords. Hugh Latimer understood Matthew 28:18, and we must as well, or else verse 19 will never be a reality in our life. As we share, we are not just doing it because we think it is a good idea! We have the authority of the Creator and Ruler of the universe! We are ambassadors for Christ, ones sent in his name with his message and his authority. The early church understood this reality, testifying, "We must obey God rather than men!" Since our Sovereign Lord has commanded us to share, mere men cannot persuade us otherwise.

Mark 16:15—The Objective

Mark 16:15 gives us the universal scope of the objective. Christ's followers are commanded to preach the gospel to all creation, or to every creature. This mandate reminds us that we are to exclude no one from our gospel proclamation and gospel witness. We are to make our objective to share with everyone in the whole world. That command is clear and simple. My objective as a disciple of Christ is to share with everyone I can. I am to exclude no one.

John 20:21—The Method

"As the Father has sent Me, I also send you." We must go to where people are. I regularly invite people to come to church and encourage my church members to do the same. And within each Sunday's message, I try to give a brief but clear explanation of the gospel message, as I am confident that there will be some in attendance who have not been genuinely converted. But we cannot put all our eggs in the attractional basket. We discussed lostness in the opening chapter when defining evangelism, but let me add two additional reminders here.

First, we should not be surprised or shocked when lost people act lost. We should be surprised when they do not act lost! Second, we must always remember that lost people are not the enemy—they are victims of our true enemy, Satan. The devil has blinded their minds, and he is holding them captive to do his will.

Luke 24:45–49—The Message

Luke 24:45–49 stands as the least well-known of the Great Commission passages, yet it is filled with key emphases, including Christ's death, burial, and resurrection, and repentance for forgiveness of sins. These verses set forth the content of the gospel and the necessary response to the gospel message.

Acts 1:8—Power

Acts 1:8 reminds us the power for evangelism flows from the Holy Spirit. As we analyze scriptural teaching on the functions of the Holy Spirit in evangelism, we see four specific functions he provides.

The Holy Spirit Guides the Witness (Acts 8)

Philip was ministering in Samaria amidst a citywide revival. People were coming to Christ right and left, and yet the Holy Spirit led Philip to leave Samaria and go out to Gaza because there was someone who needed to hear the gospel. Philip had the privilege of leading the Ethiopian to faith in Christ. The Holy Spirit guides the Christian witness. People use different terminology for this prompting of the Holy Spirit, and those "spiritual nudges" we sense are not infallible. But countless Christian witnesses have experienced this type of prompting from the Holy Spirit to talk with someone about Christ. Paul reminds us in Romans 8:14 that "all who are being led by the Spirit of God, these are sons of God." This prompting is subjective, but it is real and tangible.

Believe in a God of divine appointments. Believe in a God who sovereignly arranges circumstances for the communication of the gospel message. I had one student leave the first session of the semester-long evangelism class frustrated about the necessary witnessing reports he would have to complete during the semester. He left class to drive to work, and as he parked in a parking garage by his workplace, he decided he would speak about Christ to the first person he saw. Even though he was sure that person would tell him to go jump in a lake, at least he could say he attempted to witness.

This student spoke to the first person he encountered in the parking garage and asked him, "Is Jesus Christ your personal Lord and Savior?" To his surprise, the man answered, "No, he isn't, but I would love for him to be. Can you tell me how I can know Jesus Christ?" This student confessed his lack of faith to me in class the next day as he told me he had been reminded that God is a God of divine appointments.

When I was a relatively new believer, I was encouraged to pray every day for the opportunity to witness. Now that is a good prayer to pray. Could you imagine what might happen if every believer prayed that prayer every single day? But I quickly realized that I needed to add an element to that prayer. Some mornings I would begin by asking God to give me opportunities to witness that day, and then at the end of the day think, *Beougher, you're an idiot! God dropped three opportunities in your lap today and you were so spiritually insensitive you missed all three!* So now I begin each day praying for spiritual sensitivity to the opportunities God will bring across my path.

But even praying for sensitivity must be accompanied by walking in the Spirit and by a commitment to witness when the door opens. One of the missed opportunities in my life stemmed from my own sinfulness and selfishness. I had arranged babysitting for our children (three of them at that time) so my wife and I could travel a few hours away to attend a piano recital by one of her college professors. Sharon completed a music education degree with an emphasis in piano at UNC Chapel Hill, and her major professor had invited us to be his guests at this piano recital. I began that day praying for spiritual sensitivity to witnessing opportunities and began the day filled with the Holy Spirit.

But due to multiple frustrations (babysitter cancelling at the last minute and having to arrange another babysitter; bad directions to the recital hall resulting in lots of extra driving; and a recital that lasted far longer than I thought it should last), when we left the recital hall, I was being selfish and sinful. I said a few harsh words to my wife (something about my day being ruined), and we started our drive home in stony silence.

I had to stop for gas, and in the spirit of Murphy's Law, the pay-at-the-pump feature was broken. I thought to myself, *Two hundred thousand gas stations in the US, and I get the one where the pay-at-the-pump is broken.* My selfish, sinful heart began to pout even more with the enormous burden this situation had placed on me, so I had my own private pity party as I had to walk the few steps to go inside the store to pay for my gas.

As I was handing my credit card to the young lady behind the counter, I sensed a prompting from the Holy Spirit to talk to this woman about Christ. Because I was being sinful and selfish, I stubbornly refused. A second "spiritual nudge" followed, which I likewise rejected. As I was walking through the store to leave, I was almost knocked down by a large truck driver who was making a beeline for the store clerk. He walked right up to her, put his face close to hers (invading her personal space), and asked in a loud voice, "Ma'am, do you know Jesus?" The way he pronounced the name of Jesus made it seem like a three-syllable word.

What do you think was my immediate response? Repentance? While repentance would come, that was not my immediate response. Instead of repentance, my immediate heart response was one of criticism. My sinful, selfish heart began to criticize this man's evangelistic methodology (obviously ignoring the fact that he was seeking to witness while I had rejected the Spirit's prompting to do the same). I thought, *That's not the way you witness! You got too close to her, invading her personal space. And that question is not the best way to begin a spiritual conversation with a stranger. And furthermore, you can't even pronounce the name of Jesus correctly!*

My critical thoughts were interrupted by this woman's reply to the truck driver. "No, I don't know Jesus," she responded. "But I want to know him. Can you tell me how I can know him?" I sprinted out of the store weeping. That day I better understood the text in Luke's Gospel where it says that Peter "went out and wept bitterly." My wife saw me crying and assumed I had been convicted for how poorly I had been treating her—and yes, I had to apologize to my wife for my sinful and selfish behavior that day. But it was as if the Lord was saying to me, "Okay, Mr. Evangelism Professor. You've written books on evangelism; this man has probably never read a book on evangelism. You've taught classes on evangelism; this man probably hasn't attended a single class on witnessing. Yet when I prompt him to share, he is obedient."

We must pray for spiritual sensitivity, but then we must continue to be filled with the Spirit so we are eager to respond when we receive that "spiritual nudge." The Holy Spirit guides the witness.

The Holy Spirit Empowers the Witness (Acts 1:8)

I regularly will have church members and students say to me, "I just don't feel adequate to do evangelism." As I noted in chapter 1, whenever that happens, I grab that person by the shoulders and exclaim, "That's great! That's wonderful! You are exactly where God wants you to be! God doesn't work through people who feel they are adequate, but through those who acknowledge their weakness and need for God's empowering strength."

I first met Billy Graham back in 1990 when I was teaching evangelism at Wheaton Graduate School. I had the privilege of spending an hour with him as we walked through the museum at the Billy Graham Center on Wheaton's campus. I had envisioned this day for some time and had a long list of questions about evangelism I wanted to ask him. But when I met him, my mind went blank. I blurted out the only question that came to my mind: "Mr. Graham, do you ever feel nervous when you are witnessing to someone one-on-one?" He looked at me like that was the stupidest question he had ever heard, but when he saw it was a serious question, he replied, "Of course! Who doesn't? In fact, if I didn't feel a bit nervous I would assume I was witnessing in my own strength. God allows us to feel a bit nervous, so we will trust in him and his power."

Let's apply this principle. If the apostle Paul (see 1 Cor. 2) and Billy Graham both needed to be empowered by the Holy Spirit to do evangelism, how much more so do we need that empowering? This empowering is great news because it means we do not have to witness in our own strength. How does the Holy Spirit empower us? Through his constant presence he gives us strength to overcome fear. An evangelist told me once what when he senses fear welling up in his heart, he views that fear as a blinking red light with the Holy Spirit whispering, "Trust in me!"

The Holy Spirit Convicts the Unbeliever (John 16:8–11)

You and I cannot convict anyone of sin, righteousness, and judgment. The Holy Spirit must do that work. And guess what? He does that work well. The Holy Spirit convicts or convinces the unbeliever.

The Holy Spirit Regenerates the Unbeliever (John 3:5–7)

Just as you and I cannot convict or convince anyone, likewise we cannot convert anyone. That is the Holy Spirit's role. The Holy Spirit brings regeneration to those who are spiritually dead. The Holy Spirit affects the new birth. Only God's Spirit can raise from the dead those who are dead in trespasses and sins. Every new birth is a miracle wrought by God through his Spirit.

THE ULTIMATE VICTORY
(MATT. 24:14; REV. 5:9; 7:9; 14:6; 11:15)

Matthew 24:14 instructs us that the gospel must be preached as a witness to every nation, and then the end shall come. Revelation 5:9, 7:9, and 14:6 assure us that in heaven will be people from every tongue and tribe and nation. The Great Commission will be fulfilled! Hear this heavenly witness: "The kingdom of the world has become the kingdom of our Lord and of His Christ; and He shall reign forever and ever!" (Rev. 11:15).

We labor in the confidence that the work will be finished. Evangelism, as the heartbeat of theology, directs our energy to that goal toward which history is moving—the return of Christ and the hastening of his kingdom. Victory is certain! In the councils of eternity, the celebration has already begun. As Andreas Köstenberger and Peter O'Brien maintain, "This theme of God's saving purposes reaching the ends of the earth forms a grand envelope that contains the entire story of Scripture."[7] God's saving plan is the major thrust of the Scriptures from beginning to end.

---

7. Andreas J. Köstenberger and Peter Thomas O'Brien, *Salvation to the Ends of the Earth: A Biblical Theology of Mission*, New Studies in Biblical Theology 11 (Downers Grove, IL: IVP Academic, 2001), 26.

CHAPTER 3

THE BIBLICAL BASIS FOR EVANGELISM (PART 2)

THIS CHAPTER CONTINUES THE EXAMINATION of the biblical basis for evangelism by noting several biblical metaphors for evangelism and then by examining New Testament examples of sharing the good news.

BIBLICAL METAPHORS FOR EVANGELISM

Scripture is filled with numerous metaphors, or pictures, of the evangelistic enterprise. The paragraphs that follow highlight several of these metaphors.

Announcing the Deeds of God (1 Peter 2:4–5, 9–10)
- And coming to Him as to a living stone which has been rejected by men, but is choice and precious in the sight of God, you also, as living stones, are being built up as a spiritual house for a holy priesthood, to offer up spiritual sacrifices acceptable to God through Jesus Christ.

- But you are a chosen race, a royal priesthood, a holy nation, a people for God's own possession, so that you may proclaim the excellencies of Him who has called you out of darkness into His marvelous light; for you once were not a people, but now you are the people of God; you had not received mercy, but now you have received mercy.

Note carefully the progression in these verses. The first duty is to worship (v. 5), and the second duty is to witness: "that you may declare the excellencies of Him who has called you out of darkness into His marvelous light" (v. 9).

Sowing Seed (Mark 4:1–9)

This parable of the sower reminds us of two important truths. We are called to sow the gospel seed indiscriminately, and there will be differing responses from different people. Too often I fear we misapply this parable. Instead of sowing the seed widely, we become "soil inspectors" and only sow gospel seed where we think we find good soil. Jesus did not say, "The sower went out to inspect the soil, and where he thought he found good soil, he sowed the seed; but where he suspected the soil might be hard, or shallow, or thorny, he withheld the seed." As believers we are called to be indiscriminate sowers of the gospel seed. Live as a sower, not as a soil inspector!

Reaping a Harvest (Matt. 9:37–38)

"Then He said to His disciples, 'The harvest is plentiful, but the workers are few. Therefore beseech the Lord of the harvest to send out workers into His harvest.'" This agricultural metaphor reminds us that we go out not just to acknowledge the reality of the harvest, but to reap the harvest! Our desire is always to reap a harvest of souls, even though in some settings we end up sowing the seed instead of reaping the harvest. Jesus taught both sowing and reaping are necessary parts of the process (John 4).

Fishing for People (Matt. 4:18–20)

"Now as Jesus was walking by the Sea of Galilee, He saw two brothers, Simon who was called Peter, and Andrew his brother, casting a net into the sea; for they were fishermen. And He said to them, 'Follow Me, and I will make you fishers of men.' Immediately they left their nets and followed Him." As believers, our calling is to be "fishers of people." One key principle this illustrates is the need to regularly place ourselves where the fish are located. Missionary C. T. Studd exemplified this: "Some wish to live within the sound / of Church or Chapel bell, / I want to run a rescue shop / within a yard of hell."[1] We need to connect with lost persons in our world.

Bearing Witness (Acts 1:8)

"But you will receive power when the Holy Spirit has come upon you; and you shall be My witnesses both in Jerusalem, and in all Judea and Samaria, and even to the remotest part of the earth." This promise and command, given together in tandem, remind us that one of the reasons the Spirit was sent was to empower us for witness. We can no more restrict the command to witness to the first disciples than we can restrict the promise of the Holy Spirit. A witness is someone who tells what he or she has seen or experienced.

Creating Thirst (Matt. 5:13; Col. 4:5–6)

- You are the salt of the earth; but if the salt has become tasteless, how can it be made salty again? It is no longer good for anything, except to be thrown out and trampled underfoot by men.

- Conduct yourselves with wisdom toward outsiders, making the most of the opportunity. Let your speech always be with grace, as though seasoned with salt, so that you will know how you should respond to each person.

When commentators discuss Matthew 5:13, they point out the various uses of salt in the ancient Near East, including that salt preserves flavors. Paul's admonition in Colossians 4 adds another element: creating thirst for the water of life. Jesus created spiritual thirst with the Samaritan woman at the water well when he talked about living water.

Holding Light (Matt. 5:14–16; Phil. 2:15–16)

Another biblical metaphor for evangelism is shining the light of the gospel in the midst of a very dark world: "You are the light of the world." The darker the world seems to get, the brighter the light of the gospel will shine. We are not called to "hide" that light but to let it shine to everyone around.

---

1. Norman Grubb, *C. T. Studd: Cricketer and Pioneer* (Cambridge: Lutterworth, 2014), 154.

Liberating the Captive (John 8:31–32)

Unlike the so-called "prosperity gospel," the true biblical gospel does not promise freedom from hardship, pain, or suffering. The biblical gospel offers a reality far more significant: freedom from sin! As we share the good news of Jesus Christ in the power of the Holy Spirit, captives to sin are set free.

Radiating Fragrance (2 Cor. 2:14–16)

"For we are a fragrance of Christ to God among those who are being saved and among those who are perishing." This metaphor is one of my favorite ones for evangelism. Who doesn't like a fragrant aroma, such as the sweet smell of a lilac bush in full bloom? A faithful Christian's life not only gives off light, it also emits an aroma. That aroma proves offensive to some (an aroma of death), but to others it is an aroma of life. These verses remind us that no matter how winsomely we share the gospel, some people will reject that message of good news. And yet what a privilege is ours! God has chosen believers to "manifest through us the sweet aroma of the knowledge of him in every place."

Reconciling (2 Cor. 5:18–19)

These verses remind us that all believers have been "called to ministry"—in this instance, a "ministry of reconciliation." As followers of Christ, we have been given the "ministry of reconciliation" and have had committed to us "the word of reconciliation" (the gospel).

Serving as Christ's Representative (2 Cor. 5:20; Eph. 6:19–20)

Believers are privileged to serve as Christ's representatives, as his ambassadors. An ambassador does not invent the message he or she delivers; an ambassador faithfully delivers the message of the one who sent him or her. One of my friends uses this concept as a bridge to share the gospel. When asked what he does, my friend will reply, "I'm an ambassador!"

"An ambassador, what country?" comes the reply.
"Oh, it is much bigger than a country."
"Bigger than a country? Do continents have ambassadors?"
"Oh, it is bigger than a continent."
"What kind of ambassador are you?"

"I'm an ambassador for a kingdom—the kingdom of God. Let me share with you the message I have been commissioned to deliver."

Delivery Person (1 Cor. 15:3)

Our world is filled with delivery people, delivering everything from newspapers to Amazon Prime orders. Paul references his role as a delivery person in 1 Corinthians 15:3 and notes that he delivers his message faithfully.

JESUS AND EVANGELISM

Entire books have been written on how Jesus dealt with persons in "evangelistic" encounters. My favorite work is Robert Coleman's *The Master's Way of Personal Evangelism,* where Coleman reflects on Jesus's encounters with various people.[2] In this section I will give an overview of some key principles we can glean from the life of Jesus in relating to others, drawn specifically from John 4 and his encounter with the Samaritan woman.

Jesus was not bound by the cultural norms of his day (John 4:4).

After the Passover, Jesus starts back to Galilee. What is strange is that he goes by way of Samaria because no "proper" Jew would have any dealings with Samaritans. In Jewish eyes, the Samaritans were a mongrel race, a collection of half-breeds produced by union of wayward Israelites with Gentiles following the conquest of the northern kingdom by Assyria. So intense was the hatred of the Jews towards the Samaritans that they would seek to avoid any contact. Travelers from Jerusalem going north to Galilee would cross the Jordan River at the Samaritan boundary and journey along the eastern bank of the Jordan, bypassing Samaritan territory completely. Jews believed they would become contaminated if even the sole of their foot stepped on Samaritan soil. But Jesus ignored the cultural norms of his day and traveled through Samaria. The "need" to go through Samaria was not a geographical need but a spiritual need, as Jesus was showing the gospel was good news for all peoples.

---

2. Robert E. Coleman, *The Master's Way of Personal Evangelism* (Wheaton, IL: Crossway, 1997).

Jesus took the initiative to reach out to the Samaritan woman (John 4:7–9).

A woman comes out from the village to fill her water jar at midday. It is unusual that she would come at this time. Most women would come in the cool of the early morning or late evening. But she wanted to avoid contact with other women to avoid their piercing stares and words of rejection. This Samaritan woman is a prostitute, and she was constantly subjected to the scorn of the "respectable" people of society. And yet Jesus spoke to her, crossing religious and cultural barriers. As verse 8 reminds us, Jews studiously avoided any contact with Samaritans. In addition, in that society, a man would not converse in public with a woman, especially one with her reputation. Jesus took the initiative to speak with her.

Jesus began with common ground (water), but then pointed to spiritual realities (John 4:10–14).

People today are just like this woman in the first century: trying to satisfy their spiritual thirst with cheap substitutes that do not satisfy. Jesus offers living water—only he can satisfy—both here and now and in eternity.

Jesus responded to the issues the woman raised, but kept on track with the message (John 4:21–24).

In an attempt to turn the focus away from her sin, the woman brings up the topic of worship. Jesus briefly answered her question, but then brought the focus back to her need of a Messiah.

Jesus spoke truth and revealed to her what her real need was (John 4:15–18).

We hear regular voices in our culture saying that Christians should not be so judgmental, that we need to display love and grace. Jesus certainly displayed love and grace to this woman, but part of extending love and grace is being honest with people about their spiritual condition. Jesus was characterized as being "full of grace and truth" (John 1:14), and this encounter demonstrates that reality once again.

Jesus invited the woman to believe in him (John 4:25–26).

Jesus openly declared who he was—that he was the Messiah, the Savior of the world. John 4 continues with showing how this woman, after putting her faith in Jesus as Messiah, then went into her village and shared the good news. We see the response in verse 39: "From that city many of the Samaritans believed in Him because of the word of the woman who testified, 'He told me all the things that I have done.'"

EVANGELISM IN THE EARLY CHURCH

Michael Green begins his classic work *Evangelism in the Early Church* with this powerful reminder:

> It was a small group of eleven men whom Jesus commissioned to carry on his work, and bring the gospel to the whole world. They were not distinguished; they were not well educated; they had no influential backers. In their own nation they were nobodies and, in any case, their own nation was a mere second-class province on the eastern extremity of the Roman map. If they had stopped to weigh up the probabilities of succeeding in their mission, even granted their conviction that Jesus was alive and that his Spirit went with them to equip them for their task, their hearts must surely have sunk, so heavily were the odds weighted against them. How could they possibly succeed? And yet they did.[3]

How could they possibly succeed? Look at all their liabilities! They had no seminaries. They had no tracts. They had no lifestyle evangelism seminars on DVD. They had no national polling agencies doing demographics on the local population. They had no buildings. No choir robes. No microphones or padded pews. What caused this small band of followers who deserted Jesus at his trial to become those who "turned the world upside down"? (Acts 17:6). How did they seek to fulfill his final words to them to "Go and make disciples of all the nations"? The following is an overview of problems the early church faced as they sought to share the good news of Christ and how they responded to those challenges.

---

3. Michael Green, *Evangelism in the Early Church* (London: Hodder and Stoughton, 1970), 13.

The problem of focus: Make evangelism a top priority.

The problem of focus asks the question, "What should the church be doing?" We can see that the church can and should participate in many different activities: evangelism, discipleship, fellowship, service, prayer, worship, all of which are vitally important. I have heard that when George Sweeting was president of Moody Bible Institute he used to keep a sign on his desk that read, "The main thing is to keep the main thing the main thing." While all of the "marks of the church" are crucial, what is the one activity believers cannot do in heaven? *Evangelism!* You can *worship* in heaven, but you can't *witness!* You can *fellowship* in heaven, but you can't *witness!* The early Christians had a deep burden for the lost. They were ready to share Christ with others in season and out of season. Everyone sensed his or her responsibility for the Great Commission.

The early church had a deep conviction that people needed Christ. They ministered in a day of great religious pluralism, like our own; but far from letting that discourage them, it caused them to make evangelism a top priority—on every page in the book of Acts you see the gospel being shared with others.

The problem of powerlessness: Remain open and sensitive to the leading of the Holy Spirit.

As I have mentioned already, I often tell people that their feelings of inadequacy in evangelism can be a good thing because God wants us to recognize that we are not adequate in our own strength. He never intended for us to live the Christian life in our own power. It was the power of the Holy Spirit that transformed the disciples. Jesus knew that his disciples would be ineffective without the power of the Holy Spirit (they had already demonstrated that truth quite convincingly!). So he told them, "Do not leave Jerusalem, but wait for the gift my Father promised, which you have heard me speak about. For John baptized with water, but in a few days you will be baptized with the Holy Spirit" (Acts 1:4–5, NIV). A. W. Tozer once maintained, "If the Holy Spirit was withdrawn from the church today, ninety-five percent of what we do would go on, and no one would know the difference."[4]

---

4. Cited in R. T. Kendall, *Holy Fire: A Balanced Look at the Holy Spirit's Work in Our Lives* (Lake Mary, FL: Charisma House, 2014), 9.

The problem of apathy: Ask God to give you a burden for the lost.

I saw a bumper sticker years ago that read, "Apathy is rampant in America, but who cares?" Tragically, that is sometimes true of the church. Apathy is rampant in the church, but who cares? The answer is clear: God cares! God wants us to have a burden for those who do not know him. The early church displayed this burden for the lost.

The problem of discouragement: Don't just talk about prayer—pray!

In prayer, we take our eyes off ourselves and put them on God. We are reminded that he is able. Luke 11 records the disciples asking Jesus to teach them how to pray. The question is: Did they learn? As you study the book of Acts, you have to conclude they did. Throughout the book of Acts, you see the disciples praying. Prayer was the starting point for their evangelism. E. M. Bounds drove home forcefully the need for prayer in his book *Power through Prayer*: "What the Church needs today is not more machinery or better, not new organizations or more and novel methods, but men whom the Holy Ghost can use—men of prayer, men mighty in prayer. The Holy Ghost does not flow through methods, but through men. He does not come on machinery, but on men. He does not anoint plans, but men—men of prayer."[5] Which activity do we do more often, talk about prayer or actually pray?

The problem of methodology: Point people to Jesus.

Our goal is to point people to Jesus. He alone is the Savior. Hope is found only in him. The early church avoided needless controversies on secondary matters so they could keep the focus on Christ. We must point people to Jesus.

The problem of motivation: Let yourself be overcome with the wonder of the message.

Matthew 12:34 reminds us that "the mouth speaks out of that which fills the heart." When we reflect on the good news of the gospel—how we have been transferred from the kingdom of darkness to the kingdom of light—how can we not be motivated to share this good news with others? If Matthew 12:34 is true (and it is), then we must ask the question: What is filling our heart?

---

5. E. M. Bounds, *Power through Prayer* (Grand Rapids: Baker, 1972), 7.

Problem of "selective sharing": Believe in the power of the gospel.

Paul testifies, "For I am not ashamed of the gospel, for it is the power of God unto salvation to everyone who believes, to the Jew first and also to the Greek" (Rom. 1:16). Do we really believe that the gospel is the power of God unto salvation? We too often settle for a religion of the "possible." We give up on people too easily and write them off as prospects for salvation. There are individuals and churches all over the world who are reaching people even though others are telling them there are too many obstacles or that it is too difficult. I am convinced there are two types of attitudes among Christians and churches: (1) we can't reach people today—it has become too difficult; or (2) with God's help, we will reach people. I am convinced they both are right in their own way! Those who say, "We can't" usually don't. Those who say, "With God's help we can" usually do.

The problem of skepticism: Demonstrate the love of Christ.

People are wondering today whether following Christ makes any difference. Numerous scandals among Christian leaders in the church have made people skeptical. Jesus reminds us that one of our greatest apologetics is a changed life: "A new commandment I give to you, that you love one another, even as I have loved you. By this all men will know that you are my disciples, if you have love one for another" (John 13:34–35). The great Christian apologist Justin Martyr noted it wasn't so much intellectual arguments that convinced him Christianity was true but that he saw people with nothing in common who genuinely loved one another.

The problem of societal pressure: Live for "an audience of one."

The early believers were faithful in spite of persecution. They displayed a "holy audacity" in sharing their faith with others. Persecution could not silence their voices. They understood the lordship of Jesus Christ. To them, "Jesus is Lord" was more than a slogan; it was a lifestyle.

CHAPTER 4

THEOLOGY OF EVANGELISM

ROBERT COLEMAN TELLS OF AN ARTIST, seeking to depict on canvas the meaning of evangelism, painting a storm at sea. Black clouds filled the sky. Illuminated by a flash of lightning, a little boat could be seen disintegrating under the pounding of the ocean. Men were struggling in the swirling waters, their anguished faces crying out for help. The only glimmer of hope appeared in the foreground of the painting, where a large rock protruded out of the water. There, clutching desperately with both hands, was one lone sailor. It was a powerful scene. Viewing the painting, one could see in the storm a symbol of mankind's helpless condition. The only hope of salvation was "the rock of ages," a shelter in the time of storm.

But as the artist reflected upon his work, he realized that the painting did not accurately portray his subject. So he discarded that canvas and painted another. It was very similar to the first: the black clouds, the flashing lightning, the angry waters, the little boat crushed by the pounding waves, and the crew vainly struggling in the water. In the foreground the sailor was clutching the large rock for salvation. But the artist made one change: the survivor was holding on with only one hand, and with the other hand he was reaching down to pull up a drowning friend.

Coleman argues that is the New Testament picture of evangelism—that hand reaching down to rescue the perishing. People who grasp the truth of the gospel dare not hold on with both hands, for there are multitudes who have not yet received the message of God's redeeming grace. The very nature of our salvation makes us reach out to others with the word of life. This imperative gives rise to a theology immediately related to the propagation of the gospel. Such a theology does not rest upon a few scattered texts of Scripture but draws upon the entire scope of biblical revelation. Evangelism brings into focus the purpose of all Christian doctrine. In fact, Coleman maintains that evangelism is "the heartbeat of all Christian theology."[1]

Some in our day seem to make a keen mind antithetical to a warm heart and a focus on theology antithetical to a commitment to practical ministry. As Carl F. H. Henry said in 1967, "In these next years we must strive harder to become theologian-evangelists, rather than to remain content as just theologians or just evangelists."[2] Henry's challenge mirrors James Denney's famous dictum: "If evangelists were our theologians or theologians our evangelists, we should at least be nearer the ideal church."[3] This chapter seeks to lay out some key theological foundations for evangelism.

THE AUTHORITY OF SCRIPTURE

To summarize Francis Schaeffer, Christianity is based on two very important realities: God is there, and he is not silent.[4] He has revealed himself to humankind, and the record of both the divine acts and the divine speech is found in Scripture. A necessary foundation for theology is that God exists, and he communicates with us. The only reason we can do theology at all, at least in terms of objective truth, is that there is a God who has revealed himself to us.

Theology is not simply subjective; it is not just our own reason or our own experience. Without God being there and speaking, we would have no objective vantage point from which to view life. Anything we said would just be our opinion. The God who is there has spoken—that reality is vital—and

1. Robert E. Coleman, "Theology of Evangelism," *Review & Expositor* 77, no. 4 (1980): 479.
2. Carl F. H. Henry, "Facing a New Day in Evangelism," in *One Race, One Gospel, One Task: Vol. 1*, eds. Carl F. H. Henry and W. Stanley Mooneyham (Minneapolis: World Wide, 1967), 13.
3. James Denney, *The Death of Christ* (New Canaan, CT: Keats, 1981), viii.
4. See Francis A. Schaeffer's works, *The God Who Is There: Speaking Historic Christianity into the Twentieth Century* (Downers Grove, IL: InterVarsity, 1968) and *He Is There and He Is Not Silent* (Wheaton, IL: Tyndale House, 1972).

the God who is there is incomprehensible! We wouldn't be able to figure him out unless he revealed himself to us. Now it is true that he has not given us exhaustive knowledge of himself. God has not revealed to us all that he knows. Deuteronomy 29:29 reminds us of that reality: "The secret things belong to the LORD our God, but the things revealed belong to us and to our sons forever, that we may observe all the words of this law." Even if God did reveal all of his mysteries to us, we would not understand them!

God must take the initiative to reveal himself to us. And this reality existed even before the fall: even Adam and Eve in their sinless state in the garden needed to have revelation from God. The author of Hebrews teaches us, "God, after He spoke long ago to the fathers in the prophets in many portions and in many ways, in these last days has spoken to us in His Son, whom He appointed heir of all things, through whom also He made the world" (Heb. 1:1–2). In the past, "God spoke to our forefathers through the prophets," while in the last days, "He has spoken to us through His son." What is consistent? God spoke! He spoke through the prophets, but now there is finality.

As we reflect on a theology of evangelism, we must begin with our authoritative source: Scripture. Where we begin in theology largely determines where we end. Evangelism is but a reflection of a God who has spoken. The gospel is a message sent from heaven—a message of revelation from a father who is ever seeking to save his prodigal children. John Stott maintains, "Without the Bible world evangelization would be not only impossible but actually inconceivable. It is the Bible that lays upon us the responsibility to evangelize the world, gives us a gospel to proclaim, tells us how to proclaim it, and promises us that it is God's power for salvation to every believer."[5]

In this introductory work I will not detail the arguments for the inspiration and authority of Scripture, as many others have done that exceedingly well elsewhere. The Bible is inspired by God (literally God-breathed) and inerrant (without error), and therefore authoritative. One can believe in an inerrant Bible and yet not be evangelistic, but that problem is with the individual, not with the Scriptures. So while a high view of Scripture

---

5. John R. W. Stott, "The Bible in World Evangelization," in *Perspectives on the World Christian Movement: A Reader*, eds. Ralph D. Winter and Steven C. Hawthorne (Pasadena, CA: William Carey Library, 1981), 9.

does not itself guarantee an evangelistic lifestyle, a low view of Scripture cuts the nerve of evangelism. Harold Lindsell notes:

> Perhaps the best way to show how dramatic the missionary retreat has been is to look at the percentage decline in the number of overseas missionaries among some of the major denominations between 1962 and 1979: Episcopal Church, 79 percent decline; Lutheran Church of America, 70 percent; United Presbyterian Church in the U.S.A., 72 percent; United Church of Christ, 68 percent; Christian Church Disciples, 66 percent; United Methodist Church, 46 percent; American Lutheran Church, 44 percent.

Lindsell concludes: "Though many factors contributed to this decline, it is legitimate to reckon that these figures are a rough index of the depth of conviction about basic Christian doctrine—the nature of the gospel, the lostness of mankind apart from Christ, and the necessity of obeying biblical mandates calling for sacrifice and discipline for the sake of advancing the kingdom of Christ."[6] When people start picking and choosing what parts of the Bible they are going to view as authentic, isn't it interesting that the "hard sayings" are usually the first to be jettisoned?

A student of history observes that the degree of commitment to evangelism, whether from a church or an individual, is often commensurate with the degree of their conviction about the authority of the Bible. Prominent evangelists in the history of the church have been those who believed in the full truthfulness of Scripture. When Christians lose confidence in the Bible, they lose their passion for evangelism. Arthur Johnston noted that rationalism did not leave a heritage of evangelism.[7] Why witness if you do not have a saving message?

---

6. Harold Lindsell, "The Major Denominations Are Jumping Ship," *Christianity Today,* September 16, 1981, 16.
7. Writing about the missionary movement of the nineteenth century, Johnston explained, "No one questions seriously the evangelical stance of the missionary movement of the nineteenth century. It was known to be biblical in doctrine, godly in conduct, emphasizing personal reconciliation with God, and concerned for human and national welfare. While the Church in some countries was adversely influenced by Socinianism, rationalism, Darwin evolutionism, and finally, modernism and humanism, the forces allied with the cause of world evangelization had their moorings in the authority of the infallible Holy Scriptures." See Arthur Johnston, *The Battle for World Evangelism* (Wheaton, IL: Tyndale House, 1978), 33–34.

Even Billy Graham, in his early ministry, struggled with the temptation to doubt the truth of Scripture. A fellow evangelist by the name of Charles (Chuck) Templeton had embraced some higher critical views on the Bible during his studies at Princeton Theological Seminary. Templeton told Graham he would have to change his simple message in order to reach people.

Templeton's challenge to the authority of Scripture occasioned a struggle in Graham's heart and mind. While in California in 1949, Graham took his Bible into the woods at a retreat center. After a long period of struggle, he responded:

> Oh, God, I cannot prove certain things. I cannot answer some of the questions Chuck is raising and some of the other people are raising, but I accept this Book by faith as the Word of God. Where there are things I cannot understand, I will reserve judgment until I receive more light. If this pleases Thee, give me authority as I proclaim Thy word, and through that authority convict men of sin and turn sinners to the Savior.

Later Graham would reflect about the power of that commitment:

> [It] gave power and authority to my preaching that has never left me. The gospel in my hands became a hammer and a flame. . . . That flame melted away unbelief in the hearts of the people and moved them to decide for Christ. I felt as though I had a rapier [blade] in my hand and through the power of the Bible, was slashing deeply into men's consciousness, leading them to surrender to God.[8]

From that day forward Billy Graham's preaching was characterized by the phrase, "the Bible says." Graham's article in the first edition of *Christianity Today* (October 15, 1956) was titled "Biblical Authority in Evangelism." He made this appeal to his readers: "I am . . . fervently urging a return to Bible-centered preaching—a Gospel presentation that says without

---

8.   Billy Graham, "Biblical Authority in Evangelism," *Christianity Today* 1, no. 1 (October 15, 1956): 5–6.

apology and without ambiguity 'Thus saith the Lord.' . . . Preach the Scriptures with authority!"

Below I will outline three ways in which the Bible provides our basis for reaching the world with the gospel. The Bible gives us the mandate for world evangelization, the message for world evangelization, and the power for world evangelization.

Mandate for World Evangelization

In a world awash with pluralism, the Bible reminds us we are commissioned to take the gospel to the ends of the earth. We have already discussed the Great Commission passages in chapter 2, and they remind us of our mandate for world evangelization.

Message for World Evangelization

The Bible also furnishes the message for world evangelization. Evangelism is the announcement that salvation has come. Why witness if people are not lost? How do we know they are lost? *Because we accept the veracity of the Bible.* How do we know Jesus can save? *Because we believe the Bible.* How do we know *only* Jesus can save? *Because the Bible says so!* The authority of Scripture rests on the authority of Christ himself. Authentic evangelism is a divine mandate mediated to us through the teachings of the Bible. Thus the invitation we offer is not ours. It is his.

The only source you have for knowing about Christ is the Bible. Today we face great cultural pressure to water down beliefs about the exclusivity of the gospel, human sexuality, or the value of every person. We are told we must listen to more modern and more wise voices than the voice of Scripture. Evangelism involves the proclamation of the good news found in the Bible: the good news of what God is like and what he has done to bring forgiveness to those who have rebelled against him.

Power for World Evangelization

The Scriptures also provide the power for world evangelization. Hebrews 4:12 reminds us, "For the word of God is living and active and sharper than any two-edged sword." God has promised to bless his Word. The Spirit speaks to people through the Word. Romans 10:17 instructs us that "faith comes from hearing, and hearing by the word of Christ." Preaching the gospel is indispensable. It is the God-appointed means by which the prince of darkness is defeated, and the light comes streaming into people's hearts. There is power in God's gospel: his power for salvation (Rom. 1:16).

LOSTNESS OF HUMANITY

Another key theological foundation for evangelism is the lostness of humanity. The Scriptures remind us that ultimately there are only two categories of people in the world: lost and saved. The Scriptures teach us that without Christ, individuals are spiritually dead (Eph. 2:1).

They are alienated from the life of God (Eph. 4:18), and they are without hope and without God in the world (Eph. 2:12). Paul describes this lostness in 2 Corinthians 4:3–4: "And even if our gospel is veiled, it is veiled to those who are perishing, in whose case the god of this world has blinded the minds of the unbelieving so that they might not see the light of the gospel of the glory of Christ, who is the image of God."

Those who do not know Christ are perishing. Even John 3:16, perhaps the most widely quoted verse in the Bible, reminds us that people will perish apart from faith in Christ. Human beings have a fatal disease: sin. The soul that sins must die (Ezek. 18:20). The only remedy for that fatal disease is the cross of Jesus Christ. Without faith in Christ, we will perish in our sin. We have both an inclusive message (whosoever will may come) but also an exclusive message (Jesus is the only way to God the Father).

GOD THE EVANGELIST

Lewis Drummond correctly argues, "Evangelism begins in theology, not anthropology."[9] When we examine Scripture concerning "theology proper," or the doctrine of God, we see a clear picture of "God the evangelist."

God's Nature and Character

Love yearns to make itself known! In Luke 15 we find three parables about lostness: the lost sheep, the lost silver, and the lost son. All three parables point to the same reality: the loving heart of God toward sinners and his rejoicing over the repentance and return of those objects of his

---

9.   Lewis A. Drummond, *The Word of the Cross: A Contemporary Theology of Evangelism* (Nashville: Broadman, 2000), 98.

love. Two times in this passage Jesus states that there is great joy in heaven when a sinner repents (vv. 7, 10). In Luke 15:11–32, the spotlight is on the father's manner of receiving his lost son who returns to him. The real surprise in the story is that the fattened calf is the one who got killed! God welcomes repentant sinners into his presence.

God's Initiative

These parables also illustrate God's initiative. In Luke 15:4–7, the story of the lost sheep, the focus is on the seeking shepherd. God initiates evangelism, and he empowers evangelism. As Romans 5:8 reminds us, "But God demonstrates His own love toward us, in that while we were yet sinners, Christ died for us." What a beautiful picture of God's initiative in our salvation! He did not wait for us to get our act together, or he would be waiting a long time. No, he took the initiative in our salvation—while we were yet sinners, Christ died for us. And 1 John 4:19 teaches us, "We love, because he first loved us."

God's Plan

What is God's plan to communicate his message of redemption to the world? Think of all the possibilities God could have chosen to communicate the message of salvation. He could have written the four spiritual laws in the heavens using the stars; he could have written "Steps to Peace with Me" on stone tablets in multiple languages and scattered them across the earth; he could have used animals (talking donkeys) to communicate the good news; and he most certainly could have employed angels as heavenly messengers of the saving message of the gospel. God could have used any of those methods, yet he chose to use human beings as messengers of salvation.

THE SOVEREIGNTY OF GOD AND SALVATION

C. H. Spurgeon was once asked if he could reconcile divine sovereignty with human responsibility. He replied, "I wouldn't try. I never reconcile friends."[10] Some people who read Spurgeon's response are surprised.

---

10. J. I. Packer, *Evangelism and the Sovereignty of God* (Downers Grove, IL: IVP, 1961), 35.

What does he mean that these two doctrines are "friends?" Are they not opposed to each other? Can they really both be true and work together in God's plan?

The Bible clearly teaches the sovereignty of God. God can do anything he desires. Job affirms, "I know that you can do all things, and that no purpose of Yours can be thwarted" (Job 42:2). Psalm 135:6 teaches, "Whatever the LORD pleases, He does, in heaven and in earth, in the seas and in all deeps." In Isaiah 46:9–10 God testifies, "Remember the former things long past, for I am God, and there is no other; I am God, and there is no one like Me, declaring the end from the beginning, and from ancient times things which have not been done, saying, 'My purpose will be established, and I will accomplish all My good pleasure.'"

Yet Scripture also emphasizes that people have real responsibility and freedom in the choices they make. A person cannot blame God for his or her choices. Consider Judas Iscariot and his betrayal of Christ: "For indeed, the Son of Man is going as it has been determined; but woe to that man by whom He is betrayed!" (Luke 22:22).

Some argue that a strong belief in God's sovereignty harms evangelism. They cannot understand how a person holding a firm belief in the sovereignty of God can be evangelistic.[11] Persons making this argument usually point to someone they know who affirms God's sovereignty but who is not evangelistic.[12] A quick survey of church history shows the assertion that God's sovereignty harms evangelism is disproved *historically*. Some of the greatest pastors, evangelists, and missionaries in church history affirmed the sovereignty of God in salvation (Richard Baxter, George Whitefield, Andrew Fuller, William Carey, C. H. Spurgeon, and Lottie Moon, just to name a few). A survey of Scripture shows this assertion is disproved *biblically*. Both God's sovereignty and human responsibility are taught in Scripture, at times in the very same passage (Luke 22:22; John 1:12–13; 6:37; 6:44, 47; Acts 2:23; 4:27–28). And certainly the apostle

---

11. Many who make this argument fail to distinguish between hyper-Calvinism (which affirms God's grace in salvation but neglects an appeal to lost sinners to repent and believe) and evangelical Calvinism (which affirms God's grace in salvation but emphasizes the necessity of an "invitation" to repent and believe).

12. When individuals use this argument, I point out that I know people who are Arminian in their theology and who are not evangelistic. Should we extrapolate from the example of such persons to conclude that a strong belief in the free will of man kills evangelistic zeal?

Paul, who strongly affirmed the sovereignty of God throughout his writings (e.g. Rom. 9 and Eph. 1), was one of the greatest evangelists, church planters, and missionaries the world has ever seen (e.g. 1 Cor. 9:16, 19–23).

EVANGELISM AND GOD'S SOVEREIGNTY

I maintain a belief in God's sovereignty does not diminish evangelistic zeal but rather fuels it. I believe that a proper understanding of God's sovereignty and human responsibility will produce five results in the way we do evangelism.

A belief in God's sovereignty will make us faithful in evangelism.

Those who try to use God's sovereignty as an "excuse" not to do evangelism do not really understand the implications of God's sovereignty in their lives. I heard of a young preacher who came to a seasoned preacher and exclaimed, "I don't invite people to respond to the gospel because I believe in the sovereignty of God."

> The older preacher asked him, "Do you really believe in the sovereignty of God?"
> "Yes," the young man replied.
> The older man asked again, this time with more force, "Do you *really* believe in the sovereignty of God?"
> "*Yes, I do,*" came the adamant reply.
> "Well then, *obey* your sovereign God and call on people to repent and believe!"

Evangelism is a part of God's revealed will that he expects people to obey. Matthew 28:18–20, the passage we know as the Great Commission, begins with Jesus asserting his authority both in heaven and on earth. He then commands his followers to go into all the world and make disciples of all the nations. These verses do not contain the Great Suggestion, but the Great Commission. Evangelism is an essential part of God's plan to save people (Rom. 10:14–15, 17).

The God who ordains the ends also ordains the means. The Westminster Confession of Faith, Chapter V ("Of Providence"), contains these helpful assertions:

I.   God the great Creator of all things does uphold, direct, dispose, and govern all creatures, actions, and things, from the greatest even to the least, by his most wise and holy providence, according to his infallible foreknowledge, and the free and immutable counsel of his own will, to the praise of the glory of his wisdom, power, justice, goodness, and mercy.

II. Although, in relation to the foreknowledge and decree of God, the first Cause, all things come to pass immutably, and infallibly; yet, by the same providence, he orders them to fall out, according to the nature of second causes, either necessarily, freely, or contingently.

III. God, in his ordinary providence, makes use of means, yet is free to work without, above, and against them, at his pleasure.

In other words, God often displays his sovereignty not *apart* from the use of means but *through* the use of means. It is not an *affront* to God's sovereignty but an *acknowledgment* of his sovereignty to use the means God has given for the securing of his purposes.

No one will be saved apart from hearing and responding to the gospel message. Obeying our sovereign God will cause us to be faithful in sharing the good news and calling on persons to repent and believe. Regardless of whether one believes in election based on foreordination or foreknowledge, questions remain: "Who are the elect? How do we identify the elect?" The elect are not walking around with special marks on their foreheads. The elect are those who repent and believe. No one will be saved who does not repent and believe. So our task is not to spend all our time in theological debate and speculation but to share the gospel and call on people to repent and believe. I tell my students, "I don't care how many points you have in your theology—if evangelism is not one of them, you are not biblical!" As George Whitefield asserted, "Let a man go to the grammar school of faith and repentance, before he goes to the university of election and predestination."[13] That is good advice not only for the lost person who needs to be saved but also for believers seeking to be faithful witnesses.

---

13. George Whitefield, *The Journal of George Whitefield* (London: W. Strahan, 1740), 627. Whitefield credits this quotation to the Puritan martyr John Bradford.

Paul, in 2 Corinthians 5:20, reminds us that our role as witnesses is to be "ambassadors for Christ." He reveals the dynamic at work in our witnessing through a key phrase in verse 20 (NIV): "God . . . making his appeal through us." It is *God's* appeal, but how does he make that appeal? Through *us*—through faithful ambassadors who share the message with which they have been entrusted. What is that message? "We implore you on behalf of Christ, be reconciled to God." Faithfulness in evangelism requires not merely *informing* but also *inviting*. The invitation is clear: "Be reconciled to God."

The promise is for all who believe. John reminds us, "But as many as received Him, to them He gave the right to become children of God, even to those who believe in His name, who were born, not of blood nor of the will of the flesh nor of the will of man, but of God" (John 1:12–13). Jesus testifies, "For God so loved the world, that He gave His only begotten Son, that whoever believes in Him shall not perish, but have eternal life" (John 3:16). Romans 1:16 and Matthew 11:28–30 highlight this same emphasis. Paul affirms, "Whoever will call on the name of the Lord will be saved" (Rom. 10:13). The apostle follows that affirmation with a series of questions in verse 14: "How then will they call on Him in whom they have not believed? How will they believe in Him whom they have not heard? And how will they hear without a preacher?" He concludes in verse 15 by noting, "How beautiful are the feet of those who bring good news!" A belief in God's sovereignty makes our feet beautiful as we faithfully proclaim the good news to lost persons.

The biggest barrier people face in witnessing is the fear of others. That fear of others is tragically presented in John 12:42–43: "Nevertheless many even of the rulers believed in Him, but because of the Pharisees they were not confessing Him, for fear that they would be put out of the synagogue; for they loved the approval of men rather than the approval of God." A proper understanding of the sovereignty of God frees us from the enslaving fear of other people, which often is our greatest hindrance in evangelism.

It is wrong when someone says, "Because God is sovereign I don't need to evangelize." A proper response would be, "Because God is sovereign I must evangelize faithfully." Our sovereign God has commanded us to share the gospel with the world.

A belief in God's sovereignty will make us confident in evangelism.

Biblical hope is not "wishful thinking" but confidence—not in our own skill or ability but in God's power to change hearts. Years ago I had a conversation with a missionary friend as he was reflecting on his ministry among unconverted millions in China. He told me, "I'm still trying to sort out where I stand on God's sovereignty and man's responsibility, but I know one thing for sure—these people's *only* hope is for God to open their eyes." When we understand the spiritual condition of lost persons, we are reminded of how impossible evangelism is from a human standpoint. Paul asserts, "But a natural man does not accept the things of the Spirit of God, for they are foolishness to him; and he cannot understand them, because they are spiritually appraised" (1 Cor. 2:14). Furthermore, Paul confirms that lost persons are spiritually dead in their trespasses and sins (Eph. 2:1), that no one seeks after God (Rom. 3:11), and that "the gospel is veiled to those who are perishing" because "the god of this age has blinded the minds of the unbelievers so they cannot see the light of the gospel of the glory of Christ" (2 Cor. 4:3–4). What hope does such a person have? The good news of the Bible is that faith is a gift of God (Phil. 1:29; Eph. 2:8) and that repentance is granted by God (Rom. 2:4; Acts 5:31; Acts 11:18; 2 Tim. 2:25). God can open blind eyes; God can soften hard hearts; God can raise the spiritually dead to new life. We cannot do any of that—but God can!

Many persons who affirm God's sovereignty also are fearful of spurious conversions. Jesus warned us that in the day of judgment there would be *many* persons who thought they were saved but who were not truly saved (Matt. 7:21–23). I want witnesses to try to avoid spurious conversions, but I do not want us to be so afraid of spurious conversions that we never seek real ones! Paul reminds us that the gospel is the power of God unto salvation to everyone who believes (Rom. 1:16). We can share the good news with confidence.

We also have the confidence that the Great Commission will one day be fulfilled! In Revelation 7:9–10, the veil of eternity is pulled back, and the apostle John is given a glimpse into heaven. What does he see? "After these things I looked, and behold, a great multitude which no one could count, from every nation and all tribes and peoples and tongues, standing before the throne and before the Lamb, clothed in white robes, and palm branches were in their hands; and they cry out with a loud voice, saying, 'Salvation to our God who sits on the throne, and to the Lamb.'" God's sovereignty gives great confidence in our mission endeavors, especially among unreached people groups.

We should not depend on slick marketing or our own skills of persuasion to bring people to faith, but on the power of God. In 2 Corinthians 4:6, Paul compares the salvation of a lost sinner to the creation of the world: "For God, who said, 'Light shall shine out of darkness,' is the One who has shone in our hearts to give the Light of the knowledge of the glory of God in the face of Christ." At the beginning of creation, when there was only darkness, God said "let there be light," and there was light. God shines his light into the dark hearts of sinful persons so they can see Jesus Christ for who he really is. The God of creation, who first called light out of darkness, is the only one who has the power to overcome people's spiritual darkness and blindness. If God did not open the eyes of blinded sinners, all would perish in their sins (Rom. 9:29). The sovereignty of God is the only basis for confidence in our evangelistic endeavors. Only God can raise the dead, give sight to the blind, and turn hearts of stone into hearts of flesh.

A belief in God's sovereignty will make us patient in evangelism.

When Paul began his ministry in Corinth, he was filled with fear (1 Cor. 2:1–5). But according to Acts 18:9–10, God gave him incredible words of encouragement: "And the Lord said to Paul in the night by a vision, 'Do not be afraid any longer, but go on speaking and do not be silent; for I am with you, and no man will attack you in order to harm you, for I have many people in this city.'" God is telling Paul that there are people in Corinth who have been elected to salvation but who have not yet repented and believed. Notice Paul's response. It was not, "Since God has already chosen these people then I guess I'm not needed here—I'll head out to somewhere else." No, Paul's response was, "And he settled there a year and six months, teaching the word of God among them" (Acts 18:11). An understanding of God's sovereign work in the city of Corinth gave Paul patience. It is why he would elsewhere testify, "For this reason I endure all things for the sake of those who are chosen, so that they also may obtain the salvation which is in Christ Jesus and with it eternal glory" (2 Tim. 2:10).

Without a belief in God's power to change hearts, it is easy to grow discouraged when our efforts do not bring immediate results. But when we witness God's workings of grace in Scripture (e.g., Paul) and in history (e.g., John Newton), we are reminded that God is in the business of saving people we might have written off. In Mark 4, Jesus teaches what we know as the parable of the sower. I think we often misapply this parable. The sower did not go out to inspect the soil and sow seed only where he thought he found good soil. Rather the sower sowed the seed everywhere. In our evangelistic efforts we need to stop being soil inspectors and start being sowers of the gospel seed. Another way to phrase this truth is: "Never say 'no' for someone else." We make that mistake far too often. We decide they are not good soil, and we say "no" for them, withholding the seed of the gospel. We need to reflect on God's work of grace in the life of Lydia: "the Lord opened her heart to respond to the things spoken by Paul" (Acts 16:14). Let's stop saying "no" for other people. A belief in God's sovereignty will make us patient in evangelism.

A belief in God's sovereignty will make us prayerful in evangelism.

Prayer is a sign of our dependence upon God. Every time we pray, we are acknowledging God's sovereignty and our own limitations. When we pray for unconverted persons, we do so recognizing that only God can soften hard hearts, open blind eyes, and raise to new life those who are spiritually dead. We pray for God to open blind eyes and soften hard hearts. We ask God to save, not merely to make it possible for people somehow to save themselves. And we ask God to bring fruit to our gospel endeavors as Paul did: "Finally, brethren, pray for us that the word of the Lord will spread rapidly and be glorified, just as it did also with you" (2 Thess. 3:1). Paul's request for prayer, found in Colossians 4:2–6 and Ephesians 6:18–20, reflects his understanding of the vital connection between evangelism and prayer. So to the person who argues, "Because God is sovereign it doesn't matter whether I pray or not," the Scriptures would answer, "No, because God is in control you should pray persistently!" Because God is sovereign, he can answer our prayers.

A belief in God's sovereignty will make us joyful in evangelism.

In 2 Corinthians 4:1–2, Paul sets forth his "agenda" in ministry: "Therefore, since we have this ministry, as we received mercy, we do not lose heart, but we have renounced the things hidden because of shame, not walking in craftiness or adulterating the word of God, but by the manifestation of truth commending ourselves to every man's conscience in the sight of God." Paul saw his responsibility as sharing the gospel and then leaving the results up to God. He affirms in 1 Corinthians 3:6–7, "I planted, Apollos watered, but God was causing the growth. So then neither the one who plants nor the one who waters is anything, but God who causes the growth." But knowing that God will bring the growth caused Paul to persevere joyfully in ministry: "I will most gladly spend and be expended for your souls" (2 Cor. 12:15). In Ephesians 1:3–14, Paul notes that, in God's wisdom, all things have been designed to bring about "the praise of His glorious grace" (v. 6) and "the praise of his glory" (vv. 12, 14). We are joyful in evangelism because we know that God is using our efforts not to glorify us but himself and his glorious grace.

An important historical witness to how a belief in God's sovereignty fuels evangelistic zeal can be found in the life and ministry of Andrew Fuller. Fuller writes,

> A fleshly mind may ask, "How can these things be?" How can Divine predestination accord with human agency and accountableness? But a true, humble Christian, finding both in his Bible, will believe both, though he may be unable fully to understand their consistency; and he will find in the one a motive to depend entirely upon God, and in the other a caution against slothfulness and presumptuous neglect of duty. And thus a Christian minister, if he view the doctrine in its proper connexions, will find nothing in it to hinder the free use of warnings, invitations, and persuasions, either to the converted or the unconverted. Yet he will not ground his hopes of success on the pliability of the human mind, but on the promised grace of God, who (while he prophesies to the dry bones, as he is commanded) is known to inspire them with the breath of life.[14]

Fuller's last line in that quotation brings to mind Ezekiel 37:1–14, where Ezekiel was commanded to preach to a valley of dry bones. Ezekiel was fully aware of the futility of such preaching, but on the basis of God's command and God's promise, he preached, and the dead came to life.

As we share the gospel with dead sinners today, we recognize this same sense of hopelessness apart from God's sovereign work. Let no convert

---

14. Andrew Fuller, *The Works of the Rev. Andrew Fuller*, vol. IV (New Haven: S. Converse, 1824), 263–264.

take credit for his or her salvation. Let no witness presume to take credit for another's salvation. As Luke testifies in Acts 2:47, "And the Lord was adding to their number day by day those who were being saved." And yet as we share, we witness God bringing life from death, and as a result God receives the glory. As Paul testified in Romans 11:33–36:

> Oh, the depth of the riches both of the wisdom and knowledge of God! How unsearchable are His judgments and unfathomable His ways! For who has known the mind of the Lord, or who became His counselor? Or who has first given to Him that it might be paid back to him again? For from Him and through Him and to Him are all things. To Him be the glory forever. Amen.

CHAPTER 5

HISTORY OF EVANGELISM

WHY STUDY HISTORY? The oft-quoted phrase, "Those who fail to learn from the mistakes of history are doomed to repeat them" reminds us of the benefits of learning from those who have gone before. We could also reformulate that phrase in a more positive way: "Those who learn from the successes of history have an opportunity to repeat them." Let me suggest four benefits to studying church history, specifically the history of evangelism.

First, we are helped to become more aware of our own presuppositions. We all bring to our study of the Bible (or any other material) a perspective that is influenced by the historical and cultural situation in which we find ourselves. Often, even without being aware of it, we screen all we consider through the filter of our own understanding. As we study different historical perspectives, we learn that there are alternative ways of viewing the matter. Studying history can sensitize us to the manner in which culture affects one's thinking and one's practice of evangelism.

Second, we are encouraged to make our own formulations with a little more humility. Other believers throughout history may have viewed things differently. I remind my students, "When you enter the gates of heaven, you are not going to be met by a gauntlet of the great theologians of the past, cheering your entrance, exclaiming, 'Finally! The person who got it all right! Welcome!'" Studying history reminds us that faithful believers have differed on various means of communicating the gospel message.

Third, we can learn from what others before us have done and not done, both good and bad. We can observe common threads that contribute to evangelistic movements. We can see how each generation sought to be faithful to the Great Commission in its own particular context. We can learn lessons from the experiences of others. Wise people learn from their experiences; really wise people learn from other people's experiences.

Fourth, we can gain inspiration for Christian ministry. The church has a remarkable heritage of faithful believers throughout the centuries! This chapter presumes to fulfill a daunting task, the task of summarizing some two thousand years of church history in a handful of pages. It reminds me of trying to capture the waters of Niagara Falls with a tin cup! The reader is encouraged to look to the resources referenced in the footnotes if they desire more in-depth historical information.[1]

EVANGELISM IN THE EARLY CHURCH (TO AD 500)

Jesus and the Apostles (to AD 100)

In chapter 3 of this book, we briefly discussed how Jesus and the early church practiced evangelism. By way of review, we will briefly summarize some key points of emphasis. Jesus serves as a model evangelist, evangelizing in Galilee (Mark 1; Matt. 4; Luke 4) and in Samaria (John 4). He engaged

---

1. For starters, readers should look to classic works on church history, such as Kenneth Scott Latourette, *A History of the Expansion of Christianity,* 7 vols. (New York: Harper & Brothers, 1937) and Justo L. González, *The Story of Christianity,* 2 vols. (San Francisco, CA: HarperSanFrancisco, 1983). In addition, there are a handful of books written specifically on the history of evangelism: Robert G. Tuttle Jr., *The Story of Evangelism: A History of the Witness to the Gospel* (Nashville: Abingdon, 2006); John Mark Terry, *Evangelism: A Concise History* (Nashville: Broadman & Holman, 1994); Milton L. Rudnick, *Speaking the Gospel through the Ages* (St. Louis: Concordia, 1984); and Paulus Scharpff, *History of Evangelism* (Grand Rapids: Eerdmans, 1966). Some works cover specific periods of church history, such as C. E. Autrey, *Evangelism in the Acts* (Grand Rapids: Zondervan, 1964) and Michael Green, *Evangelism in the Early Church* (Grand Rapids: Eerdmans, 1962). Others center on geographical regions, such as Thomas P. Johnston, ed., *A History of Evangelism in North America* (Grand Rapids: Kregel Academic, 2021); William Warren Sweet, *Revivalism in America* (Nashville: Abingdon, 1944); Darius Salter, *American Evangelism: Its Theology and Practice* (Grand Rapids: Baker, 1996); Bernard A. Weisberger, *They Gathered at the River: The Story of the Great Revivalists and Their Impact upon Religion in America* (Boston: Little, Brown, 1958); and W. L. Muncy Jr., *A History of Evangelism in the United States* (Kansas City, KS: Central Seminary Press, 1945).

in both public teaching as well as personal witnessing.[2] He trained his followers in evangelism and sent them out in pairs to evangelize. He commissioned his followers to carry out the evangelization of the entire world.

As we turn to the apostles, we see Peter evangelizing across racial and cultural lines (Acts 10, 11, 15). Paul became the evangelist to the Gentiles, and his life remains a model by which evangelists can be challenged and encouraged. Paul evangelized as he traveled, and he went "house to house" to communicate the gospel message. He evangelized through preaching, at prayer meetings, during debates, through his letters, and through prison ministry (from the inside!). Many other believers were involved in evangelism as well: Steven (Acts 7), Philip (Acts 8), Barnabas, Silas, Timothy, and many unnamed persons in Acts 8:4: "Therefore, those who had been scattered went about preaching the word."

We can identify certain characteristics of evangelism in the first century. Evangelism was "aggressive" in the sense that the gospel message often was shared before relationships were built. It was clear that the early church believed the gospel to be "good news," and they sought to share that news near and far. In this period evangelism was often accompanied by the working of miracles. Witnesses were sensitive to the leading of the Holy Spirit. Writing was used to spread the gospel message.

Evangelism in the Mediterranean World (AD 100–500)

Evangelism took place during this period of time in spite of severe persecution. Why were Christians persecuted? The emperors began to realize that Christianity could not be "absorbed" as other religions had been, and therefore Christianity was seen as a threat. False charges were levelled against Christians: cannibalism (because of the Eucharist); sexual orgies (because of believers testifying of their love for one another); and "atheism" (because they worshiped an "invisible" God). Christians chose to remain separate from certain Roman activities that were tied to pagan worship, leading to charges that believers were "haters of mankind." But ultimately it was their uncompromising witness and refusal to deny Christ even under penalty of death that made Christians threats to the emperors.

---

2. For a helpful summary of Jesus's evangelistic interactions with individuals, see Robert E. Coleman, *The Master Plan of Personal Evangelism* (Wheaton, IL: Crossway, 1997).

In spite of persecution, Christians continued to witness to Christ's death and resurrection. Tertullian's famous observation shows the power of the gospel in spite of the governing authorities persecuting and killing believers: the blood of the martyrs is the seed of the church.[3] In the year AD 112, Pliny wrote to Emperor Trajan, lamenting the rapid growth and spread of Christianity in the Roman Empire: "The matter seemed to me to justify my consulting you especially on account of the number of those imperiled; for many persons of all ages and classes and of both sexes are being put in peril by accusation, and this will go on. The contagion of this superstition has spread not only in the cities, but in the villages and the rural districts as well."[4] By the year AD 300, an estimated 10 percent of the Roman Empire was considered to be practicing Christians.[5]

Evangelism took place during this period through various methods. Public preaching of the gospel message, though often dangerous, continued to be done. Personal witnessing by believers continued to take place. Literature became an increasingly utilized means, with the Scriptures being translated from Hebrew/Aramaic/Greek to languages such as Syriac, Gothic, and Latin. Various "apologists" (e.g., Justin Martyr, Irenaeus, and Tertullian) defended Christianity against false claims and boldly presented the gospel message in their writings.

Why the success in evangelizing during this time frame? The obstacles were legion. The foundational reason for the success of the church in this time period was the power of God at work through the gospel (Rom. 1:16). The message carried a tremendous appeal to the culture of that time. In an age with a great fear of death, the news that "Jesus has conquered death" was a powerful message. We must also note that the messengers "loved not their own lives even unto death" (Rev. 12:11). Polycarp's martyrdom provides one stirring example among many:

---

3. The exact quote from Tertullian is, "The Christian blood you spill is like the seed you sow, it springs from the earth again, and fructifies the more." See William Reeve and Jeremy Collier, trans., *The Apology of Tertullian and the Meditations of the Emperor Marcus Aurelius Antoninus*, Ancient and Modern Library of Theological Literature 31 (London: Griffith Farran, 1889), 143.

4. Quoted in Henry S. Bettenson and Chris Maunder, eds., *Documents of the Christian Church*, 4th ed. (New York: Oxford University Press, 2011), 4.

5. Keith Hopkins, "Christian Number and Its Implications," *Journal of Early Christian Studies* 6, no. 2 (1998): 191.

Now, as he was entering the stadium, there came to Polycarp a voice from heaven, "Be strong, Polycarp, and play the man." And no one saw the speaker, but the voice was heard by those of our people who were there. Thereupon he was led forth, and great was the uproar of them that heard that Polycarp had been seized. Accordingly, he was led before the Proconsul, who asked him if he were the man himself. And when he confessed the Proconsul tried to persuade him, saying, "Have respect to thine age," and so forth, according to their customary form; "Swear by the genius of Caesar," "Repent," "Say, 'Away with the atheists!'" Then Polycarp looked with a severe countenance on the mob of lawless heathen in the stadium, and he waved his hand at them, and looking up to heaven he groaned and said, "Away with the atheists." But the Proconsul urged him and said, "Swear, and I will release thee; curse the Christ." And Polycarp said, "Eighty and six years have I served him, and he hath done me no wrong; how then can I blaspheme my king who saved me?" But the Proconsul again persisted and said, "Swear by the genius of Caesar"; and he answered, "If thou dost vainly imagine that I would swear by the genius of Caesar, as thou sayest, pretending not to know what I am, hear plainly that I am a Christian. And if thou art willing to learn the doctrine of Christianity, grant me a day and hearken to me."[6]

Michael Green maintains that evangelism was seen as the responsibility of every follower of Christ: "It was axiomatic that every Christian was called to be a witness to Christ, not only by life but by lip. Everyone was to be an apologist, at least to the extent of being ready to give a good account of the hope that was in them."[7] These early believers also sought to live holy lives. They were called Christians ("little Christs") for a reason: they were captivated by Christ and wanted to glorify him by their words and actions. They also cared for their fellow human beings, truly believing they were lost and headed for hell apart from faith in Christ.

---

6. Quoted in Bettenson and Maunder, eds., *Documents of the Christian Church*, 11.
7. Michael Green, *Evangelism in the Early Church*, 175. Green notes their methodology: "This must often have been not formal preaching, but the informal chattering to friends and chance acquaintances, in home and wine shops, on walks, and around market stalls. They went everywhere gossiping the gospel; they did it naturally, enthusiastically, and with the conviction of those who are not paid to say that sort of thing." See Green, *Evangelism in the Early Church*, 173.

During this time frame various "corruptions" of evangelism also arose. Doctrinal corruption took place with a change in the doctrine of salvation (no salvation outside the established church; baptism necessary to wash away original sin). This reality reminds us that the church is more often destroyed from within (false teaching) than from outside (persecution). Another corruption was the union of church and state under Constantine (AD 313). Constantine made Christianity a legal religion and encouraged everyone to become a Christian. He "baptized" his army by marching them through a river and offered rewards for citizens who converted to Christianity. While initially one could argue this was good for the church (persecution ended), it had devastating long-term effects (nominal Christianity; lack of holiness in the church). Some who joined the church brought with them their pagan ideas and practices.

EVANGELISM IN THE MIDDLE AGES (AD 500–1500)

During this period of time, salvation came to be seen as sacramental, practiced through sacerdotalism. A "sacrament" is a sacred act that gives saving grace, and "sacerdotalism" is the belief that these sacraments must be mediated through a priest. The established church also made large territorial gains, and the practice known as simony (the buying of a church office) became commonplace. Bishops were not only leaders in the church but political leaders as well. Wealthy persons deeded large tracts of land to what was becoming the Roman Catholic Church.

Some individuals still emphasized spiritual Christianity and approximated biblical evangelism from within the church. Bernard of Clairvaux (1090–1153) was a strong preacher who focused on the love of Christ.[8] He wrote the moving hymn still found in hymnals today, "Jesus, the Very Thought of Thee." Francis of Assisi (1181/2–1226) renounced his wealth at his conversion, preached to the poor, and established the Franciscian Order. John Wycliffe (1320–1384) declared the Scriptures to be the sole source of Christian doctrine and published the first English translation of the Bible (various parts appeared from 1382 to 1395). John Hus

---

8. John Calvin considered him the major witness to truth between Gregory the Great and the 1500s. See Tony Lane, "A 12th Century Man for All Seasons: The Life and Thought of Bernard of Clairvaux," *Christian History Institute*, 1989, https://christianhistoryinstitute.org/magazine/article/a-12th-century-man-for-all-seasons.

(1369–1415), who likewise emphasized scriptural authority, was burned at the stake after being guaranteed a safe conduct pass. (The argument the Roman Catholic authorities made was that safe conduct passes do not apply to heretics.) Girolamo Savonarola (1452–1498) was a Catholic priest in Florence, Italy. He became upset with corruption in the Catholic Church and was converted as he studied the New Testament for answers. He preached judgment on the "wicked" city of Florence, and revival broke out! Savonarola left the Roman Catholic Church and continued preaching until he was hanged, and his body was burned as a heretic.

Others started groups outside the established church in an attempt to bring reform through the Scriptures. While groups such as the Petrobusians, Henricians, Arnoldists, and Waldenses cannot be viewed as completely evangelical in the modern sense of the term, they sought to follow the teaching of the Scriptures as they understood them.[9] During this time frame the Crusades took place, which were an attempt to recapture Jerusalem from Muslims. Some of those captured were ordered to convert to Christianity at the point of a sword. This forced evangelism remains a commonly raised issue when Christians talk with Muslims today.

This time frame also saw the rise of missionary movements. Patrick (389–461) spread the gospel message throughout Ireland. Columba (521–597) brought the gospel to the Scottish island of Iona. Augustine of Canterbury (545–605), preached the gospel throughout England, and Boniface (675–754) took the gospel message to Germany and Belgium. Monasticism, which developed as a reaction to the decline of holiness in the church, created numerous monasteries, some of which became centers of scholarship and preaching.[10]

In addition to these individuals and groups who "approximated" biblical evangelism, many unnamed believers kept the fires of the gospel burning. Workman summarizes:

> We have pointed out already that the martyrs were witnesses to the absoluteness of the Christian faith, that the religion of Jesus would have

---

9. See Mendell Taylor, *Exploring Evangelism: History, Methods, Theology* (Kansas City, MO: Beacon Hill, 1964). Taylor discusses these groups and others in chapter 4.
10. See George Hunter, *The Celtic Way of Evangelism* (Nashville: Abingdon, 2000). Hunter argues the church in the West needs to reconsider this "Celtic Way of Evangelism," namely, to allow people to "belong" before they "believe."

nothing to do with the current syncretism. Time after time we find judges, either actuated by mercy or promoted by their "philosophy," striving to draw the martyrs into syncretistic admission which would have given them their liberty. But the martyrs refused to purchase life by any compromise between their faith and "the world." Well would it be for the Church today if she could learn the lesson they taught. The fashionable syncretism of the empire has passed away; men are no longer intent on the identification of the gods of Greece and Rome. In its place we see a more dangerous fusion, the identification of the world and the Church, the syncretism of material and spiritual things. We need once more to catch the martyr spirit, a belief in the absoluteness of the Christian faith translated into facts which shall make the Church a "peculiar people," whose strength does not lie in any blending of light and darkness, but in her renunciation of and aloofness from "the world."[11]

EVANGELISM AND THE REFORMATION
(AD 1500–1600)

Prior to the Protestant Reformation, corruption had grown within the Roman Catholic Church. During late 1300s and early 1400s, multiple individuals were claiming to be pope at the same time. Alexander VI (1492–1503) secularized the papacy, having a mistress and fathering four children. Calls for reform came from the Conciliar Movement (but the popes simply ignored them or overruled their wishes) and also from individuals such as John Hus (who was put to death for his calls for reform). Abuses were rampant, particularly with the practice of selling indulgences. Johann Tetzel (1465–1519) was especially infamous as an indulgence peddler, originating the catchy phrase, "As soon as the coin in the coffer rings, the soul from purgatory springs."

The Reformation Era is seen by Protestant church historians as the period in which the gospel message was rediscovered. Luther's emphasis on justification by faith laid the groundwork for the gospel as it is generally understood in evangelical circles today. Milton Rudnick observes,

---

11. Herbert Brook Workman, *Persecution in the Early Church* (London: Oxford University Press, 1980), 143.

"Drawing especially on St. Paul and Augustine, the Protestant reformers affirmed that salvation is entirely God's work of grace (here understood as God's undeserved generosity) and in no sense that of the sinner."[12]

Magisterial Reformers

The Magisterial Reformers were those who used the magistrate—the powers of the state—to bring reform, the most notable of whom were Martin Luther and John Calvin.[13]

Martin Luther (1483–1546)

John Warwick Montgomery begins his article titled "Luther and Missions" with a humorous statement followed by a question: "A current joke has to do with a new Martin Luther doll: you wind it up and it just stands there! Did Luther just stand there . . . or did he move dynamically with a sense of mission to the lost?"[14] Paulus Scharpff, in defending Luther as an evangelist, argues:

> The history of Protestant evangelism as such begins with Luther. In a letter to Frederick the Wise on March 5, 1522, Luther said: "Your Grace knows, or if not, I herewith inform you, that I obtained the Gospel not from men but alone from heaven through our Lord Jesus Christ, and that I should like to be known and recorded as a servant and evangelist. Early the following year Luther signed a letter to Prince George of Saxony: "Martinus Luther, by God's grace, Evangelist of Wittenberg."[15]

---

12. Milton L. Rudnick, *Speaking the Gospel through the Ages: A History of Evangelism* (St. Louis: Concordia, 1984), 78.
13. While the focus of this chapter is on evangelism, many historians have noted the lack of emphasis on missions among the Magisterial Reformers. Gustav Warneck, the first great historian of the modern missionary movement, suggested eight reasons why there was an absence of overt missionary thought among the Magisterial Reformers. See Gustav Warneck, *Outline of the History of Protestant Missions*, translated from the second German edition of 1882 by Thomas Smith (Edinburg: James Gemmell, 1884), 11–23. Building upon Warnock, Kenneth Scott Latourette added three additional reasons to his list. See Latourette, *A History of the Expansion of Christianity,* 3:25ff.
14. John Warwick Montgomery, "Luther and Missions," *Evangelical Missions Quarterly* 3 (1967): 193–202.
15. Paulus Scharpff, *History of Evangelism*, trans. Helga Bender Henry (Grand Rapids: Eerdmans, 1966), 10.

While it is noteworthy that Luther desired to be called an evangelist, he certainly was not an evangelist in the mold of a Billy Graham or Luis Palau. But we can see his communication of the gospel through five main activities.

First was through his teaching. Even after being excommunicated by the pope, Luther continued to teach at the University of Wittenberg, influencing thousands of students, many of whom carried the gospel of grace throughout Europe. Second was through his preaching. Luther made the preaching of the Word the focus of the worship service. He preached the gospel of grace to the people of Wittenberg, focusing on a "cross-centered" theology.[16] Third was through his writings. Luther wrote some one hundred books and pamphlets to explain his views and spread the gospel. He understood the ability of the printed word to impact the masses. Rudnick observes,

> The printing press brought Luther and his doctrine to the attention of a large public and gained for him a host of followers. Although printing with movable type had been invented in 1484, this was the first instance of a major movement utilizing its potential. The importance of printing as a medium for disseminating the Reformation can scarcely be exaggerated.[17]

Fourth was through composing hymns. Luther's hymns carried his theology to the common people. That reality led a Roman Catholic to lament, "Luther's songs have damned more souls than all his books and speeches!"[18] In an age of rampant illiteracy, people could remember the words of songs. His most famous hymn is undoubtedly "A Mighty Fortress Is Our God."

Fifth was through translating the Bible into German. While hiding at Wartburg Castle, Luther began translating the New Testament into German. He finished the New Testament in 1522 and the complete Bible in 1534. Luther wanted to put God's Word in the language of the people so anyone could read it and find redemption. Scharpff writes, "Luther

---

16. Scharpff argues, "To one and all Luther proclaimed the sovereignty and lordship of Jesus Christ. Since apostolic days the validity and uniqueness of Christ's name had not been presented as Luther now did." See Scharpff, *History of Evangelism*, 11.
17. Rudnick, *Speaking the Gospel*, 82.
18. Quoted in Edward Dickinson, "The Hymns of Martin Luther: Their Predecessors and Their Place in History," *Bibliotheca Sacra* 52, no. 208 (1895): 700.

evangelized also through his various writings, and *above all* through his translation of the Bible whereby the Gospel was brought to the German people in their own tongue."[19]

John Calvin (1509–1564)

Calvin sought to communicate the gospel of grace through preaching. He preached on Sundays but also on Mondays, Tuesdays, and Fridays.[20] Church members were expected to attend services, highlighting the importance of the Word preached. Calvin also communicated through writing, especially his biblical commentaries and the *Institutes of the Christian Religion* (1536). Apart from the Bible, the *Institutes* was perhaps the most influential book of the Reformation era. Calvin also wrote catechisms and confessions of faith, summarizing doctrine in easy-to-remember formats for the people.[21] He founded the Academy of Geneva, which sent out evangelists. Between 1555 and 1562, Calvin's school sent out eighty-eight evangelists to France.[22] Calvin also trained John Knox, who would help reform Scotland.

Radical Reformers (Anabaptists)

A plethora of groups fell under the heading of Radical Reformers, those who did not seek to use the state to reform the church. In particular, those referred to as the "Evangelical Anabaptists" (e.g., Basil Hubmaier and George Blaurock) were active evangelists in spite of persecution from the Magisterial Reformers.[23] The Anabaptists were persecuted because

---

19. Scharpff, *History of Evangelism*, 11, emphasis added. See also A. M. Chirgwin, *The Bible in World Evangelism* (New York: Friendship Press, 1954), 29–35.
20. See John Dillenberger, ed., *John Calvin: Selections from His Writings* (Missoula, MT: Scholars Press, 1975), 233.
21. Here are Calvin's comments regarding the *Catechism of the Church of Geneva*: "Writings of a different class will show what were our views on all subjects in religion, but the agreement which our churches had in doctrine cannot be seen with clearer evidence than from catechisms. For therein will appear, not only what one man or other once taught, but with what rudiments learned and unlearned alike amongst us, were constantly imbued from childhood, all the faithful holding them as their formal symbol of Christian communion." See Dillenberger, *John Calvin*, 247.
22. For a recent work defending Calvin's missionary zeal, see Michael A. G. Haykin and Jeff Robinson, *To the Ends of the Earth: Calvin's Missional Vision and Legacy* (Wheaton, IL: Crossway, 2014).
23. Much early historiography on the Anabaptists was quite negative. William R. Estep, *The Anabaptist Story* (Grand Rapids: Eerdmans, 1963), lists historians he considers

believer's baptism was seen as a threat to the unity of church and state (where all citizens were baptized as infants).

The Great Commission was a central focus of the teaching of the Evangelical Anabaptists.[24] They saw it as binding on every Christian. Laypersons actively witnessed to others, using family contacts, natural relationships with neighbors and other acquaintances, and their occupational contacts. Women were especially active in sharing their faith, and some were chained in their homes "to keep them from going to their relatives and neighbors to witness to their faith."[25] Milton Rudnick states categorically, "No Christians of the Reformation era were more committed to and active in evangelism than the Anabaptists."[26]

The English Reformation (1520s–1600)

Luther's views spread to England in the 1520s. William Tyndale translated the New Testament into English in 1526. But it was King Henry VIII's break with Rome (over the pope's refusal to annul his marriage to his wife Catherine, who had been unable to bear him a son), that launched the Reformation in England. That context has led some to designate the English Reformation as a political reformation instead of a theological reformation. But the theological reformation was soon to follow. In the *Act of Supremacy* (1534), the King of England was declared to be the head of the church in England. The liturgy was changed from Latin to English, and English translations of the Bible were approved. However, when Henry

---

the "most offensive" at 1n2. However, due to the writings of scholars such as Harold Bender, George Williams, Franklin Littell, and Kenneth Davis, the movement tends to be viewed more positively today. Estep gives a concise introduction to Anabaptist historiography in *The Anabaptist Story* at 1–7.

24. Littell comments, "No words of the Master were given more serious attention by his Anabaptist followers than his final command." See Littell, "The Anabaptist Theology of Mission," *Mennonite Quarterly Review* 21, no.1 (1947): 18. See also Littell, "Protestantism and the Great Commission," *Southwestern Journal of Theology* 2, no. 1 (1959): 30n15, for a listing of quotes from many Anabaptist leaders on the Great Commission.

25. Donald F. Durnbaugh, *The Believers' Church: The History and Character of Radical Protestantism* (New York: Macmillan, 1968), 231–32.

26. Rudnick, *Speaking the Gospel*, 93. Karl Schornbaum documents a quote from a citizen of Heilbronn who testified before a court in 1539 that he had fled from the Anabaptists as from the devil, for "they would gladly have persuaded all of us." See Karl Schornbaum, *Quellen zur Geschichte der Taufer* (Leipzig, 1934), 61, quoted in Wolfgang Schaufele, "The Missionary Vision and Activity of the Anabaptist Laity," in *Anabaptism and Mission*, ed. Wilbert R. Shenk (Scottdale, PA: Herald, 1984), 73.

sensed the movement was becoming too Protestant, in 1539 he issued the *Six Articles,* which marked a return to Catholic doctrine.

Henry's only son, Edward VI, reigned from 1547 to 1553. Edward took the throne at the age of nine, and had as his chief advisor the Protestant Edward Seymour. In 1547 the Catholic *Six Articles* was repealed, and in 1549 the *Act of Uniformity* imposed the use of the newly minted *Book of Common Prayer* for worship. In June of 1553, The *Forty-Two Articles of Religion* became the first truly Protestant confession of faith for the Church of England.

When Edward died in July 1553, he was succeeded by his older sister, Mary, a staunch Roman Catholic. In October 1553 the Protestant statement of faith, *Forty-Two Articles of Religion*, was repealed. While many Protestants fled England for fear of their lives, others were put to death as heretics under Mary's rule. John Foxe's *Acts and Monuments* (Foxe's *Book of Martyrs*), detailed the sacrifices of the martyrs. When Mary died in 1558, her younger sister Elizabeth came to the throne. Elizabeth launched the Anglican Church, which some have called a "halfway house" between Catholicism and Protestantism. In Elizabeth's "Middle Way," *Thirty-Nine Articles* were drawn up, which all clergy had to accept (ambiguity was allowed regarding the exact significance of the sacrament in the communion service). A Bible was to be available in every church. While the path of the English Reformation did appear to proceed from the top down depending on the beliefs of the English sovereign, the printing of English Bibles and the liturgy being available in various forms in English helped promote the cause of Protestant theology, including salvation by grace through faith.

PIETISM AND PURITANISM (1600s–1700s)

Pietism was a reaction to what was perceived to be a "dead orthodoxy" in German Lutheran churches. Philip Jacob Spener launched the pietistic movement with his publication of *Pious Desires* in 1675. Spener emphasized small groups, focused Bible study, and high moral standards. Where spiritual life might seem absent in the established church, these Bible study groups displayed spiritual passion and service. One offshoot of the Pietist movement was the Moravians, a group led by Nicolaus von Zinzendorf. The Moravians became one of the forerunners in the modern missionary movement.

Puritanism began as a movement of reform within the Anglican Church. Puritans felt Elizabeth's "Middle Way" did not go far enough in its reforms, so they wanted to purify the Church of England from all vestiges of the papacy. They condemned all Catholic ceremonies as being idolatrous and stressed personal conversion as part of the covenant of grace. The movement had little success under Elizabeth, but it did succeed in convincing King James I to authorize a new translation of the Bible, what we know today as the King James or Authorized Version of the Bible (1611).

King Charles I (r. 1625–1649) was friendly to Roman Catholicism and was opposed to Puritanism. Ongoing strife with Parliament led in 1642 to the English Civil War. In 1645 the Westminster Assembly of Divines produced a new *Directory of Worship*, which was authorized to replace the *Prayer Book* in worship. Charles was tried for treason in 1649 and was beheaded, leading to the English Commonwealth under Oliver Cromwell, known as "The Lord Protector." Eventually the monarchy was restored when King Charles II assumed the throne in 1660. In the *Act of Uniformity* (1662), as well as other statutes he enacted, Puritan reforms were quickly reversed, causing several hundred ministers to leave the Church of England rather than conform to what they felt were unbiblical practices. Some believers left England for other lands, where they hoped they could worship without threat of governmental interference.

The Puritan pastor Richard Baxter (1615–1691) serves as a model of a pastoral evangelist. In his book *The Reformed Pastor* (1656), he sets forth his system of parish evangelism through going "house to house" and conversing with every individual in his parish at least once per year.[27] Baxter was also a powerful preacher of the gospel message, whose motto was to preach "as a dying man to dying men."[28] He discovered, however, that for his preaching to be fruitful, he must follow it up with direct personal

---

27. By "reformed" Baxter means not Calvinistic in doctrine (though he was basically in the Reformed camp) but renewed in practice. He sought a renewal in how pastors envisioned their calling and ministry, arguing that in addition to preaching, pastors needed to be involved in "personal work" (what we today would term "personal evangelism and discipleship"). Baxter scholar Tim Cooper has revised this classic work for today's pastors. See *The Reformed Pastor: Updated and Abridged Edition* (Wheaton, IL: Crossway, 2021).
28. Richard Baxter, *The Autobiography of Richard Baxter*, ed. N. H. Keeble (London: J. M. Dent & Sons, 1974), 26.

discourse with every family in his parish. He urged pastors to take up this ministry of personal instruction with this heartfelt plea:

> I study to speak as plainly and movingly as I can, and yet I frequently meet with those that have been my hearers eight or ten years, who know not whether Christ be God or man, and wonder when I tell them the history of his birth and life and death, as if they had never heard it before. . . . I have found by experience, that some ignorant persons, who have been so long unprofitable hearers, have got more knowledge and remorse of conscience in half an hour's *close discourse*, than they did from ten years' public preaching. I know that preaching the gospel publicly is the most excellent means, because we speak to many at once. But it is usually far more effectual to preach it privately to a particular sinner, as to himself: for the plainest man this is, can scarcely speak plain enough in public for them to understand; but in private we may do it much more. . . . I conclude, therefore, that public preaching alone will not be sufficient. . . . Long may you study and preach to little purpose, if you neglect this duty [of personal instruction].[29]

He penned numerous works on conversion to help people understand the nature of true conversion.[30]

Another Puritan evangelist was John Bunyan (1628–1688). His autobiography, *Grace Abounding to the Chief of Sinners: A Brief Relation of the Exceeding Mercy of God in Christ to His Poor Servant* (1666), gives the reader an immediate glimpse into his evangelical theology. Bunyan was imprisoned for twelve years for preaching in an "unlawful" gathering. He wrote his classic book, *Pilgrim's Progress,* while imprisoned for six months in 1675. *Pilgrim's Progress* is an allegory that describes the pilgrimage of the Christian life. The main character, Christian, is weighed down by a great burden he gets from reading the Bible. A man named Evangelist comes to direct Christian to the Wicket Gate. At the foot of the cross, Christian's burden rolls away. The remainder of the book displays the pilgrimage of the Christian life, including times of struggle and doubt, culminating in

---

29. Baxter, *The Reformed Pastor* (Carlisle, PA: Banner of Truth, 1974), 196.
30. See Timothy K. Beougher, *Richard Baxter and Conversion: A Study of the Puritan Concept of Becoming a Christian* (Tain, Scotland: Christian Focus, 2007) for an analysis of Baxter's theology of conversion and practice of evangelism.

Christian finally entering the Celestial City. *Pilgrim's Progress* is often referred to as perhaps the best-read Christian book after the Bible. Numerous persons came to faith in Bunyan's day through his writing, as well as many since his time.

THE GREAT AWAKENING (1700S)

The Evangelical Awakening in England took place in the 1700s under the leadership of men such as George Whitefield (1714–1770) and John Wesley (1703–1791). John Wesley graduated from Oxford University and came to the American colonies as a missionary but returned back to England an abject failure. His meeting a group of Moravians on board the ship led him to a Moravian prayer meeting on Aldersgate Street, where on May 24, 1738, Wesley experienced a heart change: "About a quarter before nine, while he was describing *the change which God works* in the heart through faith in Christ, I felt my heart strangely warmed. I felt I did trust in Christ, Christ alone for salvation; and an assurance was given to me that he had taken away *my* sins, even *mine*, and saved *me* from the law of sin and death."[31] Wesley preached throughout England and trained others to preach the gospel of grace. He also set up a system of societies, classes, and bands—smaller groups of believers—for purposes of evangelism and discipleship.

Wesley travelled some 250,000 miles on horseback. One of his biographers, Canon Overton, bemoaned the fact that the pace of Wesley's movements is calculated to drive a biographer to despair: "It is simply impossible to follow him step by step, although there are ample materials to enable one to do so. He seems to fly about like a meteor."[32] Wesley preached some 40,000 sermons and wrote 233 books or pamphlets, in addition to helping with the writing of over a hundred others. His life and ministry can perhaps be best summarized with his motto: "The world is my parish." When questioned as to his authority to preach all over England (violating the parish system of only preaching in one's own parish unless the bishop over other parishes gave express permission to preach there), Wesley responded that God had

---

31. John Wesley, "24th May, 1738," in *The Journal of John Wesley*, ed. Nehemiah Curnock (London: Charles H. Kelly, n.d.), 1:476.
32. John Henry Overton, *John Wesley* (Boston: Houghton, Mifflin, 1891), 86.

given it to him in commanding him to proclaim the Gospel to all creatures: "Suffer me now to tell you my principles in this matter. I look upon all the world as my parish; thus far I mean, that in whatever part of it I am judge it meet, right, and my bounden duty to declare, unto all that are willing to hear, the glad tidings of salvation. This is the work which I know God has called me to; and sure I am that His blessings attend it."[33]

Charles Wesley's (1707–1788) influence must be mentioned as well. Though Charles joined John in gospel preaching, it was his hymn writing that had the greatest impact on people. Charles took great gospel truths and set those truths forth in hymns such as "And Can It Be," "Come, Thou Long-Expected Jesus," "Hark! The Herald Angels Sing," "Christ the Lord Is Risen Today," "Jesus, Lover of My Soul," and "O for a Thousand Tongues to Sing." The doctrine of salvation he and his brother preached throughout the land were articulated in his songs of praise. Countless numbers of people learned their theology through these hymns.

What is now called "The First Great Awakening" took place in the 1740s in the American colonies through the leadership of men such as Jonathan Edwards (1703–1758) and George Whitefield. This awakening was called "great" because its impact was far-reaching, both in breadth and depth.[34] Forerunners to this awakening were preachers such as Theodore Frelinghuysen (1691–1748) and Gilbert Tennent (1703–1764). But it was in Northampton, Massachusetts, under Jonathan Edwards's preaching that the "first fruits" of the revival were seen in the mid-1730s. Eventually the awakening would sweep across the colonies. While Edwards largely remained in New England, George Whitefield preached throughout the American colonies, testifying to the gospel of grace. Whitefield's impassioned preaching of Christ, combined with his booming voice that could carry even in large crowds, resulted in many people hearing the gospel and being converted.

Whitefield was truly America's first "celebrity." Born in England and heavily influenced by being a part of the Wesleys' "Holy Club" while at

---

33. John Wesley, "Letter to James Harvey, March 20, 1739," in *The Letters of John Wesley* (London, Epworth, 1931), 1:286.
34. Mark Noll remarks, "Its currents of renewal outran the expectations of the clergy and from Nova Scotia to Georgia changed the rules of the game for the American churches." See Mark A. Noll, *A History of Christianity in the United States and Canada* (Grand Rapids: Eerdmans, 1992), 90.

Oxford, Whitefield made seven trips across the Atlantic from England to the American colonies. With much of his preaching taking place outdoors, some believe that 80 percent of the colonists in America heard Whitefield preach in person. In addition to Whitefield, there was a multitude of itinerating preachers who traveled to share the message of God's grace and mercy in Christ.

The Second Great Awakening (c. 1800–c. 1835)

The Second Great Awakening began during the 1790s in New England with scattered renewals of piety in various towns. It then gathered momentum in the early decades of the new century. The greatest outbreaks of religious enthusiasm occurred in Kentucky at the great camp meetings of 1800 and 1801, most memorably at Cane Ridge. Revival came to Yale in 1802.[35] Evangelistic methods during the Second Great Awakening were focused on circuit riders and camp meetings.

Francis Asbury (1745–1816) popularized the Methodist Circuit Rider System in America. Asbury left England for the American colonies in 1771, never to return. As American settlers began leaving the eastern seaboard journeying toward new land in the West, church leaders were confronted with a key question: How was the growing territory to the West to be reached with the gospel message? Asbury had the answer: circuit riding preachers. Asbury was an organizational genius and drew up maps of circuits for men he would recruit as circuit riders.

Where other groups' strategies involved a "settled ministry" (a pastor being assigned to one congregation in a village or town), Methodist circuit riders had multiple preaching points they served, which was known as their circuit. Thus, the name "circuit riders" or "saddlebag preachers" was given to these men. Wigger notes, "A typical Methodist itinerant was responsible for a predominantly rural circuit, 200 to 500 miles in circumference. He was expected to complete his circuit every two to six weeks, with the standard being a four weeks' circuit."[36] In addition to traveling

---

35. See J. Edwin Orr, *Campus Aflame: A History of Evangelical Awakenings in Campus Communities*, ed. Richard Owen Roberts (Wheaton, IL: International Awakening, 1994), for information on the Yale Revival and other college revivals during this time period.

36. John H. Wigger, "Holy, 'Knock-'Em-Down' Preachers," *Christian History* 45, no. 1 (1995): 23. Unlike the men in "settled" parishes, circuit riders were constantly on

and preaching, the circuit riders would meet with the Methodist classes (weekly small group gatherings for fellowship and accountability), as well as spend personal time with individuals and families. This ministry was not for the lazy or faint of heart!

The Methodist circuit riders were tireless in their pursuit of souls. A discouraged Kentucky Presbyterian once was ambitious to find a family whose cabin had not been visited by a Methodist preacher. He lamented, "In several days I travelled from settlement to settlement . . . but into every hovel I entered I learned that the Methodist missionary had been there before me."[37] Another contemporary noted that "not infrequently a Methodist circuit-rider called at the cabin of a settler before the mud in his stick chimney was dry or before the weight poles were on the roof."[38] Methodist circuit riders seemed to be everywhere, leading one New Yorker to exclaim in 1788, "I know not from whence they all come, unless from the clouds."[39] Circuit riders were so relentless in their ministry that on stormy days there was a proverbial saying: "Nobody was out but crows and Methodist preachers."[40]

Camp meetings were large gatherings of people on the frontier for the purpose of preaching.[41] These meetings were often ecumenical, with Presbyterians, Methodists, and Baptists all preaching to the gathered crowd. People would travel to the meetings and "camp out" for days to listen to

---

the move. Peter Cartwright's observations concerning this difference in strategy are clear and pointed. He writes, "The Presbyterians, and other Calvinistic branches of the Protestant Church, used to contend for an educated ministry, for pews, for instrumental music, for a congregational or stated salaried ministry. The Methodists universally opposed these ideas; and the illiterate Methodist preachers actually set the world on fire (the American world at least) while they were lighting their matches!" See Peter Cartwright, *Autobiography of Peter Cartwright*, ed. W. P. Strickland (New York: The Methodist Book Concern, n.d.), 79.

37. Albert H. Redford, *The History of Methodism in Kentucky* (Nashville: Southern Methodist Publishing House, 1868–76), 3:530, cited in Charles A. Johnson, *The Frontier Camp Meeting: Religion's Harvest Time* (Dallas: Southern Methodist University Press, 1955), 19.

38. Phares, *Bible in Pocket, Gun in Hand: The Story of Frontier Religion* (New York: Doubleday, 1964), 11–12. See also William W. Sweet, *The Story of Religion in America* (Grand Rapids: Baker, 1973), 218–19.

39. Wigger, "Holy, 'Knock-'Em-Down' Preachers," 25.

40. Bernard A. Weisberger, *They Gathered at the River* (Boston: Little, Brown, 1958), 45–46.

41. An excellent starting point in studying the topic is *Christian History* 14, no. 1 (1995), devoted to camp meetings and circuit riders.

the preaching. Thousands heard the gospel message and were converted through the preaching at these camp meetings.

Charles Finney (1792–1875), a lawyer turned preacher, became perhaps the best-known figure of the Second Great Awakening.[42] Finney utilized new approaches in his evangelistic ministry that came to be known as "New Measures."[43] Finney saw outpourings of revival during his ministry. He defined revival as "nothing else than a new beginning of obedience to God."[44]

Asahel Nettleton (1783–1844) was another prominent preacher during the Second Great Awakening. Allen Guelzo argues that Nettleton, not Finney, was "the principle figure of the Second Great Awakening."[45] In 1811 Nettleton was ordained as a Congregational itinerant evangelist. He was a powerful preacher who insisted on reverence during his meetings. He cooperated with other ministers to work toward revival (unlike Charles Finney) and had a strong emphasis on following up with the converted.

Richard Allen (1760–1831), born a slave in Philadelphia, was converted at the age of seventeen through the preaching of a Methodist circuit rider. Richard's brother was also converted. Their changed lives led to the conversion of their master and their eventual freedom. Allen became an itinerant preacher and traveled the circuit with many Methodist preachers. He returned to Philadelphia where he taught Bible classes at St. George's Methodist Episcopal Church. Observing that the majority of free blacks did not attend church, Allen had a vision to create a separate African Methodist church to reach them. Eventually that church joined with other black churches to form the African Methodist Episcopal Church in 1816.

An event known as the "Haystack Prayer Meeting" (1806) helped launch missions efforts from North America to other parts of the world. Five students from Williams College in Massachusetts were praying about

---

42. See Garth M. Rosell and Richard A. G. Dupuis, eds. *The Memoirs of Charles G. Finney: The Complete Restored Text* (Grand Rapids: Zondervan, 1989).
43. Finney sets forth his methodology in his work, *Revival Lectures* (Old Tappan, NJ: Fleming H. Revell, n.d.). Even Finney critic Richard Owen Roberts acknowledges this work of Finney's is "doubtless the most influential revival work [ever] published." See Richard Owen Roberts, *Revival Literature: An Annotated Bibliography with Biographical and Historical Notes* (Wheaton, IL: Richard Owen Roberts, 1987), 182.
44. Finney, *Revival Lectures*, 7.
45. Allen C. Guelzo, *Edwards on the Will: A Century of American Theological Debate* (Eugene, OR: Wipf & Stock, 1989), 217.

a plan to reach the unevangelized world with the gospel message. They were forced to take shelter in a haystack during a thunderstorm, and Samuel J. Mills (1783–1818), one of the five young men, gave the decisive word: "We can do it, if we will." They attended Andover Theological Seminary and were sent to the mission field by the American Board of Commissioners for Foreign Missions in 1810.

Sojourner Truth (Isabella Baumfree; c. 1797–1883) was born into slavery but was emancipated by her master in 1827. She began an itinerant speaking ministry in 1843 and took on a new name to compliment her mission, "Sojourner Truth." She became famous throughout the northern states as an itinerant preacher, abolitionist, and advocate for the poor and women's rights.

The Laymen's Prayer Revival (1857–1858)

A layman named Jeremiah Calvin Lanphier was doing outreach visitation for the North Dutch Reformed Church in New York City. In September 1857 he felt led to organize a noonday prayer meeting for businessmen and to invite them to come and pray. The prayer movement went from one location with a handful of men at the beginning to dozens of locations with thousands of people all over the city. The prayer movement spread to other major cities as well—Boston, Chicago, and Philadelphia soon had their own prayer meetings. Hundreds of thousands of people were converted through these months of prayer and sharing the gospel message.[46]

Nineteenth- and Twentieth-Century Evangelism

D. L. Moody (1837–1899) was his generation's best-known evangelist.[47] Because of a challenging family situation, his total schooling was the equivalent of a fifth-grade education. He never went to college or seminary, nor was he ever ordained. He preferred throughout his life to be called simply "Mr. Moody."

---

46. J. Edwin Orr notes that Roy J. Fish calculated a total of 996,370 persons added to church rolls in the two years of revival. See Orr, *The Event of the Century: The 1857–1858 Awakening* (Wheaton, IL: International Awakening, 1989), 326.
47. My favorite Moody biography is the one by Lyle W. Dorsett, *A Passion for Souls: The Life of D. L. Moody* (Chicago: Moody, 1997).

Moody moved to Chicago in 1856 and developed a successful shoe sales business. In 1858 he organized a Sunday school in one of the neediest sections of the city. The class soon grew to more than five thousand children, eventually becoming the Illinois Street Independent Church in 1864 (later known as The Moody Memorial Church). In 1860 he gave up his business and devoted himself to city missionary work.

During the Civil War he served as a chaplain in the Union Army. Moody had scores of opportunities for witnessing every day for nearly four years, helping him polish his evangelistic skills. On an 1867 trip to Great Britain, he was challenged by Henry Varley with these words: "The world has yet to see what God will do with and for and through and in and by the man who is fully and wholly consecrated to Him."[48] Moody committed to try his utmost to be that man.

The Great Chicago fire of October 1871 led Moody to leave church work for a ministry as a traveling evangelist. He was joined by Ira D. Sankey, whose singing added greatly to the effectiveness of Moody's preaching. Moody had a very successful preaching tour in Great Britain from 1873–1875 and, upon returning home, held massive evangelistic campaigns in major American cities until his death.

One of the approaches Moody popularized was urban evangelism. Moody wanted to reach the cities. He said, "Water runs downhill, and the highest hills in America are the great cities. If we can stir them we shall stir the whole country."[49] Moody's business background led him to focus on organization and promotion. No detail of preparation or promotion was overlooked. It was his practical wisdom in conducting his work that won for Moody the confidence and support of the most successful businessmen in America.

Moody chose to use theaters and lecture halls rather than churches for his meetings. He focused time and energy on training personal witnesses. The "enquiry room," where people with spiritual questions could go to find answers, became a regular feature of his meetings. In these rooms the people he had trained did "personal work" with the individuals seeking salvation. He understood the power of music and utilized it effectively in

48. Charles R. Erdman, *D. L. Moody: His Message for Today* (Grand Rapids: Revell, 1928), 42.
49. William R. Moody, *The Life of Dwight L. Moody* (Uhrichsville, OH: Barbour, 1985), 263.

his meetings. In addition to his meetings, he also focused on education (founding several schools), conferences (to teach the Bible and correct doctrine), and publishing (Fleming H. Revell and Moody Press). Moody captivated his audiences with a homey and sentimental style of story-telling. His message was simple, often focusing on the "Three R's": ruin by sin; redemption by Christ; and regeneration by the Holy Spirit. He focused on the love of God and often said his goal was to "love them in."

Charles H. Spurgeon (1834–1892) modeled pastoral evangelism through Christ-centered preaching and personal evangelism.[50] Spurgeon's giftedness as a preacher has earned him the title "The Prince of Preachers." Thousands of his sermons were published and made available throughout the English-speaking world. One can read them even today and sense Spurgeon's passion for the gospel message and clarity in sharing that message.

Other prominent evangelists during this period were J. Wilbur Chapman (1859–1918), R. A. Torrey (1856–1928), and Billy Sunday (1862–1935). Chapman saw great evangelistic harvests in different pastorates, leading to appeals for him to turn to full-time evangelistic work. Chapman was an organizational genius, and his planning and promotions paved the wave for successful evangelistic campaigns in numerous cities.[51] Torrey saw fruit as an evangelistic pastor and traveling evangelist. He also understood the importance of correct doctrine and the role of apologetics for evangelism and wrote books to train others to witness, including *How to Bring Men to Christ* and *How to Work for Christ*. Torrey advocated strongly for witnesses to rely on prayer and the power of the Holy Spirit. He also served as President of Moody Bible Institute and the Bible Institute of Los Angeles (BIOLA).

Billy Sunday was a professional baseball player who left baseball to preach Christ. He traveled to hundreds of cities and towns proclaiming the good news of Christ. He built large wooden tabernacles for his meetings, and to deaden the sound of footsteps on the wooden floors, he covered them with sawdust. In an era before GPS technology, loggers could easily get lost in the woods. If a fire ever were to begin, they needed to know how to escape and get back to camp quickly. They started a practice

---

50. For Spurgeon's advice on preaching the gospel message, see his *Lectures to My Students* (Edinburgh: Banner of Truth, 2011), as well as reading Spurgeon's sermons. For personal evangelism, see his admonitions in C. H. Spurgeon, *The Soul Winner* (New York: Fleming H. Revell, 1895).
51. See Muncy, *History of Evangelism,* 146–48.

of putting a bag of sawdust on their shoulder as they left camp, and then poking a hole in the bag so it would leave a "sawdust trail." In the event of danger, they could follow the "sawdust trail" to safety. Billy Sunday urged his listeners to "hit the sawdust trail" and come to the front to symbolize them receiving Christ as their Savior and Lord.

Of course Billy Graham (1918–2018) is this generation's best-known evangelist.[52] He preached the gospel in person to more than two hundred million people in more than 185 countries—more live audiences than anyone in history—not counting the additional millions he has addressed through radio, television, the internet, and the printed word. Some estimate that more than two billion people heard the gospel through his ministry. He was the author of thirty-three books and appeared on the Gallup Poll's "The Ten Most Admired Men in the World" a record sixty-one times. He had been called the pastor to presidents, and had a personal audience with every US president from Harry Truman to Barack Obama.

He quickly adapted to burgeoning technology to share the gospel, utilizing radio ("Songs in the Night" and "The Hour of Decision"), film (Worldwide Pictures produced more than 130 films), publishing (books, materials, and magazines including *Christianity Today* and *Decision*), and training (Schools of Evangelism and International Congresses for Itinerant Evangelists).

Since I serve as the Billy Graham Chair of Evangelism in the Billy Graham School of Missions, Evangelism, and Ministry at The Southern Baptist Theological Seminary, when Billy Graham died I was asked to write a brief news release that day on what we can learn from his life. The following is the content from that article, "7 Things Every Christian Can Learn from Billy Graham."

Definitive pronouncements about a person's legacy are best left to future historians, but in the case of Billy Graham, certain reliable observations can be made now. As I both mourn his passing today and rejoice that he is now with the Savior whom he deeply loved, I offer these reflections on his enduring legacy. These observations are not about the vast numerical impact of his evangelistic ministry (such as preaching to more than

---

52. Two essential books in studying Billy Graham are William Martin, *A Prophet with Honor: The Billy Graham Story* (Grand Rapids: Zondervan, 2018) and Graham's own autobiography, *Just as I Am* (San Francisco: HarperSanFrancisco, 1977).

200 million people) but about his ongoing legacy from which we can draw inspiration in our own lives and ministries today.

Billy Graham

Billy Graham believed in the authority of Scripture.

After struggling with a season of doubt, prompted by his friend Charles Templeton's skepticism, Graham made a bedrock commitment to affirm the Bible as God's certain and trustworthy Word. The signature phrase in his preaching became "The Bible Says."

Graham knew the power of prayer.

He repeatedly said "there are three secrets to my ministry. The first is prayer; the second is prayer; and the third is prayer." He pled with God for the souls of people. In his 2006 book *The Journey,* Graham gives this advice: "Every man or woman whose life has ever counted for God has been a person of prayer. A prayer-less Christian is a powerless Christian. . . . Throughout both the Bible and the history of the church, those who made the greatest impact for God were those who prayed the most."[53]

Graham knew the fullness of the Holy Spirit.

Graham documents his time in the British Isles with the great Welsh preacher Stephen Olford and how Olford helped him understand what it meant to have the fullness of the Holy Spirit fueling one's life and one's preaching. Graham said, apart from his conversion, that meeting with Stephen Olford was the most significant spiritual experience of his life. In his 1978 book, *The Holy Spirit,* Graham enunciates what was the heart of the matter for him: "It is not how much of the Spirit *we* have, but how much the Spirit has of *us*."[54]

Graham focused on the cross.

Like the apostle Paul, Graham "determined to know nothing among you except Jesus Christ, and Him crucified" (1 Cor. 2:2). In the midst of

---

53. Billy Graham, *The Journey: How to Live by Faith in an Uncertain World* (Nashville: Thomas Nelson, 2006), 117.
54. Billy Graham, *The Holy Spirit: Activating God's Power in Your Life* (Waco, TX: Word Books, 1978), 100.

growing secularism and skepticism, when other so-called "evangelists" might shy away from preaching the cross, Billy Graham made clear that without the cross (and the resurrection) we have no gospel message. He boldly proclaimed that salvation was only found through the cross of Christ.

Graham promoted personal evangelism.

He realized that God had called him to be a preaching evangelist to millions, but he also understood that the majority of people who come to Christ would be brought through the witness of faithful believers. Over the years, the Billy Graham Evangelistic Association has sponsored hundreds of training opportunities to equip Christians in sharing the gospel.

Graham prepared for the future.

He knew that should the Lord's return not happen in his lifetime, the need for ongoing gospel ministry would continue after he was no longer preaching. One of his enduring legacies that I have the privilege of being a part of is the Billy Graham School of Missions, Evangelism and Ministry here at The Southern Baptist Theological Seminary. Graham loved this school that carries his name (the only such school in the world) and was thrilled for the ongoing gospel training that men and women would receive here long after he was gone.

Graham lived a life of holiness.

Throughout his remarkable ministry, spanning some eight decades, there had never been a hint of scandal. Early in his ministry Graham made commitments to protect his life and ministry from scandal—setting high standards for both financial accountability and sexual morality. How can one explain Graham's impact? Perhaps his wife Ruth said it best when asked how to explain his worldwide impact. She observed, "Billy isn't a great preacher—but he is a holy man."

What legacy has Billy Graham left us? He has set an example of one who affirmed the authority of Scripture, knew the power of prayer, experienced the fullness of the Holy Spirit, focused on the cross, promoted personal evangelism, prepared for the future, and lived a life of holiness.

During one of his extended crusades, Billy had his brother-in-law, Leighton Ford, preach one evening so Billy could rest his ailing voice. Billy wanted to be there to pray for Leighton as he preached, so he put on large sunglasses, pulled a baseball cap down low on his forehead, and went out and sat in the audience that night.

Billy sensed that the man sitting next to him had come under conviction during the message, and when Ford gave the invitation, Billy asked this man if he wanted to go forward to commit to following Christ. The man looked at him and said, "No, I think I'll wait until tomorrow night when the 'big gun' shows up."

The world lost a gospel champion when Graham died. But Billy Graham would want to say to every believer, "Don't wait for the next 'big gun' to come along. Go share Christ with your family member, coworker, classmate, neighbor, friend, or acquaintance today."[55]

Evangelism Through Youth Movements

"Youth for Christ" emerged as an outburst of evangelistic youth rallies. Early leaders were Lloyd Bryant, Jack Wyrtzen, and Percy Crawford. By 1943, Saturday night youth rallies were a fixture in many American cities. Torrey Johnson, pastor of the Midwest Bible Church, organized the first rallies in Chicago in 1944. Billy Graham joined YFC in 1944 as its first full-time employee. In 1945, key leaders met and established Youth for Christ International. Torrey Johnson became their first president. Many Christian leaders of that era got their "start" in ministry with groups such as Youth for Christ.

The Rise of Parachurch Ministries

Evangelical parachurch ministries (*para* meaning "alongside") began to flourish in the second half of the twentieth century. They tend to be very specialized, focusing on a specific area of ministry such as church planting, mass evangelism, literature distribution, broadcasting, theological education, medicine, agriculture, relief, aviation, camping, communications, discipleship, fund raising, management consulting, orphanages, translation, and youth ministries.

In particular the rise of parachurch ministries on college campuses in the 1950s and following—groups such as Campus Crusade for Christ (now Cru), The Navigators, InterVarsity Christian Fellowship, and Student

---

55. Adapted from "7 Things Every Christian Can Learn from Billy Graham," *Southern Seminary Magazine* 86, no. 1 (Spring 2018).

Mobilization—not only saw thousands of college students come to faith in Christ but then trained and deployed those believers as missionaries, Christian workers, and godly laypersons.

Evangelism Training Programs

D. James Kennedy's Evangelism Explosion became a popular training program in the 1970s and beyond.[56] Other helpful tools were developed as well such as Campus Crusade's "Four Spiritual Laws" and Billy Graham's "Steps to Peace with God." These training programs and tools helped equip "ordinary" believers to share the gospel message.

Lessons from Studying the History of Evangelism

God raises up people in his time and in his way for his work.
Some people today are suggesting with Billy Graham's death that the age of preaching evangelism is over. Here is a quote in 1932 from a great evangelist of a previous era, Oswald J. Smith:

> Well, now, where in such a church is there room for an Evangelist? Why, he is simply crowded out, for that kind of programme doesn't need him. Think you the churches of today are pleading for evangelistic services? Could Crossley and Hunter persuade the worldly churches of this Laodicean age to close their doors and unite in a city-wide campaign? Can you picture the modernistic ministers of this generation sitting together on the same platform, lauding, praising and backing a Moody and Sankey campaign? Certainly not. Evangelism has been ruled out of court. It is no longer the order of the day. Nor will the churches ever again throw open their doors to traveling Evangelists, as they did a generation ago. That peculiar type of Evangelism has gone and gone forever.[57]

God raises up people in his time and in his way for his work. Just as the ministry of Billy Graham could not be foreseen by Smith, I would argue

56. D. James Kennedy, *Evangelism Explosion: Equipping Churches for Friendship, Evangelism, Discipleship, and Healthy Growth*, 4th ed. (Carol Stream, IL: Tyndale House, 1996).
57. Oswald J. Smith, *The New Evangelism* (Toronto: The People's Church, 1932), 10–11.

that those "doomsayers" who predict the demise or death of preaching evangelism after Billy Graham should look at the wonderful workings of God throughout history.

God uses a variety of people for his purposes.

One who studies evangelists of the past is struck by their differences in background, education, training, and the way they were "called" to be evangelists. Many did not follow what society would deem an "appropriate" career path in becoming an evangelist. Charles Finney's legal training and Billy Sunday's years spent on the baseball diamond are hardly the preparation that professional guidance counselors would suggest.

In spite of diversity, great evangelists have shared certain things in common.

It is hard to find a successful evangelist who has not had the following characteristics (albeit to varying degrees): deep personal piety, emphasis on personal Bible study and prayer, understanding of the work of the Holy Spirit, conviction regarding biblical authority, and love and compassion for people, just to name a few.

Most evangelists have devised new methods or approaches to reach people in their day.

They have struggled, as we must today, with how to achieve relevance without compromising truth. How can we become all things to all people (1 Cor. 9:22) and yet at the same time avoid preaching another gospel (Gal. 1:8)? Studying the way evangelists of the past struggled with these issues provides insight for us today.

Most evangelists of the past (and present) have been criticized.

While sometimes deserving of the criticism (and we must learn from their failures as well as their successes), other times it is the reflection of a hostile culture that sees the preaching of the cross as "foolishness." Their conviction and steadfastness in the midst of opposition provides courageous examples for us to follow. Billy Graham would want to say to every believer, "Don't wait for the next 'big gun' to come along. Go share Christ with your family member, coworker, classmate, neighbor, friend or acquaintance today."

CHAPTER 6

EVANGELISM AND POSTMODERNITY

ONE OF MY FAVORITE STORIES is about two moose hunters who chartered a pontoon plane to fly them to a specific lake in central Canada. When they landed on the water and taxied to the shore, the pilot told them, "Guys, this lake is not very big. If the plane is too heavy, I can't build up enough speed skimming across the water to take off safely. So if one of you shoots a big moose, the other one needs to shoot a small one. Or both of you can shoot medium-sized moose. But if you both shoot a big moose, I'm telling you right now, we cannot take both of them back." With that understanding, the pilot got in the plane, skimmed across the water, took off, and disappeared from their sight.

Three days later the pilot landed on the water and taxied to the shore, where he found the two hunters beside two of the biggest moose he had ever seen. He said, "Guys, I was afraid this would happen. Pick which one you want to take. We can't take both, or the plane will be too heavy to take off safely." But the two hunters got the pilot to agree to take them by assuring him they had hunted at this exact same lake the previous year, had shot two moose even bigger than these two, and the pilot had agreed to take them. Against his better judgment, the pilot agreed.

As they skimmed across the water to build up speed for a takeoff, the pilot's worst fears were realized. The plane was too heavy, and they crashed into the trees on the far side of the lake. All three men were knocked unconscious by the crash. After several moments, the two hunters regained consciousness and one asked the other, "Where are we?" The second hunter peered out the window and replied, "It looks like about a hundred yards farther than last year."

Where are we as a culture? We are not a hundred yards farther towards godliness than last year, and last year wasn't anything to write home about. Our culture finds itself in the clutches of postmodernism, with secularization growing at an alarming rate. How are believers to respond?

A Brief Glimpse at the Postmodern World

What is postmodernism? Defining postmodernism is a little bit like trying to nail Jell-O to the wall—as soon as you think you have it, it slips away. Postmodernism is an attitude, a mindset, that affirms everything is relative. According to the postmodernist, absolute truth does not exist (except of course, for the absolute truth affirmed in the statement that absolute truth does not exist). Truth is relative. What is true for you may not be true for me.

George Barna, in his survey of the religious beliefs of Americans, appropriately titled *Absolute Confusion*,[1] discovered these startling results:

- Nearly two out of three adults contend that the choice of one religious faith over another is irrelevant because all faiths teach the same basic lessons about life.
- Most Americans cannot name the first four books of the New Testament.
- Most do not know who preached the Sermon on the Mount.
- When non-Christians were asked if they knew why Christians celebrate Easter, 46 percent could not give an accurate answer.

Most do not know what "John 3:16" is or means. They have no idea that is even a verse in the Bible. When they see someone holding up a sign at a football game that reads "John 3:16," as far as they know, some man is telling his friend he is sitting in row 3, seat 16!

---

1. George Barna, *Absolute Confusion: The Barna Report* (Ventura, CA: Regal, 1994).

A 1991 article on evangelism in *Christianity Today* describes the reality of our situation: "growing Western populations who have no Christian background, memory, vocabulary, or assumptions; they are *'ignostics*,' who do not know what Christians are talking about."[2] I agree with that analysis, and three decades later find it even more true. The majority of people I talk with about the gospel are not "agnostics" as much as they are "ignostics"—ignorant of the basic truths of the Bible and Christianity. We no longer can assume a basic Christian worldview. People no longer have Christianity as their starting point for their religious explorations.

This reality presents great challenges, yet it also produces great opportunities. People are ignorant, but many of them are open. This context is not a discouraging time to be involved in evangelism—far from it! I am reminded of the story of two soldiers huddled together in a foxhole, pinned down by enemy fire. During a lull in the shooting, one soldier peeked out to survey the situation. He exclaimed to his fellow soldier, "We are surrounded by the enemy!" The second solider replied, "That's great! Let's not let any of them get away!" While we must never view unbelievers as the enemy (they are held captive by our true enemy, Satan), we certainly are surrounded by those who do not know Christ. How can we seek to not let any of them get away?

HOW SHOULD A CHRISTIAN RELATE TO THE WORLD?

Richard Niebuhr, in his classic work *Christ and Culture*, set forth different ways the church and Christians have related to culture: Christ against culture; Christ of culture; Christ above culture; Christ and culture in paradox; and Christ transforming culture.[3] Joe Aldrich, in his book *Lifestyle Evangelism*, has simplified Niebuhr's discussion. Aldrich's analysis mirrors Niebuhr's, but it uses terminology that I find more understandable for today's context. Aldrich suggests there are four different ways that Christians and churches can relate to secular culture.[4]

---

2. George G. Hunter, "Can the West Be Won?," *Christianity Today*, December 16, 1991, 43–44.
3. H. Richard Niebuhr, *Christ and Culture* (New York: Harper, 1951).
4. Joe Aldrich, *Lifestyle Evangelism: Crossing Traditional Boundaries to Reach the Unbelieving World* (Portland, OR: Multnomah, 1981), 59–65.

Rejection

This response involves withdrawal and isolation from "sinners." It was the approach followed by some in the monastic movement, as they sought to keep sin outside the walls of their monastery. This response is common among some fundamentalist Christians, based in no small part on 2 Corinthians 6:17: "come out from their midst and be separate." This position has a valid point: Christians should not be involved in sin and evil. But to adopt the rejection position—to completely withdraw from the world—means that we can no longer be salt and light.

Immersion

I may be the first Baptist you have ever read who would write against immersion, although this is a different type. Aldrich uses the term *immersion* to highlight the exact opposite response to rejection. In this position, the Christian or the church radically identifies with the culture but in so doing becomes essentially indistinguishable from the world. The salt loses its saltiness, and effective evangelism does not take place. The Christian message becomes so diluted that it loses its distinctiveness.

People who adopt an immersion approach have close proximity to lost people, but they have no distinctive message to share. They have neglected the admonition of Scripture to not let the world cram you into its mold (Rom. 12:2). The immersion approach allows the world to do just that—to cram the Christian or the church into the world's mold. It is reminiscent of the young couple who asked a pastor of a very progressive church, "What do you believe here?" The pastor replied, "What do you want us to believe?"

Split Adaptation

This approach blends the rejection and immersion options. In reality it is a form of spiritual schizophrenia. This person tries to be a citizen of two worlds and drifts with the majority opinion. This person could be described as a "Sunday-only Christian." On Sunday, he follows the rejection approach, but Monday through Saturday, he adopts the immersion approach. It is like the man who applied for a job, listing as his references his pastor, his deacon, and his Sunday school teacher. The interviewer asked, "Can I get the names of some people who know you the rest of the week?"

Critical Participation

This is the approach Aldrich advocates, and one that I agree with as well. It seeks to follow Jesus's admonition to be in but not of the world (John 17:14–16). Believers are to be spiritually distinct from the world's culture but not socially segregated from it. This position is the most challenging of the positions to adopt because the believer must always live in the tension of being in, but not of the world. The apostle Paul modeled this approach for us in 1 Corinthians 9. He writes, "For though I am free from all men, I have made myself a slave to all, so that I may win more" (1 Cor. 9:19). Paul had the status of a free man, but he made himself a slave of all. Why did Paul relinquish his rights, and become a "slave?" He tells us: "so that I may win more."

That phrase is remarkable! If you were a theology professor, you might mark Paul as having bad theology. Don't you know, Paul, that it is God who saves men, not you? Paul believed in God's sovereignty, but he also recognized that God fulfills his purposes through "secondary means," including people. How could Paul win more people by relinquishing his rights? He answers that question by giving us three illustrations.

The Jew

"To the Jews I became as a Jew, so that I might win Jews; to those who are under the Law, as under the Law though not being myself under the Law, so that I might win those who are under the Law" (1 Cor. 9:20). The Jews were under the Old Testament Mosaic law. How does Paul seek to win them to Christ? He tells us, "I became like a Jew," and "I became like one under the Law—though I myself am not under the Law." Paul doesn't offend their sensitivities; rather, he accommodates them to the degree he can so he can gain a hearing. To those who were under dietary restrictions, Paul was willing to follow their diet, though, as he says, he was not himself under the same law. Paul could have ridiculed their food customs—brought a barbecued pork sandwich into the synagogue—and argued with them, "Don't you know that because of Jesus you no longer need to be bound to dietary food laws?" But Paul did not do that. He did not create unnecessary obstacles. If the cross is a stumbling block, so be it, but let's not create unnecessary stumbling blocks!

The Gentiles (Non-Jews)

"To those who are without law, as without law, though not being without the law of God but under the law of Christ, so that I might win those who are without law" (1 Cor. 9:21). When Paul came to the Gentiles, he did not come with all the "baggage" of Jewish law. Why not? So that he might present the gospel to the Gentiles. That was why when Paul was in Antioch, he ate their food; and while he was in Jerusalem, he ate Jewish food. When Paul witnessed to Gentiles, he did not expect them to act like Jews, and he did not assume his hearers knew who Abraham or Moses was.

The Weak

"To the weak I became weak, that I might win the weak" (1 Cor. 9:22). In the context of 1 Corinthians 9, Paul seems to be referring to those who had "weak" consciences regarding eating meat. Paul relinquished his right to eat meat to impact these persons for Christ (see his argument in 1 Corinthians 8). Paul's point was that in order to achieve his purpose and calling, he was prepared to relinquish whatever right was necessary if the exercising of that right would cause someone to stumble.

Paul was not teaching situational ethics; he is not for a moment saying the end justifies the means. His accommodation was only in areas that were permissible in the moral law of God. He made clear that he was under the law of Christ. Paul was flexible in his *methods* but not in his *morals*. He was under the moral law of God. Paul is talking about accommodating only in areas where there is Christian liberty, such as eating meat offered to idols. How does that apply to us today? In matters of Christian liberty, though I may have a right to do a certain thing, I will not exert that right if it is going to be to the detriment of any individual and hinder them from coming to a saving knowledge of Jesus Christ.

All People

"I have become all things to all men, so that I may by all means save some" (1 Cor. 9:22). Paul is prepared to accommodate however he needs to in order to reach people with the gospel. He adopted a person-centered approach in his witnessing. Paul never denied the truth or compromised in the realm of morality but adjusted as much as he could to the perspective of those whom he was with. He did not adopt the approach, "When in Rome, do as the Romans do." Accommodation for evangelism does not mean the witness involves himself or herself in sinful practices. Paul did not behave like them, but he identified with them as much as he could so he could reach them. Again, Paul was not teaching that the end justifies the means. He accommodated only in those things that were not sinful. He was not committing sins to try to further the gospel, but he was sacrificing liberties for the sake of the gospel.

In 2 Corinthians 8–9 Paul deals with the theme of Christian freedom. The point Paul drives home in chapter 8 is that Christian freedom has limits. In the context of chapter 8, it is limited by our love for "weaker" Christians, those not as spiritually mature. In chapter 9 he gives us another reason why we would choose to limit our liberty. We limit our liberty for the sake of the gospel. In chapter 8 our liberty must be limited by our love for other believers. In chapter 9 our liberty must be limited by our love for the lost.

PRINCIPLES FROM ACTS 17:16–34 (PAUL AT ATHENS)

Effective evangelism today involves going "back to the future." As we reflect on the world today, much of it looks very first-century in its appearance. The early church ministered in a day when a variety of religious expressions were deemed valid, and the one option ruled "out of court" seemed to be the exclusivity of the gospel (that salvation is found only in Christ). Paul models evangelism for us in his ministry in Athens. Athens was an intellectually sophisticated city, with great cultural and intellectual influence. In its glory days, Athens had been the home of Socrates, Plato, and Aristotle. But Paul was unimpressed with its faded glory. As he walked the streets of Athens, he saw men and women in need of a Savior. We can unpack four key principles from this passage for our witness today.

The effective witness ministers out of a burdened heart (vv. 16–17).

This burden is focused in two directions: God's glory and the lost. Athens was indeed "a city full of idols." One ancient writer speculates at this time there were some thirty thousand different gods being worshiped in Athens! Paul was stirred with jealously for God's glory. He was greatly distressed to see the idolatry in Athens—to see that though there was a great deal of religion, there was no worship of the true and living God. God was not being honored by these people. He was not being loved and obeyed because these people did not know him. John Stott emphasizes the importance of this burden for God's glory: "Is this not the cause of our guilty silence? We do not speak for Christ because we do not so love His name that we cannot bear to see Him unacknowledged and unadored. If only our eyes were opened to see His glory, and if only we felt wounded by the shame of His public humiliation among men, we should not be able to remain silent."[5]

Paul had a burden for the lost that moved him to action. He "reasoned" from the Scriptures with both Jew and Gentile, seeking to point them to the gospel of grace. His burden did not discriminate between different groups of people; he understood his obligation to share the gospel with all. There must be a time when our heart becomes *broken* for lost humanity. This text reminds us that proper Christian witness begins in a burdened heart, not in feelings of superiority. Our evangelistic impulse is not a matter of intellectual pride but of spiritual concern for a lost and dying world. The effective witness ministers out of a burdened heart—a burden for God's glory and a burden for the lost.

The effective witness begins where people are in their spiritual pilgrimage (vv. 18–23).

These verses reveal several things about Paul's approach. First, he studied his audience. Paul uses descriptive phrases: "I observe" and "I was passing through and examining." He looked past what he saw on the surface and saw their real need. They were people who needed Jesus Christ. What do you see when you see people? A *barber* sees hair; a *salesman* sees shoes; a *dentist* sees teeth. What do you see when you see people? Do you see them as spiritual beings, created in the image of God? People whose lives are being ruined by sin and who stand in desperate need of the gospel?

Second, he began where they were in his witness to them. Paul's gospel proclamation brought confusion to his listeners. They accused Paul of teaching nonsense! To secular ears, the preaching of the gospel seems strange: "you are bringing some strange things to our ears" (v. 20)! The Christian witness often hears the same response today. Many secular people assume themselves to be good and decent people, and they are offended to be told they are sinners in need of redemption. They want to work out their problems on their own, but the gospel demands repentance from self-sufficiency. Paul began where they were. He did not assume they knew about the true and living God. We often make the mistake today of

---

5. John R. W. Stott, *Our Guilty Silence: The Church, the Gospel and the World* (London: Hodder and Stoughton, 1967), 22.

starting in the middle (assuming too much on the part of our hearers), instead of starting at the beginning. We must be sensitive to our audience.

Third, he zeroed in on their spiritual hunger. Paul's observations showed him the Athenians were a religious people. A deficit of spirituality was hardly the problem. Just to cover all their bases, they had even erected an altar to "an unknown god." "It just so happens I know that unknown God," said Paul. "What you worship in ignorance I now proclaim to you." This is surely a pattern for witnesses in a postmodern world. We must seek to turn humankind's spiritual hunger toward the truth of the gospel. God has placed that hunger within lost persons so that they might desire Christ. Paul Little writes, "Every person I have known who has been used of God in personal evangelism has had an attitude of expectancy to discover interested people."[6]

The devil works at keeping Christians believing that most people do not want to hear about the way of salvation. Yet look at the world around us. Why the proliferation of cults? Why the growth of the New Age movement? Why are people making appointments and waiting in lines to visit psychiatrists so they can pay them lots and lots of money to listen to their problems? Why the problems with drug and alcohol abuse? Because people are hurting and looking for answers! We must zero in on people's spiritual hunger.

The effective witness teaches the true and living God (vv. 24–29).

Paul's concern was to establish his preaching of Christ on the larger foundation of the knowledge of God in the Bible, the maker of heaven and earth. He begins with creation, which establishes mankind's accountability to God, and then moves to redemption. We learn two more facets of Paul's evangelistic strategy from these verses. First, he is focused on who God is (vv. 24–28). Verse 28 shows us that Paul knew the secular literature of his day. But he did not try to persuade his hearers by using their weapons—that was merely his starting point. Instead, he focused on who God is. He preached God the *creator* (v. 24). God is the maker and not the one who was made. God was not created by humans; he is the One who makes humans and everything else that exists in all the universe.

---

6. Paul E. Little, *How to Give Away Your Faith* (Downers Grove, IL: InterVarsity Press, 1966), 36.

He preached God as *sustainer* (vv. 25). God does not have any needs himself. He is perfect. He does not live in temples made by human hands. We do not provide for him; he provides for us. He also preached God as *ordainer* (vv. 26). God is in control of history, providentially working in the affairs of humankind. Finally, he preached God as *near* (vv. 27). He is not a God who is far off and inaccessible. Rather, he intimately involves himself in the lives of his creatures.

Second, he confronted their mistaken views (vv. 29). Witnessing is both offensive and defensive. We must present the truth *and* correct error. We must do both! Make an effort to strike the appropriate balance of both presenting truth and correcting error in your evangelism.

The effective witness points people to Christ (vv. 30–31).

Paul preached Christ as the resurrected Savior (v. 31; cf. v. 18). Although Christ's death is central to salvation, the Bible never leaves Christ nailed to the cross. Had it not been for the resurrection, who would have recognized the redemptive significance of his death? Because Jesus rose from the dead, he is who he claimed to be, and his teaching can be trusted. We must keep the focus of our message on Christ. Not a church, not a denomination, not a philosophy of life, but a person! Christ is the gospel!

Paul also called for the necessary response to his message. He gives three great truths which underscore the importance of repentance.

1. *Judgment day is coming.* God has appointed a day when he will judge the world, when every person will have to give an account of his or her life.
2. *There is an unchallengable judge.* His verdict is final. There is no higher court of appeal.
3. *God has made these truths evident by an irrefutable fact.* He raised Jesus Christ from the dead.

We must declare the gospel and then invite people to respond to God's invitation to repent and believe.

The Result (vv. 32–34)

We see three difference responses to Paul's preaching. Some people *mocked.* Mocking is the defense of pride when it has no good answer; it resorts to ridicule. If you cannot answer your opponent, try to tear him down. Some people *wanted to know more*. Perhaps this was an excuse to avoid dealing with the truth, but perhaps it showed genuine interest on their part. And some were *gloriously converted*. We should expect all three types of responses as we engage people with the gospel in our culture today.

CHAPTER 7

WHAT IS THE GOSPEL?

ACCORDING TO THE BIBLE, just what is the gospel message? Galatians 1:8–9 exhorts, "But even if we, or an angel from heaven, should preach to you a gospel contrary to what we have preached to you, he is to be accursed!" In case we missed his point the first time, Paul goes on, "As we have said before, so I say again now, if any man is preaching to you a gospel contrary to what you received, he is to be accursed!" These verses in Galatians 1 remind us of the importance of getting the gospel right. So what is the gospel message?

I want to begin with an observation made by J. Mack Stiles in his book *Marks of the Messenger*. This book is not on the gospel per se; its emphasis is more on the communicator of the gospel—the messenger. Stiles makes an historical observation on which we should reflect. Stiles notes that you tend to see a troubling pattern among religious movements. Unfortunately, after the gospel is first *accepted*, believed, and embraced, after a period of time the gospel can become *assumed*. How do you know the gospel is being assumed? When you have people saying, "Oh, we've already heard that before." Stiles notes it is not a very far cry from the gospel being assumed to the gospel being *confused*; then, it is not a far step from the gospel being confused to the gospel being *lost*.[1] We must never start

---

1. J. Mack Stiles, *Marks of the Messenger: Knowing, Living and Speaking the Gospel* (Downers Grove, IL: InterVarsity Press, 2010), 40.

down this slippery slope by assuming the gospel; we must continually believe it, share it, and live it out.

In his book, *The Explicit Gospel,* Matt Chandler notes that Scripture presents the gospel to us from two different perspectives. He calls them the view from the *ground* and the view from the *air*.[2] We can see similarities to these views and how Christ is presented to us in the four Gospels. Scholars note that in the synoptic Gospels (Matthew, Mark, and Luke), Jesus is presented from "below." We first encounter him as a man—he was born. The Gospel of John presents Christ from "above." The very first verse, John 1:1 states: "In the beginning was the Word, and the Word was with God, and the Word was God." Both viewpoints are accurate pictures of Christ, they simply have different starting points—one from below and one from above.

Similarly, Chandler says the gospel can be viewed from the ground and from the air. When we view the gospel from our perspective, from the ground, we see that the gospel is message about *God,* the gospel is a message about *man,* the gospel is a message about *Christ,* and the gospel is a message about our necessary *response.* However, Chandler notes that the perspective from above reveals the gospel is a message about *creation,* the *fall, reconciliation,* and then *consummation.* Both perspectives are pictures that Scripture gives us. In this chapter, I am going to focus on what Chandler calls the "gospel from the ground" because that's where we encounter this good news as human beings.[3]

Keep in mind the gospel also speaks not only to our justification but also to our sanctification. When we become Christians, the gospel is not something we should leave in the rearview mirror. We need to preach it to ourselves daily because it speaks not only to our initial salvation but also to our ongoing growth in the Christian life. As believers we go through a cycle of guilt and grace and gratitude; therefore, we need to constantly be reminded of the gospel message.

What is the gospel? Let me make one other introductory observation before we unpack the gospel from the ground. In Acts 2 we see Peter preaching the good news, the gospel of Christ, to believing Jews. Peter does not have to explain who God is; they already know the name Yahweh.

---

2. Matt Chandler, *The Explicit Gospel* (Wheaton, IL: Crossway, 2012), 16–17.
3. Helpful approaches to communicating the gospel message include: 3 Circles; The Bridge to Life; One Verse Evangelism (Romans 6:23); The Story; Two Ways to Live; and The Roman Road.

In essence, Peter starts "in the middle" of the gospel from the ground. He assumes a lot on the part of his audience. I bring this up because I grew up in an "Acts 2 culture," a culture where society as a whole had an understanding of the God of the Bible. In my elementary school, we had the Ten Commandments on the wall of the school right next to the American flag, and we began every day of elementary school with our teacher leading the class in prayer. That meant that the students, even if they were not churchgoers, had a basic understanding of the person of God.

Fast-forward to today. We no longer live in an Acts 2 culture. Rather, our culture more accurately reflects Acts 17. In Acts 17 we also have a preacher and an audience. Paul is the preacher this time. The audience in Athens is not composed of believing Jews; the audience is filled with pagans, with Gentiles, with those who have little to no knowledge of the true God. Paul notes that they had set up idols to all kinds of gods. Lest they miss any gods, they even set up an altar to the unknown God. Paul told them that what they worshiped in ignorance (this unknown God), he was going to explain to them. Paul did not follow the example of Peter. Instead of starting in the middle, he followed the example of Julie Andrews in *The Sound of Music*: "Let's start at the very beginning; it's a very good place to start." Paul began with creation and with who God is.

Why do I emphasize this point? Because I am convinced that we are no longer an Acts 2 culture; we are an Acts 17 culture. In our culture we can no longer assume that people have a basic level of understanding of Christian truths. That is significant because many of the evangelistic materials that are still utilized today were developed back during a time in which you could assume some knowledge of God on the part of your hearers. People used to know you were talking about the God of the Bible when you said, "God." Today when people mention God, they could mean anything. We must help people understand who the biblical God truly is.

A MESSAGE ABOUT GOD

First, the gospel is a message about God. The gospel tells us who God is, what he is like, and what he expects from his creatures. The Bible tells us that God is the holy and loving creator, and, as such, he has an absolute claim on our lives. Thus, Paul began in his witness to the Athenians in Acts chapter 17 with God the creator.

It is important that as we explain who God is to people and that we explain that he is not only loving but also holy. The pendulum has really swung in our culture to where the people who do acknowledge God seem to talk about him simply as a God of love, seldom if ever mentioning God as holy. However, if you were to look through the Scriptures to discover the predominant attribute of God, it would be his holiness. Often when people encounter God in Scripture, they cry out, "Holy, holy, holy!" They fall on their faces in worship.

When people today talk about God's love, what they describe often seems more like mere sentimentality than the true love of a father. It comes across more like the love of a heavenly grandfather. If you have children, did you witness your parents changing before your very eyes when you had kids of your own? I sure did! My wife and I were back on my parents' farm some years ago with our young children. Sharon and I got up early to walk around the farm for exercise and to enjoy the beauty of God's creation. When we re-entered the house, our four children were sitting at the breakfast table eating ice cream. I asked, "Can someone explain what is going on here?" Kristi, our oldest child, looked at me and said, "Grandpa said we could have *whatever* we wanted for breakfast." They all had chocolate-chip ice cream dripping off of their chins. I looked at my dad and I said, "Who are you? I don't know you. You resemble the man who raised me, but you're obviously not him!"

Even worse, there is an oak paddle that hangs in my parents' kitchen. It was my dad's fraternity paddle, signed by all his fraternity brothers and then laminated. I grew up hating those men because that paddle was the rod of discipline in our home, and it inflicted pain on my backside far too often. My parents were firm believers in the adage, "Spare the rod, spoil the child." That same paddle still hangs in our kitchen. However, it looks different. My mom glued a heart-shaped pillow to the paddle with "Grandma's Paddle" embroidered on it. Now that I'm the grandfather of ten grandchildren, I understand that distinction. But let us never forget that God is not a heavenly grandfather that simply says "Yes" to do whatever you want. He is a heavenly Father who loves us enough to discipline us. He is a holy father.

In his book *To Tell the Truth*, Will Metzger says, "Most of my time in witnessing is taken up with defining the nature of the biblical God."[4] In an

---

4. Will Metzger, *Tell the Truth: The Whole Gospel Wholly by Grace Communicated Truthfully and Lovingly* (Downers Grove, IL: InterVarsity, 2012), 105.

Acts 17 society we need to spend more time explaining to people who God is rather than less because until people see God as holy, they will never truly see themselves as sinful. The gospel is first a message about God.

A Message about Humanity

Second, the gospel is a message about humanity. The gospel makes clear that we are created in the image of God: "God created man in His own image, in the image of God He created him; male and female He created them" (Gen. 1:27). We are the pinnacle of God's creation, and yet we are sinful and fallen. The Bible goes on to say in Romans 3:10–12, "There is none righteous, not even one; there is none who understands, there is none who seeks for God; all have turned aside, together they have become useless; there is none who does good, there is not even one." Romans 3:23 reminds us, "For all have sinned and fall short of the glory of God," and Romans 6:23 teaches us that "the wages of sin is death." Our sin earns us spiritual death and separation from God.

The Bible says that while we were created in God's image, we haven't lived as God wants us to live; we have stubbornly chosen our own way, and we have rebelled against God's authority in our lives—that is what the Bible calls sin. That is why we need God's initiating work: because of the sinfulness of our hearts, we would never come to him on our own. Left to ourselves, we will always run *away* from God, not *to* him—like Adam trying to hide from God in the garden. But because we have lost a sense of God's holiness, we do not even see the sinfulness of our sin.

Sinful people throw out expressions such as, "If God grades on the curve, I'll be okay," or "I know I'm not perfect, but I'll take my chances." They don't really see themselves as truly sinful before a holy God. They feel the *effects* and *results* of sin, but people in our culture today tend to view their problems as horizontal, or sociological, instead of as vertical, or theological.

Richard Baxter was a seventeenth-century pastor in Kidderminster, England. He saw nearly the whole community of Kidderminster converted to Christ. His story is one of the most amazing and remarkable stories of pastoral faithfulness in Christian history. Baxter said the greatest struggle he faced in the seventeenth century was convincing the people of Kidderminster that they were sinners in need of a savior. If Baxter would say that in the seventeenth century, what do you think he would say about our world today? Baxter shares a good illustration, though a bit dated. He said to imagine a man who is on the gallows, having been convicted of a capital offense. He is about to be hanged for that capital offense. He has the noose around his neck, and the hangman has his hands on the lever. Baxter said to imagine at that moment, a messenger from the king rushes up with a parchment in his hand sealed with the king's seal. The messenger comes to this condemned man and says, "The king has pardoned you!" Baxter asked what that man's response would have been to the news of the pardon. He would be relieved and joyful but also humble. Because he was guilty of a capital offense, he knows he deserves to die, yet the king used his power of pardon to spare him.

Baxter then suggests taking that same messenger from the king and having him deliver that message to "an innocent bystander" in the crowd, someone who was there to observe the execution. The messenger would say to that bystander, "Hey, I have good news for you. The king has pardoned you!" Baxter asked how that man would respond to news of a pardon. He would be neutral at best, arguing he did not need the pardon. He might even turn hostile, saying, "I don't need a pardon. Don't offend me by suggesting I need a pardon. I haven't done anything deserving of death. I'm an innocent bystander!"

Baxter said the greatest challenge in his pastoral ministry was convincing the people in his city they were not the innocent bystander; they were rather the man on the gallows. That is our challenge today as well. Francis Schaeffer was once asked the question, "What would you do if you met a really modern man on a train and just had one hour with him to share the gospel?" Schaffer answered that he would spend forty to fifty minutes demonstrating the dilemma that he was morally dead. Then he would take ten to fifteen minutes to preach the gospel. He goes on to make this observation: "I believe that much of our evangelistic and personal work today is not clear simply because we are too anxious to get to the answer without having a man realize the real cause of his sickness, which is true moral guilt and not just psychological guilt feelings in the presence of God."[5] We are too quick to give the solution without people really understanding the true nature of the problem. People today do not really see the

---

5. Francis A. Schaeffer, *Death in the City* (Wheaton, IL: Crossway, 2002), 85–86. Cited in Metzger, *Tell the Truth*, 118–19.

horrific nature of their sin because they first do not see God's holiness. It is against the backdrop of God's holiness that we most clearly see our sin. We shoot off fireworks at night because the brilliance of the light is best seen against the backdrop of darkness. Conversely, the darkness of our sin is best seen against the backdrop of God's holiness.

A Message About Christ

Third, the gospel is a message about person and work of Christ. When sharing the gospel we must first give his credentials and then his message. We show people who he is and then what he has done.

The Person of Jesus

In John 1:29 we read about Jesus, "Behold, the Lamb of God who takes away the sin of the world!" Matthew 1:21 refers to Jesus as Emmanuel, meaning "God is with us." Jesus is fully man and fully God. As such, Jesus is the mediator between God and man. Scripture makes clear that where we have all failed, Jesus lived a perfect life. Jesus Christ stood in front of his bitterest enemies and asked them this question, "Who among you convicts me of sin?" and the Bible says they were silent (John 8:46). They could not point out anything. The author of Hebrews testifies Jesus was tempted in all things as we are, yet without sin (Heb. 4:15). God himself has come down in the person of his only Son. The incarnation and the full deity of Jesus are cornerstones of the Christian faith.

Because Jesus is God, he is able to authentically forgive sin. Because Jesus is *human*, he has an understanding of us at our deepest point of need and he serves as our true representative. Because Jesus is *both God and human*, we have in him a perfect mediator who is our go-between before God. Fulfilled prophecy proves Jesus is who he claimed to be. Here are just a few examples of the prophecies fulfilled in the person of Christ:

- Would be the "offspring of a woman" (Gen. 3:15; Gal. 4:4)
- Promised offspring of Abraham (Gen. 18:18; Matt. 1:1)
- Promised offspring of Isaac (Gen. 17:19; Matt. 1:2)
- Promised offspring of Jacob (Num. 24:17; Matt. 1:2)
- Will descend from the tribe of Judah (Gen. 49:10; Matt. 1:2–3)
- The heir to the throne of David (Isa. 9:7; Matt. 1:1)

- Born of a virgin (Isa. 7:14; Matt. 1:18)
- Place of birth (Micah 5:2; Matt. 2:1)

Christ as a person simply cannot be ignored. The witness must present Jesus as the Son of God, the one at whose name every knee will bow, the one who is King of kings and Lord of lords, who will reign forever!

The Work of Jesus

The death of Jesus was not accidental. Peter reminds us in Acts 2:23 (ESV) that it was "according to the definite plan and foreknowledge of God." It fulfilled what God had foretold through the prophets (Acts 3:18). Hebrews 9:22 (ESV) reminds us, "Without the shedding of blood there is no forgiveness of sins."

Billy Graham testifies that on one occasion at a crusade in Dallas, he lost the focus on the cross. He had preached that night not sensing God's anointing and seeing little response. He asked a friend after the service what he thought about it. His friend shared, "Billy, you didn't preach the cross tonight. You said a lot of good things, but you didn't preach the cross. That is what shows us very clearly our sin and our need for a Savior." That night in Dallas, Billy Graham made the commitment that the apostle Paul had made centuries before: "I determined to know nothing among you except Jesus Christ in him crucified."[6]

Justice and love meet at the cross; we see true justice and yet sacrificial love. As Paul explains in Romans 3:26, God is both just and the justifier of the one who believes God. Sin must be punished, but God himself takes that penalty on himself in the person of Christ. Jesus took our place and died the death we deserved. Second Corinthians 5:21 says, "He made Him who knew no sin to be sin on our behalf, so that we might become the righteousness of God in Him." In Galatians 3:13, we read that Christ became a curse for us. First Peter 3:18 tells us, "Christ also died for sins once for all, the just for the unjust," and Romans 5:8 reminds us that "God demonstrates His own love toward us, in that while we were yet sinners, Christ died for us." No wonder Jesus shouted, "It is finished" right before he bowed his head and yielded his spirit. We do not fear judgment day

---

6. Billy Graham, "Go in His Power," *Decision Magazine*, January 1989, 1.

because the one who will judge us is the one who died for us. We have good news to proclaim!

The Resurrection of Christ

Although Christ's death is central to salvation, the Bible never leaves Christ nailed to the cross. Christ lived a perfect life and died a sacrificial death, but his resurrection is a key theme in the apostolic preaching. We must proclaim not only the cross but also the resurrection. Both are absolutely vital. Had it not been for the resurrection, we would not have fully understood who Christ was in his saving significance. In Acts 17:31, Paul writes, "He has fixed a day in which he will judge the world in righteousness through a Man whom He has appointed, having furnished proof to all men by raising Him from the dead."

Was Jesus the only person to die on a cross at the hands of the Romans? No! Thousands died on a cross—at least two others that very same day. How do we know that Christ's death was different? Scripture tells us God proved or vindicated him to be the son of God by raising him from the dead. First Corinthians 15 reminds us that the gospel is not simply news about Christ's death but also about his resurrection. We must share with people the death of Christ, but we must also share his resurrection.

The gospel is a message about God, the holy and loving creator. The gospel is a message about humans, who were created in the image of God but rebelled against God as sinful, fallen, and broken creatures. The gospel is a message about Christ, his perfect life, his sacrificial death, his being raised from the dead, and his ascent into heaven to rule and reign. Finally, we see the gospel is a message about a necessary response.

A NECESSARY RESPONSE

Knowing the first three aspects of the gospel is not enough. The gospel calls for a response from each of us; the biblical response is repentance and faith. First Thessalonians 1:9 (NIV, emphasis added) reminds us of the importance of both repentance and faith in conversion. We cannot come to God still clutching idols: "They themselves report what kind of reception you gave us. They tell how you *turned* to God from idols to serve the living and true God." Notice the direction of this action: *to* God and *from* idols, not the other way around. You do not decide one day to leave your idols and then try to find God. What happens is that you discover the beauty, the glory, the greatness and majesty of God, and seeing that and wanting it, you are willing to lay aside the cheap imitation idols you have been clutching.

The gospel message, the good news, calls for a response. John 1:12 says, "But as many as received Him, to them He gave the right to become children of God, even to those who believe in His name." When you receive an invitation with the statement, "Please R.S.V.P," you are being asked to respond to the invitation. We see Jesus's gracious invitation in Matthew 11:28: "Come to Me, all who are weary and heavy-laden, and I will give you rest."

What is the response we are to make? Scripture puts repentance and faith together as different aspects of the one act of coming to Christ for salvation.

Repentance

Repentance consists of turning from sin and turning to God. What is biblical repentance? Scripture makes clear that repentance literally means a change of mind. When we truly have a change of mind, however, it will be more than a change in the way that we think. It will affect the way that we live. Here is my definition of repentance: *a change of mind, that leads to a change of heart, that results in a change of action.* Our necessary response is to repent, to think differently about sin and about God, to make a U-turn away from that sin, and to come by faith to God in Christ (see Luke 13:3 and Acts 17:30).

Repentance involves more than remorse or simply feeling sorry for wrongdoing. Remorse certainly is a starting point for repentance, but true repentance is more than that. You may have heard of the man who had trouble sleeping, so he wrote an anonymous letter to the IRS, saying, "I cheated on my taxes last year, and I'm having trouble sleeping; therefore, I'm sending a certain amount of cash. Take this and apply it to the US Treasury." Then he added, "P.S. If I still can't sleep, I'll send in the rest next week." That man experienced some remorse but not true repentance.

Faith

The gospel demands that we turn *from* sin in repentance but also *to* God in faith. We must respond to the gospel. As we share the good news, we must make clear that the gospel is not only a declaration of what God has done in Christ, but it is also an invitation to believe in him. Faith underscores the grace of God, affirming that our salvation comes as a gift from him. But it involves more than a general belief—there must be a specific response. Even the devil believes in God. James 2:19 illustrates this reality (my translation): "You believe God is one. Even the demons believe, and yet they tremble." Only when we have repented and believed can we say, "Christ is my Savior and my Lord."

Sonny Bono was an entertainer-turned-congressman in the 1990s. He died in a skiing accident in January 1998. What many did not realize is that less than a week earlier, Michael Kennedy, the thirty-nine-year-old son of the late Robert Kennedy, had been killed while skiing by running into a tree in Aspen, Colorado. Following Michael Kennedy's death, on their way to ski at Lake Tahoe, Sonny's wife, Mary, told him it would probably be a good idea for them to get helmets for skiing. Sonny said he would get one on the next trip. Sonny went skiing the next day without a helmet, crashed into a tree, and was killed.[7] What was even more tragic is that he knew what he needed to do before he went skiing—he knew that it would be a good thing for him to get a helmet, but he thought he had all the time in the world to do it. But his time ran out. Scripture compels us, "Today, if you hear his voice do not harden your heart" (Heb. 3:15; cf. Ps. 95:7–8), and, "Now is the day of salvation" (1 Cor. 6:2). The gospel is a message about our necessary response.

---

7. Bruce Fessier, "Sonny Bono: 20 Years Later, His Last Ski Run Feels 'As if It Was Yesterday,'" *The Desert Sun*, December 31, 2017, https://www.rgj.com/story/news/2017/12/31/sonny-bono-20-years-later-his-last-ski-run-feels-if-yesterday/993256001.

CHAPTER 8

MOTIVATIONS FOR EVANGELISM

MOTIVATION DIRECTLY AFFECTS GETTING A JOB DONE. When people are motivated to do a task, they will most likely do it. When they are not motivated to do it—even though they are trained and equipped—they probably are not going to do it.

IDENTIFYING SCRIPTURAL MOTIVATIONS FOR EVANGELISM

John R. W. Stott, long-time rector of All Souls Church in London, wrote more than fifty books. One of his first was a book on evangelism called *Our Guilty Silence.* He argues that we need incentives (or motivations) in evangelism: "In evangelism too we need incentives, for evangelism is difficult and dangerous work. It brings us face to face with the enemy in hand-to-hand combat. . . . Some never begin to evangelize for want of adequate incentives. Others begin, but grow discouraged and give up; they need fresh incentives."[1] Stott notes the reality of spiritual warfare and the need for incentives to continue to share the gospel.

Stott then argues that God's glory serves as a powerful incentive for evangelism, noting, "This incentive of the glory of God is the link between

---

1. John R. W. Stott, *Our Guilty Silence: The Church, the Gospel and the World* (London: Hodder and Stoughton, 1967), 13–14.

our worship and our witness."[2] He asks, "Is not this [a lack of concern for God's glory] the cause of our guilty silence? We do not speak for Christ because we do not so love His name that we cannot bear to see Him unacknowledged and unadored. If only our eyes were opened to see His glory, and if only we felt wounded by the shame of His public humiliation among men, we should not be able to remain silent."[3] Stott's observation about the glory of God providing motivation for our evangelism rings true to Scripture. Indeed, the Scriptures teach us that all things were created for God's glory (Isa. 43:7; Col. 1:16).

Billy Graham argued for three motivations for evangelism: (1) Christ's love compels us; (2) the approaching judgment; and (3) the command of Christ. Graham stated that the command of Christ is "our primary motive."[4] In addition to these motivations highlighted by Stott and Graham, I have found great motivation from Paul's admonitions in 2 Corinthians 4:16–5:21. I return to this passage of Scripture time and time again. In this passage we find ten very powerful motivations for evangelism.

An Eternal Perspective (2 Cor. 4:16–5:8)

Though the things we can see—our body, the world—are decaying and passing away, the things we can't see—our walk with Christ, our eternal destiny—are being renewed every day. Though in this world we will have suffering and affliction, in the next world we will experience unspeakable glory. Second Corinthians 4:18 provides the key: "while we look not at the things which are seen, but at the things which are not seen; for the things which are seen are temporal, but the things which are not seen are eternal." If we walk by sight, we will never become effective witnesses. Why? Because we will look at our next-door neighbor who seems very religious, one who has a zeal for God that puts us to shame, and we might begin to think he already has a pathway to God. Or we look at a co-worker who is really a good, thoughtful, kind person and assume she has found a way to God. If we do not look at that which is seen but that which is unseen, we realize that in an eternal sense the unseen world is more real

---

2. Stott, *Our Guilty Silence*, 22.
3. Stott, *Our Guilty Silence*, 22.
4. Billy Graham, "The Evangelist and a Torn World," Chapter 1 in *Choose Ye This Day: How to Effectively Proclaim the Gospel Message* (Minneapolis: World Wide Publications, 1989), 9–18.

than the world that we can see. The world that we can see is temporary and passing away. Therefore, to be effective witnesses we have to learn what it is to walk by faith and not by sight.

Paul describes our earthly bodies as tents in 2 Corinthians 5. Anyone who has camped out knows the frailty of tents. They can be blown down by a single burst of wind, and they can leak in the rain. A tent is fragile. And that is how Paul describes our bodies. But do not miss the main point: God is building an eternal *home* in the heavens for us! When death occurs, there is a replacement for the earthly tent, namely, a house from God, eternal in the heavens. We will live in a resurrected and glorified body throughout eternity!

When we live in the power of the indwelling Christ and are renewed every day, we will focus on the eternal reality of things we *cannot* see rather than on the fleeting reality of what we *can* with our physical eyes. Life is sometimes difficult! Reaching out to others is difficult! But we can reach out as we develop an eternal perspective about what really matters— not our own personal comfort but that God be glorified in and through our lives.

A Deep Desire to Please God (2 Cor. 5:9)

"Therefore we also have as our ambition, whether at home or absent, to be pleasing to Him." Some people in Christian circles criticize ambition. The reason for that criticism is obvious: many people are ambitious for the wrong things! Some people spend their lives climbing the ladder of success only to find out too late it is leaning against the wrong wall. But Paul says, "I have an ambition, I have a goal in life, and that goal is to be pleasing to the Lord." That is an ambition worth living and dying for.

I start every morning the same way. I am usually up by 5:00 a.m. I sit down at my desk and am greeted by a sign I had made years ago to remind me of an important truth. It reads, "An Audience of One." I'm reminded every morning that my goal today is to please an audience of one. If God is pleased with me today, then it does not matter if I displease other people. And it does not matter how many people I please today; if I do not please God, then the day is a failure.

Two of the saddest verses in the Bible are found in John 12:42–43: "Nevertheless many even of the rulers believed in Him, but because of the Pharisees they were not confessing Him, for fear that they would be put out of the synagogue; for they loved the approval of men rather than the approval of God." That tragic epithet is the heritage of these men. I don't want my epitaph to be, "Here lies a man who loved the approval of men more than the approval of God." I want to be a man who lives for the approval of God. We reach out with the gospel because we desire to please God, and God is pleased when we reach out to others. Live for an audience of one!

We Know We Will Be Judged (2 Cor. 5:10)

We will all stand before the judgment seat of Christ. If we have trusted Christ as our Lord and Savior, we will be judged not for our salvation but concerning our stewardship—how we have lived for him, and how we have used the talents and resources he has given us to serve him and further his kingdom. First Corinthians 3 references people who build a foundation on wood, hay, and stubble, and all their works are wiped away with fire. Others build a foundation with gold, silver, and precious stones. God calls on us to be those who build with worthwhile material. We know we are going to be judged on our stewardship. In light of that reality, we need to live our lives and spend our time in the way God desires. If God's only purpose in saving us was to get us to heaven, he could just "zap" us there at the moment of our conversion. But he has a greater plan and purpose for our lives, namely, giving ourselves in loving service to others!

C. T. Studd, legendary missionary to Africa, had his life transformed when he read the following account written from the perspective of an atheist:

Did I firmly believe, as millions say they do, that the knowledge and practice of religion in this life influences destiny in another, religion would mean to me everything. I would cast away earthly enjoyments as dross, earthly cares as follies, and earthly thoughts and feelings as vanity. Religion would be my first waking thought, and my last image before sleep sank me into unconsciousness. I should labour in its cause alone. I would take thought for the morrow of Eternity alone. I would esteem one soul gained for heaven worth a life of suffering. Earthly consequences should never stay my hand, nor seal my lips. Earth, its joys and its griefs, would occupy no moment of my thoughts. I would strive to look upon Eternity alone, and on the Immortal Souls around me, soon to be everlastingly happy or everlasting miserable. I would go forth to the world and preach to it in season and out of season, and my text would be, "What shall it profit a man if he gain the whole world and lose his own soul?"[5]

We must share Christ with that sense of responsibility. We reach out because we know we will be judged as stewards of the opportunities we have been given. The great Puritan pastor Richard Baxter almost died when he was in his thirties. Baxter claims that his illness "made me study and preach things necessary, and a little stirred up my sluggish heart to speak to sinners with some compassion, *as a dying man to dying men.*"[6]

We Understand God's Holiness (2 Cor. 5:11)

"Therefore, knowing the fear of the Lord, we persuade men, but we are made manifest to God; and I hope that we are made manifest also in your consciences." Because we understand God's holiness, we seek to persuade men. Some people are claiming that people today already know they are sinners—all they need to know is how to be saved. That assertion is simply not true. A lot of people understand something is wrong, but they do not see themselves as guilty sinners under condemnation from a holy God. Baxter maintained, "We persuade men to believe that they are sick, that they may go to the Physician."[7] Or to state it more bluntly, we must first get people "lost" before we can get them "saved." Many people think they are basically good. They say things like: "If God grades on the curve, I'll make it," or, "I'm as good as the next guy, so I will take my chances."

Because God is holy, he cannot allow sin in his presence. He must judge and punish sin. Because we understand his holiness, we reach out to others with the love of Christ. Jesus warned in Matthew 10:28, "Do not fear those who kill the body but are unable to kill the soul; but rather fear Him who is able to destroy both soul and body in hell." Jesus Christ was what some might call today a "scare preacher." He was not afraid of making people afraid of eternal punishment.

Spurgeon says:

---

5. Norman Grubb, *C. T. Studd: Cricketer and Pioneer* (Cambridge: Lutterworth, 2014), 35–36.
6. Richard Baxter, *The Autobiography of Richard Baxter*, ed. N. H. Keeble (London: J. M. Dent & Sons, 1974), 26, emphasis added.
7. Richard Baxter, *Catholick Theologie II* (London: Robert White, 1675), 221.

We rob the gospel of its power if we leave out its threatenings of punishment. It is to be feared that the novel opinions upon annihilation and restoration which have afflicted the Church in these last days have caused many ministers to be slow to speak concerning the last judgment and its issues, and consequently the terrors of the Lord have had small influence upon either preachers or hearers. If this be so it cannot be too much regretted, for one great means of conversion is thus left unused.[8]

Eternal punishment is an unpopular message in today's culture, even in today's church culture. It requires courage and confidence in God's calling to preach this truth. Phillips Brooks says, "Courage . . . is the indispensable requisite of any true ministry. . . . Courage is good everywhere, but it is necessary here. If you are afraid of men and a slave to their opinion, go and do something else. Go and make shoes to fit them. . . . But do not keep on all your life preaching sermons which shall say not what God sent you to declare, but what they hire you to say."[9] We reach out because we understand that our God is holy, that his eyes are too pure to look upon sin. First Peter 4:18 asks a piercing question: "And if it is with difficulty that the righteous is saved, what will become of the godless man and the sinner?"

Love and Concern for Others (2 Cor. 5:12–13)

Because God is holy, he must judge sin, not merely overlook it. Therefore lost persons are in real trouble! Our love for those who do not know Christ will cause us to reach out to them. Paul did not seek to impress others or to be served. What he does, he does for God and for others.

As we honestly face the truth that people outside of Christ are destined for hell, it will motivate us to reach out. People who live and die without knowing Christ are lost. They are lost now, and they will be lost for all of eternity. Jesus taught the existence of hell over and over again. In Matthew 25:46, he said, "These will go away into eternal punishment, but the righteous into eternal life." Do we ever contemplate the horrors of hell? Do we remember that persons who die apart from faith in Christ are headed there? Do we really understand what it means to love our neighbor

---

8. C. H. Spurgeon, *Lectures to My Students: Volume Two* (New York: Robert Carter and Brothers, 1889), 269.
9. Phillips Brooks, *Lectures on Preaching* (New York: E. P. Dutton and Company, 1877), 59.

as we love our own self? If we truly believe in the reality of heaven and hell, we cannot say we truly love someone if we refuse to reach out to them.

The Love of Christ (2 Cor. 5:14)

The love of Christ "controls us" or "constrains us." We do not persuade others because we want to win an argument or because we think we are better than anyone else. We persuade others because the love of Christ flows through us, giving us compassion for the lost. We reach out and share the love of Christ with others because his love has done so much for us.

Paul suffered greatly for the sake of the gospel. In 2 Corinthians 11:13 he tells us why he did it: his love and concern for other people. Robert Murray M'Cheyne was a great preacher in Dundee, Scotland, who saw many people come to saving faith in Christ. After M'Cheyne died, someone went to his church and talked to the janitor who had served under M'Cheyne. He asked him: "What was M'Cheyne's secret? How did he have such an impact on this community and town?" The janitor told him, "Come to back to his office with me and I will show you." He told the visitor to sit down behind his desk and pray for the people in this community who did not know Christ and then begin to weep. "That is what M'Cheyne did, and then he would step out into his pulpit and begin to share Christ with people—some of whom had hard hearts—and he would begin to weep. That is what M'Cheyne used to do, having a heart for other people."[10] We reach out because of our love and concern for others. The love of Christ controls us or constrains us from living for ourselves and our own selfish ambition. It drives us to give our lives in unselfish service for others in the way Christ laid down his life for us.

The Lordship of the Resurrected Christ (2 Cor. 5:15).

Because of the love of Christ, we reach out in his love. Paul builds this argument from the example of Christ. Paul claims he does nothing out of selfishness. As an example of how this, Paul reminds them of what Jesus had done. Voluntarily Christ laid down his life, both in terms of physical life and of his willingness to serve the Father's purpose. Because of this reality Paul is compelled to do likewise. Paul's "selfless" attitude toward the Corinthians

---

10. Recounted in Cortland Myers, "Things Not Shaken," in *Baptist Fundamentals: Being Addresses Delivered at the Pre-Convention Conference at Buffalo, June 21 and 22, 1920* (Philadelphia: Judson, 1920), 162–63.

is a result of Christ's love for him. If we capture the heart of what Paul is saying here, it will transform us and change the way we view life. Each day we will present ourselves to the Lord as a living sacrifice (Rom. 12:1–2).

Oscar Thompson, who wrote the book *Concentric Circles of Concern*, says, "When I am walking in submission to my Lord, I bump into more people accidentally who need Jesus than I ever could run down on purpose."[11] I find that to be true in my life! When I am walking in submission to Christ, I encounter needy people regularly. But when I am walking in sinful selfishness, I live as if life is all about me. I do not see those individuals. I do not pay attention to people who need Christ.

Most of us are quite aware of the limitations of our love. Human love runs out after a while. It is easy for us to give up on people. To keep reaching out, the key is that we no longer live for ourselves; we live for God. Many Christians do not enjoy the fullness of Christ because they are living for themselves. We reach out because of the lordship of the resurrected Christ.

Hope of a Life That Can Be Changed (2 Cor. 5:16–17)

We believe the gospel can transform the life of any person who hears it and responds to it, no matter how sinful that person currently may be. As we share the gospel, we realize this is a life that can be changed. The hope of that life being changed is one motivation for us to reach out. At times we are tempted to think that some people are so far gone that they can never change. But that is simply not true! Through the miraculous cleansing of Christ's blood, we become new creatures; we are reconciled to God.

The poem "Touch of the Master's Hand" by Myra Brooks paints a powerful picture of the transforming power of the gospel:

Twas battered and scarred, and the auctioneer
 Thought it scarcely worth his while
To waste much time on the old violin,
 But he held it up with a smile.
"What am I bidden, good folk?" he cried,
 "Who'll start the bidding for me?
A dollar—a dollar—then two, only two—

---

11. W. Oscar Thompson, *Concentric Circles of Concern: From Self to Others through Lifestyle Evangelism* (Nashville: Broadman, 1981), 63.

Two dollars, and who'll make it three?
Going for three . . . " But no—
    From the room far back, a gray-haired man
Came forward and picked up the bow,
    Then, wiping the dust from the old violin,
And tightening the loosened strings,
    He played a melody pure and sweet
    As a caroling angel sings.
The music ceased, and the auctioneer,
    With a voice that was quiet and low,
Said, "*Now* what am I bid for the old violin?"
    And he held it up with the bow.
"A thousand dollars—and who'll make it two?
    Two thousand—and who'll make it three?
Three thousand once—three thousand twice—
    And going—and gone," cried he.
The people cheered, but some of them cried,
    "We do not understand.
What changed its worth?" Quick came the reply,
    "The touch of the Master's hand."
And many a man with life out of tune,
    And battered and scarred with sin,
Is auctioned cheap to a thoughtless crowd,
    Much like the old violin.
A mess of pottage—a glass of wine,
    A game—and he travels on.
He is going once—and going twice—
    He's going—and almost gone!
But the Master comes, and the foolish crowd
    Never can quite understand
The worth of a soul and the change that's wrought
    By the touch of the master's hand.[12]

We reach out because of the hope of a life that can be changed.

---

12. Myra Brooks Welch, "The Touch of the Master's Hand," *The Gospel Messenger*, February 26, 1921.

God's Amazing Plan to Let Us Be Involved (1 Cor. 5:18–20)

Verse 20 highlights one of our roles in evangelism: we are ambassadors. God allows us the privilege of playing a part in seeing people's eternal destiny changed, of seeing people transferred from the kingdom of darkness to the kingdom of light. I have a friend who replies to the question, "So what do you do?" with this answer: "I am an ambassador!" His response always opens the door for a gospel witness. What does an ambassador do? An ambassador does not invent a message. He or she faithfully reports the message that he or she has been given. God gives us the privilege—a privilege not even angels experience—of sharing the good news of Jesus Christ with lost and needy sinners. When Corrie ten Boom was asked for the purpose of her life, she responded with this poem:

> When I enter that beautiful city,
> and the saints all around me appear,
> What a joy when someone will tell me,
> "It was *you* who invited me here."[13]

What an amazing privilege to serve as an ambassador for Christ!

"The Wonder of It All": Christ's Sacrificial Death (1 Cor. 5:21)

I have borrowed that phrase the "wonder of it all" from the life of a man named Rodney "Gipsy" Smith. Gipsy Smith was an evangelist who grew up in a gypsy family in England in the early 1900s. He gave his life to Christ at the tender age of six. As a teenager he was called into the gospel ministry and he began preaching throughout England in Salvation Army venues. He eventually ended up coming to the United States, where he preached many evangelistic services.

Vance Havner recounted an experience of hearing Smith preach:

> It was my privilege to hear the Gipsy preach at meetings which proved to be the last time he came to America. He was in his 80's. My, how he preached that night! I have never heard him any better. At the end of the meeting, I decided that this might be the last time I would see him this side of Heaven and I just had to go up and shake his hand and

---

13.   Corrie Ten Boom, *Not Good if Detached* (Fort Washington, PA: CLC, 2009), 40.

thank him. As I came near the Gipsy, an older man came up to him and I heard him say, 'Gipsy, I heard you preach when you first came to America over 50 years ago—my how you blessed my heart then. I have never forgotten it—but again tonight, how my heart was warmed and thrilled! Gipsy, tell me—what's the secret?' Gipsy replied, 'I have never lost the wonder of it all.'"[14]

I love that phrase: "the wonder of it all." That phrase is convicting because it is easy for us to lose sight of it. There are many individuals that have been Christians for decades, but there is no real excitement, vibrancy, or love for Christ. Gipsy Smith shared Christ for over eight decades because he never lost the wonder of it all.

Concluding Thoughts

Which of these motivations is the most important one for evangelism? They are all important! I believe God has given us multiple motivations because we need them all! At various points in our pilgrimage, one or more of these motivations might "rise to the surface" as most significant to us at that time, but we need constant motivation. This chapter began with a powerful observation from John Stott that bears repeating as we conclude this chapter: "In evangelism too we need incentives, for evangelism is difficult and dangerous work. It brings us face to face with the enemy in hand-to-hand combat. . . . Some never begin to evangelize for want of adequate incentives. Others begin, but grow discouraged and give up; they need fresh incentives."[15] Understanding our need for "fresh incentives," may we constantly reflect on these motivations God has provided for us.

---

14. Quoted in John Bjorlie, "Gipsy Smith," *Uplook*, January 1994, http://www.uplook.org/1994/01/gipsy-smith.
15. Stott, *Our Guilty Silence*, 13–14.

CHAPTER 9

OVERCOMING BARRIERS TO WITNESSING

WHY DON'T CHRISTIANS SHARE THE GOSPEL more often? Or, to personalize the question, why don't you witness more regularly? Why don't I? A survey was taken of participants in an evangelism training session prior to a Billy Graham Crusade in Detroit in 1976.[1] One of the questions on the survey asked, "What is your greatest hindrance in witnessing?" More than 50 percent of those surveyed said their biggest problem was fear of how the other person would react. Others felt they didn't know enough to share the gospel adequately. Other responses included being too busy, not having a consistent enough Christian life themselves, or at times lacking compassion for others.

I have encountered an additional hindrance in witnessing; namely, people who think the gift of evangelism is necessary before one can be an effective witness. In this chapter I will examine six barriers to witnessing and provide biblical and practical answers for dealing with these obstacles.

BREAKING THE BARRIER OF FEAR

Fear serves as the greatest of all barriers to overcome in witnessing. How can we break the barrier of fear in our witnessing? First, we must recognize

---

1. Leighton Ford, *Good News Is for Sharing* (Elgin, IL: David C. Cook, 1977), 15.

that we are not alone in struggling with fear in witnessing. All believers who share Christ with others have to work through the issue of fear.

Second, we need to name our fears. What is it specifically that we fear? Some people fear not knowing enough (I will deal with this issue in the next section on breaking the barrier of ignorance). Others fear in their attempt to witness they will do more harm than good. Yet the people who raise this issue often are the very ones who have the least to worry about! Why? Because they are the most sensitive when it comes to other people! But we must also recognize we cannot possibly put a lost person into a worse condition that he or she is in already! They are without Christ and without hope in the world. They are bound for an eternity in hell. We cannot put nonbelievers in a worse situation than they already find themselves in.

Perhaps the most common fear in witnessing is the fear of rejection. How will the person respond to my witness? Will he or she reject the message? Will he or she reject me?

Responses to Fear

Having identified common fears in witnessing, how should we respond? First, we must understand that to a certain degree fear is normal and can prove desirable. Fear itself is not the problem. Fear can be helpful and even necessary to keep us alert and in a spirit of prayer. Fear can be a good thing when it leads us to have a strong confidence in God, not in ourselves. But when fear keeps us from necessary action, it becomes a problem. When confronted by fear in a witnessing situation, we should see that fear as a blinking red light the Holy Spirit uses to get our attention so he can remind us, "Trust in me!"

Second, we must recognize that most of our fears are ungrounded. People generally do not respond in a hostile manner! Most non-Christians are far more willing and even eager to discuss spiritual things than most believers think they are. Of course it's true that a few people may be hostile, and some may be indifferent. But the fear that people are going to reject us and act negatively is usually not realized. Most people, if approached in a sensitive manner, will react with politeness.

Third, we must remember that fear does not disqualify or excuse us from our responsibility to witness. Even if people do respond in a less than positive manner, that does not excuse us. If we plan to wait until all fear is gone before we share God's love with others, then we will never share. Fear will always be with us. But the good news of the Bible is that fear doesn't need to control us. Over and over again in the Bible we are urged, "Do not be afraid" (e.g., John 14:27; Isa. 44:8). In commanding us not to fear, Jesus tells us we have a choice in the matter. We can choose not to be afraid, even in the face of fear.

Fourth, we need to appropriate God's resources to deal with fear. What are these resources? Through Scripture we see that God has given us many resources to deal with fear. In 2 Timothy 1:7 (NIV), Paul reminds Timothy, "For God did not give us a spirit of timidity but a spirit of power, of love and of self-discipline." How is boldness produced in the life of a believer? Acts 4 suggests three ways. Verse 13 suggests that boldness is produced through personal contact with Jesus. As we spend time with him daily, he supplies us with his strength and power. Verses 29–31 show us that boldness is also given in response to our prayers. Verse 31 teaches us that boldness is a byproduct of being filled with the Holy Spirit. God gives us his power to break the barrier of fear when we look to him.

Breaking the Barrier of Ignorance

When people say they don't know how to witness, it usually means one of two things. It may mean they are unclear about the *message* of the gospel, or they are uncertain about an appropriate *method* to share the message. We must know the message of the gospel before we can share it with others. (Chapter 7 unpacks the gospel message in a clear way that can easily be shared with others.) What about those people who know the message of the gospel but are struggling with a suitable method to share Christ with others? First, there are a variety of methods. No one particular method is the right one when it comes to evangelism. But there is a wrong method: to sit back and do nothing! D. L. Moody was confronted one day by a person who disapproved of his method of witnessing. Moody replied that he wasn't overly fond of it himself and asked, "What methods do you use?" "Oh, I don't have a method," the critic replied. "Well," Moody retorted, "I think I like the way I do it better than the way you don't!"[2]

---

2. Leighton Ford, *The Christian Persuader* (New York: Harper & Row, 1966), 68.

Too many people get sidetracked in debates over methodology. Jesus used different methods when healing blind men.[3] On one occasion he merely spoke a word (Mark 10:52), another time he used touch (Matt. 9:29), and on another occasion he placed mud on a blind man's eyes (John 9:6). Can you imagine what might have transpired had these men happened to meet together to discuss their experiences? "Isn't it wonderful how Jesus heals by simply speaking?" one would say. "You are wrong," the second man would protest. "He uses touch." The third man would interject, "You are both wrong! He doesn't use words, or touch—he uses mud to heal!" Their argument could have led them to form three new denominations: the *Touch*ites, the *Speak*ites, and the *Mud*ites. I tell people, "If you don't like a particular method of witnessing, don't waste precious time and energy criticizing it—use one you feel comfortable with and get on with the task!" Chapters 16–21 highlight several different methods of sharing the gospel.

God Uses Ordinary People

We must all begin where we are and then seek to grow. Anyone who knows Jesus can bear witness to him. Many of the people in Bible times who testified of Jesus had no training—formal or otherwise—in the Scriptures or in witnessing. One such person was the woman of Samaria, who left her water pots and told her fellow villagers about Jesus (see John 4:4–42). The man born blind (John 9) testified of Jesus to others without having any formal evangelism training.

Training Opportunities

If you are reading this book, then this point is truly "preaching to the choir." You are utilizing this resource to become better equipped to share your faith. Continue to take advantage of resources and training opportunities to learn and grow. Even though I have been practicing evangelism for more than forty years and have taught evangelism for more than thirty years, I am constantly reading books on evangelism and attending training seminars taught by others. But the bottom line is to begin where you are right now. If you wait until you have mastered every approach, anticipated every question, or read every book, you will never witness. You may feel

---

3. Ford, *Christian Persuader*, 125.

there is so much more you could know about sharing your faith. By all means take advantage of opportunities to learn more! But don't let that stop you from beginning where you are reaching out to others right now.

A Modern-Day Hero

A modern-day news story tells how one "ordinary" man responded in a crisis to save a drowning woman.[4] On January 13, 1982, Air Florida's Flight 90 crashed on takeoff and fell into the icy waters of the Potomac River. Martin Skutnik, age twenty-eight, saw the plane go down. He stood with other spectators on the riverbank watching a woman who had survived the crash and was struggling to swim in the cold water. Skutnik plunged into the river and rescued her. He had never taken a life-saving course, but he saved the woman's life. He may not have used proper form or technique when he swam to the woman's side, at least as professional swim instructors would teach it. He may not have followed the Red Cross's *Lifesaving Manual* in the method he used to grab the woman and bring her back to the safety of the shore. At that time, Skutnik was a general office worker who lived in a rented townhouse with his wife and two children. He had no training for the task he undertook that day. But he couldn't stand by idly and let another human being die without trying to help. He became a national hero on that fateful day by risking his life to rescue that drowning woman.

You may feel less than adequate for the task of witnessing to Christ's love to those around you. You may feel inadequate because of your lack of formal training. Yet, like Martin Skutnik, the urgency of the moment demands that you do what you can with what you have right now. Yes, seek to learn all you can about witnessing and to improve your skills in communicating the gospel, but don't wait until you think you've got it all together to begin sharing. Seek to share the good news with someone today!

BREAKING THE BARRIER OF APATHY

Before we discuss the importance of having a burden for the souls of lost people, we need to recognize an important truth. The Christian life was never intended to be lived solely in the realm of emotion. Yes,

---

4. James J. Kilpatrick, "Rescuer's Name Could Be Legion, for He Is Many," *The Kansas City Times*, January 22, 1982, A-9.

emotions are God-given and can be a powerful means by which he stirs us to action. But Scripture emphasizes our decisions must come from the will. We are to choose God's way whether or not we feel particularly good about following it at that time. If we base our actions on emotions, ultimately we will be frustrated. The mountaintop and valley experiences of the Christian life are not the norm; most of the Christian life is lived on the plain. We need to learn to make choices based on what we know is right, not because we necessarily feel good about doing them. But we must also acknowledge that having a burden for the lost can be a powerful motivation in our witness.

Compassion for Lost People

What exactly do we mean when we use the term *compassion*? The word comes from the Latin word *passion* (meaning "to suffer" or "to feel") and the prefix *com* (meaning "with"). Thus, when we have compassion, we suffer or feel with someone. Scripture gives us many examples of those who demonstrated a heart of compassion for others. For example, Moses said to the Lord, "Alas, this people has committed a great sin, and they have made a god of gold for themselves. But now, if You will, forgive their sin—and if not, please blot me out from Your book which You have written!" (Exod. 32:31–32).

The apostle Paul displayed a heart of compassion. We see his deep concern for others when he said, "I have great sorrow and unceasing grief in my heart. For I could wish that I myself were accursed, separated from Christ for the sake of my brethren, my kinsmen according to the flesh, who are Israelites" (Rom. 9:2–4). The supreme example of compassion for others is, of course, our Lord Jesus Christ. Matthew 9:36 records that when he saw the multitudes, "He had compassion on them."

Others who have been used of God throughout history have had this sense of burden for lost people. John Vassar, the great evangelist who ministered in Boston, once knocked on the door of a woman's home and asked if she knew Christ as her Savior.[5] She said, "It's none of your business," and slammed the door in his face. He stood on the doorstep for a period of time and wept over this woman's condition. She looked out of her window

---

5. Billy Graham, "Stains on the Altar," *One Race, One Gospel, One Task* (Minneapolis: World Wide, 1967), 155.

and saw him standing there, weeping because of her. The next Sunday morning she was in church. She said she couldn't get away from his tears. When did we last weep for lost humanity?

Developing a Heart of Compassion

One key in developing a heart of compassion is to honestly face the truth that people outside of Christ are destined for hell, separated from God for eternity (Matt. 10:28; 2 Thess. 1:9). People who live and die without knowing Christ are lost. They are lost now, and they will be lost forever. If we truly believe in the reality of heaven and hell, we cannot say we truly love someone if we refuse to share the Gospel with them. Thousands of people die each day and enter a Christless eternity. The question is, Do we care? As Christians we have the message that can deliver people from the bondage and penalty of sin.

Another step toward cultivating a heart of compassion is to recognize that time is short. James 4:14 (NIV) reminds us that our life is like "a mist that appears for a little while and then vanishes." Hebrews 9:27 (NIV) teaches that a person is "destined to die once, and after that to face judgment." George Bernard Shaw once noted that the ultimate statistic is this: "One out of one dies."[6] Have we come to grips with this reality?

A third means of cultivating a heart of compassion is to saturate your mind with Scripture. D. L. Moody once preached a sermon on compassion. A newspaper reporter asked him, "How did you prepare that sermon?" Moody said that while on his knees he read several passages of Scripture about the compassion of Jesus. As he read, he became overwhelmed with a burden for the lost. He said, "I lay on the floor of my bedroom and prayed, and read, and wept. As I did, I wrote down the thoughts that came to my mind and heart."[7]

A fourth means of developing compassion is to spend time with lost people. Too many Christians have no close non-Christian friends to whom they are reaching out with the love of Christ. As we get involved in the lives of others, we begin to see the heartaches of life firsthand. Then we are moved to reach out to them in love. We may sing on Sunday morning,

6. John Blanchard, ed., *Gathered Gold: A Treasury of Quotations for Christians* (Welwyn, UK: Evangelical Press, 1984), 60.
7. George Sweeting, "The Evangelist's Passion for the Lost," *The Calling of an Evangelist* (Minneapolis: World Wide, 1987), 37.

"Rescue the perishing, care for the dying, snatch them in pity from sin and the grave,"[8] but our actions during the week might be proclaiming, "I really couldn't care less."

A fifth means of developing compassion is to spend time in intercessory prayer. Oswald J. Smith has asked, "Can children be born without pain? Can there be birth without travail? Yet how many expect in the spiritual realm that which is not possible in the natural!"[9] We may need to pray, "God, break my heart with the things that break your heart." If we lack a burden for the lost, we should get on our knees and ask God to give it to us!

BREAKING THE BARRIER OF INTROSPECTION

This barrier can be stated in several ways. Whether it is phrased as, "First I need to get my own life in order," "I've got enough problems of my own I need to work on first," or "When I get myself straightened out, then I'll start witnessing," this barrier always points to some future point when everything will suddenly come together in our lives. At that point, we think, we'll reach out to others with the gospel.

No Perfect Witnesses

The problem with such reasoning is that we will never be perfect in this life! If we must wait until we become "good enough" to begin sharing our faith with others, we will never begin. Spiritual perfection awaits us in another world: heaven. Since there are no perfect Christians here on this earth, there can be no perfect witnesses. If perfection were a necessary qualification, then nobody would make it! The simple fact is that God uses everyone by grace.

Now it is certainly true that our life and lips—our walk and our talk—should agree. Our lives should reflect the message that we proclaim. But while recognizing that we are not perfect in our personal lives, we must nonetheless step out in faith and begin to share the gospel with others. We cannot delay our witnessing until some magical point when we finally think we have it all together. We will never attain perfection in this life! Being a

---

8. Fanny J. Crosby, "Rescue the Perishing," *Hymns for the Family of God* (Nashville: Paragon, 1976), 661.
9. Oswald J. Smith, *The Passion for Souls* (London: Marshall, Morgan, and Scott, 1950), 26.

Christian doesn't mean never stumbling, but it does mean we can honestly admit it when we do fail and seek forgiveness from God and others whom we have wronged. That in itself can be a powerful basis for witness!

The early Christians certainly did not wait until they had become spiritually perfect before they shared Christ's love with others. The Samaritan woman began telling people immediately about the love of Christ! Jesus did not select highly qualified individuals who had demonstrated deep spiritual insight to be his disciples; he chose rough, uneducated fishermen to tell his story of love. Someone has highlighted just how "ordinary" the first disciples were by composing a hypothetical memorandum that reads as follows:

TO: Jesus, Son of Joseph, Woodcrafters Shop, Nazareth
FROM: Jordan Management Consultants, Jerusalem
SUBJECT: Staff Aptitude Evaluation

Thank you for submitting the resumes of the twelve men you have picked for management positions in your new organization. All of them have now taken our battery of tests, and we have not only run the results through the computer, but also have arranged personal interviews for each of them with our psychologist and vocational aptitude consultant.

It is the staff opinion that most of your nominees are lacking in background, education, and vocational aptitude for the type of enterprise you are undertaking. They do not have the team concept. We would recommend that you continue your search for persons of experience in managerial ability and proven capability.

Simon Peter is emotionally unstable and given to fits of temper. Andrew has absolutely no qualities of leadership. The two brothers, James and John, the sons of Zebedee, place personal interest above company loyalty. Thomas demonstrates a questioning attitude that would tend to undermine morale. We feel that it is our duty to tell you that Matthew has been blacklisted by the Greater Jerusalem Better Business Bureau. James, the son of Alphaeus, and Thaddeus definitely have radical leanings, and they both registered a high score on the manic-depressive scale.

One of the candidates, however, shows great potential. He is a man of ability and resourcefulness, meets people well, has a keen business mind and has contacts in high places. He is highly motivated, ambitious, and innovative. We recommend Judas Iscariot as your controller and right-hand man. All the other profiles are self-explanatory.

We wish you every success in your new venture.
Sincerely,
Jordan Management Consultants[10]

Were these early disciples perfect? Far from it! But they recognized their inadequacy for the task and learned to rely on God's wisdom and strength. The recognition of our inadequacy can, in fact, contribute to effective witnessing if we remember that it is the Holy Spirit who must work in and through us.

What About Hypocrisy?

Even though we understand there are no perfect Christians, many in the Christian community have been embarrassed by the scandals among Christian leaders that have been front-page news in recent years. Perhaps we are a little more reluctant to share our faith with others because we don't want to open ourselves up to the charge of being a hypocrite!

What do we do when someone raises this as an issue? First, it is important to remember that while consistent living is very important, our lives are not the gospel. We invite people to trust Christ not because we are perfect Christians but because of who Jesus Christ is and what he has done. If the person you are witnessing to is hung up on the question of hypocrites, admit it! There are hypocrites in the church just as there are in every other arena of life. Some police officers are crooked. But what happens when someone breaks into your home late at night? Do you reason, "Some police officers are crooked so I'm not about to call the police! How do I know I won't get one who is a hypocrite?" Obviously, people don't reason this way in other areas of their lives.

On a recent Uber ride with my wife, our driver (James) sought to rebuff my witness by saying that he was done listening to Christians because of all

---

10. Tim Hansel, *Eating Problems for Breakfast* (Waco, TX: Word, 1988), 194–95.

the hypocrisy he had seen. I assured him that I had witnessed *far* more hypocrisy in the church than he had ever dreamed existed, and then shared an analogy that helped him with this issue. I mentioned that my wife, Sharon, has taught piano for more than thirty years. She has some students who play Mozart really well, and other students (mostly beginners) who play him poorly at times. I asked our driver (James) if we should conclude that Mozart was a poor composer based on the way some people played his music. I acknowledged that some people follow Christ's teaching and example very poorly, but that was a reflection on them, not on Christ or the truth of what he taught. James conceded that point and listened with an open mind to my gospel presentation, even requesting prayer when the ride ended.

Focus on Christ

It is helpful to focus on the person of Christ. Share with the person that Jesus wasn't a hypocrite. Say, "He hated hypocrisy as much as you apparently do." He reserved some of his harshest words for the religious hypocrites of his day! In Matthew 23, Jesus addressed religious hypocrites using terms such as "blind guides," "blind fools," "snakes," and "brood of vipers." He chastised them for their greed, sell-indulgence, and wickedness. No one could say that Jesus ever gave his approval to hypocrisy. Ultimately, the real issue is not hypocrites in the church but a person's response to Jesus Christ. Romans 14:12 teaches that every person will stand before God to give an account of his or her life. At that time, whether or not others were hypocrites will not matter in the least. Each of us will have to answer to God for our own lives.

We Are Weak, but He Is Strong

A person who is struggling in one or more areas of life can be a powerful witness to the reality of Jesus Christ. His power can be perfected in our weakness (see 2 Cor. 12:9). When we are weak, he shows himself to be strong. Satan tries to whisper to us that we need to be perfect before we can speak to others about the Savior, but this is simply another of his many tactics designed to keep Christians from witnessing. It is when we recognize that we are not adequate in and of ourselves and rely on God's strength that his power is able to flow through us.

Finally, if you know your life is out of line, do what it takes to get it back in line! Are you suffering from spiritual burnout because you have left your first love? Restore that relationship with the Lord today! Are you out of fellowship with others? Attempting to go it alone in the Christian life will always lead to failure and discouragement. God designed his church to provide support and encouragement for believers.

Evangelism Takes Faith

Begin reaching out where you are. Beginning a lifestyle of witnessing takes faith; it will stretch you and cause you to grow. It will make demands on you. Have you ever heard anyone discuss the difference between the Sea of Galilee and the Dead Sea? Both have an intake of pure water. The difference is that the Dead Sea has no outlet. The water stalls within the lake and grows stagnant and stale. Some Christians' lives are like that. Their problem is not intake but output. They are taking in good spiritual food, but with no outlet their lives are growing stale and stagnant. A consistent lifestyle of reaching out to others with the love of Christ is one of the keys to spiritual health.

A consistent life is important. But remember that it is not your life but the gospel that is "the power of God" to bring people to salvation (1 Cor. 1:18). We must point people beyond our own lives to the cross of Christ. Like Paul, our testimony must be, "We do not preach ourselves, but Jesus Christ as Lord" (2 Cor. 4:5).

BREAKING THE BARRIER OF BUSYNESS

Have you ever wished for a twenty-five-hour day? Have you ever felt it is impossible to cram everything you need and want to do into your current schedule? Do you ever find yourself saying, "I'd witness more, but I just can't seem to find the time." If you are like most people, the issue of time is a significant one. Most of us have unanswered emails, unfinished to-do lists, unfulfilled promises, and the list goes on and on. In addition to our own plans, others place demands on our time.

Making Time, Not Finding Time

In dealing with busyness, we must acknowledge an important truth. A statement we often make, "I didn't have time for this or that," is seldom true. A more accurate statement would be, "This item was not high enough on my priority list that I would set aside something else to do it." We never "find" time to do anything; rather, we "make" time. As one person has observed, "Time flies on its own. It's up to us to be the navigator." We choose how to spend our time based on what's important to us.

God's Perspective on Time and Eternity

We can break the barrier of busyness when we allow God to develop in us a proper perspective on time and eternity. Time is one of God's most precious gifts to us. Life at its longest is brief. James 4:14 (NIV) says our life is like "a mist that appears for a little while and then vanishes." Job 7:6 refers to the passing of time as "swifter than a weaver's shuttle." Is it any wonder that in light of the brevity of life Moses prayed in Psalm 90:12, "Teach us to number our days, that we may present to You a heart of wisdom"?

Our time is not our own; we are merely stewards of the time that God has given us. We are reminded in 1 Corinthians 6:19–20 that as followers of Christ, we are not our own—we have been bought with a price. In light of that, we need to live our lives and spend our time in the way God desires. God's plan for our lives is not merely existing. If God's only purpose in saving us was to get us to heaven, he could just zap us there at the moment of conversion. But he has a greater plan and purpose for our lives: that we give ourselves in loving service to others!

Have you ever stopped to ask yourself what in this world is eternal? Possessions? Positions? Prestige? Pleasure? No! *People* are eternal! Every person on this planet will exist forever, either living in heaven with God or in hell separated from him. Hebrews 9:27 tells us that everyone is appointed to "die once and after this comes judgment." In John 5:28–29, Jesus says, "Do not marvel at this; for an hour is coming, in which all who are in the tombs will hear His voice, and will come forth; those who did the good deeds to a resurrection of life, those who committed the evil deeds to a resurrection of judgment."

People are eternal. How we need for God to burden each of our hearts with this reality: there is nothing on earth more important than people. Many people are giving their time and their lives to accumulate things that God has already promised to destroy. Second Peter 3:10 tells us that when the Lord returns like a thief in the night, "The earth and its works will be burned up." Jesus challenged his followers by saying, "Do not store up for yourselves treasures on earth, where moth and rust destroy, and where thieves break in and steal. But store up for yourselves treasures in heaven, where neither moth nor rust destroys, and where thieves do not break in or steal; for where your treasure is, there your heart will be also" (Matt. 6:19–21). Where is your treasure? Scripture challenges us to make our treasure that which is eternal, not temporal.

If you are like most believers, you face a tremendous struggle when it comes to spending time with other people. You have friends at church with whom you desire to fellowship, and there never seems to be enough time for that. And yet you know you need to try to reach out to lost people as well. How can you possibly do it all? We must strive for balance. We need fellowship. We need the encouragement and support we receive from other believers. But we also need to be involved in ministry and in reaching out to others. As Paul urges in Ephesians 5:16, we need to make the most of our time "because the days are evil."

Managing Time

Here are some general principles of time management that have proven helpful to many people: identify time wasters; operate on a schedule; and be creative in your use of time. Learn to do two things at once. What activities can you do with people as you are building relationships with them? Use your leisure time creatively. Take your unsaved friends to a ball game or a concert. Suggest a family picnic together, or take the kids to a playground. Have a neighborhood barbecue in your backyard. The possibilities are endless if we will only have eyes to see!

BREAKING THE BARRIER OF GIFTEDNESS

A hindrance to evangelism not pinpointed by the survey done by the Billy Graham Association in 1976 (but that I see frequently mentioned today) relates to the "gift of evangelism." The logic goes something like this: "Evangelism is a spiritual gift, and I don't have it; therefore, God does not expect me to do evangelism."

Is there a "gift of evangelism"?

Evangelism is not listed as a spiritual gift in the three major lists of spiritual gifts in the New Testament (i.e., Rom. 12:6–8; 1 Cor. 12:8–10, 27–31; Eph. 4:11). In Ephesians 4:11, the term *evangelist* is used, most likely signifying an office and not a gift. While I cannot argue definitively against evangelism being a spiritual gift, I certainly cannot argue definitively that evangelism is a spiritual gift.

Even if evangelism is a "gift," it is also clearly a command for all believers.

I once heard a speaker tell a Christian audience, "If you don't have the gift of evangelism, stop feeling guilty about not witnessing. You will serve God in other ways. You do need to pray for those who do have the gift of evangelism, but you need to understand that witnessing just isn't your thing." I had the opportunity to talk with this speaker afterward, and I asked him if I could come speak at his church for two consecutive Sundays. The first Sunday I wanted to stand in front of his congregation and ask, "How many of you have felt guilty about giving? I'm here today to relieve you of that guilt! If you don't have the gift of giving, God doesn't expect you to give. But you do need to pray for those who do have the gift, and please pray hard, because this church has a large budget."

The second Sunday I would ask, "How many of you have felt guilty about not serving? I'm here today to relieve you of that guilt! If you don't have the gift of serving, God doesn't expect you to serve. But you need to pray for those who do have the gift, and please pray hard, because each of those people will be wearing about twenty-seven hats in this church." This man begrudgingly conceded I had a point. We know there are gifts of giving and serving, and yet God calls all believers to participate in those actions. Even if evangelism is a spiritual gift, it is clearly a command for all believers.

Do Christians see themselves as being "on mission" for Christ?

What do you call a woman who works at a hospital assisting doctors? A nurse. Suppose that nurse is a believer and flies to the Philippines to serve. What do we call her then? A medical missionary. Why do we not see her as a medical missionary here? Years ago I was visiting a church in another state and overheard a conversation that crystalized my thinking on this issue. One woman asked another woman, "What do you do?" The second woman replied, "What do I do? I am a disciple of the Lord Jesus Christ, on mission for him, cleverly disguised as an emergency room nurse." I thought, *That is the perspective we need to have!*

That identity is what we must cultivate in our own lives and in the lives of our church members. What do you do? I'm a disciple of the Lord Jesus Christ, on mission for him, cleverly disguised as a teacher, stay-at-home mom, construction worker, college student, engineer, secretary, or factory worker. Is that how you view yourself?

CHAPTER 10

DEVOTIONAL LIFE AND EVANGELISM

JESUS'S WORDS IN MATTHEW 12:34b highlight an important principle of evangelism: "the mouth speaks out of that which fills the heart." Have you seen the late-night television infomercial for grandparents? The spokesperson promotes a two-DVD set for grandparents for only $99. The first DVD trains grandparents in how to overcome the fear of talking about their grandchildren. The second DVD teaches grandparents how to bring up the topic of their grandchildren in everyday conversation.

No you haven't, and you never will. Why not? Because grandparents do not need any help or training in how to talk about their grandchildren. Grandparents love to talk about their grandchildren because "the mouth speaks out of that which fills the heart." When we struggle with witnessing, therefore, the issue is not a speech problem but a heart problem. When our hearts are not filled with Christ and his love, talking about him can seem forced. But when our hearts are filled to overflowing with Christ, we talk about him readily. So how can we make sure our hearts are filled with Christ and his love? A meaningful devotional life fuels a life of witnessing.

A Daily Quiet Time

When Christians use the phrase "daily quiet time," what exactly do they mean? Christians throughout the ages have used different terms to describe this time alone with God, such as daily fellowship with God, morning watch, or daily devotions. The daily quiet time does not serve primarily as a time of study but rather as a time of communion with God.

Those of us in ministry spend a great deal of time preparing messages for other people. We open the Bible with a view to communicate its truth to others. But first we must understand and absorb those truths into our own hearts and minds. Richard Baxter began his exhortation in *The Reformed Pastor* with Paul's opening phrase in Acts 20:28 (KJV): "Take heed therefore unto yourselves." He notes that before we can take heed to others, we must first take heed to ourselves. He writes, "Content not yourselves with being in a state of grace, but be also careful that your graces are kept in vigorous and lively exercise, and that you preach to yourselves the sermons which you study, before you preach them to others."[1] He reflects on the importance of protecting our own walk with God: "When I let my heart grow cold, my preaching is cold; and when [my heart] is confused, my preaching is confused; and so I can oft observe also in the best of my hearers, that when I have grown cold in preaching, they have grown cold too; and the next prayers which I have heard from them have been too like my preaching. We are the nurses of Christ's little ones. If we forbear taking food ourselves, we shall famish them."[2] While Baxter's words were written to pastors, they apply to all of us as we seek to share biblical truths with others. Our devotional time is when we fuel our souls for gospel witness.

The "What" of a Quiet Time

A quiet time has two key components; first of all is time in God's Word. We should begin by reading the Bible, then meditating on it, and then seeking to apply its truths to our lives. A very helpful acrostic I was introduced to as a new believer has really helped me in terms of my own reflection as I read through a passage of Scripture. The acrostic is: S-P-A-C-E.

---

1. Richard Baxter, *The Reformed Pastor* (Carlisle, PA: Banner of Truth, 1974), 61.
2. Baxter, *Reformed Pastor*, 61.

S = Sin

Is there a sin to confess? As we open our hearts and minds to God's Word, often we are confronted with sinful actions or sinful motives. When convicted of our sin, we need to confess it to God.

P = Promise

Is there a promise to claim? I heard of one believer asking a fellow believer, "What do you do with the promises of God?" The second believer responded, "I underline them in blue ink." God wants us to do more than simply underline his promises in blue ink—he wants us to claim and stand on them. As you read, ask yourself, *Is there a promise to claim from this passage or a word of encouragement as I press forward in the Christian life?*

A = Attitude

Is there an attitude to change? True outward change always begins with inward change. Jesus made clear the importance of heart attitude in the Sermon on the Mount (Matt. 5–7).

C = Command

Is there a command to obey? God's objective in giving us a command is not for us to simply agree with it, but to obey it. Understanding must be followed by obedience.

E = Example

Is there an example to follow? Or perhaps is there an example to *not* follow? Scripture honestly portrays not only the successes of believers (which we should emulate) but also their failures (which we should avoid). We should learn from positive examples and be warned by negative examples.

The second component of a quiet time is prayer. As a new believer, I was introduced to the A-C-T-S acrostic for prayer. Since then, I have followed that guide for my prayer life. This pattern ensures that my prayers do not focus only on asking God for things, but on other crucial aspects of prayer as well.

A = Adoration

- Hebrews 13:15: "Through Him then, let us continually offer up a sacrifice of praise to God, that is, the fruit of lips that give thanks to His name."

- Psalm 34:1: "I will bless the LORD at all times; His praise shall continually be in my mouth."

Adoration is praising God for who he is, for his attributes, for his character, and for his glory. Our service ultimately flows out of praise. We need to be reminded each day of who God is and we do that through adoration.

C = Confession

- Psalm 66:18: "If I regard wickedness in my heart, the Lord will not hear."

- 1 John 1:9: "If we confess our sins, He is faithful and righteous to forgive us our sins and to cleanse us from all unrighteousness."

As we are reminded of God's glory and holiness, we are confronted with our own sinfulness and need for cleansing. First John 1:9 instructs us to confess our sins. I have heard this verse described as the Christian's "bar of soap."

T = Thanksgiving

- Psalm 40:5: "Many, O LORD my God, are the wonders which You have done, and Your thoughts toward us; there is none to compare with You. If I would declare and speak of them, they would be too numerous to count."

- 1 Thessalonians 5:18: "In everything give thanks; for this is God's will for you in Christ Jesus."

Thanksgiving is thanking God for what he has done. Many people confuse praise and thanksgiving. They are related but distinct. Adoration is praising God for who he *is*, and thanksgiving is thanking God for what he has done.

S = Supplication

- 1 Timothy 2:1: "First of all, then, I urge that entreaties and prayers, petitions and thanksgivings, be made on behalf of all men."

- Hebrews 4:15–16: "For we do not have a high priest who cannot sympathize with our weaknesses, but One who has been tempted in all things as we are, yet without sin. Therefore let us draw near with confidence to the throne of grace, so that we may receive mercy and find grace to help in time of need."

God gives his children the privilege of bringing our requests to him. Because of what Christ has done on our behalf, we are able to approach the throne of grace with confidence and boldness.

The "How" of a Quiet Time

Following are few general principles that I have found helpful in my own devotional life.

Time

The adage is true: "If you aim at nothing, you will hit it every time." We schedule that which is important to us. We enter the day/time into our phone or write it down on our calendar. Why? Because we never find time for those things that are important; we must make time. I have my daily quiet time the first thing in the morning because it is typically the only time of the day that I can protect from interruption. As my day unfolds, my cell phone rings with calls or buzzes with text messages, and my email box fills up continually. But early in the morning, I have the opportunity to have uninterrupted and unhurried time with the Lord.

Some people respond, "Well, that sounds fine, but I'm not really a morning person." It has been said that there are two different kinds of people: those who wake up and say, "Good morning, Lord," and others who wake up and say, "Good Lord, it's morning." You may be the latter. I would encourage you to at least begin the day in some way with a focus on the Lord, even if it is brief. For your daily quiet time, figure out what time works best for you, and then make a commitment.

Place

Have a designated place, and prepare it the night before. This will vary according to your personality. My sacred place is at my desk in the basement office of my home. I go down there each morning after pouring a cup of coffee. I sit down at my desk and meet with God. I have my Bible and prayer journal already out from the night before so I can immediately enter into the presence of the Lord. My wife likes to sit in an armchair in our den and enjoy fellowship with the Lord. Determine what works best for you.

Preparation

When I open God's Word, I pray the prayer of the psalmist in Psalm 119:18: "Open my eyes, that I may behold wonderful things from Your law." That verse is a prayer for illumination. It is a prayer saying, "God, I need your help to understand your Word. Open my eyes. Give me illumination. Help me to see what is here, and how I should understand it and apply it."

Reading

I believe quality is more important than quantity at this point. I follow a Bible reading plan to help me read through the entire Bible each year (about three chapters per day), but my goal is not to race through the Bible. Rather, it is to learn from it and have it change my life. A daily dose of Bible reading is better than a longer period of reading once per week. I often tell my church members, "Seven days without God's Word makes one week." That is a play on words—it not only "makes one *week*" but also "makes one *weak*." We need daily intake of God's Word to be spiritually strong.

Writing

I like to journal insights to keep track of what I am learning from the Word. I have heard it said, "The palest of ink is better than the most retentive memory." Those daily journal entries from decades of days spent with God are precious treasures to me. The key is *consistency* rather than *length*. I believe it is more helpful to our spiritual life to spend ten to fifteen minutes a day in Bible reading and prayer than it is to spend two hours one day a week. I have also heard it said, "Don't worry if you miss a day. If you miss one day, God will know; if you miss two days, you will know it; if you miss three days, everyone around you may know." The most important thing you can do today is to meet with God!

SUMMARY

A daily quiet time fuels our witness as it refreshes our heart and our mind with the Lord and his Word. And yet a daily quiet time is not a "magic bullet." If circumstances prevent you from beginning your day with meaningful communion with Christ, it does not mean that day is a failure or that God cannot use you to impact others. And beginning the day with God must be followed by walking with him moment by moment throughout the day.

.

CHAPTER 11

PRAYER AND EVANGELISM

A. R. GESSWEIN POWERFULLY ARTICULATES the relationship between prayer and evangelism: "Prayer is the lifeline of New Testament evangelism, the oxygen for its holy fire. The New Testament was born in prayer. It knows no evangelism without prayer and no prayer which does not lead to evangelism. God has joined these together in one piece, and no man must separate them."[1] Dick Eastman echoes that thought as he maintains, "I am convinced that when we stand before God . . . we will discover that every soul ever brought to a knowledge of Christ was in some way related to intercessory prayer."[2] We must not separate prayer from evangelism. They are joined together in God's economy.

THE ROLE OF PRAYER IN EVANGELISM

Examine the witness of the New Testament. Note how much time Jesus spent in prayer and how much he encouraged prayer in his teaching. He gave numerous promises to encourage those who would pray (Matt. 7:7–11; 18:19; 21:22; Mark 11:24; John 14:13–14; 15:7; 16:23–24). His prayer in John 17:20 was not only for his current disciples but was also for lost

1. Armin R. Gesswein, "Prayer and Evangelism," in *Evangelism: The Next Ten Years*, ed. Sherwood Wirt (Waco: Word, 1978), 93.
2. Dick Eastman, *Love on Its Knees* (Old Tappan, NJ: Chosen, 1989), 19.

persons who would come to faith through the disciples' witness: "I do not ask on behalf of these alone, but for those also who believe in Me through their word." Jesus specifically told us we should pray that the Lord of the harvest would send out laborers into the harvest fields (Matt. 9:37–38).

The apostles were men of prayer. As you study the book of Acts, you observe they had set times of prayer; they prayed for boldness and witnessed with great courage; and they prayed before crucial decisions (such as selecting the men who presumably were the first deacons in Acts 6). The apostle Paul both taught and modeled prayer. He exhorted others to pray and requested prayer for his own ministry. In 2 Thessalonians 3:1 Paul requests prayers for the success of his evangelistic endeavors: "Finally brethren, pray for us, that the word of the Lord will spread rapidly and be glorified just as it did also with you."

Paul began most of his letters discussing his own prayer life and uses powerful words and phrases such as: "I am praying for you without ceasing"; "I am always praying for you"; "thanking God always on your behalf"; "I cease not to give thanks for you"; "I thank my God always in my every prayer for you all"; "We give thanks, praying always for you; For this cause we do in prayer"; "We give thanks always for you, remembering without ceasing"; "We are bound to thank God always for you"; "Also we pray always for you"; "I thank God that without ceasing I have remembered you in my prayers, night and day" (Rom. 1:9–10; 1 Cor. 1:4; Eph. 1:15–16; Phil. 1:3–4; Col. 1:3, 9; 4:12; 1 Thess. 1:2; 2:13; 2 Thess. 1:3, 11; 2 Tim. 1:3, my translation). Gesswein was correct: prayer is the lifeline of New Testament evangelism.

WHY IS PRAYER IMPORTANT IN EVANGELISM?

Prayer is commanded.

The command to pray for evangelistic endeavors originates with Jesus himself (Matt. 9:35–38). Jesus teaches us that a vital link between unsaved humanity and the kingdom of heaven is prayer—not random or sporadic prayer, but a specific plea for more harvesters to be found who will go into the fields and perform this vital task of evangelism. Jesus tells us to pray for more harvesters. As Jesus commands us to pray to the Lord of the harvest, he also promises to give us all we need in our labors for his kingdom (John 14:13–18). God answers and empowers us when we seek to obey his commands.

Evangelism involves spiritual warfare.

When we share the gospel of Christ with unbelievers, we engage in spiritual warfare. Satan opposes evangelism because every soul that comes to Christ is one that he does not own. Samuel Chadwick maintained, "The one concern of the devil is to keep Christians from praying. He fears nothing from prayerless study, prayerless work, prayerless religion. He laughs at our toil, mocks at our wisdom, but trembles when we pray."[3] Satan's strategy is to immobilize evangelism. Prayer is our weapon against spiritual darkness: "Evangelism is regaining territory that has been taken by the enemy. It is not a process of intellectually convincing people of truth but of releasing them from prison."[4]

Paul discusses spiritual armor in Ephesians 6, and then boldly challenges believers, "With all prayer and petition pray at all times in the Spirit, and with this in view, be on the alert with all perseverance and petition for all the saints" (Eph. 6:18). Prayer is needed for unbelievers for several reasons.

- They are spiritually blind (Rom. 3:11; 2 Cor. 4:3–4).
- They are captives of Satan (Col. 1:13; 2 Tim. 2:25–26).
- They are without understanding (1 Cor. 2:14).
- They are spiritually dead (Eph. 2:1).
- They are condemned (John 3:36; Eph. 2:3).
- They will experience the judgment of God (Matt. 7:13; John 3:36).
- They are helpless (John 6:44; Eph. 2:12).
- They are the reason Christ came (Luke 19:10).

Prayer unleashes spiritual power.

Evelyn Christenson recounts the story of an elderly lady in her late eighties who served on the board of her organization:

---

3. Quoted in Paul Billheimer, *The Mystery of God's Providence* (Carol Stream, IL: Tyndale House, 1983), 78.
4. Clive Calver, et al., eds., *A Guide to Evangelism* (Basingstoke: Marshall, Morgan, & Scott, 1984), 35.

I can still see my almost ninety-year-old (now deceased) board member Edith sitting in board meetings with a little pile of pictures in her lap. She couldn't stand it until she had shown us that month's pictures. Of what? Children, grandchildren, birthday parties, vacations? Oh, no. Missionary friends from her "special mission field" regularly sent her the names and pictures of those they were trying to win to Jesus. Edith would then pray, by name, for them until they accepted Jesus. In her sleepless, pain-filled nights, Edith often prayed all night. The pictures were that month's harvest of her new converts! Her pain-ridden wrestling for those souls was the power that produced their release from Satan's evil kingdom.[5]

Billy Graham often articulated that his ministry "success" was entirely dependent upon prayer. The first time I met Billy Graham in 1990, he told me there were three secrets to his ministry: prayer, prayer, and prayer. The Billy Graham Evangelistic Association solicited prayer support for up to a year before each crusade. Many of those who came forward in an evangelistic crusade had already had their hearts softened through prayer. Pearl Goode was one of those who prayed consistently and boldly for Billy's crusades. Ruth Graham spoke at her funeral, saying,

> From 1954 until her death Pearl Goode was at every one of the Billy Graham crusades. She came not to join in the inspiring and festive atmosphere that often accompanies the meetings. Instead, she quietly remained in her hotel room praying—sometimes all night—for the spiritual success of the outreach. Without fanfare or publicity, she poured out her heart to God on behalf of the efforts of thousands of men and women each of whom had a part to play. Only God can say how many souls are now part of His kingdom because of the prayers of Pearl Goode.[6]

Paul reminds us that if we want spiritual results, we must use spiritual weapons in our warfare: "For though we walk in the flesh, we do not war according to the flesh, for the weapons of our warfare are not of the flesh, but divinely powerful for the destruction of fortresses" (2 Cor. 10:3–4).

---

5. Evelyn Christenson, *Battling the Prince of Darkness* (Wheaton, IL: Victor, 1990), 107–8.
6. John Pollock, *Billy Graham: Evangelist to the World* (Minneapolis: World Wide, 1979), 113.

HOW TO PRAY EVANGELISTICALLY

George Peters maintains, "Reaching the unreached will, first of all, mean for us, not only to lay hold of it in faith, but to develop thousands and thousands of prayer cells in America and elsewhere that will commit themselves wholeheartedly to prayer until the victory will be won."[7] Andrew Murray states his belief in the role of prayer for evangelism: "The man who mobilizes the Christian church to pray will make the greatest contribution in history to world evangelization."[8]

Pray Regularly

Ephesians 6:18 exhorts us, "With all prayer and petition pray at all times in the Spirit, and with this in view, be on the alert with all perseverance and petition for all the saints." Pray regularly—at all times.

Pray Specifically

We should pray specifically for several things:

- For conviction of our own personal sin. Sin hinders us in ministry, including our ministry of intercession: "Behold, the LORD's hand is not so short that it cannot save; nor is His ear so dull that it cannot hear. But your iniquities have made a separation between you and your God, And your sins have hidden His face from you so that He does not hear" (Isa. 59:1–2).
- For specific people who are not believers (Rom. 10:1)
- For God to bring effective witnesses (including you) across their paths (Col. 4:2–4)
- For God to arrange circumstances in their lives to point them to Christ (Rom. 8:28)
- For the Holy Spirit to convict them of their sin and lostness (John 16:8–11)

---

7. Quoted in David Bryant, "Concerts of Prayer: Waking Up for a New Missions Thrust," *Missions Frontiers* 5, no. 3–4 (1983), 8.
8. Quoted in Dick Eastman, *The Jericho Hour: The Church's Final Offensive* (Lake Mary, FL: Creation House), 143.

Pray Fervently and Persistently

James 5:16 encourages us, "The effective prayer of a righteous man can accomplish much." Don't give up praying! George Mueller, a noted prayer warrior, advises:

> The great point is to never give up until the answer comes. I have been praying for fifty-two years, every day for two men, sons of a friend of my youth. They are not converted yet, but will be! How can it be otherwise? There is the unchanging promise of Jehovah and on that I rest. The great fault of the children of God is, they do not continue in prayer; they do not go on praying; they do not persevere. If they desire anything for God's glory, they should pray until they get it. . . . He has given me, unworthy as I am, immeasurably above all I had asked or thought! I am only a poor, frail sinful man; but He has heard my prayers ten thousands of times, and used me as the means of bringing tens of thousands into the way of truth. . . . These unworthy lips have proclaimed salvation to great multitudes, and very many have believed unto eternal life.[9]

Mueller also prayed for a personal friend for sixty-three years to be converted. According to David Shibley, this friend accepted Christ as Mueller's casket was being lowered into the ground: "There, near the open grave, this friend surrendered his heart to the Lord. Persistence had paid off!"[10]

Pray Boldly and Expectantly

Hebrews 4:16 reminds us, "Therefore let us draw near with confidence to the throne of grace, so that we may receive mercy and find grace to help in time of need." And the apostle John testifies, "This is the confidence which we have before Him, that, if we ask anything according to His will, He hears us. And if we know that He hears us in whatever we ask, we know that we have the requests which we have asked from Him" (1 John 5:14–15).

---

9. Abbie Morrow, *The Work of Faith Through George Mueller* (Cincinnati: M. W. Knapp, 1899), 149.
10. David Shibley, *A Force in the Earth: The Charismatic Renewal and World Evangelism* (Altamonte Springs, FL: Creation House, 1989), 79.

Evelyn Christenson watched her mom pray boldly for family members. When her mom became a Christian, no one else was a believer in her family. Evelyn writes:

> And my mom had the privilege of leading every single one of them to Jesus Christ before they died. And she prayed for twenty-five years for my dad, and she prayed thirty years for my only brother to find Jesus. That was my mom. When she died at the age of ninety-one they all said that my mother had won more people to Jesus Christ in her town than all of the pastors put together. Because she was some great, wild evangelist? [Oh no]. My mom was a simple little lady who knew how to pray. . . . I was rather surprised when I got a little older and realized that plans and programs and projects somehow replace the power.[11]

Pray for Laborers

Matthew 9:37–38 remind us of our need to pray for laborers: "Then He said to His disciples, 'The harvest is plentiful, but the workers are few. Therefore beseech the Lord of the harvest to send out workers into His harvest.'" We must pray for God to raise up more laborers who work in the harvest fields of the world by both sowing and reaping. Specific prayers include:

- For those who proclaim the gospel (Eph. 6:19–20)
- For opportunities/open doors to share Christ (Col. 4:2–4)
- For boldness (Acts 4:29, 31; Eph. 6:19)
- For sensitivity, wisdom, and clarity (Col. 4:2–4)
- For individuals to be convicted and saved (Rom. 10:1; 1 Thess. 1:5; 1 Tim. 2:1–4)
- For more witnesses and harvesters (Matt. 9:38; Rom. 10:14–15)
- For common ground to tell them of Christ (1 Cor. 9:19–23)

Practical Suggestions

Pray using a list. We all struggle with our recall and with remembering even that which is important. A prayer list helps keep our prayers focused and on target.

---

11. Address given at Wheaton College, Wheaton, Illinois, on April 9, 1991.

"Joshua Walks." These are prayer walks by an individual or group whose purpose is to ask God to "break down walls." These prayer walks can be done in your own neighborhood, the neighborhoods surrounding your church, or by walking around a city. Sharon and I have done these prayer walks in our neighborhood, and our church has taken groups of streets to walk down and pray for each individual home/family. The website BlessEveryHome.com offers resources to pray for neighbors by name.

Prayer chains. With the advancement of technology, this means is effective at getting prayer needs out ASAP. One person at a church is the coordinator who compiles specific requests and communicates them to the members of the prayer team. Communication is usually done by text, email, or social media, but it can also be done by phone.

Praying over each seat before church services or evangelistic events. For years I have had faithful church members come to the church sanctuary on Saturdays to pray over each pew, asking God to bring lost and hurting people to sit in that pew and that their hearts would be touched by the gospel as it is proclaimed on Sunday morning.

Using pictures or pictorial directories to pray for a group. I use my church pictorial directory to pray for my church members each week. Yearbooks or directories can be used to pray for class rosters or members in any organization.

Inviting church members to share the first names of lost family members and friends, and adding them to the church prayer list. Church prayer meetings have often been described as "organ recitals," with most if not all prayers directed to the physical needs of church members and their loved ones. As someone has observed, "The church seems to spend far more time praying to keep saints out of heaven than sinners out of hell." There certainly is nothing wrong with praying for physical needs. We can and should pray for those needs. My favorite definition of "minor surgery" is "that which is done on someone else." It is never minor when it affects us or our loved ones. But if we really believe the spiritual must take priority over the physical, why do our prayer meetings often not reflect that reality?

Prayer triplets. The Billy Graham Evangelistic Association, as well as many other churches and organizations, has long made use of this approach. For evangelistic purposes, it is a simple way of getting in groups of three to pray for specific people to come to Christ. Each of the three believers will have three names of lost persons, so the total number of people they commit to pray for is nine. They meet regularly, either in person, or through the use of technology, to pray for those lost persons by name.

Praying with lost persons about specific needs. In chapter 15, one of the "Bridges to the Gospel" I propose is the prayer bridge. The prayer bridge simply asks the question, "Is there anything I could pray about for you?" Here are a few suggestions from Kevin Harney about praying with an unbeliever:

- Keep your prayer brief.
- Use common language.
- Extend a hand if it is appropriate.
- Pray for the person's specific need or joy.
- Pray in the name of Jesus.
- Check in to see how things are going.
- Be sensitive to location and volume.[12]

CONCLUSION

When we pray for lost persons, we are pleading with God, "You must go before us! If you do not open blind eyes and soften hard hearts, all our efforts will be in vain." As the oft-quoted expression reminds us, "We need to talk with God about people before we talk to people about God." R. A. Torrey maintained, "The most important human factor in effective evangelism is prayer."[13] J. Oswald Sanders affirms,

If it is our genuine desire to be used in cooperation with the Holy Spirit in leading men and women to faith in Christ, we must in some degree master the holy art of intercession. If the Master wept and prayed over

---

12. Kevin G. Harney, *Organic Outreach for Ordinary People: Sharing Good News Naturally* (Grand Rapids: Zondervan, 2009), 114–15.
13. R. A. Torrey, "The Place of Prayer in Evangelism," in *The Fundamentals,* eds. R. A. Torrey, et al., 4 vols. (Grand Rapids: Baker, 1917), 3:218.

the lost, then His servant should partake of His spirit. Prayer should always have an important place in our programme, since the salvation of a soul is not a human, but a divine work, and it is prayer that releases the power of God.[14]

God alone can save. God alone can change a sinner's heart. But God has ordained that our prayers are part of the means he uses to accomplish his ends. When we pray, we are joining our frail hands of clay with God's mighty omnipotent hands. Charles Spurgeon exhorts us with these powerful words: "If sinners will be damned, at least let them leap to Hell over our bodies. And if they will perish, let them perish with our arms about their knees, imploring them to stay. If Hell must be filled, at least let it be filled in the teeth of our exertions, and let not one go there unwarned and unprayed for."[15] As Helen Shoemaker testifies, "Praying always. Here is the fruit of New Testament evangelism. It bore fruit in the first century—it bears fruit today."[16]

S. D. Gordon, in his classic work *Quiet Talks on Prayer*, maintains:

The greatest thing anyone can do for God and for man is to pray. It is not the only thing. But it is the chief thing. The great people of the earth today are the people who pray. I do not mean those who talk about prayer; or those who say they believe in prayer; nor yet those who can explain about prayer; but I mean those people who take time to pray. These are the people today who are doing the most for God: in winning souls; in solving problems, in awakening churches.[17]

The first disciples did not ask Jesus to teach them to preach, perform miracles, or feed the hungry. They asked Jesus to teach them to pray (Luke 11:1). May we do likewise!

14. J. Oswald Sanders, *Effective Evangelism: The Divine Art of Soul-Winning* (Waynesboro, GA: STL, 1937), 30.
15. Charles H. Spurgeon, *Spurgeon at His Best*, ed. Tom Carter (Grand Rapids: Baker, 1991), 67.
16. Helen S. Shoemaker, *Prayer and Evangelism* (Waco, TX: Word, 1974), 113.
17. S. D. Gordon, *Quiet Talks on Prayer* (Westwood, NJ: Fleming H. Revell, 1967), 11.

CHAPTER 12

CONCENTRIC CIRCLES
OF CONCERN

DR. OSCAR THOMPSON, former professor of evangelism at South-western Baptist Theological Seminary in the 1970s, was an extremely passionate personal evangelist. He died from cancer at a relatively young age, and his widow, Carolyn, took his teaching notes and published them in the book, *Concentric Circles of Concern: From Self to Others through Life-Style Evangelism*.[1]

Thompson always began his personal evangelism classes by asking this question: "What is the most important word in the English language?" How would you respond to that question? Many people would say "love." Many Christians would say "Jesus." Oscar Thompson's answer to his own question, however, was "relationship" because apart from relationship, there is no love. Some people think about evangelism as going out to witness to person X, someone they have not yet met. We always need to be prepared to witness to person X. But, as Oscar Thompson pointed out, God has already placed around us a whole array of people who don't know Christ and need the gospel. Because they are within our concentric circles, we may be the person that God intends to share with them.

---

1. W. Oscar Thompson, *Concentric Circles of Concern: From Self to Others through Life-style Evangelism* (Nashville: Broadman, 1981).

Family/Relatives

Who in your family does not know Christ? Start with your immediate family—your mom, dad, and your siblings. If any of them do not know Christ, make that a daily matter of prayer. Pray that God would give you opportunities to communicate the good news with them. The "relation-ship bridge" is a wonderful bridge to use with a family member to be able to say something like this: "I'm not sure I have ever really explained to you in depth what happened to me in college or why I left my career in engineering and decided to study theology instead. Could I share that with you?" I promise you the answer will be yes.

Every single year at least one student in my classes has had the privilege of introducing either their mom or dad, or both, to Christ simply by laying the foundation of prayer and then taking the initiative to ask, "Can I explain to you in depth what it means to know Christ?" Your family is the first circle. Ask yourself, "How can I communicate the gospel to them?" If you do not live close to family, you may have an opportunity over a holiday to talk to them. But personal evangelism can occur over the phone, Zoom, Skype, Facetime, or other social media.

Close Friends

The next circle is that of close friends. Don't just think about those whom you would consider to be your close friends, but also think about people that would consider you to be their close friends. The world is filled with lonely people! If you as a Christian are simply friendly to others, they may have you on their short list of good friends. You can include close friends going back to college or even back to high school. I recently had my fortieth high school class reunion and had the privilege of interacting with some of my classmates I had not seen since graduation. I was not a genuine follower of Christ when I graduated high school, even though I was a professing Christian. I had the opportunity to have several wonderful conversations over a two-day period of time with friends that I hadn't seen in forty years but who needed Jesus. Forty years has a way of stripping away a lot of pretense in a person's life. A lot of the hopes and dreams people had during high school had been dashed on the rocks. I found some very willing ears to the message of hope that is found Christ. Think about close friends in your life, and start praying for them.

Neighbors

The next circle is your neighbors. Neighborhoods will vary. My wife grew up in large cities, while I grew up on a farm in Kansas. My closest neighbors were a mile away in every direction. Whatever your neighborhood looks like, who lives around you? According to Acts 17 your neighbors are not there by accident. Paul, in his sermon in Athens, taught that God determines people's places of habitation (Acts 17:26). How do you begin to connect with neighbors? Emily Post (an etiquette guru from the past generation) would say when someone new moves into your neighborhood, take the initiative to go and introduce yourself, acquaint them with the neighborhood, offer various kinds of help, provide a meal for them, and things such as that. But in our changing culture, many people have lost the sense of what it is to be "neighborly."

The first home Sharon and I bought was in Geneva, Illinois, a western suburb of Chicago. We bought the last home in a brand-new subdivision of eighty-seven small starter homes. As we moved into our home, our neighbors did not come over to help us unload nor did they introduce themselves or acquaint us with the neighborhood. So we took the initiative to reach out to them. We baked dozens of chocolate chip cookies and took them to our neighbors just to introduce ourselves and meet them. A good rule of thumb is when you are new in an area, it is okay to be friendly—at least for a couple of weeks!

We went from house to house, and I would say, "Hi, my name is Tim and this is my wife, Sharon. We just moved in at 831 Howell Drive. We are so glad to be a part of this neighborhood. We wanted to meet our new neighbors and bring a plate of cookies as a 'new neighbor' gift." They would give us their names, and, as we walked away, I would pull out a little note card and write down their name (e.g., John and Betty Smith, 816 Division Avenue). That became our list of people to pray for in our neighborhood over the course of the next six years. We had the privilege of seeing eight of our neighbors come to faith in Christ.

You may ask, "What if I have lived in the same place for a couple years and haven't yet really connected with my neighbors?" Follow the biblical principle of repentance and say, "Lord, I am sorry I have not reached out to my neighbors." Then go and turn on your oven to 350 degrees, bake chocolate chip cookies, and take them to your neighbors. You can say something like this: "You know, life gets so crazy and hectic; we've lived here for a couple of years, and we always seemingly running in different directions. It dawned on us recently that we haven't been very good neighbors, and we just wanted to come over and meet you. I know we wave to each other as we're coming in and out of our driveways, but I wanted to finally take the time to meet you. Hi, my name is Tim, and this is my wife, Sharon. We live down the street at 1308." That simple act then establishes a basis for ongoing communication. We need to take the initiative to meet our neighbors; they typically are not going to take the initiative to meet us even if we are the "new kids on the block." Get to know your neighbors to build a foundation for future ministry opportunities.

Coworkers/Classmates

The next circle is composed of those with whom we work. Every work environment is different, but many believers work alongside nonbelievers for multiple hours each day. One important principle about witnessing to people at work is to avoid robbing your employer. Do not take company time where your employer is paying you and your coworker to do a job if your conversation distracts from that duty. If that is the case, take advantage of breaks, lunch times, or invitations to a hangout after work. But there are some lines of work where you can work and talk at the same time.

I spent one summer doing all kinds of construction jobs, including roofing. When you are on a roof hammering nails, you can talk about everything. It was not taking away from our employer to have conversations because as we talked, we were still being productive in our job. However, if you work as an accountant preparing tax returns and you are trying to have a gospel-centered conversation at that same time, you are setting up your poor client for an IRS audit. You know you are not going to do either task well, and you are stealing from your employer.

How do you reach out to people at work? Be friendly; take the time to meet people and learn their names. Some people are more gifted than others in remembering names, but you can develop that art. Look for opportunities to get to know your coworkers better. Find out their interests and their passions. I love to spend time with unbelievers and have gospel conversations. One of my mentors taught me early on that if you buy someone's lunch, you can witness to him or her any day of the week.

So get to know your co-workers and talk about grabbing lunch, or invite them to your home. For many students, schoolwork is their "work." Students can identify others in their classes and seek to build meaningful relationships with them. Countless lives, mine included, have been transformed on college campuses due to the caring and intentional ministry of Christian students.

ACQUAINTANCES

The last category consists of acquaintances. An acquaintance is not person X; he or she is not a complete stranger. Acquaintances are people you have met, people you know but perhaps not very well. When we lived in the Chicago area, our kids were in the public school system, and Sharon and I got involved in the Parent Teacher Organization. Did you know that unbelievers care about their children's education too? That organization became a focal point of contact for us with nonbelievers. Sharon and I then had an opportunity to rub shoulders with five other couples in the leadership of the PTO, leading to friendship and gospel opportunities.

Our kids also played sports, and we had them involved in the community leagues, providing an opportunity to connect with other families. Because we buy used cars and then "drive them into the ground," we see auto repair mechanics on a regular basis. My wife connects with people at the various stores where she shops. (How can I discourage her from shopping when she is doing evangelism?) Sharon has unbelievable people skills and the gift of mercy. She seeks out the same salespeople at the various stores and gets to know them. She is always looking for opportunities to share.

How can you cultivate meaningful relationships with unbelievers? What might that process look like for you? Years ago I joined a bowling league in order to be around unbelievers. I had gone from being surrounded by unbelievers on a secular college campus to living in seminary housing, taking classes on campus, and then working for a Christian organization the rest of the day. Most of my waking hours (and even my sleeping hours), I was surrounded by Christians! Someone suggested I might be able to connect with non-Christians at a bowling alley, and were they ever correct! The bowling alley was filled with people who did not know Christ. My two years in that bowling league provided countless opportunities to connect with people and share the hope found in Christ.

Another way I have sought to connect with unbelievers is by playing golf. I love being out in God's creation, and I love competition. Golf is a sport that I always looked down on, something I thought "real" athletes didn't play. I played basketball, ran track, and played football, tennis, and baseball, and I thought golf was something you played if you couldn't do anything else. After multiple knee surgeries, I couldn't do anything else, so I took up golf. I thought, *How hard can this game be? The ball is not moving, nobody is guarding you, and no one is trying to knock you down.* Well, it is the hardest sport I have ever played. Do you know that a lot of unbelievers like to play golf too? I have shared the gospel many times on the golf course.

When our youngest daughter headed off to college, my wife went through a serious case of "empty nest syndrome." As soon as the taillights headed out, I was jumping up and down, celebrating that we had raised our children and sent them off. But my wife was over in the corner sobbing. As we entered into our new season of life, we decided to look for some new things to do together as a couple. I met another man at the golf course and found out that he and his wife taught ballroom dancing. So, guess what? Sharon and I took up ballroom dancing lessons. Ballroom dancing was never on my bucket list, but Sharon loved it and had always wanted to take lessons.

The ballroom dancing class was taught by a husband and wife, and we had five other couples taking lessons with us. We now had a new mission field with these new acquaintances. We took the instructors to dinner before class the second week and had a wonderful conversation. At some point, I was asked, "Tim, what do you do?" I told him I was a minister.

"What group are you with?" was his stunned query.

"Baptist," I replied.

"And you can dance?" he asked with amazement.

"Obviously not, since you saw me in the class last week!" I rejoined.

"No, I mean you are allowed to dance?" he asked.

"Well, yes. We are in the class!"

He was still stunned when the dance class began after dinner. Before the class started, he made an announcement to everyone to make sure they knew I was a preacher and that Sharon was a preacher's wife. Two of the couples' nonverbal reactions told us they wanted nothing to do with us since we were "religious," but the rest of us became friends. We have dinner together and discuss spiritual things.

PERSON X

The final circle is person X. We need to always be on the alert for divine appointments, when God will lead us to begin a spiritual conversation with a complete stranger. But we also need to open our eyes and see that "the fields are white unto harvest." God has already placed people in our circles of influence. Are we praying for them and seeking to share the good news with them? Are we looking to build meaningful relationships with them, all for the glory of God? Think about your last week and your last month. How much time have you spent with unbelievers in social settings? Jesus was known by sinners as a friend. Can unbelievers say the same thing about us?

PART 2

PRACTICING EVANGELISM

CHAPTER 13

EVANGELISM AS A WAY OF LIFE

TWO DIFFERENT "CAMPS" OR "PHILOSOPHIES" about how to approach the task of evangelism have arisen in recent years. On the one hand are those who emphasize "initiative" evangelism,[1] arguing that believers should be ready and willing to witness to anyone, anywhere, at any time.[2] Another approach advocates for "lifestyle" evangelism, emphasizing the importance of building a relationship with persons before you share the gospel with them.[3] This chapter will examine the strengths and weaknesses of these two approaches, and then set forth what I believe is a balanced approach.

BIBLICAL BASIS AND EXAMPLES OF EACH APPROACH

Advocates for the initiative position point to verses such as Colossians 4:5–6: "Conduct yourselves with wisdom toward outsiders, making the most of the opportunity. Let your speech always be with grace, as though seasoned with salt, so that you will know how you should respond to each person." These verses, along with many others, direct believers

---

1. I use the term "initiative" rather than the more pejorative labels sometimes assigned to this approach, such as "confrontational" or "intrusional."
2. Mark McCloskey, *Tell It Often—Tell It Well: Making the Most of Witnessing Opportunities* (San Bernardino, CA: Here's Life, 1985).
3. Joseph C. Aldrich, *Lifestyle Evangelism: Crossing Traditional Boundaries to Reach the Unbelieving World* (Portland, OR: Multnomah, 1981).

to be prepared to talk to people referred to as "outsiders"—those outside the church and outside the faith. There is no indication of the necessity of building a relationship of trust with these outsiders before sharing the gospel with them.

The lifestyle approach focuses on verses such as Matthew 5:16: "Let your light shine before men in such a way that they may see your good works, and glorify your Father who is in heaven." Here the emphasis is on the witness's lifestyle, the good works that others can see in the life of the believer. Lifestyle evangelism advocates note that the gospel can flow naturally through a network of relationships of trust. Aldrich argues, "Christians are to *be* good news before they *share* the good news."[4]

Beyond biblical admonitions, do we see examples of each of these approaches in Scripture? Are there examples where the gospel was shared with someone where there was no preexisting relationship of trust, and are there examples where the gospel flowed naturally through existing relationships?

The Initiative Approach

Philip's witness in Acts 8:26–40 serves as an example of the initiative approach. When Philip was directed by the Lord to leave Samaria and go to a desert road, he encountered an Ethiopian traveling on that road. Philip had no preexisting relationship with this man. They were not golfing buddies or members of the same country club. Philip did not one day blurt out, "You know, we've been golfing buddies now for six years, and I need to share something important with you." The first time they ever met, Philip shared the gospel!

Peter's sharing with Cornelius (Acts 10) was not based on a long-standing friendship. Peter and Cornelius were not members of the same supper club, where they had shared meals together multiple times and become close friends. Their very first encounter, Peter boldly shared the gospel with Cornelius.

Paul and Silas's witness to the Philippian jailer in Acts 16 serves as another example. This jailer, who had no preexisting relationship with these men, cried out to them, "What must I do to be saved?" (Acts 16:30). Paul and Silas did not respond, "Well, we're sorry, but we just met you. We need to build a relationship of credibility and trust before we can share this

---

4. Aldrich, *Lifestyle Evangelism*, 20 (emphasis original).

good news with you, so we will have to postpone that conversation." No! They gladly shared Christ with him.

Jesus got right to the issue of spiritual concerns, taking the initiative in his conversations with people. In the case of the Samaritan woman, even "intrusion" might not be a strong enough term to describe Jesus's interaction with her. Jesus's commissioning of the twelve (Matt. 10) and the seventy (Luke 10) can hardly be regarded as teaching lifestyle evangelism. The mission was to be that of gospel excursions in numerous towns for the sole purpose of confronting strangers with the dramatic news of the approach of the kingdom.

In Scripture we see many examples and admonitions for initiative evangelism, taking the lead to share the gospel with someone you have just met. In fact, the majority of gospel conversations in the Gospels and Acts are what could be categorized as initiative evangelism. This refers to sharing the gospel without the benefit of a preexisting relationship between the witness and the one being witnessed to.

Why emphasize these examples of the initiative approach? Because you will hear people today making comments such as, "People don't care how much you know until they know how much you care,"[5] or, "You should not talk to somebody about Jesus until you first build a relationship of trust with them." Those statements do not fit with the pattern we find in the New Testament, where we see both the admonition and the example of being prepared to talk to people about Christ the very first time you meet them.

The Lifestyle Approach

Lifestyle evangelism advocates argue that the chances that a nonbeliever will come to a true understanding of the gospel with a person with whom they have an established relationship are higher than when a person shares Christ with a stranger. Do we see any biblical examples of lifestyle evangelism, of the gospel being shared through preexisting relationships?

The New Testament gives accounts of believers who shared the gospel with others they knew, often members of their own family. Timothy came to faith through his mother and his grandmother, through their faithful

---

5. Aldrich attributes this quotation to Floyd McClung, but does not cite his source. See Aldrich, *Lifestyle Evangelism*, 35.

witness in the home (2 Tim. 1:5). Lydia expressed faith in Christ and then shared with her whole family, and they were baptized (Acts 16:15). The Philippian jailer, who was brought to Christ through initiative evangelism, brought Paul and Silas to share with his family, and the entire family was saved (Acts 16:32–34). The Samaritan woman went into her town and shared with the people there, "Come, see a man who told me all the things that I have done" (John 4:29). In John 4:39 we find these words: "From that city many of the Samaritans believed in Him because of the word of the woman who testified."

A biblical example of a brother-to-brother evangelism exists in Andrew and Peter. Andrew is the one who brought Peter to the Lord. That fact may surprise some people, as Peter is always the one out front, the natural leader, the one who seemingly always wants to be first to answer Jesus's questions. Andrew operates more in the background, more in the shadows. For example, in the feeding of the five thousand, where was Peter? Scripture doesn't tell us, but we can be certain he was right up front with Jesus, making sure everyone there knew he was Jesus's right-hand man. Where was Andrew? John's account of this miracle (John 6) informs us it was Andrew who brought the little boy and his lunch to Jesus. Andrew was out in the crowd with people. The result was that this little boy's lunch, after being blessed and multiplied by Jesus, ended up feeding the massive crowd that day. Peter was your type-A personality, up front, always the one speaking out. Andrew was your behind-the-scenes person, just quietly talking with people, getting to know them.

Christians tend to celebrate those who have the personality of a Peter. They are the ones who are always up front leading and get all the affirmation; they are the ones who are always asked to speak. And yet, I've observed over the years that more transformation in evangelistic ministry tends to get done by Andrews than by those with the personality of Peter. So, if you find that your personality is more like Andrew than like Peter, celebrate the way God has shaped you. Significant ministry often takes place in the shadows, not in the limelight. Remember it was Andrew who brought Peter to Jesus, not vice versa. If your personality is more that of an Andrew than a Peter, rejoice and be thankful. Do not try to be something you're not. Serve God in that role. And all of us should celebrate the Andrews in our churches—those who work behind the scenes unselfishly out of love for the Lord and love for people.

Potential Problems with Each Approach

It is helpful in reflecting about contrasting philosophies to think about the potential problems of each approach.

Potential Problems with the Initiative Approach

1. It can be insensitive. Joseph Aldridge, in his book *Lifestyle Evangelism*, uses terms like "spiritual ambush," "spiritual mugging," and "intrusive evangelism" to describe witnessing to strangers. He says that "buttonholing a stranger" demonstrates a "fundamental lack of respect for human dignity and personality."[6] There may be some gospel witnesses who are like bulls in a china shop, but is this the biggest problem that we have in our churches? For every one Christian who perhaps could be charged with being "too aggressive" in evangelism, there are thousands of believers who don't open their mouths to tell anyone about Christ. The answer to this potential problem is quite simple: practice sensitivity when doing initiative evangelism! If you begin witnessing to a person, and the person does not want to talk you, respect him or her, and do not try to force that conversation against their will. Initiative evangelism need not be offensive! It is not a choice between high-pressure salesmanship and nothing. Paul did not offend people because he took the initiative. Rather, when others were offended, it was by the gospel message itself. McCloskey maintains, "Our communication is purposeful and persuasive, but we also realize that there is a point where the nonbeliever must decide for himself. Here is where we must respect the moral responsibility of each person created in God's image and the behind-the-scenes work of the Holy Spirit in the conversion process."[7] McCloskey continues: "A man convinced against his will is of the same decision still. . . . The person must have the genuine freedom to disagree, or to postpone his decision. We are not out to win an argument, but a person."[8]

---

6. Aldrich, *Lifestyle Evangelism*, 80, citing James Jauncey, *Psychology for Successful Evangelism* (Chicago: Moody, 1972), 123.
7. McCloskey, *Tell It Often—Tell It Well*, 61.
8. McCloskey, *Tell It Often—Tell It Well*, 62, 53.

2. Follow-up may not occur. Aldrich notes that if you already have a preexisting relationship and someone comes to Christ, you have an automatic, built-in follow-up matrix.[9] Aldrich's point is valid, and yet I know people who have come to Christ in Christian families with no discipleship whatsoever. I also know people who have come to Christ in good churches in which there was no follow-up. Follow-up with new believers must be *intentional* whether there is a preexisting relationship or not; the fact there is a preexisting relationship does not guarantee follow-up will take place, nor does the fact there is not a preexisting relationship mean that follow-up will not take place.

3. It can be a "cop-out" in terms of living a consistent Christian life to those around us. Aldrich points out that a weakness with some initiative evangelism is that it stems from a type of fortress mentality, where Christians will go across town to knock on the door of a total stranger but have never walked across the street to say hello to their neighbor. Aldrich believes that for some proponents of initiative evangelism, their activity can be a substitute for having to pay the price of living a consistent Christian life in front of those who know them best. He writes, "Evangelism for those living in such an evangelical ghetto is seen as a regular lowering of the drawbridge and a charge out into enemy territory followed by a quick retreat back across the moat."[10] Aldrich's point no doubt has validity in some cases, but it doesn't necessarily follow that all practitioners of initiative evangelism automatically neglect people around them.

Potential Problems with the Lifestyle Approach

As I mention potential problems with the lifestyle approach, be sure to understand that by "lifestyle" I am referring to the proponents of lifestyle evangelism who say you must have built an existing relationship of trust before you seek to share the gospel.

1. Whose life is good enough? Our lives are not the gospel. Leighton Ford maintains, "But while evangelism is never *mere* words, isolated from the total life of God's people, it must always include the telling of the

9. Aldrich, *Lifestyle Evangelism*, 80.
10. Aldrich, *Lifestyle Evangelism*, 80.

story of Jesus. Episcopal pastor-evangelist Samuel Shoemaker once asked, "Whose life by itself is good enough to speak of Jesus?" And he pointed out that while our lives must back up our words, it takes words to tell about the life and death and resurrection of Jesus Christ.[11] McCloskey asks, "How can we expect the non-believer to know that we are a reflection of the good news until they know what the good news is?"[12]

2. The gospel may never be shared verbally. Evangelism must include the message of the gospel! How shall they believe unless they hear? (Rom. 10:14). Lifestyle evangelism can degenerate into all lifestyle (living a committed Christian life) but no evangelism (verbal witness). Too much of a focus can be put on building the relationship and then waiting for that perfect opportunity. In describing a lifestyle evangelism approach, Aldrich writes, "It *usually* means that at some point in time a person will have to share the words of the gospel."[13] As a student of mine observed about some believers he knew who were practicing "lifestyle" evangelism, "They spend so long building a bridge of friendship they become afraid to carry the gospel over that bridge lest it damage the friendship."

3. It can sap urgency. Aldrich notes that a lifestyle evangelism strategy is "low pressure, long range. . . . If presence is really felt, and is positive, the unbeliever will ask you the reason for your hope!"[14] I agree with Aldrich that we should take a "long range" approach to evangelism, not quickly giving up if the person doesn't immediately respond to the gospel, but his implication that we should live a committed Christian life and then wait for unbelievers to ask us for the reason for the hope we have seems to me to go beyond what Peter was setting forth in 1 Peter 3:15. Peter was not giving that verse as the totality of our evangelism strategy; rather, he was exhorting us that when we are asked, we need to be prepared to give a response. Scripture does not put the burden on the unbeliever to approach a Christian and ask about the gospel. The burden is on believers to communicate the gospel with those who do not know Christ.

---

11. Leighton Ford, "How Shall They Hear?" quoted in Sherwood Wirt, *Evangelism: The Next Ten Years* (Waco, TX: Word, 1978), 23.
12. McCloskey, *Tell It Often—Tell It Well*, 181.
13. Aldrich, *Lifestyle Evangelism*, 85 (emphasis mine).
14. Aldrich, *Lifestyle Evangelism*, 84, 85.

4. It can eliminate a large group of people from potential Christian witness. There are scores of people around all of us who do not have a Christian family, a Christian neighbor, or a Christian friend. If the only way to reach them is through building a relationship of trust, some people are never going to hear the gospel. We should do all we can to build relationships. Christians, of all people, ought to be in the ministry of relationship building, meeting new people, caring for people, and loving people. But if we adopt the viewpoint that we should not talk to someone about Christ until a relationship of trust has been built, countless numbers of people will never hear the gospel. McCloskey powerfully argues:

> There are just too many people who need to know Christ as soon as possible to insist that effective evangelism must be relational in approach. Not everyone is blessed to have Christian friends who can "flesh out" the life of Christ. Not everyone is fortunate enough to witness the life-changing power of the gospel and new life in Christ as it is manifested corporately in the local church.
>
> Thus, a philosophy of evangelism that insists on the presence of a relational element (as a normative practice) will unfortunately exclude those not privileged to have meaningful exposure to Christian friends or the corporate witness of the church. This is why many groups practice initiative evangelism and employ strategies that encompass masses of people. It is not that they are against the relational element in evangelism, but they do not allow it to determine the scope of their outreach. Let's reach our friends. Let's do whatever it takes to communicate authentically to them. But let's not forget that others also need to hear the gospel.[15]

A Balanced Approach

After examining these approaches, let me suggest a balanced approach. I realize that like beauty, balance is in the eye of the beholder. Someone once remarked that "the only Christian in perfect balance is the one on his

---

15. McCloskey, *Tell It Often—Tell It Well*, 171.

or her way to the other extreme." It is easy to swing to one extreme or the other, while maintaining balance is often much harder for us to do.

I believe we need to learn from both of these approaches. These philosophies are not mutually exclusive. Both are encouraged and exemplified in Scripture. Perhaps proponents of these approaches have created something of a false dichotomy. How can you take the initiative and share the gospel with someone other than incarnationally? And no matter how long you have had an existing relationship with someone, isn't sharing the biblical gospel by its very nature confrontational?

Following are three admonitions from Scripture that serve as a faithful guide as we strive to practice evangelism as a way of life.

Biblical evangelism must be done with urgency.

More than seven billion souls live on this planet. All seven billion will die and enter eternity. If the biblical message is true (and it is!), then hell is a tragic conclusion for those who have not come to God through Christ. Richard Baxter, the great Puritan pastor in seventeenth-century England, was given a death sentence by a doctor when he was in his thirties. He was coughing up blood, and the doctor told Baxter he was going to die. Baxter decided that if he was going to die, he wanted to spend the remaining weeks of his life not in smog-filled London, which seemed to make his cough worse, but instead in the countryside. He traveled to Rous Lench (a village in Worcestershire) and stayed in the home of a friend as he prepared to die.

How did he prepare to die? He meditated on Scripture; he looked at what Scripture had to say about heaven and about glory. He did not die but ended up living almost to the age of seventy-six. He published his reflections on heaven, and it turned out to be an eight-hundred-page book called *The Saints' Everlasting Rest*. It was a runaway bestseller in the decade of the 1650s in England. In the preface, Baxter notes that he wrote this book with one foot in the grave, and he talked about how being given a death sentence tends to focus one's attention on things that matter.

After he recovered, he made a commitment that from that moment on, he would speak to sinners with compassion, "as a dying man to dying men."[16] Baxter realized through that experience that every time he preached it could be his last sermon, and he wanted to make sure he pointed people to Christ in his sermons. He knew that the next sermon people hear may be their last, and they had better hear about Christ and the way to salvation. Evangelism must be done with urgency.

Biblical evangelism must be done with sensitivity.

Jesus approached people differently. He did not approach people with a "one size that fits all" mentality.[17] When talking to the rich young ruler, he let the man walk away. And the text emphatically says he "felt a love for him" (Mark 10:21). Evangelism must be done with sensitivity to and respect for the individual. McCloskey notes:

> The first-century church . . . realized that the message of the gospel traveled along the two-lane highway of boldness *and* sensitivity. With no boldness, the gospel would be silenced by persecutors, suffering, inconvenient circumstances and the fears of the evangelist. It would never reach the ears of unbelievers.
>
> Without sensitivity, the gospel might be heard, but not truly understood. The goal of the first-century Christians was not merely to get unbelievers within earshot of the gospel, but to help them truly understand its content and personal implications. Therefore, they boldly took the initiative—in a spirit of sensitivity.[18]

Biblical evangelism must be done with integrity.

We must avoid bait and switch tactics; we must reject any kind of trickery. In 2 Corinthians 4:2, Paul says, "but we have renounced the things hidden because of shame, not walking in craftiness or adulterating the word of God, but by the manifestation of truth commending ourselves to every man's conscience in the sight of God." Biblical evangelism must be done with urgency, sensitivity, and integrity.

---

16. Richard Baxter, *The Autobiography of Richard Baxter*, ed. N. H. Keeble (London: J. M. Dent & Sons, 1974), 26.
17. A helpful study in Jesus's approach with individuals is Robert E. Coleman, *The Master's Way of Personal Evangelism* (Wheaton, IL: Crossway, 1997).
18. McCloskey, *Tell It Often—Tell It Well*, 196 (emphasis original).

THE RELATIONSHIP BETWEEN A
CHRISTIAN'S WALK AND TALK

In chapter 1 we noted that our life is not the gospel, that the gospel must be shared verbally. We critiqued the quote often (but mistakenly) attributed to St. Francis of Assisi, "Preach the gospel at all times; use words if necessary." We argued that words *are* necessary to communicate the gospel message because our life is not the gospel. However, the lifestyle evangelism advocates do make an important contribution to our witness, and that is the reminder that in some of our relational contexts our walk does carry a lot of weight. If you live a committed Christian life but never share the gospel verbally, how does your non-Christian neighbor know the source of your hope? And conversely, if you communicate the gospel verbally but are a complete jerk in the process, those words of eternal life may well fall on deaf ears.

I maintain that both are important, but their relative importance is dependent on the relationship between the witness and the person being witnessed to. When a person is a family member or someone who knows you very well, your life is going to speak loudly to that individual (versus your words only). Remember the context of 1 Peter 3. Peter is writing to wives who have unbelieving husbands and tells them the way to reach their unbelieving husbands is not by continually preaching to them or trying to nag them into the kingdom. Peter instructs them to communicate the good news and then to let their lives reinforce the gospel. With a family member or close friend, your walk will carry a lot of weight, but note the gospel must still be shared verbally for evangelism to have taken place.

But with acquaintances or complete strangers, the Christian's walk becomes less significant in relation to their talk. The person doesn't know us well (or at all) and therefore cannot reflect deeply on the Christian character that might be present in our life. But even the way we approach that person, whether an acquaintance or a stranger, will communicate loudly to them. We can share the good news of the love of Christ with others, but if we do it in a harsh, unloving manner, the message might be ignored. What is the relationship between a Christian's walk and talk? Both are always necessary. Live out the hope found in the gospel at all times, and use words because they are necessary.

Keeping Evangelism as a Lifestyle

How can we keep evangelism as an everyday part of our life, not something that we just engage in at sporadic times? Let me suggest the following ways.

Commit yourself to a lifestyle of evangelism.

A lot of things happen by accident, but evangelism is not typically one of them. We must commit ourselves to a lifestyle of sharing the good news with others. Be ready anywhere and anytime. Commit to share the good news "in season and out of season."

Pray for sensitivity to others and opportunities.

Each morning lift up your eyes and see that the "fields are white unto harvest." We need that reminder, because left to ourselves when we wake up each morning our focus is too readily on all our struggles, troubles, and to-do lists. Pray that the Holy Spirit would make you sensitive to witnessing opportunities throughout the day. That is a prayer that God delights to answer! Beginning each day with that prayer sensitizes us to opportunities we might have otherwise overlooked.

Pray for compassion and boldness.

These are two struggles we often have in terms of sharing the gospel. We too easily lose our sense of compassion, and when we look upon the lost multitudes instead of having compassion as our Lord did, we look on them with criticism, condemnation, callousness, and coldness. Pray often, "Lord, give me the heart of compassion that you have." Pray also for boldness. The early church prayed for boldness. Why? Because they needed it. God delights to answer prayers for compassion for others and boldness to share the gospel. We don't have to end those prayers with, "Lord if it be your will."

Never say "no" for someone else.

It is too easy for us to assume that people we encounter throughout our day would not be interested in hearing the gospel and that they would never respond positively to a gospel presentation. If they say no to Christ, that is one thing, but let's stop saying "no" for them by not even seeking to share with them. I have said "no" for far too many people in my life, and I don't want to live that way.

Be a sower, not a soil inspector.

This principle was highlighted earlier in this book but bears repeating here. Mark 4 recounts the parable of the sower who went out to sow. As he sowed, seed fell on all different kinds of soil. Notice Jesus did not say, "The sower went out to *inspect* the soil, and *then* where he thought he found good soil he sowed the seed; but where the soil did not look good he withheld the seed." I am afraid that is sometimes exactly the way that we approach sowing the seed. We somehow feel like there must be a limited amount of seed because we sow it very sparingly. No, when the sower went out to sow he sowed indiscriminately. Yes, some of it fell on hard soil, but some of it fell on good soil. Determine to be a sower and not a soil inspector.

Cultivate your daily walk with Christ.

The most definitive verse related to personal evangelism is Matthew 12:34, where Jesus said, "The mouth speaks out of that which fills the heart." If we are having trouble talking about Christ, the Bible would say that is not really a speech problem but rather a heart problem. When we are really passionate about something, we do not have trouble talking about it. Continue to cultivate your love relationship with Christ. When you are head over heels in love with Christ and his love is overflowing in your life, talking about him is as natural as breathing.

Work at building relationships.

Being friendly to others is not a sin! Work at meeting people, getting to know them, and looking for opportunities to share with them. People are eternal. Whatever business you are in, make sure that you major in the people business. People matter to God!

CHAPTER 14

BRIDGES TO THE GOSPEL

FOR MANY BELIEVERS, the hardest part of witnessing is getting started. A few years ago there was a solar eclipse that seemingly had everyone in America talking about it. It was easy to talk about what was happening in the heavens, even with complete strangers. But how do we go from talking about what we see happening in the heavens to a conversation about heaven? Talking about gardening is easy, but how do we move from talking about gardening to talking about God? How can we transition from talking about sports to discussing the Savior?

GETTING STARTED

Dozens of people over the years have told me they really want to share their faith, but they just do not know how to do so. When I inquire further, in almost all cases, they know the gospel message well enough to share it. When they say they don't know how to witness, what they are really saying is they do not know how to get started. How can they transition from everyday conversations to eternal realities in a way that seems natural and not strained? I learned a process many years about that has helped me immeasurably in having gospel conversations. The process involves three steps: explore, stimulate, and share.

Explore

By "explore," I mean trying to understand the person you are talking with. There are two helpful ways to explore. First, make it a point to *observe* all you can when you meet someone. Study them to see what you can learn about them. For example, if you have the chance to go into someone's home, you can tell what is important to them by the pictures on their wall. If you come into the living room in my home, you will see a picture of me standing on the famous Swilcan Bridge on the eighteenth hole of the Old Course in St. Andrews, Scotland, the home of golf. Every great golfer in the world has stood on that bridge—and some not-so-great ones.

Through simple observation immediately you would know a few things about me. You would know that I am a golfer, and you would know my wife must really love me because she lets me put a golf picture in our living room. As you looked at other pictures, you would see that family is a priority to me, as the other pictures on the wall are of our children and grandchildren. If you looked at the books in our bookcase, you would conclude we are religious because our bookcase is filled with religious books and Bibles. When you saw the *Game & Fish* magazine on my coffee table, you could surmise I like fishing and perhaps hunting. You get the idea. Simple observation can tell you a lot about a person.

Second, as you observe, *ask questions*. If you ask good questions and pay attention, people will tell you a lot about themselves. Listening—really listening—to their answers helps you get to know that person better. I ask a lot of questions and let the other person talk far more than me. They will usually say something that gives me an avenue or an "open door" to bring spiritual things into the conversation. The starting point in this process of sharing is to explore—to find out what you can about the other person through observation and through asking good questions. When I see someone with a tattoo, I ask them, "Can you explain the meaning of your tattoo?" I have yet to meet the person who wasn't happy to share the story behind their tattoo, and that story often leads to deeper conversation about life issues.

Stimulate

We have heard the old adage, "You can lead a horse to water, but you can't make him drink." But as one sage added, "But you can salt the oats!" In Colossians 4:6, Paul talks about having our speech "seasoned with salt."

We bring spiritual salt into the conversation to see if it produces spiritual thirst. We bring spiritual salt into the conversation by making a statement or asking a question that points to spiritual realities. (We will provide numerous such questions later in this chapter.) This is where we move from the "secular" to the "sacred."

Share

After we have gone through these steps, we then share the good news of what God has done for us in Christ.

This simple three-step process has served me well for more than four decades in personal evangelism. It has become my default setting as I meet new people and engage them in conversations. Let me give one example of how this process has played out in my personal witnessing encounters.

I was flying from Chicago to Houston for a speaking engagement. On the flight I ended up in the bulkhead row with a young mom, Susan, and her very hyperactive seventeen-month-old daughter. Susan started apologizing to me before I had even fastened my seat belt: "Sir, I'm so sorry. My daughter is really excited about this flight, and she's a little out of control." Well, that was not true. She was a whole lot out of control! Before the plane took off, she had managed to slap my tie with her sucker (leaving a big sugar stain)—twice.

How would you begin a conversation in those circumstances? Following the process, I began by asking her if Chicago or Houston was home. She replied, "Houston." I asked what had brought her to Chicago. She replied, "Grandparents." We continued the conversation with me asking questions and with her continually apologizing for her daughter's frenzied activity in the bulkhead row. I finally said, "Susan, I have four children, and if you are with someone who has children, you do not need to explain your child's behavior. Been there, done that, got the T-shirt! And for people who don't have children, no amount of explanation is going to do any good. So just relax. I'm fine with your daughter."

A few moments later Susan asked me a question that caused me to move from the "explore" step to the "stimulate" step and bring spiritual salt into the conversation. She asked, "You have four children? *How in the world do you manage with four children?* I can't even handle one child." I shared with her that raising four children was not easy—that parenting was the hardest job I had ever had. But I told her there was one thing that has made all the difference in the world, and that was that we were basing our child-raising off of principles we learned from the Bible.

Her reaction was one of shock and disbelief. "The Bible?" she asked. "What does the Bible have to do with raising children?" Since she asked me a question, I felt it was my duty to answer it! So I spent the next several minutes walking Susan through the main message of the Bible (the gospel message). I had progressed through the "explore" and "stimulate" steps and was now in the "share" step. I talked about who God is, the holy and loving Creator, and how we are created in God's image but are sinful and fallen, which causes us to hurt even people we love. I asked her if she ever got really angry with her daughter. She replied, "You mean like right now?" I asked her why that was the case. Could it be that she didn't love her daughter? She bristled at that suggestion and exclaimed, "I would die for my daughter." To which I replied, "I don't doubt that. And yet you get so angry at her. How do you explain that?" She replied, "I can't explain it—it doesn't make sense." I told her how the Bible explains that situation: it is because we are sinful and broken and separated from God, and that reality causes us to sin against other people—even those we love.

We spent most of the two-hour flight discussing spiritual truths, and when we landed, she thanked me profusely, acknowledging that she had always believed religion was something private but had learned so much about God, herself, and forgiveness and was very thankful for the conversation. And yet I am quite confident she did not get on that plane with the intention of having a religious conversation. In fact, had a reporter asked her before she boarded the flight, "On your trip to Houston today would you like to have a lengthy conversation with a religious fanatic?" I'm quite sure her answer would have been, "Absolutely not! I'd rather walk!" I am convinced what made her open to the conversation was the process I have outlined.

I could have started the conversation with another approach, such as, "If this plane were to crash on the way to Houston, do you know for sure where you would spend eternity?" I have asked that type of diagnostic question of many people over the years, but I do not believe that would have been the best starting point for a spiritual conversation with Susan. Susan's greatest felt need was that she felt like a failure as a mom. Instead of bringing the gospel into the conversation through the door of a possible plane crash, I simply brought it through the door of parenting, using her felt need to explain what her greatest real need was and how God has provided an answer to it.

Bridges to the Gospel

Several years ago I ran across the concept of "bridges to the gospel" in a fine book on evangelism by Dick Sisson.[1] A bridge to the gospel is a statement or question that helps us move naturally from general conversation to talking specifically about spiritual things. Following are several different categories of how we can bridge from the secular to the sacred, with examples given for each of the various bridges.

Church Bridge

- "Were you brought up in a particular religious tradition?"
- "Do they talk about heaven much in your church?"
- "What does your church teach about the way a person can have his/her sins forgiven?"

Increasingly, there are people who answer the first question "no," but many people still have some type of religious background. If a person identifies with a church, then the next two questions can move the conversation from "churchianity" to "Christianity." I particularly love the third question, "What does your church teach about the way a person can have his/her sins forgiven?" Note the nuance in this question. You are not asking them what they believe (which can seem too personal) but what their church teaches. But the answer they give about what their church teaches will most assuredly tell you what they believe.

Personal Experience Bridge

- "Through the years have you come to know Christ in a personal way, or are you still on the way?"
- "What is your current level of interest in spiritual things?"
- "Where are you in your own personal search for meaning and purpose in life?"

---

1. Dick Sisson, *Evangelism Encounter* (Wheaton, IL: Victor Books, 1988), 136–38.

Sometimes I will tie this personal experience question with the church bridge if they indicate they have a church background. For example, "Through your time at Faith Lutheran Church, have you ever come to know Christ in a personal way, or do you feel like you're still in process?" You are not directly asking them, "Are you a Christian?" Before I understood some of these concepts, I remember asking one lady in Texas, "Are you a Christian?" She looked at me and said, "Well, I live in Texas and, you know, I'm not one of those Buddhists or Hindus or Muslims. I'm a Texan, so of course I'm a Christian." To her, identifying as a Christian was simply a cultural expression of not being an adherent of another religion. In her mind, if you are born in America (or at least in Texas), then of course you are a Christian.

I don't typically use the bridge asking about their current level of interest in spiritual things, because if the person says zero or none, it is harder to continue. But sometimes, spiritual matters come up early in the conversation, and that is a way to bridge into a deeper spiritual discussion.

Intellectual Bridge

- "Is there a specific question or concern that is hanging you up in your spiritual journey?"
- "Has anyone ever shared with you what the Bible teaches about . . . ?"
- "Has anyone ever shared with you how to have a personal relationship with God?"
- "Has anyone ever shared with you the main message of the Bible?"
- "Do you consider yourself a seeker of truth?"

I find this bridge very beneficial when witnessing on a college campus. Students fancy themselves as intellectuals and thoughtful individuals. I have found the intellectual bridge questions helpful in cutting through a lot of intellectual fog and getting to the heart of the matter. One of my seminary professors was converted as a college student when a professor challenged him to read "the world's all-time best-selling book, the Bible." He read through the entire Bible, and by the time he finished, he had met Christ in the pages of Scripture.

You may have friends or family members who fancy themselves to be intellectuals and think religion is something only uneducated people believe in. I have approached intellectuals before with this question: "How intellectual is it when you reject something out of hand, without even studying it? That sounds more like a fundamentalist approach to me than an intellectual approach." I remind them that the Bible is the world's all-time best-selling book, and that it would be rather close-minded to reject it without even understanding its main message.

Personal Opinion Bridge

- "In your personal opinion, what is a Christian?"
- "What do you think of . . . ?" (God, Jesus Christ, religion, the Bible, meaning of life, etc.)

It never ceases to amaze me how pollsters can discover people with no opinion! In my experience, I find that people are more than happy to share their opinion. Using this bridge, you simply ask their personal opinion on what it means to be a Christian. You are not asking them to define what it means according to the Baptist Faith and Message 2000; you just ask them what they *think*. Their answer will reveal where they are spiritually.

Quite often, after they give their opinion, they will turn the question back to you: "In your personal opinion, what is a Christian?" At that point I shift the focus of the discussion. I tell them I like to base my opinions on spiritual questions on what the Bible teaches. I ask them, "May I briefly share with you how the Bible answers that question?"

Current-Issues Bridge

- "The Bible is a remarkably relevant book. Would you like to see what it has to say about this issue?"
- "May I share with you some great news that you won't find in today's newspaper?"

I once heard Billy Graham say he believed Christians should begin their day with a Bible in one hand and a newspaper in the other. Why would he say that? Because as we seek to be witnesses, it is helpful for us to know what people are going to be talking about in the breakroom at work or on the sidelines of the soccer game. Whatever is on the front page of the newspaper (or the lead story on cable news or on internet news sites) often will be a topic of conversation among people. Believers should strategize about how the Bible and a Christian worldview speak to that issue. We can begin each day prepared to let our speech "always be with grace, as though seasoned with salt" (Col. 4:6).

Sports Bridge

- "Did you know that [name of well-known athlete] is a Christian?"

Obviously, this bridge must be used with caution, as a prominent athlete professing faith in God one day may be on the front page of the paper for less-than-spiritual reasons the next day. You must choose your Christian athletes carefully. With that caveat, I still believe this is a helpful tool in one's toolbox, especially in witnessing to men who think Christianity is fine for women and children, but "real men" don't need God. I have been able to have gospel conversations with a handful of men over the years because they respected an athlete as "a man's man," but did not know he was a Christian. I don't use this bridge often, but it is available in my evangelistic toolbox if the situation warrants.

Felt-Needs Bridge

- "You know, I still have my share of problems, but having a personal relationship with Jesus Christ has made all the difference in how I handle them!"
- "Yes, Mary, I have experienced great loneliness in my life. I used to wonder if anyone would miss me or even care if I died. But I have found a special friend who loves me just as I am, who will never leave me."

"Felt" needs are not the same as "real" needs. But a felt need may serve as a doorway through which you approach the real need. When I talked with Susan on the airplane, her felt need was that she felt like a failure as a mom. In her mind, her greatest need was to be a better mother. I did not address her felt need by giving her ten tips on practical parenting. I pointed her to her *real* need, which was Christ. The phrase "felt needs" is anathema in some circles because some churches focus simply on felt needs and never get to real needs. Please do not throw the baby out with the bathwater. Felt needs are often a wonderful doorway through which to enter into addressing a person's real needs.

Prayer Bridge

- "Is there something I could pray about for you?"

I use this bridge all the time. The prayer bridge is delightfully simple. You simply ask someone if you can pray about anything for them. Remembering Jesus's observation that "the eyes are a lamp to the soul," I will often look into someone's eyes and see pain and heartache. I will often initiate a conversation with them in this way: "I don't mean to intrude, but you look like you have the weight of the world on your shoulders. Is there anything I could pray about for you?" I have found that half the time the answer is something like, "No, I'm fine," but the other half of the time, the person's eyes will fill with tears because they are hurting. I have started hundreds of gospel conversations over the years by asking a person if I can pray for him or her.

Relationship Bridge

- "Bill, we've been friends for a while now. We have talked together about so many things, yet there is a very important part of my life I have never shared with you. May I share with you about my spiritual pilgrimage?"

The relationship bridge works very well if you have family members or friends who knew you before you came to Christ. God led me to this bridge as I was getting ready to graduate from Kansas State University. I had the privilege, while an engineering student, of sharing Christ with many of my fellow engineering students and even with a few of my professors. But there was one student, Tony, with whom I had never shared the gospel. Why? Because Tony was constantly mocking Christians, and I assumed if I shared the gospel with him, he would immediately reject it and begin mocking me.

A few weeks before graduation, I came under deep conviction about my failure to witness to Tony. We had taken classes together for four years and had been regular study partners. I had spent countless hours with him and yet had never opened up my mouth to speak about Christ. I cried out to the Lord for wisdom on how to approach Tony after four years of failed silence. I sensed the Lord was prompting me, "Just do it! Just tell Tony there is an important part of your life you've never shared with him, and ask his permission to do so."

A few nights later we were studying for an exam, and as we were wrapping up our study session, I said something like this to him: "Tony, we've been friends for four years now. We've made it through engineering physics and thermodynamics together. But there is a really important part of my life I've never shared with you. Could I share that with you now?"

"Of course," was his immediate reply, and I took the next twenty minutes to share the gospel message and how Jesus Christ had changed my life. When I finished, Tony replied, "You don't know how good that makes me feel." When he saw my surprise at his comment, he continued. "Tim, I know you are a Christian. And I know you talk to other people all the time about your faith. And all this time I've wondered why you never talked with me. And the only conclusion I could come to is that you thought there was no hope for me. You don't know how good it makes me feel that you think there is hope for me."

Tony did not trust Christ for salvation that night, but he heard the gospel message. I had been his biggest stumbling block during his college days. If I, the one "real Christian" he knew, thought there was no hope for him, then God must feel the same way—there is no hope for Tony. Underneath that rough, mocking exterior was a heart that was searching, and I had squandered dozens of opportunities to share with him.

You may have family members or friends who know your life has changed, but you have never sat down with them to explain the gospel message and the reason for those changes. The relationship bridge is a wonderful way to start that spiritual conversation, especially if you have procrastinated for a long time and aren't sure how to begin. For example, "Mom and Dad, I know that I have never fully explained to you all that happened in my life my junior year of college. Could I do that?" I promise you the answer will be a resounding yes. You can use this bridge with friends and family members who have known you a long time but have not heard the gospel from you. Just yesterday a former student stopped me and told me he had used the relationship bridge to share with his elderly grandmother last year, and she had trusted Christ for salvation. Several months later she died, and he had the privilege of preaching her funeral and sharing about the hope she had found in Christ.

History Bridge

- "In all of history, what person has had the greatest impact on the world? Why?"

I am a history buff and love to read and study history. The obvious answer to the above question is Jesus. Even secular historians will acknowledge Christ's impact on the world. If you ask this question, be prepared for any answer. (A man once told me "Columbus.") After they give their answer, you can share why you believe Christ has had the greatest impact on the world. You may not use this bridge often, but tuck it away in your evangelistic toolbox for the right occasion.

Heaven Bridge

The heaven bridge is a series of four questions:

- "Do you think heaven is a perfect place?"
- "How close have you come to living a perfect life?"
- "If God were to let you into heaven as you are, what would happen to heaven's perfect record?"
- "Do you have the hope found in 2 Corinthians 5:17?"

I will often use the heaven bridge after a famous person has died. People talk about this celebrity as if he or she is now in heaven regardless of what they believed or how they lived.

In asking if heaven is a perfect place, I have never had anyone answer that question with a "no." Most people will say heaven is a perfect place. Next, if you ask how close they have come to living a perfect life, they will almost never say they are perfect. (If they do, ask their spouse, their children, or their friends for a second opinion.) Then when you ask about what would their being let into heaven to do to heaven's perfect record, a light bulb often goes off. As I have asked that question of people, I have seen the blood drain from their face as for the first time in their life they are confronted with their sinfulness, that their "goodness" isn't "good enough." Finally, you can ask if they see the hope found in 2 Corinthians 5:17, "Therefore if anyone is in Christ, he is a new creature; the old things passed away; behold, new things have come."

Tattoo Bridge

- "That is an interesting tattoo. What is the story behind it?"

When someone gets a tattoo, they do so for a reason. There is always a story behind the tattoo, whether a joyous occasion or a painful experience. I have never encountered anyone with a tattoo unwilling to share with me the story behind it, and that has opened up wonderful conversations.

Diagnostic Questions from Evangelism Explosion

Dr. D. James Kennedy, in his training program for evangelism known as Evangelism Explosion, popularized the use of two key diagnostic questions to begin gospel conversations.[2]

- "Have you come to a place in your spiritual life where you *know for certain* that if you were to die you today you would go to heaven?"
- "Suppose that you were to die tonight and stand before God and he were to say to you, 'Why should I let you into heaven?' What would you say?"

These questions are helpful in "diagnosing" the person's spiritual condition, and what he or she is trusting in for salvation.

Responsibility Bridge

- "I am a follower of Jesus Christ, and one of our responsibilities is to tell others about Jesus. Could I briefly share you what the Bible says about him?"

---

2. D. James Kennedy, *Evangelism Explosion* (Wheaton, IL: Tyndale House Publishers, 1983), 16.

This bridge can be a "fallback" bridge if you want to be able to introduce the gospel to someone, and you can't figure out which bridge to use. Owning your responsibility as a witness may be another way to start a gospel conversation.

CONCLUSION

If the hardest part in witnessing is getting started, and may people confirm that issue to be true in their situation, then the approach in this chapter provides an easy process to follow in conversations. Select several bridges to the gospel that you would feel comfortable using, and then memorize them so you have them available as you talk with people.

CHAPTER 15

GOSPEL BOOKLETS

GOSPEL BOOKLETS (OR TRACTS) ARE ANOTHER HELPFUL tool to put in your toolbox for evangelism. Some tracts are not sound theologically, and others use a bait-and-switch approach. But that does not mean we should abandon the use of booklets. A booklet is a tool just like a hammer is a tool. A hammer can be used for many different things, but we do not stop using hammers because some people misuse them. Rather, we use them properly. Do not allow the reality that some people may misuse gospel booklets keep you from using them appropriately.

BENEFITS OF USING A GOOD GOSPEL BOOKLET

I have found nine different benefits for using a theologically sound gospel booklet.

It presents the gospel clearly.

With this assertion I am of course making a major assumption, and that is that you are using a good booklet.[1] A good booklet will present the gospel clearly; a poor one will not. Cults produce booklets with their own version of the "gospel," but a good booklet—one rooted and grounded in

---

1. The gospel booklet I recommend is "Experiencing God's Grace," which is available at www.10ofThose.com.

Scripture—will present the gospel clearly. And after all, isn't that our goal: to present the gospel clearly?

It helps give you confidence when you may be nervous.

Someone once defined evangelism as a conversation between two people, both of whom are nervous. I think that is probably a fairly accurate description of many, if not most, witnessing conversations. Do you remember the very first time you had the privilege of sharing the gospel with someone? I do. The first time for me was when I was a college student. I was a relatively new believer, having only been a follower of Christ for about two months. I went on a weekend retreat with a collegiate campus group (Baptist Student Union), and the focus of that retreat was evangelism. As a young Christian I was taught to share my faith. (I learned how to share my faith before I discovered that most Christians don't do that!) One of the approaches they taught that weekend was using a gospel booklet to share Christ with others. They then gave us three booklets and challenged us to write down the names of three lost friends and then pray that God would give us an opportunity to share that gospel booklet with them over the next thirty days. I wrote down the names of two guys in my dorm and one guy that was in a class with me, and began to pray that God would open doors of opportunity.

I got home from that retreat on a Sunday evening, and the following Tuesday, Kerry, one of the men on that list I'd been praying for, was in my dorm room studying for an exam. We finished studying, and I said, "Hey, Kerry, if you have a few extra minutes I'd love to share this helpful booklet I got at a conference this past weekend. It's like a summary of the main message of the Bible." He said, "Sure," so I reached over and grabbed the booklet. My hand was shaking so bad Kerry had to reach out and help hold the booklet steady so we could read it together.

That night in my dorm room, I had the privilege for the very first time in my relatively young Christian life of sharing the good news with someone else. Kerry didn't come to faith in Christ that night, but I had the privilege of sharing with him. Even though I was nervous, I had a tool that enabled me to share. A good gospel booklet gives you confidence when you may be nervous.

It gives you a guide to keep you on the subject.

We can begin a gospel conversation, and the next thing we know we're discussing the number of men in Gideon's army. It is easy for us to get sidetracked off of the gospel message. A good gospel booklet functions like railroad tracks; it serves as a guide to keep us on the subject of the gospel.

It presents the claims of Christ clearly without getting sidetracked on other issues.

This benefit is related to the one just discussed. It helps avoid "chasing rabbits." If you're using a gospel booklet, and someone asks a question, you can simply affirm, "That's a good question," write that question down, and tell them you will come back to it when you have finished sharing the booklet. This approach enables you to keep from getting sidetracked in extraneous discussions.

It has the Bible verses printed out in case you forget.

A good booklet highlights key verses of Scripture that explain the gospel message. With a booklet in front of you, you do not need to rely on your memory to list the relevant verses and quote them accurately. A good booklet displays key verses that the Spirit of God uses to bring conviction and understanding of the gospel message.

It gives visual help.

When I was in school, people assumed there was only one kind of learner: auditory. Everyone was supposed to listen and absorb content simply by hearing it. We now understand pedagogically that many people are more visual learners than auditory learners. If they simply hear something, they don't process it as well as if they hear it and see it. A good gospel booklet not only allows the gospel to be heard but also seen, giving visual help as well as verbal.

It offers suggestions for Christian growth.

A good gospel booklet offers suggestions for Christian growth for someone who trusts Christ. I will highlight this benefit more fully later in this chapter by sharing an example of how these suggestions for Christian growth functioned in the life of one man with whom I shared a gospel booklet.

It can easily be taught to other Christians.

Unfortunately, many Christians have never shared their faith with an unbeliever even one single time. How are we to mobilize believers to begin sharing their faith with others? A very simple approach is to train them in how to share a gospel booklet with someone. (That is how I first learned to share my faith!) One of the benefits of a gospel booklet is that it can easily be taught to other Christians. If someone can read and turn pages, they can utilize this tool. It is that simple. You don't have to have memorized dozens of verses or a detailed outline; you can utilize this tool as a brand-new Christian.

To illustrate this concept more fully, I had the privilege of leading a young man named Bert to faith in Christ one evening. To solidify his commitment and to help prepare him to share with others, I walked him through a gospel booklet and showed him how he could share his newfound faith with others. I gave him three gospel booklets that night. We connected by phone a few days later, and he asked if I could give him more booklets. As a brand-new Christian, he had already shared his faith with three people in less than three days! There was a lot about Christianity he didn't know, and if asked almost any Bible question, he would not have had the answer. But he had experienced the power of the gospel in his own life, and, using a simple tool, he was now sharing the good news with others.

A simple means of training church members how to share the gospel using a booklet is to hold a one-hour training seminar. I have led this one-hour training on a Saturday morning, on a Sunday morning during Sunday school, on a Wednesday night during prayer meeting, and in small group settings during the week. You can determine which time and format works best for your church. In the first fifteen minutes of the training, I explain how you can utilize a good gospel booklet to share Christ with someone else. For the next thirty minutes, I have the participants pair off and spend fifteen minutes practicing sharing the booklet with the other person. I utilize the last fifteen minutes to answer questions, and then I send them out with three to five booklets each. During the next week, I have always had a church member text or email to request more booklets. They have discovered the simplicity of using this approach and want to share with more people.

The person with whom you are sharing will have something to take with them so they can look it over later.

I begin far more gospel conversations than I am able to finish. Whether due to time constraints or interruptions, many times I am unable to completely share the gospel message with the person I am talking with. When that happens, I always give them a booklet to take with them. I tell them, "This booklet summarizes the main message of the Bible. If you will read it, I am confident it will answer a lot of your questions about God and forgiveness." Even when I have had an opportunity to present the entire gospel message to someone, if they do not respond positively, I seek to put a booklet in their hands. They may not be interested that particular day, but when the time comes that they are interested, they will have the gospel message with them in that booklet.

THE POWER OF THE GOSPEL IN BOOKLET FORM

I want to give three quick anecdotes of how God hammered into me the power of the gospel through booklets. My roommate my first semester of seminary (before I got married) was Enos. Enos grew up in rural Kenya. One day while walking home from primary school, he found a gospel booklet (in Swahili) along the path. He took it home and gave it to his father. His father read it and gave his life to Christ, as did his mother, his siblings, and Enos himself. The entire family came to faith in Christ through a gospel booklet!

Enos came to the States for theological studies, and I had the privilege of getting to know him. He returned to Kenya and had a part in planting more than forty churches before he was martyred by Muslim extremists. Enos led hundreds of people to faith in Christ and taught thousands of believers how to share their faith. How did his faith journey begin? Through a gospel booklet.

Another seminary friend, William, came to faith through a gospel booklet. When he was a rebellious teenager, he crashed his car and broke three ribs. While he was in the hospital for observation, he was taken to the radiology department for X-rays of his ribs. While he was gone from his room, a hospital chaplain stopped by to see him. Finding him gone, the chaplain simply placed a gospel booklet on his bed for when he returned.

When William returned from the radiology department, he saw the booklet on his bed. He knew it had something to do with God, and he wasn't even remotely interested, so he picked it up to throw it in the trash can. I don't know if you have ever tried to throw something with broken ribs. I've never had broken ribs, but I have had bruised ribs, and a throwing motion is excruciatingly painful. Due to the pain, William didn't complete the throwing motion all the way to the trash can, and the booklet ended up flying into the drawer of his bedside table. He left it there, figuring that was as good as a trash can.

The next morning when he was released, his mom packed up his things, and somehow that gospel booklet made it home in his gym bag. He found it as he was unpacking the bag and picked it up to throw it in the trash can by his dresser. The booklet sailed over the trash can and went behind his dresser. He started to pull the dresser away from the wall to throw the booklet away, but his ribs hurt so badly that he just left it there.

That booklet remained behind his dresser for six months, gathering dust. But one night he had come to the end of his rope. He drove home knowing there was a booklet behind his dresser that talked about hope. He got home, pulled the dresser away from the wall, read the booklet, and gave his life to Christ. He was my accountability partner in seminary and is one of the most gifted personal witnesses I know. How did he come to faith in Christ? Through the commitment of a hospital chaplain who wanted to share the good news of Jesus Christ through any means possible. William now serves as a missions pastor. He has led hundreds of people to faith in Christ and has trained thousands in how to share the gospel.

As a final example, I want to share one of my experiences in sharing a gospel booklet. When I began seminary, I bought a new pair of dress shoes. The manager, a man named Phil, was the only other person in the shoe store. There were no other customers and no salespeople. As I tried on shoes, I talked to Phil about Christ. He politely expressed he was not interested. As I paid for my shoes and prepared to leave the store, I handed Phil a gospel booklet and said, "Phil, I respect the fact that you say you are not interested today. But when the day comes that you are interested, this booklet will help you know what it means to follow Christ." I wrote my name and phone number on the back of the booklet and gave it to Phil, encouraging him to call me if he had any questions.

Five years later I was in Chicago working on my doctorate. One evening the phone rang, and a voice at the other end said, "You probably don't remember me, but five years ago you gave me a booklet in a shoe store in Fort Worth. I have given my life to Christ, and I am calling to thank you." Amazed, I asked Phil to share his story.

Phil told me that, as I left the store, he was holding the booklet and was getting ready to drop it in the trash when my words came back to him: "When the day comes that you are interested, this booklet will be helpful." So Phil stuck the booklet in his shirt pocket, and that evening, when he returned home, he threw it in his desk drawer. The booklet remained in that desk drawer for over four years. One day when he came home for lunch, his wife had left him a note that read, "Dear Phil, I don't love you anymore. I'm not sure if I ever really loved you, but I'm sure I don't love you now. I have met my 'soul mate,' and I am leaving town with him. Don't try and find me. Our relationship is over."

As Phil's heart filled with despair, he remembered the gospel booklet in his desk drawer I had given him four years earlier, a booklet that talked about hope. Phil pulled out that desk drawer and dumped the contents on the floor, rummaging for that booklet. He found it, read it, and repented and believed. I mentioned as a seventh benefit of a good gospel booklet that it offers suggestions for Christian growth. Phil got to the end of the booklet and read, "What now? You should go to a church where the Bible is preached and where Christ in honored."

So Phil got out the Yellow Pages (the way we found churches before the internet) and began searching. He was quickly overwhelmed with the number of options for churches in the Fort Worth area. Finally he saw a church located not far from his house, so he picked up the phone to dial the number. When the receptionist answered, Phil, still holding the booklet, asked her a question: "Is yours a church where the Bible is preached and where Christ is honored?" He said there was a long pause on the other end, and the receptionist finally said, "That really doesn't describe our church." She was an honest receptionist!

He went back to the Yellow Pages and continued his search and discovered an ad for a Bible church. He thought, *This church has "Bible" in its name, so surely they will fit the description.* When the receptionist answered, Phil asked her the question prompted by the booklet: "Is yours a church where the Bible is preached and where Christ is honored?"

"Absolutely," she replied. "That describes our church wonderfully. May I get your information so a couple of members from our church can stop by your home and tell you more about the church?"

So Phil ended up being baptized and joining the church in Fort Worth. A year later he was in a men's Sunday school class that was studying the book of Acts. When they discussed Acts 9, the teacher noted that he was aware of the conversion testimony of some of the twenty-five men in the class, but not all of them. He suggested they take the next two Sundays and hear each man's conversation story summarized in three to four minutes.

The first week half the men shared, and the second week it was Phil's turn. It so happened (providentially) there was a guest in the Sunday school class that day, a man named Bruce who worked with the Navigators. When Phil shared his testimony, he held up the booklet and said, "I have tried to call the number Tim wrote down for me, but the people who answered said they had never heard of him." (I had moved to Chicago over a year earlier and had changed phone numbers.) As Phil held up that booklet, Bruce said, "I know him! There can't be that many Tim Beoughers in the world!" So Bruce tracked down my new phone number for Phil, and one cold, snowy November night in Chicago, Phil called me to say, "Thank you! Thank you that even though I told you I wasn't interested, you still placed a gospel booklet in my hands. Even though it took four years, God used that booklet to bring me to faith in Christ. Christ has transformed my life!"

I hung up the phone that night and wept tears of joy. I was so grateful I had given Phil that booklet that day in the shoe store. But I also thought about other times where I could have given someone a gospel booklet and didn't do so. I recommitted myself to try to always leave someone with a booklet they can take and look over later.

GENERAL PRINCIPLES FOR USING AN EVANGELISTIC BOOKLET

You cannot share a booklet you do not have.

Carry gospel booklets with you wherever you go—in a pocket, wallet, briefcase, or purse. I keep gospel booklets in my hunting pack, golf bag, gym bag, and glove compartment of my car. I keep them with me all the time and always have one in my pocket. I know there are many times when I don't have the opportunity to have a full gospel conversation, but I have a chance to get started and to place a booklet in someone's hands.

Never give away a booklet you have not read.
The importance of this principle should be self-evident. We all know the expression, "You can't judge a book by its cover." You can't judge a booklet by its cover either. Cults, other religions, prosperity preachers, and other false teachers produce booklets. You want to make sure the booklet's content is biblically based and gospel centered. Don't give away a booklet until you have read it and you are sure that it is solid theologically.

Be enthusiastic about the contents when you give it away.
You can improve on these suggestions, but here are a few ideas to get you started:

- "The greatest love story the world has ever seen is explained in this booklet."
- "The material found in this booklet has changed my life, and I'd love to give it to you as a gift."
- "This little booklet summarizes the main message of the Bible. I'd love to give it to you to read and then discuss it with you."

Don't say something such as, "You know, I've been carrying this booklet around for a long time trying to find somebody to pawn it off on, and you look like a good prospect. Can I just dump this off on you and get rid of it?" That is less than enthusiastic!

Ask the person if you can explain the contents to them, and if they agree, take them through it one page at a time.
What do I mean by one page at a time? Fold over the booklet so you are focused on one panel, as opposed to having it open where there is a left- and right-hand page. Our natural human tendency is to not focus on what is in front of us but to be looking ahead. Folding the booklet over and covering one page at a time helps to ensure that you both are truly on the same page together.

In some cases you may want to give the person your name and phone number for future contact.

I have a wife and four daughters, plus a daughter-in-law who is just like a daughter. They all seek to be faithful gospel witnesses as they go through life. But when my wife is traveling, for example, and has an opportunity to share Christ with the man sitting beside her on the airplane, I don't really want her giving that man her contact information. But she can give him my contact information or our church name and number. At our church, we print a label with our church information and simply put it across the back of the booklet so that people can contact us if they have questions.

CONCLUSION

I know many Christians have given up on using gospel booklets because they have seen them misused or think perhaps they are not effective anymore. If you have been reluctant to use booklets in your witnessing for these or other reasons, I hope this chapter has changed your mind. Gospel booklets should not be the only tool in your evangelistic toolkit, but they should be one of the tools you utilize. Someone may come to faith on the spot after working through a gospel booklet (like Enos), or it may be six months later (like William)—or even four years later (like Phil). The gospel is the power of God unto salvation, and one means of getting that good news into the hands of unbelievers is through the use of gospel booklets.

CHAPTER 16

PERSONAL TESTIMONY

SHARING YOUR CONVERSION TESTIMONY is another tool in your toolbox to share your faith. A personal testimony is just you telling the story of how you became a Christian and what Christ has done in your life since then. Criticism of this approach often stems from the testimony focusing a great deal on the person and very little on Christ. However, one's conversion testimony serves as a helpful tool as long as the gospel is clearly communicated in the testimony.

THE VALUE OF A PERSONAL TESTIMONY

Why utilize this approach? What value does it have? I would like to suggest three reasons why using a personal testimony is valuable.

It has a high degree of human interest.

I have never subscribed to *Reader's Digest*, but whenever I see my doctor or dentist, I usually can skim several issues while waiting on my appointment. Surveys have shown the most popular section in *Reader's Digest* is "Drama in Real Life." Those stories about human drama captivate our interest. We as human beings are fascinated by other people's lives; we are interested in other people's stories. Sharing your personal testimony gives you an opportunity to use your life to talk about Christ's life, death, burial, and resurrection.

It is easy to share.

Why is it easy to share? It is easy to share because it is simply your story. You don't have to have memorized a detailed outline or multiple verses of Scripture to be able to share your personal testimony. In John 4:7–30, we find the account of Jesus's interaction with the Samaritan woman. After Jesus had a conversation with her where he exposed her sin and revealed himself as Messiah, this woman went back to her village. John 4:39 says, "Many Samaritans from that town believed in him because of the woman's testimony." Here is a woman that had not set foot on a seminary or Bible college campus, and who had not participated in any personal evangelism training at the local church. But she had encountered the Lord Jesus Christ and simply through testifying of what she knew many came to believe in him.

It helps others to be more willing to share their lives with you.

If you are transparent about your own struggles in life, it often leads others to be more vulnerable about their lives. When people meet me and find out that I am a pastor and a seminary professor, they often assume I have smooth sailing all the time and never have any challenges in life. Sharing points of pain in your life about your own struggles helps people to be more open.

Biblical Basis: Paul's Testimony

We see a clear biblical example of the use of a conversion testimony as a means of sharing the gospel in the life of the apostle Paul. Paul refers to his own spiritual pilgrimage three times (Acts 9, 22, and 26). He follows a basic pattern here that many use as a pattern for a testimony outline:

1. Paul's life before becoming a Christian (Acts 22:3–5; 26:4–11)

2. Paul becomes a Christian (Acts 22:7–16; 26:12–18)

3. Paul's life after becoming a Christian (Acts 9:19–22; 22:21; 26:19–20)

It is a very simple outline: my life before Christ, how I met Christ, and what Christ has done in my life since that time.

SPECIAL HELPS FOR THOSE WHO
BECAME CHRISTIANS AT AN EARLY AGE

I have had many believers tell me they really do not have a testimony, often because they came to Christ at an early age (and therefore do not have a "Damascus Road" type experience to share). Below are some helpful tips for those who came to Christ at an early age on how to share their testimony.

Realize that you do have a testimony.

When I was in college, I shared my conversion testimony one night at a gathering of students. My roommate told me later that he would never be asked to share his testimony because he did not really have one. He grew up with godly parents and came to Christ at the age of six. He said, "I'm sure I probably pushed my sister at some point in my young six-year-old life. I'm sure I lied about eating candy at some point to my parents. But I hadn't done anything really wild. I really have no testimony." I remember grabbing him by the shoulders and saying, "I wish I had your testimony. I wish I could have gone through my high school years being more concerned about what God thought about me than other people. I did things in high school that I didn't really want to do, things I knew were wrong, but because of peer pressure I did them because I loved the approval of men more than the approval of God. You were able to stand up against peer pressure because you knew Christ. What a great testimony!" If you came to Christ at an early age, celebrate that you do have a testimony!

Suggested areas on which to focus

Focus on your home, the people who influenced you, and your early Christian experience. Focus on your early understanding of what following Christ meant. You might not have even been able to pronounce, understand, or spell the words *justification* or *sanctification*, and yet you somehow knew that you were a sinner and that Christ was the only Savior, and you trusted him to save you from your sin. Share specific areas where Christ has made a difference in your life, such as being able to keep you from peer pressure. Your life after Christ in the outline will just be longer in your testimony than your life before Christ.

What if you do not remember the exact time of your conversion?

I heard a speaker ask once, "How can you meet the King of the universe and not remember when you meet him?" Another preacher/evangelist maintained that if you cannot remember the hour you first believed, then you are not a Christian. How should we respond to these assertions?

If people argue that you cannot possibly be spiritually alive unless you remember the moment of your spiritual birth, ask them if they remember the moment of their physical birth. The obvious answer, of course, is that none of us remember the moment of our physical birth. You can then tell them they cannot possibly be alive because they do not remember the moment of their physical birth. Their reply will be something like this: "But I am alive! I know I am alive because I manifest the signs of physical life!"

Scripture never encourages us to base our assurance of salvation on remembering the moment of our spiritual birth. Rather it encourages us to base our assurance first and foremost on the promises of God; second, on the inner witness of the Spirit; and third, on the evidences that Christ is present and working in our life—the fruit that we see and the change of direction in our life. Billy Graham's wife Ruth could not identify the hour she first believed. Ruth grew up on the mission field in China where her father, Nelson Bell, was a medical missionary. She knew she came to Christ as a young girl, but looking back, she could not pinpoint the exact date. In reflecting on her experience, she once quipped, "I don't know when the sun came up, but I know it's shining."

I trust that quote will be an encouragement to some of you that have been made to feel guilty about not knowing the specific time and day of your conversion. The key question is not, "Do you remember the hour you first believed?" but "Do you show the signs of spiritual life now?"

DO'S IN GIVING YOUR PERSONAL TESTIMONY

Begin your testimony with an attention-getting sentence.

Here are some examples of some attention-getting sentences:

- I used to think I really knew what was going on in life. Boy was I wrong!
- I used to be afraid of dying but not anymore.

- I grew up in a church but did not understand its purpose until a few years ago.
- I wasn't always this interested in Christian things. . . .

Beginning a testimony with a statement like one of these helps create interest in what you are going to say.

End your testimony with a response question.

Ending with a response question puts the ball back in their court and gives them something specific to which they can respond. Here are a few response questions I have found helpful:

- That is how I became a Christian. Does what I said make sense to you?
- Do you feel like you've come to know Christ in a personal way, or do you feel like you are still on the way?

Adjust your testimony so others can identify with you. Identify with weaknesses and needs as honestly as you can.

When I say adjust, I do not mean that you should change your testimony but that you should adjust it (to the degree you can) to better identify with the person. For example, I do not normally discuss fear of death in the opening of my testimony, but that was a component in pointing me to Christ. If the person I am talking with has a fear of death, I can adjust my testimony to that end.

Use Scripture! (2 Tim. 3:16–17; Heb. 4:12)

Scripture is the Word of God. It is living and active and more powerful than any two-edged sword. When I say to use Scripture, I do not mean you have to give the Scripture reference every time you mention a verse. But weave God's Word into your testimony.

Present Christ, not yourself.

Christ should be the focus of your testimony, not your deeds or misdeeds. Critics of the use of personal testimony in evangelism point to the fact that many people make themselves the central focus in their story. A good conversion testimony uses *your* story to tell *Christ's* story, the good news of the gospel message.

Stress the personal relationship you have with Christ.

Many people have "religion" but do not have a "relationship." Make sure you clearly indicate that what you are talking about is a relationship with Jesus rather than merely a set of rules to follow.

Don'ts in Giving Your Personal Testimony

Avoid using church and "Christian talk."

As Christians we often speak the language of "Christianese." We use words and phrases that make sense to other believers but that do not communicate with those outside the faith. For example, I heard the following testimony given by a man at a Sunday evening church service. In describing how he came to faith in Christ, this man said, "When the preacher gave the invitation, I was convicted. I stepped out into the aisle and was washed in the blood of the Lamb. I came forward and took the preacher's hand and was immediately seated with Christ in the heavenlies."

Did you understand what that man was saying? I do—it is a mixture of biblical phrases and church culture. However, imagine what an unbeliever might have been thinking when she heard these words:

> When the preacher gave the *invitation* (*It must have been to a party*) I was *convicted. (That must have been some party! I wonder how long he spent in jail!).* I stepped out into the *aisle. (Okay, I understand this one because they have aisles at football games).* I was *washed in the blood of the Lamb. (Why in the world was there a dead sheep in the aisle?)* I took the preacher's hand and was immediately seated with Christ in the heavenlies. *(That makes no sense at all to an unbeliever.)*

We have to be able to communicate deep spiritual truths in ways that unbelievers can understand them without using "Christianese."

Do not be too wordy.

Do not be too wordy as you share a conversion testimony. Three to four minutes is ideal. You will find it easier to share your testimony in thirty minutes than in three minutes, but the listening span for one-on-one interactions is approximately five minutes, not thirty.

Do not overemphasize how bad you used to be.

We have all heard dramatic testimonies with creative themes such as "From Crime to Christ," "From Marijuana to the Master," or "From the Bottle to the Bible." Sometimes in these testimonies people just glorify the sin in their life before Christ. Even though Paul did not write Romans 5:20 as a guide for how to structure our personal testimony, it does give us a helpful paradigm: "Where sin increased, grace abounded all the more." That is a great principle for sharing our testimonies. Do not have sin so abounding in your testimony that grace seems like an afterthought. Do not go into all the gory details and glorify sin. When we talk about our life before Christ, it ought to be with a broken heart.

Do not mention denominations, churches, or people in a derogatory manner.

Over the years I have heard many people share their testimony and begin by throwing a church or denomination under the bus because they did not hear the gospel there. What if the person you are sharing with is a member of that group, or his or her family has been a part of that denomination for generations? You have created a needless offense. If people stumble over the cross, so be it. Let us make sure we do not create a needless stumbling block.

Avoid giving the impression that the Christian life is a bed of roses, and you are perfect.

Paint an accurate picture. Christ said that we could have an abundant life, but he never promises that it would be easy. Avoid giving the impression that coming to Christ solves all your problems. Instead, emphasize that Christ is one who was tempted in all ways and yet did not sin, or that he is the comforter and the friend who gives you strength through the hard times.

Don't preach—share Christ.

Our testimony ought to be conversational and not preachy. In an evangelistic testimony, you want the focus to be on that person's response of repentance and faith. You may well have another opportunity to share an extended testimony of your life's spiritual pilgrimage with someone, but with an unbeliever, keep a laser-like focus on the gospel.

CHAPTER 17

EVANGELISTIC BIBLE STUDIES

EVANGELISTIC BIBLE STUDIES are another helpful resource for our evangelistic toolbox. They provide a setting for people to see firsthand what the Bible teaches, to examine the claims of Christ, and to explore the gospel. Some people might never attend a church, but they might participate in a small-group Bible study. The field that is white for harvest could well be the homes or apartments right around where you live or the co-workers in your office.

An evangelistic Bible study, composed of believers and nonbelievers, meets to discuss in an open and nonthreatening way the claims of Jesus Christ. The goal of an evangelistic Bible study is to present the gospel message and give the unbeliever an opportunity to discover for him- or herself the person and work of Jesus Christ. The facilitator of these studies seeks to guide the discussion to focus on our need for a personal relationship with Jesus Christ. This type of Bible study is not intended to produce a deep discussion on the finer points of doctrine but to clearly communicate the good news of what God has done for us in Christ.

Increasing numbers of people in our society seem to have concluded that the church is out of touch with real life and, therefore, have no desire to ever enter the doors of a church. Even those individuals who are searching spiritually may feel threatened to show up for a worship service at a strange church about which they know nothing. Those of us who have been in church for years may forget how intimidating it can be to attend for the first time.

A small-group evangelistic Bible study provides an informal atmosphere and encourages openness and discussion. Meeting in a small group usually fosters relationships with neighbors or with coworkers. The care and concern shown in a Bible study can provide a marked contrast to the hustle and bustle of life or to the challenges and stresses of the workplace. An evangelistic Bible study takes the gospel message to unbelievers in a format that encourages them to be open and expectant about the material.

When I was a resident advisor in my dormitory in college, I held evangelistic Bible studies in my dorm room using material developed by the Navigators, a parachurch ministry that focuses on evangelism and disciple-making. Using the Navigators' inductive bible study on the Gospel of John, I had the privilege of seeing several men on my dorm floor come to Christ as they encountered him in the pages of Scripture. Subsequently, I have utilized material produced by Neighborhood Home Bible Studies[1] out of Illinois and *Christianity Explored* material from All Souls Church in London (an inductive study through the Gospel of Mark).[2] I also developed an "Overview of the Bible" study (five sessions) and have seen several neighbors come to faith in Christ.

A variety of formats can be used to do evangelistic Bible studies. You can do a study in a one-on-one format where you read Scripture and ask questions about the text's meaning and its personal application for today. I used this format to walk through the Gospel of Mark with an acquaintance during a weekly lunch meeting. After four months, my acquaintance had become a dear friend and brother in Christ. You could offer a potluck meal each month at your office or in your neighborhood to facilitate relationships/friendships and then do a study on the person of Jesus. Or you could offer an evangelistic Bible study for inquirers after a sermon series or a special event.

Keep in mind that those who come to your study do not need to have any prior theological commitments. You simply are inviting them to explore the person of Jesus Christ and the claims of Christianity. You are

---

1. Neighborhood Home Bible Studies has transitioned into a ministry called "QPlace," symbolizing a safe place to ask spiritual questions and receive answers. For more information, visit www.qplace.com.
2. See christianityexplored.org for more information

giving them an opportunity to look for themselves at the primary source material for facts about Jesus.

Leading an Evangelistic Bible Study

The following are several tips for leading an evangelistic Bible Study.

Pray for the study.

Prayer is the foundation for all evangelism. All forms of evangelism involve spiritual warfare. Pray for those whom you invite by name. Pray that God will open hearts to the gospel. Enlist prayer partners who will pray regularly for the study as it progresses.

Do not let fear prevent you from starting.

Bob Jacks observes, "I, and everybody I have worked with in Bible studies, have been gripped with fear in launching a new group. But the new groups were started because of a willingness to walk by faith, regardless of the fear. It takes someone with a burden for people that's bigger than his fear."[3]

Organize the study.

If possible, try to get at least one person/couple to open their home, one person/couple to lead the study, and someone to organize refreshments. You can decide whether you want a coleader or not, but it is wise to have a small team involved with you.

Decide whom to invite.

The study will be focused on seekers and non-believers. Think through neighbors, coworkers, and friends. Ask the Lord to reveal whom you should invite. Then invite them! Be upfront that you are having a Bible study. Do not bait-and-switch people into agreeing to study the Bible. Be clear in your invitation that it is a study designed to see what the Bible has to say about God and Jesus.

---

3. Bob and Betty Jacks, *Your Home a Lighthouse* (Colorado Springs: NavPress, 1989), 30–31.

Include questions in the invitation such as: Have you ever considered the claims of Jesus? Do you know the main themes of the Bible? Invite them to explore the Christian faith firsthand in a low-pressure environment. Stress that you are not forcing them to believe anything but to examine the Christian faith for themselves. Make sure the invitation is attractive but clear. Specify the place, date, time, length of study, topic for discussion, childcare (if applicable), and who will be leading the study.

Prepare your home.

Think through any distractions that could interrupt—keep the pets outside or in another room, silence cell phones, and look around for other possible distractions. Arrange seating for everyone, and have water, tea, or coffee to offer as guests arrive. This preparation will help settle the inevitable awkwardness as people get to know one another. Prepare (or enlist someone else to prepare) refreshments to serve after the study to allow time for informal visiting.

Set a clear beginning and ending time.

Make sure the times are clear, and then follow them by starting and ending on time. Show your sensitivity to everyone's schedule. One of the fears people might have about agreeing to a Bible study is that the study session will last too long. Start and end on time.

Determine the length of the study.

In addition to communicating the time frame for each study, let people know the duration of the study. Will it be four weeks? Six weeks? Eight weeks? People are more willing to commit to something if they know the schedule up front.

Share ground rules.

Remind people that the goal of the study is to let the Bible speak for itself. The goal of the study is to understand what the Bible teaches, not to mandate that everyone agree with that teaching. We want to make sure we understand what the Bible is teaching us about God, ourselves, Christ, and salvation. Also communicate that no one will be put on the spot or required to speak unless they want to do so. Emphasize this study will follow a discussion format, not a strict lecture format.

Provide copies of the Bible.

Use a translation that is easy to understand. When you refer to Scripture passages, it can be helpful to use page numbers of the copies of Scripture you provide to prevent guests from feeling embarassed because they cannot find the book of Leviticus. Do not call on people by name to read out loud or to answer questions. Instead, ask for volunteers to read.

Choose a study that focuses on the gospel.

I have taught studies from the Gospel of John (it presents clearly the claims of Jesus) and from the Gospel of Mark (a Gospel written to Gentiles and therefore devoid of many of the Jewish practices found in the Gospel of John). The "Overview of the Bible" study that I wrote begins in Genesis and highlights God's redemptive story throughout the Old and New Testaments.

Ask questions.

Help people discover truth for themselves. Encourage questions from the group, but do not always be quick to answer them. Refer questions back to the group. Do not be intimidated by silence. Questions to ask could be:

- What can we learn about God or Jesus from this passage?
- What can we learn about humankind from this passage?
- What is the setting, and who are the characters?
- What is happening in the story?
- What do you think the passage is saying?
- How does this teaching apply to us today?

Observe general principles for small group leaders.

- Maintain eye contact. Look at the person who is speaking to help him/her feel accepted and that what he/she has to say is of value.
- Always affirm questions the person may have. Never embarrass anyone by criticizing a question or comment. A helpful phrase I have used often is, "That is an interesting observation. Where in the passage do you find that?"
- Be humble. If you are asked a question and do not know the answer, tell them you will research it and answer it at another time. If you are

asked a question that moves the discussion totally off the subject, seek
to postpone it, and say you will return to it later.

- Do not criticize other churches or denominations, as that criticism
  may create unnecessary stumbling blocks. If someone stumbles, we
  want it to be over the cross, not over us criticizing a church or denomination they hold in high regard.
- Never argue; the group's purpose is to discuss, not to debate. Winning an argument may offend or alienate the guest. You should not
  agree with wrong views, but try to keep the discussion moving. Always point the discussion back to the text.
- If someone tends to dominate the discussion time, you may need to
  talk to him/her privately and encourage him/her to allow others more
  of an opportunity to participate.

Summarize the main points at the end of the study.

End with application and/or thought-provoking questions. When you
begin the next study, review what was covered during the previous study
to bring everyone up to speed.

Make yourself available.

Offer to meet with participants at other times to answer any questions, or just to strengthen the relationship you have with the other person.
People are typically more open to share questions/concerns/doubts one-
to-one than in a small group.

"Overview of the Bible" study

As mentioned earlier, I developed an overview of the Bible study for
an evangelistic Bible study we had in our neighborhood in Geneva, Illinois. We had been planning a neighborhood evangelistic Bible study using
already existing materials, but a conversation with one of my neighbors
caused us to change directions. When I asked one of our neighbors if he
and his wife would be interested in coming to a neighborhood Bible study
in our home, his response was swift and decisive: "No way. Not a chance."
When I inquired as to why, he told me it had nothing to do with Sharon or
me (he said he and his wife loved and respected us). He said he would not
come because he did not know *anything* about the Bible and did not want
to appear stupid and uninformed in front of all the neighbors.

When I floated the idea of a study that would be an overview of the Bible containing material such as how we got our Bible, why there is an Old Testament and a New Testament, why there are sixty-six books, why are there so many different translations, and so on, his eyes lit up. "We would come to a study like that," he exclaimed. "In fact, my company just mandated that all of us in management positions have to take some kind of continuing education course each year for personal growth. I can use this study for that!"

Here were the elements in the invitation letter we delivered to all eighty-six homes in our neighborhood:

> Does the Bible sometimes seem like a large or intimidating book? Or have you read parts of it, but feel your understanding is incomplete on how all the pieces fit together? Then this five-part "Overview of the Bible" is just right for you. We'll look at the main events of the Bible in chronological order and examine a handful of major themes that appear throughout the Old and New Testaments. Valuable overview charts and other handouts will be provided for notetaking and future reference.
>
> The study will be taught by Tim Beougher, who is a professor at Wheaton Graduate School. Each session will last about ninety minutes, allowing time for questions. The study is not designed to promote one particular point of view but to allow us to examine the world's all-time bestselling book for ourselves. No prior Bible knowledge is necessary; we are all here to learn. No one will be put on the spot or asked to contribute opinions unless they want to. You are welcome to bring a Bible, or we will have extra copies here for your use.

You can see in the invitation that we tried to anticipate questions/objections that might come up in the minds of our neighbors. We rejoiced when thirteen of our unbelieving neighbors agreed to participate in the study, and we rejoiced even more when eight placed their faith in Christ as a result of the study.

The five sessions were developed as follows:

1. Creation through Abraham
2. Abraham through "the wanderings"
3. Joshua through the end of the Old Testament

4. The New Testament life of Christ
5. Acts through Revelation

As we progressed through the Bible, beginning in Genesis, we asked, "Who is God, and what is he like?"; "Who are we as human beings, and what is our greatest need?"; "How has a gracious God made provision for sinful human beings to be reconciled to himself?"; and "What is our necessary response to God's provision?" In examining the sacrificial system over and over again throughout the Old Testament, we emphasized that because of our sin, we need atonement, a covering for sin in order to be reconciled to God. When we got to the New Testament and discussed Christ's crucifixion, I asked the question of the group, "Why was it necessary that Christ shed his blood?" In unison all thirteen of our neighbors replied, "Because without the shedding of blood there is no forgiveness of sin." The study was the most evangelistic Bible study I have ever led because we stuck to the key themes of creation, fall, redemption, and consummation.

Conclusion

Remember the goal of an evangelistic Bible study is to introduce people to Christ. Pray that seekers meet Christ and become his disciples. I recently received the following email from a student who began an "Overview of the Bible" study at his office (the study was held over the lunch hour and was completely voluntary):

> I wanted you to know that I'm on my third seven-week study that stemmed from your Personal Evangelism class. It all started in my office with five people last fall. I used (clearly stole) your Overview of the Bible outline. Two in attendance had never done a Bible study before. One hadn't touched a Bible in fifty years. One gentleman had never touched a Bible. We are now up to ten attending. Thank you for encouragement to do so. We jump into the Gospels next Tuesday!

Committing to invite neighbors or colleagues at work to an evangelistic Bible study is a step of faith. Take encouragement from the following admonition by James Nyquist and Jack Kuhatschek:

Leading a Bible discussion can be an enjoyable and rewarding experience. But it can also be *scary*, especially if you've never done it before. If this is your feeling, you're in good company. When God asked Moses to lead the Israelites out of Egypt, he replied, "O Lord, please send someone else to do it!" (Ex. 4:13) . . .

The list goes on. The apostles were "unschooled, ordinary men" (Acts 4:13). Timothy was young, frail, and frightened. Paul's "thorn in the flesh" made him feel weak. But God's response to all of his servants—including you—is essentially the same: "My grace is sufficient for you" (2 Cor. 12:9). Relax. God helped these people in spite of their weaknesses, and he can help you in spite of your feelings of inadequacy.[4]

His power truly is perfected in our weakness.

---

4. James F. Nyquist and Jack Kuhatschek, *Leading Bible Discussions* (Downers Grove, IL: InterVarsity: 1985), 5.

CHAPTER 18

GOSPEL APPOINTMENTS

ONE OF THE BEST WAYS TO HAVE GOSPEL CONVERSATIONS is to *plan* for them by actually *scheduling* them! We schedule other important events in our life, making sure we write them down on our calendar or type them into a reminder app on our phone. We create time in our schedule for all kinds of things: work, exercise, eating, and recreation. But we somehow rarely seem to schedule any time for evangelism. Why not schedule one of the most important things we can do in life: sharing the good news of Jesus Christ with others?

Paul Worcester serves as National Collegiate Evangelism Director for the North American Mission Board of the Southern Baptist Convention. Prior to that role, he led Christian Challenge, an evangelism and discipleship ministry to college students, at Chico State University in California. He has developed an approach called "Gospel Appointments," which is reproduced below.[1] While launched and fine-tuned in a university setting, this approach can be used anywhere with anyone.

---

1. Paul Worcester, "How Do I Set Up a Gospel Appointment?" www.GospelAppoint ments.com. Used by permission.

Benefits of Gospel Appointments

Worcester notes, "Gospel appointments are one of the most effective ways to share the gospel because they are intentional and relational. Gospel appointments are intentional because you are clearly explaining the good news and giving them a chance to respond to Christ. They are highly relational because you are building trust with someone by spending time with them." He lists several benefits to this approach.

- *They are simple to set up.* All you need to do is ask the person to join you for lunch or for a cup of coffee.
- *They are an ideal setting to get to know someone.* You display care and build trust when you spend time with people, getting to know who they are as individuals.
- *They minimize distractions that often arise when sharing Jesus in other settings.*
- *They show a person that you sincerely care as you discover their story and share your story.* At the beginning of the meeting, focus on getting to know the person as an individual. Then you can ask them about their spiritual background, leading very naturally to you having the opportunity to share your experience with God.
- *They emphasize the importance of this good news*! When you meet with someone about a particular topic it demonstrates that it is worth the time investment.
- *They provide time to share a complete gospel presentation.* They also provide time to confirm that the presentation has been understood, as well as time for questions and discussion about each point.
- *They lead naturally into follow-up meetings or friendship evangelism.*
- *Anyone can be trained to do a Gospel Appointment*! All you need to be able to do is invite someone to meet for a meal or coffee, listen to someone's story, and know how to share a simple gospel presentation. Worcester notes there is spiritual power when the gospel is shared with people, and says he has never seen anyone offended by someone initiating a gospel appointment.

How to Set up a Gospel Appointment

1. *Start a conversation with a non-Christian or someone you are not 100% sure where they are at spiritually and talk about any topic you want.* Follow the F.I.R.E. acrostic: Find common ground; Interests; Relationships; Experience with spiritual things.
2. Take advantage of any opportunity to *identify with Christ.* This can be something like "I just got back from a fun trip that helped my relationship with God" or "I heard the most amazing message in church yesterday!" Don't worry about the exact words—just say something! Something is better than nothing.
3. *Ask them a quick spiritual question,* like "Do you have any interest in spiritual things?" or "Did you grow up going to church or anything like that?" (See chapter 15 in this book on "Bridges to the Gospel" for other helpful questions).
4. *Try to set up a meeting.* No matter how they answer, you can follow it up with something like, "That's interesting. Hey, I have been learning some pretty helpful things about having a relationship with God. Maybe we could get together sometime for lunch or coffee and talk more about this?" After you ask this question, be quiet and wait for them to respond. If they say yes, try to set it up right then and figure out a time to meet. If they can't think of a time off the top of their head just say, "OK, I will call or text you sometime later and we can set it up."
5. *Go back to a casual conversation and just hang out with them.* Maybe something like, "So what are your plans for this weekend?"

What to Do After You Have Scheduled a Gospel Appointment

1. *Pray like crazy*! Pray for an open, receptive heart for your friend. Pray you will have boldness and clarity of speech as you share. Recruit other believers to pray for you before and during your meeting.
2. *Make sure to confirm the meeting time and location that day through a phone call or text message.*

3. *Bring your gospel lesson or whatever you need to share the good news with them.* Bring a pen, paper, Bible, or booklet. It might be good to also bring an extra Bible you can give them just in case they don't have one

4. *Start by talking casually and building a relationship with the person,* but jump in pretty quickly talking about deeper things such as family and upbringing. Then walk through the three-story outline:

   » *Their Story:* Ask them to share their story about their experience with spiritual things as soon as possible. Just say something like, "So what's your background when it comes to spiritual things?" Most people have something to share.
   » *Your Story:* Share your testimony briefly.
   » *God's Story:* Introduce the Bible lesson or illustration. You can say, "I would love to share with you from the Bible how we can have a personal relationship with God" or "I have this illustration that explains the big story of God. . . ."

5. *Pull out the gospel lesson and just read it with them.*[2] Make sure to sit close enough that both of you can comfortably see it. You don't need to add a lot to it. Simply take them through the lesson or illustration to communicate the good news of what God has done for us in Christ.

6. *Make the invitation clear.* If your gospel presentation includes a sample prayer of commitment, ask them, "Why don't you read this prayer? Don't pray it yet. Just read it and see if it reflects the desire of your heart." Wait and give them time to read it and think about it. Then ask, "Would you like to commit your life to Christ right now?"

7. *If they say "no," respectfully ask what is keeping them from making this commitment.* Don't be pushy or try to force a response. Continue to cultivate the relationship. Ask if they would like to do an investigative study through the Gospel of John or the Gospel of Mark to study the life of Jesus firsthand.

8. *If they say "yes" to Christ, show your excitement and lead them to pray to God out loud, based on the sample prayer.* Encourage them to make it their own prayer, because it is not magic words but the attitude of

---

2. Worcester provides a sample gospel presentation at https://www.challengecsuc.com/assets/pdfs/gospel-(updated).pdf.

their heart. I usually open in prayer thanking God for our time and then ask them to pray to God out loud.

9. *Celebrate and set up a follow-up meeting.* Tell them this is the most important decision of their lives. Then say, "This was fun. There are some other things like this that we could look at if you want to start meeting. Does this same time next week work for you?" Make sure you have a time to meet again before you leave. Thank and praise God.

CONCLUSION

We schedule and make time for important events in our life. Why not adopt this approach when it comes to sharing our faith, and schedule a gospel appointment with a family member, relative, friend, neighbor, classmate, work associate, or acquaintance? Paul Worcester maintains, "If I had to choose just one evangelistic tool to use for the rest of my life I would immediately choose gospel appointments. They are by far the most liberating evangelistic tool I have ever discovered."[3]

---

3. Paul Worcester, "Gospel Appointments, Part 1," *Collegiate Collective* (blog), September 22, 2014, http://collegiatecollective.com/gospel-appointments-part-1/#.XYPTSyV7njB.

CHAPTER 19

SERVANT EVANGELISM

THE GOAL OF EVERY-MEMBER MOBILIZATION

WHAT IS THE GOAL OF BELIEVERS sharing their faith? I would argue it is "every-member mobilization." The Great Commission commands every believer to evangelize. Every believer needs to know the gospel, be equipped in how to communicate the gospel, and then share it on a regular basis. Unfortunately, in most churches, people are still in process toward that goal. People are not interested in evangelism for a variety of reasons. Some have had a bad experience in evangelism and therefore avoid it completely. My mother (who died of cancer several years ago) was deathly afraid of water. When our kids would go swimming at the swimming pool, she would sit on the bench and never get in the water. She had what to others seemed like an irrational fear of water. However, it was not irrational to her because when she was in high school, she almost drowned.

I have known people deathly afraid of evangelism because they had a similar experience with evangelism. One friend of mine was taken out witnessing the day he made his profession of faith in his church. He was asked to share his testimony (he was not even sure what that word meant) and his favorite verse of Scripture (he did not even have John 3:16 memorized yet). This experience so embarrassed him he spent decades running from evangelism and any type of evangelism training.

My friend reluctantly agreed to participate in a servant evangelism project (handing out lightbulbs in a neighborhood). Having a positive experience in this "entry-level" approach transformed his views on evangelism. He now actively and joyously shares his faith with others. While I am not guaranteeing this type of transformation in the life of everyone who participates in a servant evangelism project, I have seen it happen over and over again. Servant evangelism is an excellent starting point for people who have never shared their faith or who have been burned by a bad experience.

What Is Servant Evangelism?

Servant evangelism is intentionally sharing Christ by modeling biblical servanthood. The concept of servant evangelism was popularized by Steve Sjogren's book *Conspiracy of Kindness*.[1] Sjogren shares how their church grew by reaching out through servant evangelism projects: going out to meet the needs of people in their community and serving in the Lord's name. Servant evangelism is more than just service. The Peace Corps does acts of service, but they do not do them in Jesus's name. Servant evangelism is the joining together of service and a gospel witness. Servant evangelism is sharing the love of God in a practical way, combining simple acts of kindness with pointing people to Christ. In servant evangelism, the love of Christ is seen and felt as well as heard. It is not social ministry but evangelism.

Who Is Involved in Servant Evangelism?

The beauty of servant evangelism is that anyone can be involved! You do not need a lot of training or preparation before going out. Church activities often separate family members (children, youth, women, men), but servant evangelism projects can be done by families. Projects also can be done by Sunday school classes or small groups as a way for the group to minister together outside the walls of the church.

Servant evangelism also involves those to whom we minister. As you get out in your neighborhoods, you will discover people who are lost,

---

1. Steve Sjogren, *Conspiracy of Kindness* (Ann Arbor, MI: Vine, 1993).

confused, and hurting. Servant evangelism sometimes provides an opportunity for deeper witness and reaping of an evangelistic harvest, but it often serves as a way to plant seeds.

WHEN CAN BELIEVERS DO SERVANT EVANGELISM?

Part of the beauty of servant evangelism is that it can be done anytime. If you want to do a Christmas outreach, obviously you would do it in December. If you want an Easter outreach, then spring would obviously be the best time. While some servant evangelism projects are calendar specific (shoveling snow in the winter or raking leaves in the fall), many projects can be implemented during any month of the year.

WHERE SHOULD SERVANT EVANGELISM PROJECTS TAKE PLACE?

While it is certainly not wrong to host some type of servant evangelism project on your church campus, I believe it is far better to get out into the neighborhoods where people live. It is usually preferable to meet people on their turf. When we ask people to come to our church property to receive something, they may hear us saying, "If you come to us, we will serve you." Jesus tells us to "go out into the highways and along the hedges, and compel them to come in" (Luke 14:23).

For example, in one church where I pastored, I challenged our youth to begin reaching out and to choose a servant evangelism project. They decided they wanted to serve the community by providing a free car wash at the church. But rather than making people from the community come to us, they had it at a local store parking lot that allowed nonprofits to use their facilities. When they had the car wash, people would ask, "How much is it?" When told it was free, they would always ask why. The youth then responded, "Just as our cars get dirty and need to be washed, in a much greater way our lives are dirty because of sin and need to be cleansed. The Bible emphasizes that only Jesus can cleanse us from the sins in our life. We are doing this free car wash to remind people of Jesus's sacrifice for sin." They washed about forty cars and planted many seeds for the gospel.

Why Do Servant Evangelism?

We are following the example of Christ when we serve.

Jesus said, "The Son of Man did not come to be served, but to serve, and to give His life a ransom for many" (Matt. 20:28). When we serve others, we are following our Lord's example.

We will encounter receptive people.

Jesus told the disciples in John 4:35 to "lift up your eyes and look on the fields, that they are white for harvest." As you go through a neighborhood knocking on doors, you will encounter receptive people. At one church where I served, we provided free leaf raking for neighborhood families. We merely said, "We as a church want to serve our community and show the love of Christ in a practical way."

Those who could not rake leaves brought their rakes to borrow, or donated lawn garbage bags. Others offered to babysit children during the project so parents could go out and rake leaves or simply come be part of a prayer team to pray for those going out. On this occasion, one team came to a house where a man was out in the yard raking leaves. He had a huge yard and was barely making a dent. The team offered to rake the leaves for him, and he declined, saying that he could not afford it. It took a few minutes for him to comprehend that they were offering to do it for free. His wife had wanted their family to go to the zoo for a rare family day, but he had told her that he had to rake leaves. They finally convinced him to take his family to the zoo, and they would rake his yard for him. The family came home to a yard completely free of leaves, with bags piled up at the curb several feet high. This family showed up at the church the next day to say thank you. I arranged a visit in their home on Tuesday evening that week, and two weeks later I had the privilege of baptizing the couple. They were receptive to a gospel witness from me because of how our church had served them.

It is easy to do.

Servant evangelism is easy to do since it simply involves going out and lovingly serving people. Participants do not have to memorize forty verses of Scripture or go through sixteen weeks of witnessing class training to be able to go out and say, "Our church is out seeking to show the love of Christ in a practical way."

It doesn't require a lot of time or money.

Most servant evangelism projects do not require a lot of time or money. How can you impact a community for Christ when you don't have a large budget line item for outreach? Most servant evangelism projects require a minimal investment of time and money, with many of them simply utilizing "sweat equity."

It can involve everyone.

Someone does not have to be an extrovert to participate in servant evangelism. Anyone can hand out a light bulb or rake leaves. It also allows families to serve together and partner in the gospel.

It can overcome stereotypes.

Servant evangelism overcomes the negative stereotypes some people have about Christians. When a pastor knocks on someone's door, it is often assumed that the pastor is after money. Servant evangelism totally flips that narrative. When we go out, we communicate that we are not there for money. We want to show the love of Christ in a practical way by serving.

Servant evangelism projects also help overcome negative stereotypes Christians have about neighborhood outreach. Some believers fear that if they ever knocked on someone's door on behalf of Christ and the church, they would be ridiculed, berated, and perhaps thrown off the front porch. Yet most people respond respectfully when approached via servant evangelism.

Servant Evangelism Projects

A goldmine of ideas for servant evangelism can be found online.[2] I will mention a few projects below, but go to the online article to gain more ideas.

Light Bulb Distribution

Everyone needs light bulbs. My wife and I recently reached out in a neighborhood near our church. Here was our script: "Hi, my name is Tim Beougher and this is my wife, Sharon. We are from West Broadway

---

2. Steve Sjogren, "94 Servant Evngelism Ideas for Your Church," https://www.stevesjogren.com/94-servant-evangelism-ideas-for-your-church.

Baptist Church just across the road here, and we are in the neighborhood handing out free light bulbs today to remind people that Jesus is
the light of the world." We went to a hundred homes, found sixty-three
people home, and handed out more than fifty light bulbs (and a packet of
information about our church).

A few people did not want the free light bulb. One conversation involved a woman who declined the light bulb, explaining she was Jewish.
I responded, "Well, this isn't a Christian light bulb; this is just a regular
GE light bulb. Do you use light bulbs?" She smiled and accepted it, and we
ended up having a great conversation. This type of outreach seeks to build
a relationship of trust between the church and her neighbors.

At another church we did light bulb distribution in a rather affluent
neighborhood, handing out several hundred free lightbulbs. A year and a
half later we had a family from that neighborhood who visited our church.
When filling out a guest information card asking how they found out
about our church, this family wrote, "We received a light bulb." This light-
bulb distribution had taken place eighteen months earlier. The family had
experienced two major crises the previous week, and they decided to attend a church on Sunday. (In this case the adage proved true: "There are no
atheists in foxholes.") There were dozens of churches within a brief drive
of their house, and yet they chose to go to "the light bulb church." A few
weeks later the whole family placed their trust in Christ for salvation.

Now, how did all of that happen? It all happened because one of the
members of our church knocked on their door a year and a half earlier and
handed them a light bulb. There did not appear to be any immediate fruit
from that servant evangelism project. But a year and a half later an entire
family met Christ because of that project.

Laundromat

Another example concerns a woman who was doing her laundry at the
closest laundromat and observed a family having to spend their meager resources on washing clothes even though their children were hungry. This
woman began a servant evangelism project through her church where
every Monday night, she showed up with a bucket of quarters and offered
to pay for people's laundry. When people asked why she was doing that,
she would respond that just as our clothes get dirty and need to be washed,
in a much greater way the Bible says that our lives are dirty because of sin.

There is only one way to have our sins washed away, and that is through the Lord Jesus Christ. Every Monday night people from the community would show up, and church members would pay for their laundry, feed them (potluck), and share God's Word with them. A church was planted in that neighborhood out of the simple act of seeing a need and seeking to meet it through servant evangelism.

Christmas Gift Wrapping

At Christmastime, many malls will have a kiosk that will wrap your newly purchased Christmas gifts—for a price. One church member noticed one December that her mall no longer provided that service and suggested the church might be able to meet a need. So the church rented a kiosk and put up banners declaring "Free Christmas Gift Wrapping." When asked why they would wrap presents for free when most mall kiosks charged for the service, the response was, "We are doing this service to remind people Jesus is the reason for the season." Many people heard the good news of great joy at Christmastime through this simple servant evangelism project.

Free Water Bottles

We did a servant evangelism project by going to the local jogging trail where there was a three-mile stretch with no water. We set up a booth to give away free water. That led to many conversations about how we wanted to share the love of Christ in a practical way and how Jesus is the living water. We had our church logo and information on the water bottles, and for the next several months, we would have people who would show up at church because they were handed a bottle of water as they were out walking in the heat.

REMINDERS BEFORE GOING OUT

Trust that God has prepared the way.

When you go out to knock on a door, remember the Holy Spirit has already gone before you. You are not going out alone, so trust that God has prepared the way.

Be sensitive to people.

Your goal is not to force a conversation. Your goal is not the "hardcore salesman approach" where as soon as they crack open the door, you jam your foot in the opening so the door cannot shut all the way until you can make your sales pitch. The goal is simply to be friendly and neighborly. Two men who went out on light bulb distribution in a neighborhood returned two hours later apologizing that they had only made it to one home. They explained they spent the full two hours listening, reading Scripture, and praying with a man who was grieving the loss of his wife. Yet their morning was a resounding success. They found a need, and they helped meet that need. As you go out, be sensitive to people. What God has planned may be different than what you have planned.

Trust God to use you in people's lives.

In another church where I served as interim pastor, I led the youth on a servant evangelism project, something I called a "mystery missions project." I told the young people I would buy them ice cream if they completed the project. When they arrived at the church on Friday evening to receive instructions about the project, I explained the concept of servant evangelism. I told them their "mystery missions project" for the evening was to do a servant evangelism project for area gas stations: offering to clean their toilets.

The leader among the youth was a young man nicknamed Kev, who was more rebellious than he was spiritual. He immediately protested, "We can't do that! We don't know how to clean toilets!" I had anticipated that response, so I took the youth to the basement restroom in the church and demonstrated how to clean a toilet. "Are you really going to make us clean toilets?" one youth asked. I told them I was not going to make them do anything, but if they wanted ice cream later, they needed to go out and clean toilets.

While at one gas station, an elderly couple pulled up with a flat tire. They had been driving and sensed the tire was going flat and had prayed that God would get them to a gas station where someone could help them put on the spare tire. Since it was not a full-service gas station, the attendant said he could not help them, but Kev offered to change the tire. As he was changing the tire, the elderly man said to Kev, "You are an answer to prayer! You are an angel!" When Kev showed up for ice cream that night, he came over to me, grabbed me in a bear hug, and soaked my shirt with his tears. He said, "I have never seen God use me before. I want to get right with God." God used this servant evangelism project to bring a rebellious prodigal back to himself.

CONCLUSION

Some people criticize servant evangelism because it seems heavy on service and light on actual evangelism. But as long as a verbal witness is shared alongside loving acts of service, it is evangelism! It is true that in some cases it might more closely approximate pre-evangelism than evangelism (because the full gospel message is not shared). Yet people have come to Christ both directly and indirectly through the witness given in servant evangelism projects. Furthermore, many Christians have discovered that servant evangelism provided an excellent starting point for them in cultivating a lifestyle of witness.

CHAPTER 20

EVANGELISM AND THE INTERNET/SOCIAL MEDIA

WHEN SOMEONE TESTIFIES, "I came to know Christ through social media," we are reminded of the incredible impact electronic communication can have in our world. Social media has become a key means of communication in our culture. With a few quick keystrokes, any immediate thought or response can be transported to the world instantly. Social media creates possibilities to share the gospel with masses of people. The internet provides a means for the gospel message to penetrate even unreached people groups.

Witnessing the reach of technology should motivate us to strategize the possibilities of using the internet to share the gospel. Ron Haggerty, from The Orleans Marketing Group, highlights some fascinating facts about technology, including:

- More than 40 percent of the world's population uses the internet.
- More than eight billion devices are connected as of 2020.
- More than 570 new websites are created every minute.
- More than 500 million tweets are sent every day.
- Facebook has more than two billion active users.[1]

---

1. Ron Haggerty, "35 Technology Facts and Stats," Orleans Marketing Group, January 12, 2018, https://orleansmarketing.com/35-technology-facts-stats.

These facts challenge us to consider how to use the internet effectively for the Great Commission.

The Christian Broadcasting Network highlights the internet as an important tool for outreach. When Jesus told his followers to preach the gospel, "the disciples were on foot. There was no television, no radio, no airplanes, and certainly no internet. What a difference two thousand years can make! Or for that matter, ten years. Today, more and more people are coming to faith in Christ by logging onto the World Wide Web."[2] Craig von Buseck declares that pornography is the number-one searched topic on the internet, but religion is second. When asked how important the internet is in terms of reaching the world for Christ, he replied, "Right now more than one billion people are online, and what that means to us today is that any Christian who can log onto a computer can reach 1/6 of the world's population from their dining room table."[3]

Using social media to share the gospel involves more than citing Bible verses in the midst of other posts. Believers still should seek to build rapport with the persons with whom they are sharing, using many of the same principles found in relational evangelism. The difference is that they are using electronic means to apply these principles.

For many individuals, the internet and social media have taken the place of seeking wisdom from parents, teachers, pastors, and other authority figures. For example, when exhibiting symptoms of an illness, the internet becomes the first source to which many people turn. When people are seeking information on a particular illness or malady, they may trust a discussion on the internet filled with "advice" from total strangers more than they trust the word of an actual doctor. If a person breaks up with their significant other, the internet often provides the first arena to check for sympathy or to find a new significant other. Persons with spiritual questions can Google their query and receive hundreds of different answers. Christians must see the evangelistic potential of being able to provide biblically correct answers.[4]

2. Wendy Griffith, "Internet Evangelism: Casting a New Kind of Net," *Christian Broadcasting Network*, https://www1.cbn.com/churchandministry/internet-evangelism-casting-a-new-kind-of-net.
3. Griffith, "Internet Evangelism."
4. Walter Wilson argues that many people "will not come to church, but they will log onto a site in search of comfort. At this very moment, there are millions of people looking for answers to the problems that haunt them. You can reach them as never

THE PURPOSE OF INTERNET EVANGELISM

Matt Queen maintains, "The purposes of internet evangelism are three-fold in that 1) it should glorify God; 2) should serve as a means to perform the Great Commission; and 3) should be used to influence the information generation."[5] Scripture commands: "Whatever you do, do it all to the glory of God" (1 Cor. 10:31). That admonition certainly includes internet evangelism.

Internet evangelism follows many of the principles as other means of evangelism. Jesus commands his followers to be his witnesses "in Jerusalem, and in all Judea and Samaria and to the ends of the earth" (Acts 1:8). Social media opens evangelism up to the whole world. A member of our church, Steven Kunkel, graduated from Boyce College in Louisville and then left for the mission field in Japan. During his three years of study at Boyce, he devoted himself not only to his studies but also to internet evangelism. Steven is fluent in several languages and interacted with people all over the world, asking questions, having virtual conversations, and boldly sharing the gospel. He would update us regularly about his evangelistic conversations with an atheist in Japan or a Hindu in India. He took (and continues to take) the gospel message to "the ends of the earth." (At the end of this chapter Steven will share some of what he has learned doing this type of evangelistic ministry.)

THE CHALLENGES OF USING
SOCIAL MEDIA IN EVANGELISM

The challenges of using social media for evangelism are legion. First, too many people use the internet as a platform to criticize, vent opinions, and broadcast emotions. Be consistent in what you are trying to do, and seek to display the character of Christ through your posts and interactions. Avoid the temptation to share off-color jokes and anything inappropriate. This admonition includes posting any hateful articles, political views, and negative opinions about other believers. You also should avoid a "preachy

---

before through electronics." See Walter P. Wilson, *The Internet Church: The Local Church Can't Be Just Local Anymore* (Nashville: Word, 2000), 138.

5. Matt Queen, *Handbook for Internet Evangelism* (Alpharetta, GA: North American Mission Board, n.d.), 5.

tone" as you seek to witness; rather you should relate conversationally, as if you are sharing with another person (which you are!).

Second, using the internet can easily consume large chunks of time. Statistics are rising constantly about the number of hours the average person spends on mobile devices. People can waste hours surfing the internet or checking to see the latest on Facebook or Twitter—making sure they don't miss what someone had for dinner or the picture of their neighbor's cousin's new puppy. Be careful that the initial desire to use social media to witness does not lead to hours of wasted time.

Third, being on the internet can open the door to spiritual warfare and attacks by the evil one to try to lead you into sinful thoughts and attitudes. Having a computer software program for accountability/protection is important in doing anything with the internet. Do not let the intention to practice internet evangelism become the gateway to sin.[6]

PRACTICAL SUGGESTIONS

Prayer is the starting point, as always. Pray that God will guide you, that he will give you divine appointments online, and that he would give you wisdom as to what to say (as well as what not to say). Then consider sharing your testimony of how Jesus has changed your life. You can share your testimony on a public post, as well as sending it in a more personal manner via email or direct message. Encourage questions and interaction.

Avoid "Christianese." Do not use Christian jargon that nonbelievers would not understand. As you use scriptural terminology (e.g. "atonement"), explain what that term means in a way that persons not familiar with the Bible can understand. Remember Paul's prayer request in Colossians 4:3–4, asking his fellow believers to pray that as he shared the mystery of Christ he might "make it clear."

Do not let other content you post or careless words typed hastily in response to someone else harm your witness. If someone is reading your post about the gospel but then reads other material you have posted that

---

6. Current internet accountability software companies include Net Nanny, Accountable2You, X3 Watch, Ever Accountable, Lion, and Covenant Eyes. I use Covenant Eyes on all my electronic devices.

is insensitive and offensive, your credibility as a witness can be damaged. The gospel may prove offensive to people, but let the message be offensive, not the messenger.

Cultivate relationships with people. Convey a genuine interest in your followers and work personally on being a caring friend. Encourage those online with you to seek out a church or seek relationships in person. Remember that online users can respond in harsh and argumentative ways. Follow Peter's admonition and respond to them "with gentleness and reverence" (1 Peter 3:15).

Depend on the Holy Spirit. Our role is to plant seeds. God is the one who brings the harvest. This ongoing ministry will require patience, prayer, and discernment. Seeds planted do not always bear fruit immediately.

Finally, always consider linking to an online gospel booklet or gospel video that explains the gospel in greater depth. Your providing that link that someone chooses to click may result in them understanding and responding to the gospel message.

WEBSITES FOR GOSPEL PRESENTATIONS

Many websites contain helpful gospel presentations. I am listing a few of these websites here, with the recognition that as soon as this book is published, many more will be produced. Do your best to keep up to date with the best resources available. Here are some websites to consider:

- Need Him Global: https://needhim.org
- Flash multimedia gospel presentation: http://www.gotlife.com/launchpres.html
- Internet Evangelism Coalition's Web Evangelism Training: http://www.gospel.com/ministries/internet-evangelism-coalition
- Evangelistic resources: https://www.cru.org/us/en/train-and-grow/share-the-gospel.html
- Answers to questions about the Christian faith: https://www.gotquestions.org
- "Seeking" college students: http://www.everystudent.com
- Digital, copywrite free, Bible and Bible Study helps: Bible.org
- Free online courses to help understand the Christian faith: https://goingfarther.net

Evangelism Tools and Apps for Your Smartphone or Other Device

Again, by the time this book is published, there will be other helpful apps developed for gospel witness. Here are a few I have found particularly helpful:

- The Gospel App
- The Story (ViewTheStory.com)
- 3 Circles: Life Conversation Guide
- 1Cross
- Two Ways to Live

I want to share an article I asked Steven Kunkel—a current seminary student and church member—to write on this topic. Currently on mission for Christ in Japan, Steven uses his available free time to share the gospel on social media. He communicates to unbelievers regularly via social media and in internet chat rooms. Consider the following advice and encouragement from a real-life practitioner.

Internet Evangelism, by Steven Kunkel

Regarding internet evangelism, people can say the world wide web is a place of connecting/networking with others, or the internet is a dangerous place from which to stay away. Either way, we should admit that the internet is very unavoidable and is needed for school, business, and medical purposes. However, the main purpose of this article is that internet evangelism is an important component of personal evangelism. Most Christians in the United States and in other countries may think they need to witness more, but instead focus more on their iPhone, iPad, Android or any other device for entertainment purposes. The internet can be a time waster, but it is also a powerful tool for people to share the gospel with unreached people groups.

In my internet evangelism, I usually go to language learning apps where people would chat with me in order to learn and practice English, Spanish, Portuguese, or even Japanese; I would use these apps not only to make language contacts, but to be intentional to share the gospel with them, whether or not I would ever get a chance to meet them. Realizing people of different faiths try to share their religious views to some of these same people, I focus on reaching and gaining the trust of unbelievers to share with them the gospel through the social media.

As an example, one day, I invited those using a certain language app to join a gaming event; one of the people using this app saw my post and said he wanted to join. I decided to connect with him and ended up meeting him one day at a local Starbucks so that he could practice his English. As we conversed, I shifted the topic from language and culture to religion and the gospel, as I asked him about his thoughts on eternity. He was very open to know more about Christianity, and he went to church with me and started reading the Bible in order to learn more about Jesus. Although he is still an unbeliever, he has an increasing understanding of Christianity and a positive opinion of it. This same type of scenario happens often with other people in my circle of influence as I share the gospel and interact with people using the internet and social media—even in restricted countries where the gospel is forbidden.

Another example in which I shared the gospel is when one of my contacts, through the language app, saw that I had posted some Bible verses on the app and asked me why I was a Christian. I took the opportunity to share not only my testimony, but also how Jesus can save the unbeliever who asks. First Peter 3:15 challenges us to always be ready to "make a defense to everyone who asks you to give an account for the hope that is in you, yet with gentleness and reverence." Despite the person rejecting the gospel, he had the opportunity to hear the gospel (as well as many others with whom I have been able to interact).

As I seek to share the gospel using the internet, I start by praying for God's guidance, for God's work, and for God's power to convince the person to come to faith in Jesus, realizing God's gospel is a free gift to everyone who receives it (John 3:16–17; Rom. 6:23). Then, I try to seek those in whom God may already be at work.

The point of internet evangelism is for people to know the gospel. We need not be ashamed of the gospel because it is the power of God for salvation for everyone who believes (Rom. 1:16). Whether you are on the mission field, at home, or on the internet, God gave you the responsibility to share his message to unbelievers—his message of grace and love by what Jesus did on the cross. Therefore, let us share the gospel on social media and on the internet for God's glory.

CHAPTER 21

CALLING FOR A RESPONSE

IN OUR CHAPTER TITLED "WHAT IS THE GOSPEL?" we argued that the gospel message must always include explaining the necessary response of repentance and faith. If someone shares the gospel but does not discuss the necessary response, he or she has not truly shared the gospel message. The gospel message includes the necessary response of repentance and faith. But beyond explaining the necessary response, what is the witness's role in "calling for a response?" Does exhorting someone to repent and believe infringe upon God's sovereignty? Are witnesses to plead with sinners to repent and believe, or should they explain the gospel and then step back, allowing God to work in the person's heart and mind?

A helpful verse in this discussion is 2 Corinthians 5:20: "Therefore, we are ambassadors for Christ, as though God were making an appeal through us; we beg you on behalf of Christ, be reconciled to God." Paul begins verse 20 with a "therefore" to point us back to verses 18–19. In those verses he reminds believers we have been given the "ministry of reconciliation" and have been entrusted with the "word of reconciliation." In response to those realities, Paul gives all believers a job description: "we are ambassadors for Christ." Ambassadors are not free to make up their own message; their responsibility is to faithfully communicate the message with which they have been entrusted. Notice how Paul continues his description: "as though God were making an appeal through us." Whose appeal it is to repent and believe? Not ours—it is God's appeal. We did not create that message, but we seek to faithfully announce it to others in our role as Christ's ambassadors.

Observe how Paul applies this truth: "we beg you on behalf of Christ, be reconciled to God." Paul did not hesitate to beg, implore, beseech, and plead with sinners to repent and believe. Consider Acts 28:23 (NIV 1984): "From morning till evening he explained and declared to them the kingdom of God and tried to convince them about Jesus," and Acts 18:4 (NIV 1984), referring to Paul's ministry in Corinth, he "reasoned in the synagogue, trying to persuade Jews and Greeks." Mounce's observation bears repeating here:

> The kerygma was not a dispassionate recital of historical facts—a sort of nondescript presentation of certain truths, interesting enough, but morally neutral. It was, rather, the existential confrontation of man with the inescapable dilemma of having put to death the very One whom God exalted to universal Lordship. Was there any way by which man could escape the inevitable result of his blasphemous conduct? Only one—Repent! Therefore, the apostolic sermon invariably led up to a call for repentance.[1]

Leighton Ford comments, "The only right we have to ask people to commit their lives for time and eternity is that God is calling them. The gospel message is both an announcement and a command: It tells what God has done and calls people to respond."[2] And as J. I. Packer notes, biblical evangelism includes the desire to see a positive response to the gospel: "Evangelizing includes the endeavour to elicit a response to the truth taught. It is communication with a view to conversion. It is a matter, not merely of informing, but also of inviting. It is an attempt to gain, or win, or catch, our fellow-man for Christ."[3]

A common objection with regard to calling for a response has to do with the use of Revelation 3:20: "Behold, I stand at the door and knock; if anyone

---

1. R. H. Mounce, *The Essential Nature of New Testament Preaching* (Grand Rapids: Eerdmans, 1960), 84.
2. Leighton Ford, "How to Give an Honest Invitation," *Christianity Today*, May 19, 2004, https://www.christianitytoday.com/pastors/leadership-books/preachingtoconvince/ldlib08–11.html.
3. J. I. Packer, *Evangelism and the Sovereignty of God* (Downers Grove, IL: IVP Books, 1961), 50.

hears My voice and opens the door, I will come in to him, and will dine with him, and he with Me." Some argue that the context of this verse is Jesus speaking to a church, and therefore it is inappropriate to use it in an evangelistic context, while others argue there was obvious unbelief in the church, and therefore it is legitimate to use this verse in an evangelistic encounter.[4]

John Eddison writes of the circumstances of John Stott's conversion experience, "While at Rugby School in 1938, Stott heard Eric Nash (nicknamed "Bash") deliver a sermon entitled 'What Then Shall I Do with Jesus, Who Is Called the Christ?'"[5] Nash pointed Stott to Revelation 3:20, and Stott describes the impact this verse had on him:

> Here, then, is the crucial question which we have been leading up to. Have we ever opened our door to Christ? Have we ever invited him in? This was exactly the question which I needed to have put to me. For, intellectually speaking, I had believed in Jesus all my life, on the other side of the door. I had regularly struggled to say my prayers through the key-hole. I had even pushed pennies under the door in a vain attempt to pacify him. I had been baptized, yes and confirmed as well. I went to church, read my Bible, had high ideals, and tried to be good and do good. But all the time, often without realising it, I was holding Christ at arm's length, and keeping him outside. I knew that to open the door might have momentous consequences. I am profoundly grateful to him for enabling me to open the door. Looking back now over more than fifty years, I realise that that simple step has changed the entire direction, course and quality of my life.[6]

---

4. For an excellent presentation of both sides of this issue, see Walter Steitz, "The Proper Use of Revelation 3:20 in Evangelism" (ThM thesis, Dallas Theological Seminary, 1983). Steitz offers his own conclusion on page 32: "In conclusion the recipients of Christ's message in Revelation 3:14–22 were members of the local church in Laodicea which was represented by the figure of the angel of that church. When Christ spoke to the angel, He spoke to that local church and not to the universal church.

   A local church can contain unbelievers, and some of the other six local churches of Revelation 2 and 3 did contain unbelievers. Just because individuals were in the local churches in Revelation 2 and 3, did not guarantee that they were genuine believers. The overall spiritual condition of the Laodiceans and Christ's offer of salvation in Revelation 3:18 indicates that many of the Laodiceans were unbelievers."

5. John Eddison, ed., *A Study in Spiritual Power: An Appreciation of E. J. H. Nash (Bash)* (Crowborough, UK: Highland, 1992), 82.

6. Timothy Dudley-Smith, *John Stott: The Making of a Leader* (Leicester, UK: Inter-Varsity Press, 1999), 95.

Whether one agrees with the use of Revelation 3:20 as an invitation to salvation verse or not, Stott's experience reminds us there are many people in the same situation he was in: believing in Christ intellectually but never having trusted him as their personal Savior and Lord.

REFLECTING ON THE HARVEST

Do you not say, "There are yet four months, and then comes the harvest?" Behold, I say to you, lift up your eyes, and look on the fields, that they are white for harvest. Already he who reaps is receiving wages, and is gathering fruit for life eternal; that he who sows and he who reaps may rejoice together. For in this case the saying is true, "One sows, and another reaps." I sent you to reap that for which you have not labored; others have labored, and you have entered into their labor. (John 4:35–38)

We can discern several key principles about the spiritual harvest from this passage of Scripture. We see that the harvest is ripe, meaning it is ready now. We tend to view it as being in the future. We think, "Four months from now, I'm sure I will have a perfect opportunity to witness to my family member/neighbor/co-worker/friend." I love the way Ken Taylor paraphrases Ecclesiastes 11:4 in the Living Bible: "If you wait for perfect conditions, you will never get anything done." We seldom if ever will have perfect opportunities to witness. We need to capitalize on all available opportunities, not wait for perfect ones!

Another observation from this passage is the need for us to "lift up our eyes." Why the need for this command? What is the normal, default position of our gaze? Is it not for our eyes to be focused on ourselves, our needs, and our problems? We must make a conscious effort to lift up our eyes and see the harvest fields of the world. Another observation is that sowing takes place before reaping. The seed must be planted before the harvest can be gathered.

Another observation is the teamwork involved: "one sows, and another reaps." We may be involved in the sowing process or the reaping process with a particular individual, or perhaps we participate in both of those processes. A final observation is to be reminded that the objective is to reap the harvest. Yes, sowing is necessary, for without sowing there will be no reaping. But the goal is not to sow the seed and then declare, "Mission accomplished." The goal is always to reap the harvest.

WHAT IS "CALLING FOR A RESPONSE?"

There is nothing magical or mysterious about calling for a response. It is to practice what believers have done for two thousand years, and that is to share the gospel message and invite people to repent and believe. Not to decide is to have already decided! Scripture reminds us of the two roads people are traveling: the broad road and the narrow road. There are two human conditions: lost and saved. There are two spiritual states: darkness and light. There are those who are spiritually blind and those who can see spiritual realities. There are those who are far off from God and those who are near. There are two ultimate destinations: everlasting life and everlasting punishment.

John Stott reflects on the work of the Holy Spirit in regeneration and conversion:

> The essential distinction . . . is that regeneration is something which *God* does, while conversion is something which *we* do ourselves (although not by ourselves) . . . conversion is what we do, when we "turn" to God, as in Acts 9:35; 11:21, and 26:20. . . . Since the turn from idols and sin is called *repentance*, and the turn to God and Christ *faith*, we conclude that repentance plus faith equal conversion.[7]

Repentance and faith are two aspects of the same action, together forming the process known as conversion.[8] Paul Little explains the response using the symbolism of a bride and groom:

> It is significant that marriage is one of the illustrations the New Testament uses for being and becoming a Christian. It is obvious that merely believing in a fellow or a girl, however intense that belief might be, does not make one married. If, in addition, we are emotionally involved and have that "all gone feeling" about the other person we still

---

7. John R. W. Stott, *Our Guilty Silence* (Chicago: Inter-Varsity Press, 1967), 100–101.
8. See chapter 7, "What Is the Gospel?" for a more complete discussion of these terms.

will not be married! One finally has to come to a commitment of the will and say, "I do," receiving the other person into his life and committing himself to the other person thereby establishing a relationship. It involves total commitment of intellect, emotions and will. One must believe in Jesus Christ; and personally receive Him into one's life; and thus become a child of God. The pattern is the same in marriage; a fellow first believes in a girl, then must receive her into his life and thus becomes married. Mere intellectual assent to facts does not make a person a Christian any more than mere intellectual assent to facts makes a person married.[9]

WHAT STEPS SHOULD PRECEDE CALLING FOR A RESPONSE?

Before we call for a response we want to be sure the person clearly understands the gospel message. Do they have a clear understanding about God, humanity, Christ's person and work, and their necessary response? I have found the following four categories of questions to be helpful in calling for a response:[10]

1. *Recognize*: Now that you have admitted the problem, let's be sure you understand God's solution. Do you recognize that Jesus Christ died on the cross to pay for your sins?
2. *Repent*: Do you understand that you have a sin problem you cannot solve by yourself? Do you really want Christ to deliver you from your sin? Are you ready to repent of your sins and follow him?
3. *Respond*: Saving faith is the choice we make to rely upon Christ. Do you place your trust in Jesus Christ as your Savior and Lord right now?
4. *Receive*: Salvation is a free gift from Christ. Do you receive this free gift of salvation with empty, open hands?

---

9. Paul Little, *How to Give Away Your Faith* (Downers Grove, IL: InterVarsity Press, 1966), 59.
10. Michael Green describes the response in four ways: something to admit, something to believe, something to consider, and something to do. See *Evangelism through the Local Church* (London: Hodder and Stoughton, 1992), 277.

What about "the Sinner's Prayer"?

Many gospel presentations end by asking the person to pray a prayer, which has come to be known as "the Sinner's Prayer." Here is one sample of this prayer:

> "Jesus, I know that I am a sinner, and I am sorry for my sin. I believe You died for my sins. I want to invite You to come into my heart and life. I want to trust and follow You as my Lord and Savior. Amen."[11]

Many believers today testify that they were converted when praying this prayer. Wayne Grudem affirms its usefulness:

> What shall we say about the common practice of asking people to pray to receive Christ as their personal Savior and Lord? Since personal faith in Christ must involve an actual decision of the will, it is often very helpful to express that decision in spoken words, and this could very naturally take the form of a prayer to Christ in which we tell him of our sorrow for sin, our commitment to forsake it, and our decision actually to put our trust in him. Such a spoken prayer does not in itself save us, but the attitude of the heart it represents does constitute true conversion, and the decision to speak that prayer can often be the point at which a person truly comes to faith in Christ.[12]

Yet, there are also multitudes of people who testify as to having prayed this prayer with seemingly no spiritual transformation in their life. Several observations are in order.

We must emphasize that we are not saved by prayer but by grace through faith (Eph. 2:8–9). There is nothing magical about saying the words of any prayer, including the Sinner's Prayer. Also, we do not find this exact prayer in the Bible. We do find examples of sinners crying out for mercy and being

---

11. Paul Chitwood, in his PhD dissertation research, found more than a dozen different versions of the Sinner's Prayer in popular usage today. See Paul Chitwood, "The Sinner's Prayer: An Historical and Theological Analysis," Ph.D. diss., The Southern Baptist Theological Seminary, 2001.
12. Wayne Grudem, *Bible Doctrine: Essential Teachings of the Christian Faith* (Grand Rapids: Zondervan, 1999), 312.

assured their prayers were heard (Luke 18:1–14; 23:39–43), and we are promised "whoever calls on the name of the Lord will be saved" (Rom. 10:13; Acts 2:21). We are instructed in Romans 10:9–10, "that if you confess with your mouth Jesus as Lord, and believe in your heart that God raised Him from the dead, you will be saved; for with the heart a person believes, resulting in righteousness, and with the mouth he confesses, resulting in salvation."

We do not find what we today call "the Sinner's Prayer" in the Bible. The variance in wording of the various scriptural prayers reminds us that the Lord listens to the heart, not the lips. We see in Scripture that words can be uttered without true meaning. Jesus observes in Matthew 15:8, "This people honors Me with their lips, but their heart is far away from Me." In Matthew 7:21, Jesus warns, "Not everyone who says to Me, 'Lord, Lord,' will enter the kingdom of heaven; but he who does the will of My Father who is in heaven."

What is prayer? Prayer is talking to God. I am not opposed to a sample prayer when introduced something like this: "Here is a prayer that others have found helpful in expressing their desire to repent and believe." What I believe we need to avoid is the phrase, "If you want to become a Christian, pray *this* prayer." The suggestion one must pray *this* prayer (as opposed to any other prayer) reeks of sacramentalism. In fact, some witnesses use the prayer in that very way. They tell people, "Pray *this* prayer," and then assure them afterward that they are Christians and that all their sins are forgiven now and forevermore. J. D. Greear maintains: "It's not the prayer that saves; it's the repentance and faith behind the prayer that lays hold of salvation. My concern is that over-emphasizing the prayer has often (though unintentionally) obscured the primary instruments for laying hold of salvation: repentance and faith."[13]

As a new believer, I was taught to use the Sinner's Prayer as the way to lead someone to faith in Christ. My "aha" moment came one day when I sensed a young man named Manuel was ready to follow Christ after four months of gospel conversations. I instructed Manuel that if he wanted to become a Christian, he needed to "pray *this* prayer." I handed him a copy of the Sinner's Prayer to read aloud. As he was praying, he stumbled over one of the words, and looked up at me with a look of panic on his face.

---

13. Trevin Wax, "Stop Asking Jesus into Your Heart? A Conversation with J. D. Greear," Kingdom People (blog), accessed March 30, 2021, https://www.thegospelcoalition.org/blogs/trevin-wax/stop-asking-jesus-into-your-heart-a-conversation-with-j-d-greear.

His expression suggested he was thinking, "Did I just blow it? Did I just mess up my one chance to be saved?" I had in no way intended to convey to Manuel that this prayer was sacramental—that if he just got the words correct then he would be magically converted *ex opera operato*.[14] But in hearing my specific instructions to "pray *this* prayer," he interpreted the prayer as something efficacious if he could manage to say it correctly.

I have made hundreds of visits in homes of church members whose names were on the church roll but who were not active in the church. Some of them had not participated in any type of spiritual activity for decades. When I raised questions about their spiritual condition, the over-whelming response I heard was, "Don't worry about me, pastor. I still re-member the day I prayed 'that prayer.' The pastor told me I was forgiven now and forevermore. Thanks for your concern, but I'm good." On what were they basing their assurance? On the fact that they prayed the Sinner's Prayer and were immediately given assurance by their pastor at that time. Some parents of wayward children place their hope in the remembrance that their child prayed the Sinner's Prayer. I do not believe utilizing the Sinner's Prayer always results in spurious conversions. But I fear it does far too often.[15] Let's avoid the sacramental language and point people to put their trust in Christ, not in a specific prayer. Greear comments:

> Salvation does indeed happen in a moment, and once you are saved, you are always saved. The mark, however, of someone who is saved is that they maintain their profession of faith until the end of their lives. Salvation is not a prayer you pray in a one-time ceremony and then move on from; salvation is a posture of repentance and faith that you begin in a moment and maintain for the rest of your life.[16]

Instead of asking people to repeat the words of a prayer, encourage people to *follow* Jesus. Stress that salvation involves a response.

---

14. *Ex opere operato* is a Latin expression meaning "from the work performed." The Roman Catholic Church uses it to emphasize that the sacraments derive their efficacy, not from the minister or the recipient, but from the power of the sacrament itself.
15. Greear cites a 2011 Barna study that shows almost one-half of the adults in America claim to have prayed such a prayer, yet their lifestyle does not display any measure of belief. See J. D. Greear, *Stop Asking Jesus into Your Heart: How to Know for Sure You Are Saved* (Nashville: Broadman & Holman, 2013), 6.
16. Greear, *Stop Asking Jesus into Your Heart*, 8.

CHAPTER 22

EVANGELISM AND APOLOGETICS

THE MENTION OF APOLOGETICS STRIKES FEAR and uncertainty into the hearts of too many people. Caricatures of the discipline abound in the form of lofty argumentation and ungodly drive toward pride. Picture a competitive debater whose aim rests purely in the defeat of his counterpart. The worst examples of Christian apologetic activity drive away otherwise thoughtful evangelical Christians from considering the use of apologetics in their rhythms of spiritual conversation and formation. The apologetic task remains a daunting prospect for some despite the exaggerated examples. Apologetics demands clear, logical thinking that advances ideas, not egos.

For those who consider apologetics a practically untouchable or superfluous endeavor, consider how Jesus responded to one pharisaical lawyer's question about the greatest commandment in the law: "And He said to him, 'You shall love the LORD your God with all your heart, and with all your soul, *and with all your mind.*' This is the great and foremost commandment. The second is like it, 'You shall love your neighbor as yourself'" (Matt. 22:37–39, emphasis mine). Here Jesus defuses a detractor's agenda and reminds his disciples that loving God involves both heart and mind.

Apologetics helps to train minds to love Christ by thoroughly thinking through the claims of Scripture. Jesus's second citation from the law includes the admonition to love others. Apologetics helps believers to think clearly and with a purpose—that is, to love others enough to point them to Christ. At its best, apologetics helps in the process of making disciples for Jesus. It is that holy task at which this chapter aims. The purpose of this chapter is to dispel the mystique of using apologetics within gospel conversations and encourage Christians to utilize apologetic tools in their evangelistic work. Specifically, this chapter builds a definition of apologetics, explores how and when apologetics intersects with evangelism, and provides a brief primer on apologetics.

DEFINITION OF APOLOGETICS

The word *apologetics* derives from the Greek word *apologia*, which means a defense or an answer given in reply. *Apologia* occurs eight times in the New Testament, and its verb cognate *apologeomai* occurs ten times in the New Testament.[1] The passage most associated with the exercise of apologetics is 1 Peter 3:15: "But sanctify Christ as Lord in your hearts, always being ready to make a defense to everyone who asks you to give an account for the hope that is in you, yet with gentleness and reverence." Here Peter writes to believers calling them to humility and harmony. In no way does the readiness to defend conviction imply an arrogant spirit; rather, the advancement of reasons for hope should be done winsomely.

The Bible sheds more light on the apologetic task across several key passages. First, Paul addresses the Corinthian church over the issue of his apostolic authority and acknowledges the spiritual warfare that exists in his task. He says, "For the weapons of our warfare are not of the flesh but divinely powerful for the destruction of fortresses. We are destroying speculations and every lofty thing raised up against the knowledge of God, and we are taking every thought captive to the obedience of Christ" (2 Cor. 10:4–5). This passage helps further define apologetics by identifying the true adversary in terms of spiritual strongholds and lofty opinions. Apologetics never views the skeptic or unconverted as the enemy, but rather defends and advocates Christian beliefs.

Second, Paul argues similarly to the church in Colossae, "See to it that no one takes you captive through philosophy and empty deception,

---

1. Some uses of *apologia* can be found in Acts 22:1, 25:16; 1 Corinthians 9:3; 2 Corinthians 7:11; Philippians 1:7, 16; and 2 Timothy 4:16. *Apologeomai* can be found in Luke 12:11, 21:14; Acts 19:33, 24:10, 25:8, 26:1, 26:2, 26:24; Romans 2:15; and 2 Corinthians 12:19.

according to the tradition of men, according to the elementary principles of the world, rather than according to Christ" (Col. 2:8). Paul warns the church about a christological error, and his exhortation includes an active measuring of teaching against the standard of Christ. This passage continues to add a dimension to the understanding of apologetics. It includes clear, logical thinking as an antidote to the pervasive empty philosophies of the world. One aspect of apologetics this passage highlights is the development of approaches for defending the faith.

Finally, Jude writes, "Beloved, while I was making every effort to write you about our common salvation, I felt the necessity to write to you appealing that you contend earnestly for the faith which was once for all handed down to the saints" (Jude 3). Jude makes a case to the Christian community that they should actively contend for the Christian worldview, considering the presence of those who deny Jesus Christ. Although Jude's statement is two thousand years old, it remains a fresh exhortation to subsequent generations to maintain the apostolic doctrine. Doing apologetics strongly implies a continual struggle to make the best arguments during the onslaught of attacks on the Christian worldview.

Here is a working definition of apologetics based on this brief survey of these biblical passages: *Apologetics is an area of Christian thought preoccupied with the defense of the faith and developing approaches for defending the faith in hopes of seeing the skeptic convinced of the lordship of Jesus Christ and Christians nurtured in the faith.* Two purposes or kinds of apologetics are embedded in the aforementioned definition: apologetics that is belief-forming and apologetics that is belief-sustaining. Apologetics that is belief-sustaining is an approach meant to disciple or train biblical Christians in the best arguments for the faith. This method helps Christians grow in the faith and receive training in how to respond to challenges to Christianity. Apologetics that is belief-forming concerns itself with establishing the Christian worldview as credible through thoughtful explanations of the validity of the biblical worldview. Here apologetics is used as a tool for evangelism, and it is the focus of what follows.

APOLOGETIC EVANGELISM

At times apologetics and evangelism have had a strained relationship. In the current cultural milieu, the relationship between the two needs reviving. Each epoch in human history presents challenges to the Christian worldview, but none proves insurmountable to the forward march of the gospel (Matt. 16:18). The current challenges of humanism and secularism, among other philosophies, demands a strong apologetic gospel-telling. Certainly, apologetics and evangelism are not synonymous terms, but evangelism needs to be apologetic. It has been said that apologetics is the handmaiden to evangelism. While the two work together, they remain distinct tasks.

Evangelism as defined in this book is: *The compassionate sharing of the good news of Jesus Christ with lost people, in the power of the Holy Spirit, for the purpose of bringing them to Christ as Savior and Lord, that they in turn might share him with others.* Notice that the work of evangelism involves the verbal witness of the good news in the power of the Holy Spirit. The gospel is the power of God for salvation to everyone who believes (Rom. 1:16). Lost people are born again not because of impeccable argumentation but by the will and power of God working through the verbal witness (2 Thess. 2:13). Apologetics serves evangelism. In fact, apologetics can be viewed as a type of pre-evangelism. If evangelism, narrowly defined, is the verbal witness and offer of the gospel, then apologetics must seize the opportunity to lay the groundwork (or pre-evangelism) that anticipates the sharing of the good news.

The great theologian and apologist J. Gresham Machen offers wonderful words of counsel in this regard:

> It would be a mistake to suppose that all men are equally well-prepared to receive the gospel. It is true that the decisive thing is the regenerative power in connection with certain prior conditions for the reception of the Gospel. . . . I do not mean that the removal of intellectual objections will make a man a Christian. No conversion was ever wrought by argument. A change of heart is also necessary . . . but because the intellectual labor is *insufficient*, it does not follow that it is *unnecessary*. God may, it is true, overcome all intellectual obstacles by an immediate exercise of His regenerative power. Sometimes He does. But He does so very seldom. Usually He exerts His power in connections with certain conditions of the human mind. Usually He does not bring into the kingdom, entirely without preparation, those whose mind and fancy are completely

contaminated by ideas which make the acceptance of the Gospel logically impossible.[2]

I believe Machen is correct; just because apologetics is insufficient in bringing someone to faith does not mean it is unnecessary.

The pre-evangelistic work of apologetics takes a variety of shapes. A commitment to utilize a basic apologetic approach while steering a conversation toward spiritual topics will help a Christian be more persuasive in his or her evangelism. The present cultural context is quickly abandoning what once was a generally accepted biblical worldview. People, even though unconverted, at least had categories for "God" or "sin" or "Jesus." While some places still do, many have long since left such categories. So, to speak of the holy God being offended by the sin of every human being is not only met with skepticism and unbelief but outright offense. Yet, well-meaning Christians want to begin evangelism at a place that often is a nonstarter for the lost. A gentle and persuasive approach that begins to establish the basics of a Christian worldview will go a long way when presenting the gospel.

Paul's encounter with the philosophies of his day at Mars Hill in Acts 17:22–34 illustrates this kind of pre-evangelistic apologetics. Paul observes the pagan trappings of his surroundings and uses that as a bridge to explain who the one, true, and living God is. He takes the Athenians' best philosophical attempt to explain the world in reference to "an unknown god" and skillfully introduces the Christian worldview before calling on people to repent. Essentially, Paul identifies the shortcomings in the Athenian worldview and shows how the biblical worldview is coherent. Today's world is ripe with faulty philosophies that Christians would do well to observe, identify the holes in, and lovingly retell in light of the glorious Christ.

One common hurdle among skeptics and the lost is the authority of the Bible. Christians, rightly, go to the Scriptures when evangelizing because it is sharper than a double-edged sword (Heb. 4:12), but many people do not acknowledge revelation from God as either possible or necessary. Consider the following excerpt from a spiritual conversation:

---

2. J. Gresham Machen, "The Scientific Preparation of a Minister," *Princeton Theological Review* 11, no. 1 (1913): 1, emphasis added.

EC (Evangelical Christian): The Bible is God's special revelation and is a legitimate source of truth.

UB (Unbeliever): How do you know the Bible is true?

EC: The Bible offers the most comprehensive worldview that explains events and life in the world in a convincing and coherent way. What do you rely on when determining if something is true or not?

UB: Well, I prefer to look at hard evidence—things I can see or hear or observe in some way. Plus some things just make logical sense in the world.

EC: Certainly, those things can convey truth, but can they explain everything—things like love and hate or spiritual realities?

UB: You can't really measure those nonphysical things, but they seem innate to human life.

EC: Things we observe can conflict with what is supposed to be innate or rational. The world seems to be filled with those kinds of conundrums.

UB: That still does not tell me about the validity of the Bible.

EC: All I'm saying is some things in the world are not well explained by science or rationality, and the Bible can offer some explanation to things that other truth sources cannot. What would happen if people completely ignored a source of truth like the Bible?

This conversation can take any number of turns from this point, but notice how the evangelical Christian was able to make a brief defense of the validity of the Bible. This example is merely one demonstration of how to navigate a conversation about the validity and coherence of the Bible.

While apologetics can assist in laying the groundwork for an evangelistic conversation, it can also serve the evangelistic conversation itself by answering objections that may arise. Apologetics attempts to render the

Christian faith persuasive to the unbeliever. Some push back on the use of persuasion in an evangelistic context that utilizes apologetics. Critics of persuasive methods confuse persuasion with manipulation. Manipulating people or the gospel for a desired outcome is unethical. Persuasion used rightly in the context of evangelism occurs several times in the Bible.[3] In his second letter to the Corinthians, Paul says that he persuades people to Christ given the impending judgment on those who do not receive Jesus (2 Cor. 5:11). The important thing to remember is that persuasive arguments or clever words do not in and of themselves cause conversion. Believers should use arguments, personal testimonies, and clear gospel presentations. As well as those may be articulated, however, some people do not come to Christ. The missing piece is the work of God who brings sinners to himself (John 6:44). The Great Commission task assigned to believers is to communicate the gospel as clearly, graciously, and persuasively as possible and let God use these efforts to draw people to himself.[4]

The goal of evangelism should always be to bring people to Christ and invite them to trust Christ as Savior and Lord. Jesus's encounter with the rich young ruler illustrates the kind of commitment that believers call unbelievers to when evangelizing. When the rich young ruler inquires of Jesus what he must do to be saved, Jesus tells him he must keep the commandments (Matt. 19:16–17). After he affirms his obedience, Jesus tells him he must sell his assets and give to the poor, and the young ruler goes away grieving (Matt. 19:18–22).

This event in the Gospel teaches what genuine faith is. When it comes to faith, three aspects exist that help further illustrate true biblical faith.[5] The first aspect of faith is *notitia*. *Notitia* refers to the content or cognitive element of faith. The rich young ruler certainly had this aspect of faith in that he apparently was familiar with the law (Matt. 19:18). When using an apologetic method to share the gospel with an unbeliever, some will have heard the gospel multiple times over years of attendance at church yet never have faith beyond the intellectual knowledge of the events surrounding the gospel. While intellectual knowledge is necessary, it is incomplete.

---

3. Acts 17:4, 18:4, 18:13, 19:8.
4. Gregory Koukl, *Tactics: A Game Plan for Discussing Your Christian Convictions* (Grand Rapids: Zondervan, 2009), 37.
5. See the helpful discussion about these three aspects of faith in Richard A. Muller, *Dictionary of Latin and Greek Theological Terms* (Grand Rapids: Baker, 1985), 115–16.

The second aspect of faith is *assensus*. *Assensus* involves assent to the intellect. It goes beyond mere knowledge to the recognition that the content of faith is true. The rich young ruler not only knew the law, but he was willing to recognize the truthfulness of what Jesus commanded (Matt. 19:20). Using apologetics in evangelism will undoubtedly yield some people who know the content of the gospel and even assent to its truthfulness but never come to genuine faith. This point can be frustrating for the Christian evangelist to have an unbeliever who knows the truth and yet does not believe. This aspect of faith is best illustrated by the enemy and his demons, as James writes, "You believe that God is one. You do well; the demons also believe, and shudder" (James 2:19). Assenting to the truthfulness of the gospel alone still does not indicate regeneration.

The third aspect of faith is *fiducia*. *Fiducia* refers to one's personal trust that goes beyond the mind to impact the heart, the will, and the affections. The rich young ruler's faith did not rise to the level of total commitment to Christ (Matt. 19:22). This aspect of faith is justifying because it penetrates beyond the intellect to produce life change. Apologetics helps to advance clear thinking on the ideas of Scripture. The witness must position those ideas and principles in an argument that clearly and winsomely conveys the beauty of the gospel. Apologetics requires diligent preparation on the part of the witness to best wield this particular tool for evangelism. The believer who commits faithfully to this labor will reap a crown of unfading glory.

WHY DO PEOPLE ASK QUESTIONS?

As we get involved in evangelism, we quickly discover that good evangelistic conversations are not monologues but dialogues, and that includes persons asking questions. Why do people ask questions in witnessing situations? I have observed two main reasons why people ask questions: an unwillingness to forsake sin, or as an honest expression of doubt and confusion. In the first case, the questions the person is asking are not really serious questions to them. They are simply "playing games." Their mind is closed, not open. They are raising questions as a smokescreen to avoid having to deal with their sinfulness. But not all persons who raise questions are playing games. In the second case, some people ask legitimate questions because they genuinely are seeking answers. Francis Schaeffer argues, "It is not more spiritual to believe without asking questions. It is not more

Biblical. It is less Biblical and eventually will be less spiritual because the whole man will not be involved."⁶ He goes on to say, "Christianity demands that we have enough compassion to learn the questions of our generation."⁷

We need to remember that faith in Jesus Christ is not a "leap in the dark" as it is sometimes described by skeptics. Faith in Jesus Christ is instead a "step into the light." We have good reasons for believing what we believe! When people ask genuine questions, we need to seek to answer those questions. Paul Little quotes John Stott as offering a wonderful balance with this observation: "We cannot pander to a man's intellectual *arrogance*, but we must cater to his intellectual *integrity*."⁸

PRIMER ON APOLOGETICS

Much more should be said about apologetics that goes beyond the scope of this chapter. What follows is a basic tutorial that offers a familiarity with the forms that apologetics takes, its purpose, the approaches to apologetics, and some practical tips. These items have been culled together from some of the leading thinkers in this important area of evangelism.

Forms of Apologetics

In the previous section, the relationship between apologetics and evangelism was introduced in the context of pre-evangelism and evangelism. The following four items give further color regarding how apologetics is fleshed out in the evangelistic context. First, some approaches to apologetics seek to explain the foundations and principal points of the biblical worldview. This form of apologetics represents the most basic understanding of the apologetic task. When Paul evangelized Corinth, he did so by reasoning with the Jews and later testified that Jesus is the promised Messiah (Acts 18:4–5).

Second, apologetics clarifies misunderstandings or misrepresentations about Christianity. In an evangelistic dialogue, questions or concerns from skeptics are likely to arise that may be based on false information or

---

6. Francis A. Schaeffer, "Form and Freedom in the Church," in *Let the Earth Hear His Voice*, ed. J. D. Douglas (Minneapolis: World Wide, 1975), 368.
7. Schaeffer, "Form and Freedom in the Church," 373.
8. Cited in Paul E. Little, *Know Why You Believe* (Downers Grove, IL: InterVarsity Press, 2009), 25.

data. The witness takes advantage of the opportunity by correcting false information about Christianity.

Third, apologetics takes the form of handling objections, criticisms, and other questions from unbelievers. The most common type of question deals with alleged contradictions in the Bible (e.g. textual variants across translations). A significant part of using apologetics in evangelism is preparation for these questions.

Fourth, apologetics points out differences in world religions and cults. In an increasingly pluralistic culture where many ways to God—or no way to God—is valued, it is with great urgency that Christians should be prepared to speak to these issues. With growing media attention and prominence attached to a pluralistic culture, Christians will need to distinguish a biblical worldview from the many religious roads.

Purpose of Apologetics

Apologetics is a multi-faceted tool for the witness, and, because it can become complex, it is important to keep apologetics in perspective. Apologetics serves evangelism. Evangelists use apologetics. However a Christian employs apologetics, he or she needs to remember the purpose of apologetics. The first purpose is not to win an intellectual argument but to give the skeptic good reasons to embrace the Christian worldview. A 2019 Barna study showed that 44 percent of non-Christians say they might be more interested in Christianity if they had more evidence.[9] Consider the opportunity equipped believers have to provide evidence (or reasons) to lost people. According to this survey four out of ten non-Christians could be persuaded to embrace Christ if someone were to thoughtfully engage them.

The second purpose of apologetics is ultimately to persuade people to apply the truth of the gospel to their lives. Apologetics apart from a conscientious desire to see people come to Christ becomes more about the apologist than his Lord.

The third purpose of apologetics is to help people see the outcomes of their belief. This purpose serves an important evangelistic function. Many people do not consider the impact of their belief system in the long-term or

---

9. Barna Group, *Reviving Evangelism: Current Realities That Demand a New Vision for Sharing Faith* (Ventura, CA: Barna Group, 2019), 13.

the logical consequences of their convictions. A witness using apologetics will skillfully discern the ultimate result of a belief system and be able to gently guide the conversation to a natural conclusion that the unbeliever or skeptic would regret. When the unbeliever recognizes the fallacy, he or she may be more willing to listen.

Approaches to Apologetics

The field of apologetics is broad enough to include several schools of thought regarding application. This section will discuss four approaches to apologetics that have gained broad acceptance among evangelicals. Usually believers will gravitate toward one or two of these approaches, but each brings with it a set of strengths and weaknesses. In fact, nuances within each approach distinguish some of their proponents. Each of these streams of thought on apologetics takes seriously the evangelistic purpose of apologetics. This section will introduce these approaches and some of their more prominent advocates.

The first approach to apologetics is the classical approach. The classical approach emphasizes logical criteria and the use of rational arguments in determining the validity of religious philosophies. Classicists rely heavily on philosophical (e.g. ontological, cosmological) arguments for the existence of God as a primary starting point before other religious issues are adjudicated. Paul's apologetic approach in Acts 17 remains a foundational text called upon as evidence of a classical approach in Scripture. Logical reasoning also has a way of building bridges to the lost and establishing common ground with non-Christians. The classical approach also contains a significant following in church history beginning with figures such as Justin Martyr, Anselm, and Thomas Aquinas. Each of these men contributed uniquely to what is now known as the classical approach. Recent years have yielded classicists such as C. S. Lewis, Norman Geisler, and R. C. Sproul. Each have contributed greatly to the understanding of the faith through the classical approach to apologetics.

The second approach is the evidentialist approach. The evidentialist approach attempts to ground the Christian faith in verifiable facts. Such facts typically include empirical evidence—that is, things that are strictly measurable or historically verified. The evidentialist defends the Christian faith as inherently reasonable. Evidentialist apologists tend to attract unbelievers because of their ability to gather and present evidence. The world values the scientific method which is based in large part on evidence gathered through sensory perception and rationality. This approach may appeal to those ingrained in the scientific method. Popular evidentialists include Joseph Butler, Josh McDowell, Gary Habermas, Clark Pinnock, John Warwick Montgomery, and Richard Swinburne. Evidentialists stress factual evidence for the Christian worldview

The third approach is the Reformed approach (presuppositionalism). The Reformed approach presupposes God's existence and the truth of Scripture. This school of thought generally eschews efforts to prove the faith based on reason or fact. Rather, the Reformed approach focuses heavily on epistemological factors in belief and revelation. Significant presuppositionalists include Cornelius van Til, Abraham Kuyper, and Gordon Clark. The emphasis of the Reformed apologist centers around the idea that God revealed himself in the Bible. Reformed apologists defend the notion that revelation is a legitimate source of truth and will critique the empiricist and rationalist approaches to truth on the basis of their inability to explain all of life. The Reformed apologist argues that revelation offers a broad and coherent worldview that explains life.

The fourth approach to apologetics is the fideism approach. Fideism refers to belief apart from any reasoning or evidence. Some argue that the fideist approach does not belong within the field of apologetics. The fideist emphasizes faith and little else. Fideists will, however, explain in their apologetic approach why reason or evidence falls short of explaining reality. Famous fideists include Tertullian, Martin Luther, Søren Kierkegaard, and Karl Barth.

These four approaches to apologetics tend to have rather fluid boundaries. While they are defined enough to stand alone, the practical application of these approaches sometimes overlap. For example, William Lane Craig (prominent evangelist-apologist) is firmly in the classical school of apologetics, but much of his reasoning can be taken as evidential. Some even view evidentialism as a subset of the classical approach. This blending, in fact, helps the overall task of apologetic evangelism because it integrates the best of various schools of thought. On the other end, the Reformed and fideist approaches tend to bleed well together since both rely heavily on the revealed Word of God and downplay reason as an apologetic tool. The mixing of approaches should not be seen as inherently confusing or betraying to a camp. Observers have assigned the use of two or more approaches as an integration approach. Integrationists use the best of the varying approaches to chart a way forward.

Some evangelists and thinkers are difficult to pin in one category or another. Francis A. Schaeffer was a well-respected evangelist whose apologetic could be perceived as fitting into any one of the four formal approaches. Schaeffer's retreat center in the Swiss Alps, L'Abri, was a place where apologetic evangelism conversations could occur. His approach to the existence of God reflects that of a classical approach to apologetics. He also affirmed the use verifiable facts of history to argue for the validity of the biblical worldview, which is reminiscent of an evidential approach. Yet, Schaeffer was profoundly influenced by the Reformed tradition and the supremacy of the Bible as the basis for an apologetic evangelism. While Schaeffer was often critical of fideists like Kierkegaard and Barth, he advocated that the best apologetic method was the practice of the truth. One can see that Schaeffer, for example, was difficult to categorize at times. The fact that he was not so committed to a particular approach reveals where his heart truly resided. Schaeffer put it this way: "I'm not an evidentialist or a presuppositionalist. You're trying to press me into a category of a theological apologist, which I'm not. I'm not an academic, scholastic apologist. My interest is in evangelism."[10]

Let Schaeffer's commitment be instructive. One of the greatest Christian thinkers of the twentieth century avoided the intramurals of apologetic classification and preferred to use whatever method of apologetics to inform his evangelism ministry. The most helpful takeaway for Christians and the use of apologetics is to remember that the focus of apologetics is evangelism.

Practical Tips

If evangelism is going to be apologetic, it must begin with local churches. The Lord Jesus assigned the church the task of making disciples through the proclamation of the good news. As the local church gathers to equip and make disciples, apologetics will help. Training in apologetics strengthens the faith of believers and equips them to give a reason for the hope that is within them. Churches today stand at an important cultural

---

10. Cited in Jack Rogers, "Francis Schaeffer: The Promise and the Problem," *Reformed Journal* 27, no. 5 (May 1977): 12–13.

moment with an opportunity to speak Christ to a world seduced by empty philosophy. Churches must surely prepare Christ-followers to integrate an apologetic method in their evangelism. Church leaders would be wise to consider several challenges when it comes to incorporating apologetics into the life of the local church.

First, the church needs to clarify its truth claims. Christians fall into the trap of insider language, and, even worse, some people assume the gospel message in conversations. Do not assume the gospel. Clarify and defend what is meant by truth, the gospel, and Jesus. The present world vies for the affections of souls, so declare an unvarnished, biblical Jesus who rescues the lost, and give reasons why the church is willing to stake everything on it.

Second, the church should consider removing the obstacles that block a person from coming to Christ. In other words, know the people who will hear the gospel and anticipate any intellectual barriers. This task necessitates knowing and loving someone enough to discern the obstacle(s), present the truth, let the Holy Spirit bring conviction of sin, and be ready to point to the cross where forgiveness lies.

Third, the church ought to avoid platitudes and speak specifically to the skeptic's worldview. The pastors and teachers of the church can incorporate this kind of direct specificity by clearly stating an argument, illustrating the truth, and applying the concept to demonstrate the relevance of the truth claim. A church that teaches its teachers to do this will go a long way to better equip the people for an apologetic evangelism.

Fourth, the church will benefit from striking a balance between the heart and mind. Focusing too heavily on the technicality of various arguments will sidestep the heart of the listener and give the appearance of cold legality. Emphasizing emotionalism at the expense of the mind will make for empty and unrooted believers. Pastors and other church leaders who draw near to their people with gentleness and respect will have many opportunities to touch hearts and minds with the gospel. When that happens, the church becomes the place people go to get help in making sense of a painful world. The church becomes the place that helps people make sense of reality and take them from despair to hope in the declaration that truth has a name, and he is Jesus.

CHAPTER 23

WITNESSING TO CHILDREN

THE PICTURE OF BABY OBED bouncing on Naomi's knee at the end of the book of Ruth vividly illustrates family evangelism as God intended it to be. This child of God-fearing parents would grow up to father a new generation of God-fearing children that would include Jesse, the father of King David, a man Scripture calls "a man after God's own heart." From earliest times, God intended for families to be founded on love and devotion to him. Parents should naturally incorporate his word and plan for their lives into every aspect of child-rearing.

Timothy gives us a good example of the impact of the gospel message in the home. Scripture tells us that Timothy's mother was a believer, but his father was not (see Acts 16:1). Timothy learned the Scriptures from his mother and grandmother, and Paul notes, "For I am mindful of the sincere faith within you, which first dwelt in your grandmother Lois and your mother Eunice, and I am sure that it is in you as well" (2 Tim. 1:5).

We must look for opportunities to share the gospel message with children. According to a George Barna survey, almost half (43 percent) of Americans responded to the gospel before the age of thirteen, while two out of three believers responded to Christ before they were eighteen.[1] Barna explains: "It is during those years that people develop their frames

---

1. "Evangelism Is Most Effective among Kids," *Barna*, October 11, 2004, https://www.barna.com/research/evangelism-is-most-effective-among-kids.

of reference for the remainder of their lives—especially theologically and morally. Consistently explaining and modeling truth principles for young people is the most critical factor in their spiritual development."[2]

Parents must accept their responsibility to evangelize and disciple their children. Church members also need to be challenged to help parents fulfill their responsibility. Too many parents leave it up to the children's minister or the youth minister to teach spiritual insights to their children. Churches must help train parents to do this teaching and training for their own children.

In considering the subject of witnessing to children, there are extremes at each end of the discussion. Some people argue it is impossible for children to believe, and we should not be witnessing to children. Some on the other end seem to think that anytime a child expresses any interest at all in Christ we should automatically pronounce them converted. What guidance does Scripture give us in witnessing to children?

CHILDREN AND CONVERSION

I have read thousands of personal conversion testimonies written by college and seminary students. A significant number of these students shared their story using phrases such as, "I was baptized at age eight, but I really didn't know what I was doing. It wasn't until later that I truly came to know Christ," or "I went forward during an evangelistic invitation because my friend said to me, 'I'll go if you go.' While at the time I believed that was my conversion, I now have doubts that I genuinely knew the Lord then." These accounts of adult believers questioning their "childhood conversion" raise doubts in many people's minds. Can children really genuinely be converted?

Matthew 18:3 teaches us that conversion occurs at the level of a child. Jesus said, "Truly I say to you, unless you are converted and become like children, you shall not enter the kingdom of heaven." An adult might say to a child who expresses spiritual interest, "Wait until you're an adult." But Jesus says to adults, "Become like a child." Children are not saved in adult-like fashion; rather, adults are saved in childlike fashion.

---

2. "Evangelism Is Most Effective among Kids."

Matthew 19:13–15 highlights how much Jesus valued children: "Then some children were brought to Him so that He might lay His hands on them and pray, and the disciples rebuked them. But Jesus said, 'Let the children alone; and do not hinder them from coming to Me; for the kingdom of heaven belongs to such as these.' After laying His hands on them, He departed from there." The disciples rebuked those who brought the children to Jesus, perhaps because they thought the children would annoy Jesus, or that they were too young. Jesus laid his hands on them, showing how much he esteemed children.

Humility is an essential quality for conversion.

The passage in Matthew 18 goes on to say in verse 4, "Whoever then humbles himself as this child, he is the greatest in the kingdom of heaven." Humility is at the heart of salvation because it is our pride that keeps us from coming to Christ—our pride in our own innate goodness, our pride in our works, or our pride in the religious ritual we have performed. Humility and dependence are inherent in children.

A little child can believe in Jesus.

Jesus himself tells us that a child can believe. In Matthew 18:6, Jesus refers to "one of these little ones who *believe* in Me" (emphasis added). The word here is the same word for *believe* in John 3:16, Acts 16:31, and Romans 10:9–10. This verse is not teaching that every single child who expresses an interest is automatically converted, but it is saying that it is possible for a child to believe.

PRINCIPLES TO KEEP IN MIND

These are principles I first learned in my personal evangelism class (taught by Dr. Roy Fish) decades ago when I was a student. I have found these helpful in dealing with my own children and as a pastor relating to children in the church.

Like adults, children become Christians through responding to the gospel message with repentance and faith.

There is not a "separate" gospel message for children, nor is there a "different" necessary response to the gospel.

Don't assume anything.

When a child starts asking questions, they may or may not understand the gospel or be ready to receive Christ as Lord and Savior. Do not pressure a child into a response he/she is not ready to make.

A distinction should be made between the internal experience of conversion and the external expression of that experience.

We must distinguish between salvation and the external expression of that salvation (baptism or joining the church). Some children seem to think that conversion is only about getting baptized and have a view that it is baptism that produces salvation. We must be careful not to give the impression that good behavior, church activities, having prayed a rote prayer, or having raised their hand in vacation Bible school are the things that change a person's heart.

Avoid fear (or bribery) tactics.

We must avoid sensationalism with impressionable children. While we must explain the consequences of our sin (spiritual death and separation from God), avoid stoking fear by declarations such as, "God is going to get you if you don't respond tonight!" The other side of this equation bears mentioning as well. Candy tactics also should be avoided. Do not promise candy to anyone who comes to the front to become a follower of Christ. Many kids will sprint down the aisle if there is candy awaiting them.

Every child must be dealt with individually.

Every child has a different timetable in terms of their development. Stick to the basic issues, but also answer their questions. Listen to what they might be saying by asking certain questions, and it may give insight as to where the child is spiritually.

Sometimes children can be emotionally impacted by a Bible story. But that does not necessarily mean they are ready to accept Christ; we must be careful to deal with each child individually. I mentioned earlier how many adult believers discount the "conversion experience" they had as a child. I believe in some of those instances, that adult is correct—he/she did not experience genuine new birth as a child. But I also believe there are children who genuinely met Christ in conversion but were not given any counsel or follow-up about spiritual growth and, therefore, had doubts about the legitimacy of their childhood experience. They may have genuinely put their faith in Christ but never really began to grow in that relationship with him.

The religious background of a child must be taken into consideration.

I experienced the reality of this principle with my own children. My oldest child, Kristi, began asking spiritual questions when she was six years old. Sharon and I answered them one by one. Then one day she came to me and said, "Daddy, I want to follow Jesus. I want him to be my Lord and Savior. I want to turn from my sins and put my faith in him." As her dad I thought she was too young and probably did not really understand, so I kept putting her off. Then one day she came to me with tears streaming down her face and said, "But Daddy, didn't Jesus say '*whoever* believes in him?'" I realized I was being a stumbling block to my own daughter.

I have never since questioned my daughter's salvation or her commit-ment to Christ. The next day when she got home from elementary school, I asked her, "How was school today?" She replied, "Great! At recess today I told everybody in my class about Jesus!" Why should it have surprised me that my daughter at a young age wanted to follow Christ? She had grown up in a home where she was taken to church at least three times a week, the Bible was taught and studied, and we were constantly singing about the Lord in our car as we traveled. By the time my daughter turned seven years old, she had been exposed to more Bible content than some people get their entire lifetimes! On the other hand, if the child lives in a home where there has never been any teaching about Christ or the Bible, he/she may need extra conversations, teaching, and direction. A child's religious background should be taken into consideration.

The gospel must be explained in terms understandable to a child.

Sharing the gospel with children is not the time to try to impress them with your deep theological vocabulary. Explain the gospel using terms a child can understand. The Methodist circuit rider Sam Jones said the greatest compliment he ever received in his ministry came from a young boy. Jones had preached and was preparing to leave, when he heard this young boy say to his dad, "I want him to come back, because he is the only preacher I ever listened to that I can understand every thing . . . he says."[3] Jones knew that if he had communicated at a level where this young boy could understand, that meant everyone else there could understand as well.

Drs. Paul Stringer and Sharon Thompson offer examples for simplifying definitions without compromising the meaning:

- *Sin:* when you know what you should do, but you choose not to do it. It is choosing your way instead of God's way. Sin separates you from God.
- *Repent:* being sorry for the wrong choices you have made. You decide to do things God's way, not your way.
- *Obeying God:* choosing to live God's way
- *Christian:* one who has asked God to forgive him/her and be in charge of his/her life
- *Savior:* Jesus is Savior because he saved you from being separated from God because of your sin; Jesus did for you what you could not do for yourself.[4]

Never discount an expression of interest on the part of a child.

Taking a child seriously and paying genuine attention to the child's interest does not mean that that child is ready to accept Christ. It does not necessarily mean that that child understands completely. But take advantage of teachable moments. Do not expect a child to answer questions with the theological precision of a seminary graduate. But also do not assume they are ready to follow Christ just because they are asking questions.

Avoid questions that have a yes/no answer.

Children will usually answer "yes" if they are asked whether they understand. They want to please their parents and their teacher or pastor. Ask open-ended questions. Instead of asking "Do you know why Christ died on the cross?" ask, "What do you understand about Christ's death on the cross?" Or, instead of, "Do you understand what sin is?" ask "How would you explain what sin is?"

3. Sam Jones, *Sam Jones' Own Book: A Series of Sermons, with an Autobiographical Sketch* (Nashville: Southwestern, 1886), 36.
4. Paula Stringer and Sharon Thompson, "Painting Pictures of Jesus," cited in Will McRaney, *The Art of Personal Evangelism* (Nashville: Broadman & Holman, 2003), 145.

In my decades of serving as a pastor, I have had many parents bring a child to me with great excitement, believing that their child is ready to follow Christ. Sometimes the parents will have done some coaching, trying to anticipate my questions and helping their child think through how to answer those questions. If I ask a child why she wants to talk with me, and she replies, "I want to accept Christ's substitutionary atonement for my forensic justification, and to begin the process of progressive sanctification, culminating in ultimate glorification at the eschaton," I know she has had a bit of coaching from her parents.

The question I use with children (and it is not a bad question to use with adults either) is, "Tell me in your own words what that means." Children do not have an extensive theological vocabulary, but they can convey their sense of sinfulness, their need of a Savior, and how they believe Christ is that Savior. I do not want them simply repeating something they have heard others say without having a true understanding of what they are saying.

Children should be taught the responsibilities as well as the benefits of the Christian life.

Again, a child is not going to fully understand everything about the cost of discipleship. Not even adults fully understand every aspect of repentance. One of God's great gifts to us is he does not show us every aspect of our sin at the moment of conversion or we would be undone, we would be overwhelmed. Sanctification is *progressive* sanctification, but there must be an understanding of turning from sin and coming to Christ, and some understanding of the cost of discipleship and what it means to follow Christ. Children need to know the responsibilities as well as the benefits of the Christian life.

EVANGELISM POINTERS FOR PARENTS

You as a parent are responsible for the spiritual foundation of your child.

It is not primarily the job of the pastor, the children's minister, or the teachers at church. They are your partners in providing a spiritual foundation, so let them talk to your child as well. However, the primary responsibility for your child's spiritual well-being rests with you.

Share your testimony with your children.

Share how Jesus impacts your daily life. Look for teachable moments with them. Recall that in Joshua 4 the parents were to be prepared to answer when their children asked them, "What do these stones mean to you?" (v. 6). Share your conversion testimony and your spiritual pilgrimage with your children. My wife would use the many hours per week she was in the car singing Scripture songs with the kids, having them memorize Scripture verses, asking spiritual questions, and using that time to nurture them. Besides the car, the dinner table, bedtime, and family worship are other opportunities to have good spiritual conversations.

Share the gospel with your children in an age-appropriate way clearly and often.

Talk about the gospel in a natural way. Ask questions when you read Bible stories to them. Plan strategic times to talk to them—perhaps at bedtime when you are alone with them.

Let your children see you share the gospel with those in your circles of influence.

Let your children see how important it is to you to share Christ with others. Let your children go with you to invite friends or neighbors to evangelistic events, praying with them before and afterward. Make a list of friends and family you pray for regularly to come to know Christ. Let them see you being intentional about having unsaved neighbors over for a meal. Let them see you ask the waiter or waitress if you could pray for him/her. Let your children see how you try to incorporate evangelism into your daily life.

Keep the Bible as the source of authority in your home.

Read the Bible daily with your children. Talk about Scripture as you encounter various situations. If you see a beautiful scene, thank God for his creation, and read a psalm about the glory of his creation. If your child's feelings get hurt at school, bring in a verse about being kind, tenderhearted, and forgiving. If your child disobeys you, share God's command to honor and obey parents. If you yell at your child, ask forgiveness, and share how you need God's forgiveness.

Plan mission-oriented family activities.

Pray regularly for missionaries at your church or friends who are missionaries. Explain to your children the privilege we have to be ambassadors for the king of kings and reinforce the gospel message. Plan some mission activities to do with your children, giving them a meaningful role. Examples could be visiting a nursing home, providing clothes and toys for a needy family at Christmas, taking your children along to help clean an elderly person's home, or grocery shopping for someone who struggles to get out. The ideas would depend on the age of the children, life circumstances, and the amount of time you have.

Be joyful about your walk with the Lord.

A relationship with Christ is not a list of "Thou shalt not"s. Exhibit joy, even in the midst of trials (James 1:2–4). Speak often about God's love, and help them see your delight in Christ.

CHAPTER 24

WITNESSING TO FAMILY MEMBERS

FROM THE VERY BEGINNING GOD chose to work through families to bring his truth to humanity. In the Old Testament, the family served as the vehicle through which God's Word was passed on from generation to generation. The Old Testament clearly instructs what parents were to do in terms of teaching their children:

> Hear, O Israel! The LORD is our God, the LORD is one! You shall love the LORD your God with all your heart and with all your soul and with all your might. These words, which I am commanding you today, shall be on your heart. You shall teach them diligently to your sons and shall talk of them when you sit in your house and when you walk by the way and when you lie down and when you rise up. You shall bind them as a sign on your hand and they shall be as frontals on your forehead. You shall write them on the doorposts of your house and on your gates. (Deut. 6:4–9)

Jesus's ministry provides examples of entire households coming to faith. When Jesus healed the demoniac, he said in Luke 8:39: "Return to your house and describe what great things God has done for you." In John 4:46–54, we see Jesus healing the son of a Roman officer. As a result, the Roman officer and his whole house believed (John 4:53). When Jesus went to the home of Zacchaeus, Luke 19:6 reports, "And he [Zacchaeus] hurried and came down and received him gladly," and as a result, his whole family became believers.

The book of Acts evidences several instances of evangelism in a household. We read in Acts 20:20 that whole families had come to Christ in Ephesus, and Paul taught them by households. When Peter went to Cornelius in Acts 10, Cornelius had his whole family listen to what Peter had to say. In Acts 16, Lydia and her entire household believed and were baptized. Also in Acts 16, the jailer in Philippi accepted Christ and Paul and Silas spoke the word of the Lord to his family: "And after he brought them out, he said, 'Sirs, what must I do to be saved?' They said, 'Believe in the Lord Jesus, and you shall be saved, you and your household.' And they spoke the word of the Lord to him together with all who were in his house" (Acts 16:30–32).

From the very beginning God has worked through families to bring truth to humanity. However, many people find it hard to talk to their family members about Christ. Our families are the ones who know us inside and out. They know our strengths, but they also know our weaknesses. We realize they could label us as a hypocrite faster than anyone else. They might respond angrily to our witnessing attempts, which can lead to strained relationships within the family. Yet we must learn to set aside our fears and look for opportunities to share the good news with family members.

GENERAL PRINCIPLES

Witnessing to family members follows many of the same principles as witnessing to anyone; however, because of the closeness of family relationships, there are some added considerations.

Pray!
The starting place, as in every form of evangelism, is prayer. Do not give up. Keep praying. I know children who have prayed for their parents for decades and vice versa. Pray for God to work in their hearts as you prepare to share the gospel with them.

Share spiritual truths as a part of natural, everyday conversations.
Bring the subject of Christ into normal, everyday conversations. You can share how he is working in your life, answers to prayer, or a specific

verse of Scripture that has encouraged you. Assure your family members you will pray for them for different circumstances in their lives.

Be honest about wanting to share the gospel.

You can be straightforward with your family member and yet be at ease. You can start the conversation by telling them that you want to ask their opinion on something spiritual (i.e., "Who do you think Jesus Christ is?"), or ask if you can share something very personal that you have not shared before. Then give your personal testimony of how you came to know Christ.

Avoid any type of "holier than thou" attitude.

We are recipients of God's grace, and we must be ready to share that grace with others. If they are lost and acting like a lost person, remember they are lost! It should never surprise us when lost people act like lost people. Speak to them in patient and understanding ways. Remember that but for the grace of God, you would still be lost yourself.

Reflect Christ in your behavior and attitudes.

Peter reminds us that we are to answer questions "with gentleness and reverence" (1 Peter 3:15). Seek always to display the spirit of Christ as you are sharing the gospel of Christ.

Forgive them.

One of the first things you may need to do in witnessing to family members is to forgive those who have wounded you. I once heard Elisabeth Elliot share, "When you release your pain to God, then your hands are able to receive what he wants to give you."[1] When we release our bitterness, God can then fill us with more love and compassion for others. Paul gives us this admonition: "Be kind to one another, tender-hearted, forgiving each other, just as God in Christ also has forgiven you" (Eph. 4:32).

---

1. Elizabeth Elliot, "Evangelism and Missions," Women and Evangelism Conference, Wheaton College, Spring 1991.

Share the gospel message.

What do you include in the gospel message as you share with family and friends? The gospel message! There is not a different gospel for family members than there is for other people. Share the good news of what God has done for us in Christ.

Be intentional.

We need to be intentional with our family members. Life can pass by quickly while we are waiting for a perfect opportunity to talk with them. Do not wait for a perfect opportunity; seize opportunities when they present themselves.

Give Christian resources.

Books can be a tremendous way to open the door of communication. Those who enjoy intellectual conversations may enjoy C. S. Lewis's *Mere Christianity* or Tim Keller's *The Reason for God.* Those needing help in marriage or parenting may read a Christian book on that topic. Directing family members to a helpful online sermon or podcast on a particular issue could help point them to Christ.

Be sensitive to how and when to share your faith with family members.

Let the Holy Spirit guide your words. Be sensitive to opportunities. Your family knows you very well. To give you an example, when one member of my extended family heard I was leaving engineering and going into the ministry, he remarked to another family member, "I guess Tim isn't half as smart as I thought he was." Later, I had the opportunity to talk to this individual. I shared the story of E. Stanley Jones, the great Methodist missionary to India.[2] Jones once spoke at a Hindu university, sharing the claims of Christ. When he finished, the president of the university stood up and commented to the students, "If what this man has just said is *not* true, then it doesn't really matter; but, if what this man has said *is* true, then nothing matters more."[3] I shared with him that the reason I left

---

2. Jones's autobiography is titled *With Christ on the Indian Road* (Nashville: Abingdon, 1925).
3. E. Stanley Jones, *In Christ: Devotions for Every Day of the Year* (Franklin, TN: Seedbed, 2017), Kindle loc. 493.

engineering to follow God's call is that I am convinced the gospel is true and therefore nothing matters more.

Witnessing to Parents

Scripture commands us to honor our parents: "Honor your father and mother . . . so that it may be well with you" (Eph. 6:2–3). Scripture does not give a time limit on honoring them. The Bible does not say to honor them until age eighteen or age twenty-one, and then you no longer need to show them honor. We need to honor them our whole life.

Pray!

As stated above, prayer is always the starting point. We need to pray that we model Christ's love and character to them but also pray for God to soften their hearts and bring opportunities. Remember that patience is key. Evangelism is a spiritual battle—only God can change hearts! We always must go back to prayer. If your parents do not know the Lord, they should be the first people you pray for every day. Ask God to be at work in their hearts and minds.

Don't act superior to them.

Beware of an arrogant "I found it, and you don't have it" attitude. Having a superior attitude to your parents can be a stumbling block in witnessing. Your parents raised you; don't make them feel like they have failed you by not taking you to church or reading the Bible to you. This mistake is often made by young people who come to Christ in college. Their first trip home, they have a tendency to preach to their parents, sometimes in a way that communicates disrespect instead of honor.

Do not give the impression you are rejecting your family for "the family of God."

Do not cut yourself off from occasions important to your family or reject your family's heritage and traditions. I am not suggesting that you participate in something unbiblical; I am talking about going to family reunions and doing activities that build relationships. I have known new believers who have told their parents they cannot go to their annual family reunion because they have to go to a Bible study that day. Do not become so involved in Christian activities that you never see your family. When you go home, do not just hang out with your Christian friends and fail to spend any time with your parents.

Forgive them.

You may need to forgive them. No one can be a perfect parent. Some parents have deeply wounded their children, and these painful scars can cause bitterness to dwell in the child's heart. A major part in communicating the gospel to your parents is to set aside bitterness and display a forgiving heart toward them.

Show respect.

The verb form of *honor* means "to esteem, admire, compliment, commend, and show reverence." When we seek to honor someone that obviously means, we do not try to dishonor them. We do not shame them, humiliate them, or speak to them or about them negatively. Tim Challies shares this helpful advice: "Dennis Rainey goes so far as to call children to write a formal tribute to their parents, to present it to them and to read it aloud in their presence. We can honor our parents by esteeming our parents."[4]

Ask for input when making decisions.

Ask your parents for their input when making decisions. Even if you end up not taking their advice, asking them their counsel honors them by showing you respect their opinion.

Admit your failures.

Living the Christian life means humbly asking forgiveness for the many times you fail to honor Christ and others. Jesus teaches us, "A prophet is not without honor except in his hometown and in his own household" (Matt. 13:57). Why is that reality true? Our parents know us very well and can see how and when we fall short; therefore we must be quick to apologize and confess when we fail.

---

4. Tim Challies, "5 Practical Ways to Honor Your Parents," *Challies* (blog), December 21, 2016, https://www.challies.com/articles/5-practical-ways-to-honor-your-parents.

Be patient.

First Corinthians 13 reminds us that love is patient and long-suffering. It may take days, weeks, months, or years, but be patient and continue to pray for your family. Continue to share the gospel with your lips, and reinforce the gospel with your life.

Keep the channels of communication open with your parents.

As our kids left home, Sharon and I loved to get a note, a phone call, an email, or text from them. Parents always enjoy hearing from their children, no matter what the age. Lines of communication will provide opportunities for you to testify of Christ.

FAMILY TREE EVANGELISM

Make a family tree chart.

I mentioned this approach in the chapter on concentric circles. Sketch out your family tree: your parents, siblings, grandparents, aunts, uncles, and cousins. After you chart your family members, try to determine where they are spiritually.

Ask questions.

Here are some questions that are helpful to ask:

What felt needs are your relatives experiencing? Felt needs could be insecurity, boredom, lack of purpose, guilt, loneliness, bitterness, indifference, parenting problems, marriage problems, and fear of death. I am not suggesting we simply put a bandage on their felt needs. But many times, the felt need becomes a doorway to addressing the real need.

Someone may be hard-hearted today toward the gospel today, but the circumstances of life have a way of breaking up hard hearts. We have all heard the adage, "There are no atheists in foxholes." While that dictum is not universally true (some people become even more hardened during adversity), when someone's life begins crumbling around them, they are often more open to spiritual realities.

What needs could you meet in their lives? Serving others provides a wonderful opportunity to show our love and concern for them. How might you be able to serve your family members?

What are their misunderstandings about Christianity? Part of evangelism is trying to discern the real reason they are rejecting the gospel. Many think religion is the same thing as Christianity. They believe they should just try to follow the Golden Rule, and they will be okay. They need to see that being a Christian is all about a relationship with Christ. It may be they are spiritually ignorant and do not really know what the gospel is. It could be they are angry with God because of some painful circumstances in their life. Ask them about their understanding of Christianity.

What mutual interests could lead to conversations about Christ? See if you can participate in activities that would interest your family members. Maybe it would be going to a sports game; going fishing or shopping; or having a game night. Take advantage of holidays, anniversaries, birthdays, and graduations. You may need to write these on a calendar to intentionally remember them. Maintain contact with family members.

WITNESSING TO AN UNSAVED SPOUSE

The first couple, Adam and Eve, give us a vision of what God originally intended for spouses. Before the fall, life in the garden of Eden was perfect in every way. God designed that spouses base their marriage on a mutual commitment to him and obedience to his Word. Before the fall, Adam and Eve were at peace with themselves, each other, and their surroundings.

Unfortunately, because of the fall, the same cannot be said about marriages today. Discord rather than harmony often characterizes the relationship between husbands and wives.

This discord can be magnified when one partner is unsaved. Sometimes a believer knowingly marries an unbeliever, thinking that the marriage will bring the unsaved spouse to Christ. At other times, one spouse becomes a Christian after the marriage begins. Still others really think they are marrying a Christian, only to discover later that this was not true. Whatever the circumstances leading up to a marriage with an unsaved person, the challenge is what the saved spouse should do now. How can a believing spouse witness to an unsaved spouse?

Begin with yourself and your motives.

Reflect on your motives. Do you want your spouse to become a Christian simply so that it will be easier for you and so that you do not have to sit in church all by yourself? Evangelism should not be based on self-centered desires. Are your motives pure? Your primary motive should be concern for his/her lost soul. We must all examine our motives in everything to strive for a pure heart. I think about the man who brought his child to Jesus for healing, and Jesus said to this man, "All things are possible to him who believes" (Mark 9:23). The man's reply was, "I do believe; help my unbelief" (v. 24). The man was saying that though he had *some* faith (demonstrated by his action in bringing his child to Jesus), he knew his faith was not perfect. His heart still had unbelief mixed in with faith. We all struggle with having completely pure motives. We can pray in the spirit of this man and say, "Lord, I really want my spouse to be saved for his/her good and for your glory, but I also realize my motives are intermingled with selfishness." Begin with yourself.

Pray.

Again, prayer is vital. Living with an unbelieving spouse can be a difficult and demanding task. You need to pray not only for your spouse's conversion but also that your life will be a witness to the reality of Christ. Marriage can be hard enough when you live with a believer. Gary Thomas, in his book *Sacred Marriage*, writes, "View marriage as an entryway into sanctification—as a relationship that will reveal your sinful behaviors and attitudes and give you the opportunity to address them before the Lord."[5] In context, he is talking about marriage to a believer in whom the Spirit of God is also at work. You can imagine how much more challenging being married to an unbeliever can become! Pray and ask God to do a work of grace in your heart daily. Ask God how you can be a better spouse; also, pray for God to do a work in your unsaved spouse's life.

---

5. Gary Thomas, *Sacred Marriage* (Grand Rapids: Zondervan, 2000), 97.

I remember one Sunday I was coming out of my office headed to the sanctuary, and a woman in our church whose husband was not a believer stopped me in the hall. We had been praying for him for several months and inviting him to church, but he had never come. She said to me, "He's here! He's here! My husband is here in church this morning!" Then she pointed her finger in my face and said, "Don't blow it!" I had to remind her that conversion is a work of the Holy Spirit, and that it was not up to me. I encouraged her to pray that the Lord would take the words of the gospel and apply them to her husband's heart. The believing spouse is never responsible for the conversion of the other spouse—nor is it the pastor's job. Conversion is a work of the Holy Spirit.

Remember the walk/talk balance.

First Peter 3:1 says: "In the same way, you wives, be submissive to your own husbands, so that even if any of them are disobedient to the word, they may be won over without a word by the behavior of their wives." The walk/talk balance does not mean that the believing spouse should never talk about God or share the gospel; it does mean they should not preach in a nagging manner. Trying to preach your spouse into the kingdom almost always creates conflict. With an unbelieving spouse, often actions will speak louder than words. Communicate the good news, but then seek to daily live out the good news.

Live the life of a servant.

Look for ways to serve your spouse. Serving your spouse in humility and love displays the character of Christ to them.

Never imply that the Christian life means perfection.

If you ever imply that the Christian life means perfection, your spouse may take delight in pointing out your mistakes; you will most certainly fail. When you do fail, ask for forgiveness, and keep serving. This pattern requires sacrifice, and it is not an easy road. But hopefully the unsaved spouse can see the reality of Christ in your life—not perfectly, but clearly.

Deal with conflict in a godly way.

Show by the way you live that God is at work in you. Be gentle and respectful, and deal with conflict in a godly way. Admit your faults, and ask for forgiveness when you fail. If you need help, ask for it! Go to a pastor or a counselor. Compliment and build your spouse up; do not tear him/her down. Even though he/she is not a believer, be his/her best friend and give him/her the emotional support he/she needs. Enter every area of his/her life unless what he/she is doing is compromising the Bible. Learn everything you can about how to have a good marriage and then apply it. Seek to focus on the things you have in common. The depth of your sacrificial love will be the most impactful influence you can have.

Invite your spouse to special events at your church.

Invite them to go to with you to church, even if they often refuse. Invite them to special events, conferences, seminars, musicals, and especially activities that involve the children.

WITNESSING TO GRANDPARENTS/OLDER RELATIVES

If you are sharing with relatives or close friends older than you, be respectful! Remember that they may not appreciate being preached to by a younger person. Do not make it sound like you are speaking down to them; they have much more life experience than you do. Show them respect! They may have grown up in a church where personal faith was a private matter and never discussed. Try sharing your testimony with them and include the key points of the gospel in your testimony. Share that you are a sinner and that everyone sins—and end with how, by his grace, God saved you when you repented of your sins and put your faith in Christ alone for salvation.

CONCLUSION

Matthew 10:35–36 warns us that the gospel can turn a man against his father and a daughter against her mother. Families can and will divide over spiritual realities. You must be willing to bear your cross in order to live by the two great commandments of loving God and loving others. Trust God. You are to be faithful; it is God who will bring the harvest. Only God can bring salvation.

CHAPTER 25

WITNESSING TO CULT MEMBERS OR ADHERENTS OF OTHER RELIGIONS

WHILE THE PRIMARY FOCUS OF THIS CHAPTER is on witnessing to cult members, most of the principles will also apply in conversing with adherents of other religions.

WHAT IS A CULT?

In defining the word *cult* we must recognize that people have used this word differently throughout history. The term therefore can carry a variety of meanings. Sociologists have used the word to describe how groups emerge without denoting any negative connotations such as aberrant theology. Because the term *cult* today typically carries a negative connotation, sociologists tend to use different terms such as *alternative religions*, *emerging religious movements*, or *minority religions*. But it is helpful to note that early uses of the term *cult* referred to the way groups emerge without assigning positive or negative connotations to particular groups.

Some have defined cults psychologically. This definition was very prevalent in the 1960s and 1970s when observers accused some religious movements of engaging in mind control and even brainwashing their followers.

A technique known as "deprogramming" became popular during this time frame, where measures would be used to try to help a person who held a controversial belief system to change those beliefs, including abandoning allegiance to the particular group associated with the belief system.

Evangelicals define cults theologically. The definition I use for a cult is "any group that deviates from Christian orthodoxy." Immediately some people will ask, "What about world religions? Don't they deviate from Christian orthodoxy?" Yes, world religions also teach false doctrine, but they tend to be categorized as "world religions" instead of "cults." Thousands of different cult groups exist today around the world, some with millions of followers and others with only a handful of adherents.

Basic Patterns in Cults

One way to summarize basic patterns in cults is to use mathematic formulas. First, cults *add* to the Word of God. They have their own "revealed truth" that they view as superior to the Bible. While they might claim that the Bible is one of their authoritative books, whenever there is a conflict between the Bible and one of their other authorities, the Bible usually loses. Cults add to the Word of God.

Second, they *subtract* from Jesus Christ. They teach that Jesus is not fully God, and they deny his deity. Cult members may argue that Christ may be someone special—such as a prophet or great moral teacher—but they deny that he is God (part of their denying the doctrine of the Trinity). Cults subtract from Jesus Christ.

Third, they *multiply* the requirements for salvation. In addition to some type of faith in their beliefs, they all add works to their system, whether they are good works, religious works, being baptized by proxy for someone else, or being baptized for yourself. They add religious rituals people must go through to be right with God.

Fourth, they *divide* the loyalties of their members between God and their organization. They apply tremendous pressure to adherents to never to leave their organization. They equate salvation with being a part of their particular group. That is why it is so hard for people to leave. They are told if they leave, they are not simply leaving a group but losing their salvation. Pressure to remain, especially from friends and family members, can be quite strong.

A few years ago I had an ongoing four-month conversation with a cult member in Louisville. We met together every week for four months to study the Bible and to discuss doctrine. At the end of our study, he told me I had convinced him that what he had been taught was wrong. But he said he could not leave his group because his family would disown him. He was a single dad, and he said his mom would never speak to him again and would quit providing childcare while he worked. He said, "The cost is too great."

Why Should We Study Cults?

Because cult members need the Lord Jesus Christ as their Savior

Cult members are lost. They may display great devotion, they may appear sincere in their beliefs, but their beliefs do not save. Cult members need to hear the gospel and repent and believe in Christ alone for salvation.

Because we are called to make a defense for our faith

First Peter 3:15 commands us, "But sanctify Christ as Lord in your hearts, always being ready to make a defense to everyone who asks you to give an account for the hope that is in you, yet with gentleness and reverence." We are to be prepared to make a defense of our faith at all times. We are to be prepared to make a defense to all people. We must make our defense respectfully. This command is for every believer; is it not just a suggestion for a selected few super-Christians.

Because cults use our vocabulary, but their dictionary

Cult members utilize a lot of biblical terminology, such as "faith," "salvation," "Jesus Christ," "heaven," and "assurance," but they redefine those terms to fit their own doctrine. They can sound very orthodox in their vocabulary, but when you clearly define the way they are using those terms (their dictionary), you see they are espousing false teaching.

Because studying the doctrines of cults will enable us to understand and define our own beliefs better

Studying what cults teach (and why their teaching is false), helps us to understand and define our own beliefs. As we study their denial of Jesus Christ as divine, we clarify why they are wrong and why we believe in

Christ's deity. What cults teach can sound right until it is placed alongside orthodox Christian belief, just as a counterfeit bill can look genuine until it is placed alongside a real piece of currency. Then the differences become apparent.

Because regardless of whether or not you go to them, cultists are going to come to you

Whether or not you seek out cult members to share the gospel with them, you can be assured they will be seeking you out (and your neighbors and fellow church members) to convert you and them. Whereas many evangelical churches have ceased going door-to-door in neighborhoods (because it does not seem as effective or produce the same number of results as it used to), cult groups continue to knock on door after door, seeking to gain new adherents to their beliefs. They are persistent in their efforts.

PRINCIPLES FOR WITNESSING TO CULT MEMBERS

Be grounded in Scripture and Christian theology.

Cult members get the majority of their adherents from nominal Christians.[1] A typical approach is as follows. Two very polite, well-dressed young men or women knock on someone's door. They introduce themselves and mention they are surveying the neighborhood to gauge interest in a Bible study. If the person who answers the door says he attends church, they might ask him, "Has your pastor ever sat down with you to help you study the Bible?"

"Well no," the man might respond. "I'm not sure my pastor even knows who I am."

"Well," one of the cult members will reply, "we are trained in how to study the Bible and we love to help other people learn to study it for themselves. There is no cost—we don't charge anything for our time. Our reward is the joy of knowing we are helping people to better understand the Bible. Do you think you would be interested in a study like that? We could come right here to your home, at a time convenient for you, and help you."

---

1. I have heard this claim acknowledged by both cult group leaders and Christians involved in witnessing to cult members.

The next thing you know, that man is studying the Bible with these cult members, and a few months later he has left his church and joined their group.

One day as I was waiting in an airport terminal for my flight to depart, I struck up a conversation with the man sitting next to me. After a few minutes of conversation, we both stopped and smiled. Each of us realized at the same time that the other person was seeking to bring spiritual matters into the conversation! He asked, "Okay—what flavor are you?" (He was not asking my favorite type of ice cream but what religious group I was with.)

I replied, "Baptist."

We were in an airport in a southern city, so he followed up by asking, "Southern Baptist?"

"Yes," I replied. "I am Southern Baptist."

He grinned from ear to ear as he told me, "I'm Mormon. Southern Baptists make our best converts!"

Many nominal Christians know enough to know the Bible is important, but the church has often done a poor job in teaching believers how to study the Bible. Nominal Christians are "easy targets" for cults because they are not grounded in the truth.

Define terms—both yours and theirs.

I mentioned earlier in this chapter that cults use "our vocabulary" but "their dictionary." That is why it is crucial to define the terms being used in the discussion. Cult members often talk about Jesus, faith, and salvation, but they mean something very different when they use those terms. Whichever cult you are dealing with, familiarize yourself with their "dictionary." How do they "redefine" basic Christian words and concepts?

Agree on an "equal time" approach.

This principle may be the most helpful insight whether talking with a cult member or an adherent of a world religion. When I am in a spiritual conversation, and each of us identifies with our particular group, I ask the person if we can take time to share our beliefs with each other. I suggest we do this in a respectful way. I tell this person, "I would really like to know what you believe about how we can have our sins forgiven. Why don't you take the next twenty minutes and share with me what you believe. I will not attack your beliefs, and I will not interrupt you or argue with you. I will only ask a question if there is something you say that I do not understand. Then I'd like for us to switch, and I'd like to share with you what I believe."

I have found this approach to work far better than the technique I used in my earliest attempts at discussions with cult members. Our conversations quickly degenerated into passionate disagreements where there was more "heat" than "light" shared. The equal-time approach allows you to have a thoughtful conversation. Cult members and adherents of world religions are often eager for the opportunity to talk about what they believe. I always let them go first to show I do care what they have to say, but also to determine how well they understand their own group's teaching. Not every cult member or adherent of a world religion understands what their group teaches. I want to discover how well they understand their own group's beliefs as that understanding will help me in how I share the gospel message with them.

For several years I helped lead a group of college and seminary students on a study tour of England and Scotland. We would visit historical sites related to Christianity as well as attend church services and discuss outreach strategies with our brothers and sisters in Great Britain. One of the highlights of the trip each year for me was the opportunity to join in the evangelistic ministry of Jay Smith in London. Jay has a polemic ministry among Muslims in Hyde Park. Each Sunday afternoon at Speaker's Corner in Hyde Park, Jay would stand on his "soapbox" (actually a small folding ladder) and compare Christianity to Islam. Because of his topic and his God-given booming voice, he quickly garnered the largest crowd among all the speakers there. Many Muslims would come to harass, to argue, or to listen. We would stand on the outskirts of the crowd and seek to strike up individual conversations with Muslims who were there.

I approached one Muslim man and asked him, "What do you think of this speaker?"

He replied, "I do not like him. He is an angry man."

I responded, "Could be anger, but it also could be passion."

To which he replied, "Fair enough, but I think it is anger. Besides," he said, "that man is a Christian. All Christians want to do is to kill Muslims."

I reached out and put my hand on his shoulder and said, "My friend, that is simply not true."

He quickly started talking about the Crusades and how Christians have gone out of their way to slaughter Muslims. I acknowledged that had happened and told this man that both Christians and Muslims have parts of their history that are not particularly flattering. I told him we could debate what we perceive as the other group's failings but that I would rather have an honest conversation. I presented the equal-time opportunity to him, and he accepted. We went a short distance away to a park bench and had a wonderful conversation for the next forty-five minutes, during which I was able to explain the Christian gospel message to him.

Be loving.

Being loving is always the right thing to do. Ephesians 4:15 exhorts us to "speak the truth in love." Displaying love to a cult member is also strategic; they are often taught they will be persecuted by Christians. I have had Mormon missionaries tell me they are regularly "nudged off the road" by cars while riding their bicycles, and they are accustomed to having professing Christians slam doors in their faces.

How can we cultivate a heart of love toward those who hold false beliefs? By remembering they are not the enemy—they are victims of our true enemy, Satan. Satan has blinded their eyes and holds them captive to do his will. Ephesians 6:12 reminds us, "For our struggle is not against flesh and blood, but against the rulers, against the powers, against the world forces of this darkness, against the spiritual forces of wickedness in the heavenly places." Your goal is to win a person, not an argument. When you treat a cult member with love, it is disarming to them.

Become familiar with their material.

You can get a brief introduction to witnessing to members of cults and world religions at NAMB.org/Apologetics. Particularly for cults, the most helpful website is Watchman.org. This website serves as something of a "clearing house" of information, especially with its helpful "Index of Cults and Religions" and "Profiles" sections. A few hours spent on these websites will help Christians understand the belief systems of various cults/world religions.

Pray.

We could put this principle at the beginning, at the end, and everywhere in between. Engaging cult members and adherents of world religions is a spiritual battle. Satan has deceived cult members into believing lies. God is the only one who can open spiritually blind eyes, so we must saturate this process in prayer.

Stress the uniqueness of the gospel

The way I always finish a conversation with a cult member or with an adherent of a world religion is to stress the uniqueness of the gospel. I do this with a simple spelling lesson. You can spell every religion in the world with the letters D-O; *do* this, and you shall live. Every world religion or cult has certain beliefs you must hold, but they have a long list of works you have to do in order to hope that you have life after death or some reward. Christianity is spelled D-O-N-E. Salvation has been accomplished for us through Christ, and all we do is receive his gift of forgiveness with open hands.

CHAPTER 26

EVANGELISTIC PREACHING

FOR THE SCRIPTURE SAYS, "Whoever believes in Him will not be disappointed." For there is no distinction between Jew and Greek; for the same Lord is Lord of all, abounding in riches for all who call on Him; for "Whoever will call on the name of the Lord will be saved." How then will they call on Him in whom they have not believed? How will they believe in Him whom they have not heard? And how will they hear without a preacher? How will they preach unless they are sent? Just as it is written, "How beautiful are the feet of those who bring good news of good things!" However, they did not all heed the good news; for Isaiah says, "Lord, who has believed our report?" So faith comes from hearing, and hearing by the word of Christ. (Rom. 10:11–17)

While this textbook focuses primarily on personal evangelism, since some readers will also have a preaching/teaching ministry, it will prove helpful to say a few words about evangelistic preaching. Many helpful resources address this particular type of preaching, and I commend them to the reader.[1] This chapter will focus on several characteristics of a good

---

1. Helpful resources include Roger Carswell, *Evangelistic Preaching* (Leyland, UK: 10Publishing, 2015); C. H. Spurgeon, *Lectures to My Students* (Edinburgh: Banner of Truth, 2011); David L. Larsen, *The Evangelism Mandate: Recovering the Centrality of Gospel Preaching* (Wheaton, IL: Crossway, 1992); Ramesh Richard, *Preparing Evangelistic Sermons* (Grand Rapids: Baker, 2005); John Chapman, *Setting*

evangelistic message. These characteristics can be applied in various preaching/teaching contexts.

Characteristics of a Good Evangelistic Message

Bible-centered

First Corinthians 15:3–4 reminds us of the scriptural foundation for the gospel message: "For I delivered to you as of first importance what I also received, that Christ died for our sins according to the Scriptures, and that He was buried, and that He was raised on the third day according to the Scriptures." In John 5:39 (NIV), Jesus affirmed, "These are the very Scriptures that testify about me." God has promised to bless his Word. The Spirit brings conviction through the Word: "For the word of God is living and active and sharper than any two-edged sword, and piercing as far as the division of soul and spirit, of both joints and marrow, and able to judge the thoughts and intentions of the heart" (Heb. 4:12). When we preach/teach the biblical text, we can assert with confidence, "Thus says the Lord!"

John Stott gives this helpful clarification of biblical/expository preaching:

> I venture to say that all true biblical preaching is expository preaching. I know, of course, that some textbooks on homiletics supply a list of different kinds of preaching, one being "textual," another "topical," a third "expository," and sometimes others besides. In this context, "expository preaching" is usually a technical term for the detailed verse-by-verse exposition of a lengthy passage. But it is a pity to restrict the expression to this one type of preaching. "Exposition" means to bring out of Scripture what is there. Its opposite is "imposition," which is to read into Scripture what is not there, but what one would like to find there if only one could. The paramount function of true preaching is to be so subservient to the biblical text that God's Word is heard to

Hearts on Fire: A Guide to Giving Evangelistic Talks (Kingsford, UK: Matthias, 1999); Roy Fish, Al Fasol, Steve Gaines, and Ralph Douglas West, *Preaching Evangelistically: Proclaiming the Saving Message of Jesus* (Nashville: Broadman & Holman, 2006); Lloyd Merle Perry and John R. Strubbar, *Evangelistic Preaching* (Chicago: Moody, 1979).

speak from it. Whether one's text is a single word, a sentence, a verse, a paragraph, a chapter, or even a whole book, still the truly Christian preacher is an expositor.[2]

In Jeremiah 23:29 we read: "'Is not My word like fire?' declares the LORD, 'and like a hammer which shatters a rock?'" God's Word is like fire that melts, like a hammer that breaks up hard hearts. Romans 10:17 reminds us that "faith comes by hearing, and hearing by the Word of God."

Christ-centered

Christ is the Gospel, and a good evangelistic message focuses on him. Spurgeon gives this wise counsel to preachers:

> Of all I would wish to say this is the sum; my brethren, preach Christ, always and evermore. He is the whole gospel. His person, offices, and work must be our one great, all-comprehending theme. The world needs still to be told of its Saviour, and of the way to reach him. Justification by faith should be far more than it is the daily testimony of Protestant pulpits. . . . Blessed is that ministry of which Christ is all.[3]

Christ alone is the way to God (Acts 4:12; John 14:6), and we must proclaim this truth boldly. We are not presenting a theory but a person. And not just any person, but Immanuel, which translated means "God with us" (Matt. 1:23). Like John the Baptist, we announce Jesus as "the Lamb of God who takes away the sin of the world" (John 1:29).

Years ago during a summer break I read through *The Journals of John Wesley*. This evangelist's zeal for proclaiming the gospel has been seldom matched. As Wesley chronicled his journeys throughout England, he wrote phrases such as the following:

> I there offered Christ; I offered the grace of God; I offered the redemption that is in Christ Jesus; I proclaimed the name of the Lord; I proclaimed Christ crucified. I proclaimed the grace of our Lord Jesus

---

2. John Stott, "Biblical Preaching is Expository Preaching," in *Evangelical Roots,* ed. Kenneth Kantzer (Nashville: Thomas Nelson, 1978), 159–69.
3. Spurgeon, *Lectures to My Students,* 79.

Christ; I declared the free grace of God; I exhorted the wicked to forsake his way; I invited all guilty, helpless sinners.[4]

Wesley understood a good evangelistic message is Christ-centered.

Cross-centered

An effective evangelistic message is cross-centered. It is sometimes said, "Take your text and make a beeline for the cross."[5] The apostle Paul displayed this characteristic in his preaching: "God forbid that I should glory except in the cross of our Lord Jesus Christ" (Gal. 6:14, my translation), and, "For I determined to know nothing among you except Jesus Christ, and Him crucified" (1 Cor. 2:2).[6] Paul understood that the preaching of the cross was "foolishness" to the world, but he also understood it to be "the power of God" (1 Cor. 1:18).

Robert Mounce, after discussing persecution in his book *The Essential Nature of New Testament Preaching*, observes:

> Over against these hardships, which were mostly external, there was another type of opposition. This was the subtle temptation somehow to avoid the stigma that came from espousing a socially objectionable cause. To the Jews, the Cross was a stumbling block. To the Greeks, it was folly. How inviting to alter the message just enough to rid it of its objectionable quality. But the herald is forbidden to tamper with the proclamation. He must resist the constant pressure to conform. As a result he is harassed from every quarter; persecuted from without, tempted from within.[7]

---

4. John Wesley, *The Journal of the Rev. John Wesley, A. M.*, ed. Percy Livingstone Parker, 4 vols. (London: J. Kershaw, 1827).

5. John Piper cautions preachers about applying this principle in an unhealthy way. See John Piper, "Should We 'Make a Beeline to the Cross'?: A Caution for Gospel-Centered Preaching," *Desiring God* (blog), January 7, 2019, https://www.desiringgod.org/articles/should-we-make-a-beeline-to-the-cross.

6. Yet in keeping with Piper's helpful caution referenced in the previous footnote, Paul also made sure he "preached the whole counsel of God" (Acts 20:27).

7. Robert H. Mounce, *The Essential Nature of New Testament Preaching* (Eugene, OR: Wipf and Stock, 1960), 57.

Christ's death was not accidental; it was according to the definite plan and foreknowledge of God (Acts 2:23). The cross fulfilled what God had foretold through the prophets (Acts 3:18). The author of Hebrews testifies, "Without shedding of blood there is no forgiveness" (Heb. 9:22). The cross was God's plan to deal with man's sin. God displays that he is both "just and justifier of the one who has faith in Jesus" (Rom. 3:26). Christ died as our substitute. He died in our place. He died the death that we deserve: "For Christ also died for sins once for all, the just for the unjust, in order that He might bring us to God" (1 Peter 3:18).

Response-centered

Mounce's observation about the kerygma bears repeating here:

> The kerygma was not a dispassionate recital of historical facts—a sort of nondescript presentation of certain truths, interesting enough, but morally neutral. It was, rather, the existential confrontation of man with the inescapable dilemma of having put to death the very One whom God exalted to universal Lordship. Was there any way by which man could escape the inevitable result of his blasphemous conduct? Only one—Repent! Therefore, the apostolic sermon invariably led up to a call for repentance.[8]

Mounce summarizes: "God speaks: man must respond. The demand for decision is inescapable."[9] As we have discussed in previous chapters, the gospel is a message that demands response. The necessity of proclamation and persuasion can be summarized as follows:

- Declaration without persuasion is simply instruction.
- Persuasion without declaration is simply manipulation.
- Declaration with persuasion is evangelistic preaching.

C. E. Autrey says: "It must be remembered that if a pastor fails to invite his listeners to accept Christ, he is departing from the practice of the New

---

8. Mounce, *The Essential Nature of New Testament Preaching*, 83–84.
9. Mounce, *The Essential Nature of New Testament Preaching*, 155.

Testament church."[10] Notice how Paul concludes his sermon on Mars Hill: "Therefore having overlooked the times of ignorance, God is now declaring to men that all everywhere should repent, because He has fixed a day in which He will judge the world in righteousness through a Man whom He has appointed, having furnished proof to all men by raising Him from the dead" (Acts 17:30–31). Paul sets forth three great truths which underscore the importance of repentance. First, judgment day is coming. God has appointed a day when he will judge the world, when every person will have to give an account of his or her life. Second, there is an unchallengeable judge. His verdict is final. There is no higher court of appeal. Third, God has made these truths evident by an irrefutable fact: he raised Jesus Christ from the dead.

We must declare the gospel and then invite people to respond to the gospel. Spurgeon observes, "Those who never exhort sinners are seldom winners of souls to any great extent."[11] Stott argues, "We must never make the proclamation without then issuing an appeal. . . . We are to find room for both proclamation and appeal in our preaching if we would be true heralds of the King. . . . It is not enough to teach the gospel; we must urge men to embrace it."[12]

Simple

Evangelistic preaching is not a time for the speaker to try to demonstrate his brilliance. Paul warned that trying to "prop up" the message with cleverness of speech would void the preaching of the cross (1 Cor. 1:17). Simple does not denote simplistic. It means the great gospel truths should be communicated so that even a child can understand. Richard Baxter said it was hard to speak too plainly to the masses of people.[13] James Stewart argued, "You never preach the gospel unless you preach it with simplicity. If you shoot over the heads of your hearers, you don't prove anything except you have poor aim."[14] James Denney states the matter bluntly: "No man can bear witness to Christ and to himself at the same time. . . . No man can give at once the impression that he is clever and that

---

10. See *Basic Evangelism* (Grand Rapids: Zondervan, 1959), 129.
11. Spurgeon, *Lectures to My Students*, 383.
12. John Stott, *The Preacher's Portrait* (Grand Rapids: Eerdmans, 1961), 57.
13. Richard Baxter, *The Reformed Pastor* (Carlisle, PA: Banner of Truth, 1974), 96.
14. James Stewart, quoted in Billy Graham, "Ministry: We Set Forth the Truth Plainly," Preaching.com, https://www.preaching.com/sermons/ministry-we-set-forth-the-truth-plainly.

Christ is mighty to save."[15] The people must leave our services saying not "What a preacher," but "What a Savior!"

Clear

Though similar to simplicity, clarity is distinct. Something can be simple and still not be clear. Part of clarity is using words people can understand and defining terms and concepts that might be difficult to understand. John Wesley, a graduate of Oxford University, practiced his sermons to an uneducated servant girl to make sure he was using simple words and phrases. By this practice, the highly educated preacher developed the language of the marketplace. Tens of thousands throughout England heard the gospel in terms they could understand and apply.

A good evangelistic message is clear. Part of that clarity involves warning people to "flee from the wrath to come." Spurgeon observes:

> We rob the gospel of its power if we leave out its threatenings of punishment. It is to be feared that the novel opinions upon annihilation and restoration which have afflicted the Church in these last days have caused many ministers to be slow to speak concerning the last judgment and its issues, and consequently the terrors of the Lord have had small influence upon either preachers or hearers. If this be so it cannot be too much regretted, for one great means of conversion is thus left unused.[16]

Richard Baxter emphasized, "Fear must drive, as love must draw."[17]

Compassionate

As we noted in the chapter "What Is Evangelism?," it was said of D. L. Moody that he never spoke about lost souls without tears in his eyes. Compassion undergirds the spirit of evangelism. Moody's motto was "Love them in,"[18] and those who listened to him preach sensed his love and compassion

---

15. James Denney, *Studies in Theology: Lectures Delivered in Chicago Theological Seminary* (London: Hodder and Stoughton, 1895), 161.
16. Spurgeon, *Lectures to My Students*, 339.
17. Richard Baxter, *The Life of Faith* (1669), in *The Practical Works of Richard Baxter* (London, Virtue, 1838), 2:665.
18. Note the title of Stanley N. Gundry's book on Moody: *Love Them In: The Life and Theology of D. L. Moody* (Chicago: Moody, 1999).

for the lost. Proclamation should flow out of a heart of love and compassion. John Stott maintains:

> I constantly find myself wishing that [contemporary] preachers could learn to weep again but either our tear-springs have dried up or our tear-ducts have become blocked. Everything seems to conspire together to make it impossible for us to cry over lost sinners who throng the broad road which leads to destruction. Some preachers are so preoccupied with the joyful celebration of salvation that they never think to weep over those who are rejecting it.[19]

Preaching out of a heart of compassion does not mean avoiding hard subjects, such as sin, judgment, and hell. We love people enough to tell them the truth (Eph. 4:15), even when that truth may be hard for them to hear. The key is our "tone" in preaching. Does it appear that we are preaching at people or to them? In the midst of ongoing culture wars, some preachers seem to constantly denounce the sinful actions of sinful people without pointing to the only hope we have, as individuals and as a world. Roger Carswell articulates it well: "Whilst there is so much in society that upsets Christians, nevertheless we are not called primarily to be protestors, but proclaimers of good news."[20]

Urgent

In our chapter on "Motivations for Evangelism," we noted how the great Puritan pastor Richard Baxter almost died when he was in his thirties. Baxter notes that his close brush with death "made me study and preach things necessary, and a little stirred up my sluggish heart to speak to sinners with some compassion, *as a dying man to dying men*."[21] As we have the privilege of preaching/teaching the gospel message, it serves us well to remember that particular sermon/talk may be the last gospel message we ever deliver—so we want to share it clearly and passionately! And in terms of our audience, it serves us well to remember some people may

---

19. John Stott, *Between Two Worlds* (Grand Rapids: Eerdmans, 2017), 215.
20. Carswell, *Evangelistic Preaching,* 25.
21. Richard Baxter, *The Autobiography of Richard Baxter*, ed. N. H. Keeble (London: J. M. Dent & Sons, 1974), 26, emphasis added.

be hearing the gospel message for the first time, but others for the last time—so we want to share it clearly and passionately!

Baxter thought most preachers needed more urgency in their preaching:

> If we were heartily devoted to our work, it would be done more vigorously, and more seriously, than it is by the most of us. How few ministers do preach with all their might, or speak about everlasting joys and everlasting torments in such a manner as may make men believe that they are in good earnest! O sirs how plainly, how closely, how earnestly, should we deliver a message of such moment as ours, when the everlasting life or everlasting death of our fellow-men is involved in it! . . . What! speak coldly for God, and for men's salvation? Can we believe that our people must be converted or condemned, and yet speak in a drowsy tone? In the name of God, brethren, labour to awaken your own hearts, before you go to the pulpit, that you may be fit to awaken the hearts of sinners. . . . Oh, speak not one cold or careless word about so great a business as heaven or hell. Whatever you do, let the people see that you are in good earnest.[22]

D. L. Moody preached a sermon one Sunday night in Chicago and then gave his hearers an opportunity to leave the service to think over the question, "What will you do with Jesus?" The next morning Chicago lay in ashes. That fateful day of October 8, 1871, the great Chicago fire had begun. To his dying day, Moody regretted that he had told the people to wait:

> I have never dared to give an audience a week to think of their salvation since. If they were lost, they might rise up in judgment against me. I have never seen that congregation since. I will never meet those people until I meet them in another world. But I want to tell of one lesson I learned that night which I have never forgotten: and that is when I preach to press Christ upon the people then and there, and try to bring them to a decision on the spot. I would rather have that right hand cut off than to give an audience a week now to decide what to do with Jesus.[23]

---

22. Baxter, *The Reformed Pastor*, 147–48.
23. Quoted in William R. Moody, *The Life of Moody Dwight L. Moody* (Uhrichsville, OH: Barbour, 1985), 145.

CONCLUSION

These eight characteristics of a good evangelistic message serve as a helpful guide as we prepare and preach/teach the gospel message. Spurgeon reminds us: "The only thing we have to do with Christ Jesus crucified is just to lift him up and preach him. . . . Let each of us who are called to the solemn work of the ministry remember that we are not called to lift up doctrine or church governments or particular denominations. Our business is to lift up Christ Jesus and to preach him fully."[24]

24. Charles Haddon Spurgeon, *The Treasury of the New Testament* (Grand Rapids: Zondervan, 1950), 2:279.

CHAPTER 27

LOCAL CHURCH EVANGELISM

HOW CAN A LOCAL CHURCH FULFILL its calling and thrive as an evangelistic church? Pastors are called to equip believers for the work of ministry (Eph. 4:11–12), which includes evangelism. How can pastors and other church leaders motivate, equip, and encourage church members to engage in personal witnessing? Following are eleven key areas I believe are crucial in leading a local church in evangelism.

CLARITY: CASTING A VISION FOR EVANGELISM

Pastors must preach on the mandate to witness and be involved in personal evangelism themselves as a "player-coach." A recent survey by George Barna found that when asked if they had previously "heard of the Great Commission," half of US churchgoers (51 percent) say they do not know this term.[1] Pastors need to talk often about the Great Commission and how every believer is to be involved in sharing the gospel with others to "make disciples of all the nations." Create or revise the church's vision/mission statement to emphasize outreach. My current church's purpose statement reads: "The purpose of our church is to love

1. Barna Group, "51% of Churchgoers Don't Know the Great Commission," *Barna* (blog), March 27, 2018, https://www.barna.com/research/half-churchgoers-not-heard-great-commission.

God, love each other, and love our world. We seek to fulfill that purpose by: loving God through worship and prayer; loving each other through discipleship and fellowship; and loving our world through evangelism and ministry." We highlight that purpose statement often to remind us what is important.

Church members must know the church exists primarily for those not yet a part of it. Pastors should communicate by both words and deeds that the Great Commission is a priority for the church. The gospel should be shared regularly from the pulpit along with the reminder that believers are called to share this good news with others.

CONVICTION: BELIEVING THAT PEOPLE ARE LOST AND NEED CHRIST

If we do not maintain a biblical view that people are lost and that trusting Christ in this life is their only hope for salvation, we will not witness. Why risk a conversation with someone if it does not ultimately matter in the end? The Bible makes clear the gospel does matter: "Jesus said to him, 'I am the way, and the truth, and the life. No one comes to the Father except through me'" (John 14:6). We are all called to be Christ's ambassadors to share this message of hope (2 Cor. 5:20).

That conviction should also be reflected in the church's budget. I have seen church budgets with no line item for outreach at all, and other church budgets that had an "evangelism" category but only a token financial commitment. Our pocketbooks reflect our priorities as individuals, and a church's budget reflects its priorities as a church. What does your current church budget say about your church's priority toward evangelism?

COMMITMENT TO BEING AN EVANGELISTIC CHURCH

In an attempt to overcome our natural tendency toward self-centeredness, my current church has adopted the motto: "It is *so* not about us!" It is about the Lord, first and foremost—then it is about others, especially those who don't know Christ. We constantly talk about how the church is the only institution in the world that exists primarily for those not yet a part of it. Romans 10:14 (NIV) reminds us, "How, then, can they call on the one they have not believed in? And how can they believe in the one of whom they have not heard? And how can they hear without someone preaching to them?"

The pastor must also show a commitment to personal evangelism. We cannot expect church members to do evangelism if they do not see the pastor doing evangelism. Part of this commitment to be an evangelistic church is a commitment to prayer. Pray for boldness and clarity in witness, and pray for receptive hearts to the gospel message.

Climate: Cultivating a Friendly Atmosphere

I do not believe a lost person should feel comfortable at an evangelical church's worship service. For that matter, if we are truly preaching the "whole counsel of God," and the Lord's holy presence is with us, believers should not feel comfortable either! Lost people should not feel *comfortable* in our churches, but they should feel *welcome*. Regardless of what they look like or how they are dressed, we should welcome them with open arms. Churches should be friendly to guests! We often talk about how the church should be a safe place to hear a dangerous message. Jesus declared he had not come to call the righteous, but sinners (Luke 5:32).

At one church where I served as pastor, we dedicated a year to the theme, "Company is coming—and people are worth it!" We discussed what happens in most of our homes when we get a phone call that company is headed our way. We stop what we are doing and make sure the house is picked up, vacuumed, and clean. We are okay to live from day to day in the house in its "normal" condition, but when company is coming, we want to put our best foot forward.

Part of creating an evangelistic climate is to realize that God is drawing people to himself, and that means that company is coming. And we must also believe that people are worth it. We willingly get out of our normal comfort zone to get ready for company. As the saying goes, you never get a second chance to make a good first impression. We want guests to feel welcome when they enter the doors of our church. We want them to be met by friendly greeters who convey the love of Christ with their words and by their actions.

Connecting: Identifying the Lost Persons God Has Placed Around Us

We regularly highlight Oscar Thompson's concept of "Concentric Circles of Concern." God has placed people in our lives—family, friends, neighbors, work associates, classmates, and acquaintances. Acts 17:26 (NIV) instructs us, "From one man he made all the nations, that they should inhabit the whole earth; and he marked out their appointed times in history and the boundaries of their lands." We need to identify those whom God has placed in our concentric circles to receive the gospel message. We should also provide opportunities for people to connect with the church through affinity groups. Getting to know believers through participation in sports or other meetings hosted by the church can connect unbelievers with the church.

Caring: Displaying Concern for Others and Serving Them

Based on Thompson's concept of concentric circles, we have church members submit the first names of people who need Christ so we can pray for those individuals as a church. Prayer meetings in churches tend to focus on the needs of members, typically health concerns. And we should pray for those concerns! When you or a loved one is experiencing a health crisis, you covet the prayers of others. But we must not let physical needs dominate spiritual needs. Jesus reminds us of the priority of the spiritual: "Do not be afraid of those who kill the body but cannot kill the soul. Rather, be afraid of the One who can destroy both soul and body in hell" (Matt. 10:28, NIV).

In addition to praying, we encourage serving in tangible ways by meeting practical needs. Unbelievers tend to be more open to the gospel message when they see it lived out. Servanthood is a key way to display love and concern for others.

At my current church, we subscribe to a service that provides a weekly update of new people who have moved into the general area surrounding the church. Outreach team members visit these newcomers and take a loaf of homemade bread, a gospel booklet, information about our church, and a Bible. We also ask those we visit if there are any needs for which the church can pray, and we invite them to church. Regular outreach in the neighborhoods around your church sends a message to your community that you are there to serve and to help meet people's needs.

Calendaring: Identifying Specific "Harvest Days" and Special Events

I preach expository sermons verse by verse through books of the Bible. While I seek to communicate the gospel each week as part of my message, some passages of Scripture focus on the gospel more directly than others. When I am about to preach one of those passages, I alert my church members via email that this Sunday would be a great time to invite an unbeliever to come with them (not that there is ever really a bad time!) We also seek to utilize special events as a "doorway" to the gospel and the church. Dr. Thom Rainer's research among the unchurched shows that more than 80 percent of unchurched persons would respond positively to an invitation to attend church from someone they knew.[2] Ephesians 5:15–16 (NIV) challenges us, "Be very careful, then, how you live—not as unwise but as wise, making the most of every opportunity, because the days are evil."

Our church has a Halloween "Trunk or Treat" event in our parking lot every October. We have every family register at a table outside as they come and invite them to have a bowl of chili and a hotdog. An hour later, we open the parking lot, where we have volunteers who have decorated the trunks of their cars. These volunteers hand out candy that has been collected from all the church members the preceding few weeks. This event provides good relationship-building and great contacts with unbelievers.

In addition to organizing events at the church where members can invite the community to attend, members should also be encouraged to participate in community events organized by others. When people in the community see that members of your church are willing to help them with their activities and support them, they see not only see an attitude of a servant, but they also feel cared for by the church.

The church can also allow community organizations to use the church facilities for a community event. Our church regularly hosts a blood drive

---

2. Thom Rainer, *Surprising Insights from the Unchurched* (Grand Rapids: Zondervan, 2001).

sponsored by the Red Cross. This event is a good way to familiarize out-siders with the church and to break down the barrier of entering a church building. We have church members who help work the blood drive, wel-coming those persons coming to donate blood and being available to an-swer questions about the church.

One other perspective about calendaring relates to a church's overall schedule of activities. Some churches offer numerous activities and then expect (either explicitly or implicitly) that church members participate in all those activities. What results from this activity-driven church schedule? Often it is church members who seemingly have no time to spend with their unbelieving friends, coworkers, or neighbors.

I had a friend on staff at a church where the pastor declared that for one calendar year, the church would not have any meetings at the church building except on Sundays and Wednesdays. That was a paradigm shift from the church's normal practice of there being some type of meeting or ac-tivity at the church every night. The pastor encouraged the church members to pick one night per week where they could spend time with unbelieving friends, deepening their relationship and seeking to share the gospel with them. That year, that church recorded their highest number of conversions in their history! Why? Perhaps it was because the church calendar changed to allow time for building relationships with those outside the church!

COURAGE: OVERCOMING THE BARRIER OF FEAR

Perhaps the greatest single reason we do not witness more (or witness at all) is fear. It can be scary to talk about one's faith with an unbeliever. We em-phasize relying on the power of the Holy Spirit to give us boldness in sharing Christ with others: "But you will receive power when the Holy Spirit comes on you; and you will be my witnesses in Jerusalem, and in all Judea and Sa-maria, and to the ends of the earth" (Acts 1:8, NIV). Pastors should regularly talk about fear in witnessing and how to overcome it with the Lord's help.

COACHING: PROVIDING REGULAR
TRAINING IN SHARING THE GOSPEL

We are blessed today with a plethora of wonderful witnessing helps. Try to provide regular training in the use of various methods to share the gospel. I liken these different approaches to different tools in one's toolbox. Growing up on a farm, I have amassed a varied assortment of tools. Some are specialty tools that I have only used once, but they are there if I ever need them. I encourage people to fill their witnessing toolbox with various tools (evangelistic approaches) so they have one they can pull out that fits their current witnessing opportunity.

At our church we have trained people in the 3 Circles Conversation Guide, the Romans Road, One Verse Evangelism (Romans 6:23), sharing one's personal testimony, *2 Ways to Live*, *The Story*, and how to share a gospel booklet (we utilize the "Experiencing God's Grace" booklet, produced by the Billy Graham School at Southern Baptist Theological Seminary). A few years ago, as a church we read together Jeff Iorg's wonderful book *Unscripted: Sharing the Gospel as Life Happens.*[3] We followed up with a brainstorming session on how we could apply basic evangelism principles in our personal lives and in the corporate life of our church.

Pastors need to constantly ask themselves, "What tools have I provided for my people to use in witnessing?" Can we really expect people to witness if we are not equipping them in how to do so? Short-term mission trips are a great means to provide training, both before the trip and during the trip. Many times, being exposed to a different cultural context has increased people's passion for sharing the gospel.

CELEBRATING: APPLAUDING THOSE WHO ARE REACHING OUT WITH CHRIST'S LOVE

We celebrate those who are being faithful to step outside their comfort zone to share Christ with others. We encourage one another with the reminder found in Galatians 6:9 (NIV), "Let us not become weary in doing good, for at the proper time we will reap a harvest if we do not give up."

Make use of testimonies at baptisms to celebrate evangelism. Have each person who is going to be baptized either read their own testimony, or have someone read the testimony that they wrote, ideally the person who introduced them to Christ. This gives a great opportunity to reinforce the message of the gospel. Take time to share witnessing stories and

---

3. Jeff Iorg, *Unscripted: Sharing the Gospel as Life Happens* (Birmingham, AL: New Hope, 2014).

celebrate. Periodically, have a member of the church share a faith story (conversion testimony) during a worship service to remind people that the gospel still changes lives.

CHRIST: MAKE KNOWING CHRIST AND MAKING HIM KNOWN THE CONSUMING PASSIONS IN OUR LIVES

Witnessing is fueled by the overflow of our daily walk with Christ. Jesus testified, "Out of the abundance of the heart the mouth speaketh" (Matt. 12:34, KJV). As we discussed in an earlier chapter, grandparents do not need training when it comes to talking about their grandchildren. All a person needs to do is give them a moment of pause in the conversation, and they will find a way to bring up the topic of their grandchildren. Why? Because their mouths are speaking out of that which fills their heart. Grandparents find it easy to talk about their grandchildren because their hearts are filled with love for them. When love for Christ fills our hearts on a daily basis, it will be natural to talk about him to others.

Evaluate your own personal life and your church context. Which of these eleven items are happening now? Which may need to begin? Which may need to be revisited? None of these eleven areas will happen by accident. They must be emphasized, reemphasized, and then reemphasized again. We never drift toward evangelism—we constantly drift toward fellowship, but we never drift toward evangelism. We must be intentional if evangelism is to be a part of our individual lives and a part of our local church's ministry.

The church is one of the only institutions in the world that exists primarily for those not yet a part of it. Pastors must encourage and equip their people in personal witnessing. Church leaders must model a commitment to evangelism in their own lives, where they do not end up conveying, "Do as I say, but not as I do." Let us constantly pray to the Lord of the harvest to "send out workers into His harvest" (Matt. 9:38) for his glory, honor, and praise.

PART 3

PRESERVING
EVANGELISM

CHAPTER 28

THE PROCESS OF MAKING DISCIPLES

IMAGINE YOU HAVE A RICH UNCLE WHO DIES, and in his will, he leaves you a shoe factory. You know nothing about running a shoe factory, but you show up the next day eager to learn the operation. You witness all kinds of frenzied activity—forklifts carrying huge rolls of leather, workers running machines in an assembly line, and supervisors hustling around the factory checking on their employees. But when you get to the end of the assembly line to view the finished product, there is nothing there. A shoe factory should produce shoes, correct? That account illustrates an important principle: activity does not equal productivity. A shoe factory may display lots of activity, but if no shoes are produced, it is failing in its task. Activity does not equal productivity.

Now imagine you have a rich aunt who dies, and in her will she leaves you a chicken farm. You know nothing about chicken farms, but you are anxious to learn. You arrive and discover that your chickens are laying hundreds of eggs each day, which are sold for a handsome profit. But if you want to expand the business, what do you need to do? You need more chickens, correct? That account illustrates another important principle: production does not equal reproduction. In order to grow your business and produce even more eggs, you need more chickens. Production is not the same thing as reproduction.

Now imagine a steeple on top of that shoe factory and that chicken farm. The church is called to make disciples. But activity is not the same thing as production. Churches can be involved in all types of frenzied activity, but are they producing disciples? Activity is not the same thing as productivity. And if disciples are being produced, are they being trained to reproduce new disciples? Production is not the same thing as reproduction.

I often wonder how some churches would quote the Great Commission from Matthew 28 if their citation reflected the actual ministry practices of their church. Perhaps some would cite the Great Commission in this way (notice the italicized type has been changed from the actual text of Scripture):

> And Jesus came up and spoke to them, saying, "All authority has been given to Me in heaven and on earth. *Therefore, I want you to be busy and active in whatever you decide to do*; and lo, I am with you always, even to the end of the age."

While that "translation" may seem harsh, would not that change reflect the way some churches seem to interpret (or at least to apply) Jesus's words?

Other churches, if their citation of this verse reflected their actual practice, might quote the Great Commission in this way:

> And Jesus came up and spoke to them, saying, "All authority has been given to Me in heaven and on earth. Go therefore and *make decisions* of all the nations; and lo, I am with you always, even to the end of the age."

But the command in the Great Commission is not to make decisions, but disciples:

> And Jesus came up and spoke to them, saying, "All authority has been given to Me in heaven and on earth. Go therefore and *make disciples* of all the nations, baptizing them in the name of the Father and the Son and the Holy Spirit, teaching them to observe all that I commanded you; and lo, I am with you always, even to the end of the age." (Matt. 28:18–21)

As individuals and as churches, we need to be reminded that activity does not equal productivity and that production does not equal reproduction. We are called to make disciples. If that is our task (and it is), we need to ask and answer a series of questions. This chapter will follow a very basic outline: what, why, and how. What is a disciple? Why should we make disciples? How can we make disciples?[1]

What Is a Disciple?

What is a disciple? The word means different things to different people. Defined biblically, the word means one who is a learner or a follower. A disciple is a person in process, one who is growing in love for and obedience to Christ.[2] A disciple is a person who has a supreme love for, loyalty to, and obedience to Christ. Christ must be supreme.

When our daughter Karisa started kindergarten, Sharon and I went to the orientation session held by her teacher, Mrs. Clark. With all twenty eager students sitting at the front of the classroom, and with parents huddled at the back, Mrs. Clark introduced herself by means of a "shoebox biography." She pulled items one by one out of a shoebox to highlight who she was: a porcelain cat (she loves cats) and an apple (she loves apples but also loves teaching). The last item she pulled out of the shoebox was a picture of her husband. She exclaimed, "This is my husband—he is my best friend!" Without warning, our daughter Karisa leaped to her feet and asked with a voice filled with astonishment, *"Even more than Jesus?"* Mrs. Carter smiled as she said to my daughter, "No, sweetheart, not more than Jesus." Karisa said, "Okay," and sat back down.

That night Sharon and I laughed but also shed tears of joy over that episode. Karisa was only six years old. There was a lot about life she still did not understand, and we were far from perfect parents. But somehow we had gotten the message through to her tiny mind that Jesus must always be supreme. Yes, she loved her mommy and daddy, but not as much as she loved Jesus.

That incident illustrates what it means to be a disciple of Christ. He has first place in our affections, he is supreme, and we seek to love and

---

1. A recent work that addresses these issues cross-culturally is Ajith Fernando's *Discipling in a Multicultural World* (Wheaton, IL: Crossway, 2019).
2. Several verses in the Gospels highlight different characteristics of being a disciple of Christ: Matthew 10:24 (humility); Luke 6:40 (obedience); Luke 14:26–27, 33 (forsaking all for the sake of Christ); John 8:31 (abiding in the Word); John 13:34–35 (loving other believers); John 15:8 (bearing fruit).

obey him. That description of a disciple is what we are called to "make" in the Great Commission—devout learners and wholehearted followers of Christ. A disciple is one who responds to the question, "Do you love me more than these?" by affirming, "Yes, Lord, you know that I love you—I will follow you."

Why Make Disciples?

Why should individual Christians and churches be involved in making disciples? Let me suggest five reasons.

The Command of Christ (Matt. 28:18–20)

Jesus commanded us to make disciples! The question is, do we *believe* commands, or do we *do* them? If you asked people in the typical evangelical church if they believed the Great Commission, I am convinced every single hand would go up in agreement. But the issue is not agreement—it is obedience! Are we obeying Christ by seeking to make disciples? In Matthew 28:18–20 the only imperative is the word translated "make disciples." The main verb (make disciples) tells *what* is to be done, and the participles (going [as you go], baptizing, teaching) tell *how* it is to be done. That means, as a Christian, I have to be consumed with making disciples, not just decisions. Billy Graham has stated, "Decision is five percent; following up the decision is ninety-five percent."[3]

The Example of Christ and the Early Church

Jesus poured his life into the twelve disciples. Mark 3:14 (NIV) instructs us, "And He appointed twelve that they might be with him and that he might send them out to preach." Jesus modelled discipling others, so when he gave the command to "make disciples," his followers knew what he meant. And we see the New Testament church took this command seriously!

Look at this example from the life of the apostle Paul: "And after they had preached the gospel to that city and had made many disciples, they returned to Lystra and to Iconium and to Antioch, strengthening the souls

---

3. Billy Graham, cited in Waylon B. Moore, *Multiplying Disciples: The New Testament Method for Church Growth* (Tampa, FL: Missions Unlimited, 1981), 41.

of the disciples, encouraging them to continue in the faith" (Acts 14:21–22). Or this account: "After some days Paul said to Barnabas, 'Let us return and visit the brethren in every city in which we proclaimed the word of the Lord, and see how they are'" (Acts 15:36).

Notice Paul's objective in Colossians 1:28–29: "We proclaim him, admonishing every man and teaching every man with all wisdom, that we may present every man complete in Christ. For this purpose also I labor, striving according to his power, which mightily works within me." What was Paul's objective? He states it clearly: to present every person complete (mature) in Christ. Paul was preoccupied with making disciples. He was not satisfied simply with seeing people come to Christ—he wanted them to grow to the point in their Christian life where they could begin to encourage and disciple others!

The Vulnerability of New Believers (1 Peter 5:8)

First Peter 5:8 reminds us, "Be of sober spirit, be on the alert. Your adversary, the devil, prowls about like a roaring lion, seeking someone to devour." Satan is out to destroy us! The Christian life is not a game, it is a battle! Genuine converts have experienced a new birth, but it is only a birth. New believers are vulnerable to the enemy's attacks. They need to be nurtured and cared for as they are maturing in the faith.

The Stewardship of Life (James 4:14)

Romans 14:12 instructs us that each of us will have to give an account of our life. And James 4:14 reminds us our life is like a "vapor"—like a quick puff of smoke that appears for just a moment and then is gone. Life at its longest is brief when compared to eternity. I was reminded of the brevity of life one day while I was in high school. Jim Croce was a popular singer/songwriter at the time, and his song "Time in a Bottle" was playing on the radio as I drove to school one morning. The chorus of the song has these haunting lyrics: "But there never seems to be enough time, to do the things you want to do, once you find them." I heard later that day that Jim Croce had been killed in a plane crash. He, like every person before him and after him, was unable to capture "Time in a Bottle."

William James has noted, "The great use of life is to spend it for something that outlasts it."[4] What is eternal? The Scriptures remind us only three things are eternal: God (Ps. 90:2); God's Word (Isa. 40:8); and people (Matt. 25:46). If we are to be good stewards of the life God gives us, however long that earthly life might last, we must invest in eternity. People are eternal!

Max Lucado exhorts believers to "make major decisions in a cemetery."[5] What does he mean by those somber words? He is reminding us that life at longest is brief and that we will soon be dead and buried. How will we wish that we had lived, and what will we wish that we had done, when we are dead and they lower our body into the ground? Lucado suggested that believers should consider their end and let it determine how they live today.

A pastor friend of mine in Florida read that line in Lucado's book and encouraged his people to apply that principle. He secured a large granite bench and had it placed on the edge of the church's property facing a cemetery. He then preached on the concept of living for eternity—of making major life decisions in a graveyard. I spoke with him six months after that sermon, and he said that principle had begun to transform his church. He said there had not been a single week that had passed when, as he was entering the church property or leaving, that he did not see someone sitting on that granite bench praying. Individuals, couples, and entire families had gathered on that bench to make a major life decision in light of eternity.

To Advance the Kingdom of God (2 Tim. 2:2)

Paul gives us a concrete example of spiritual multiplication in his relationship with Timothy. He writes, "The things which you have heard from me in the presence of many witnesses, entrust these to faithful men who will be able to teach others also" (2 Tim. 2:2). We see four generations represented in this verse: Paul, Timothy, faithful men, and others. Multiplication is the best strategy to reach the world for Christ, but the church often relies on addition. We are all here because of physical multiplication. God's first command was, "Be fruitful and multiply, and fill the earth" (Gen. 1:28). The reason why multiplication works in the physical realm is

---

4. Quoted in Perry Ralph Barton, *The Thought and Character of William James, Volume 2: Philosophy and Psychology* (London: Oxford University Press, 1935), 289.
5. Max Lucado, *In the Eye of the Storm: Jesus Knows How You Feel* (Nashville: Thomas Nelson, 2012), 108.

because each generation has the ability to produce more offspring. Each generation must reproduce itself to perpetuate the next.

Reflect on the spiritual realm. How did you become a follower of Christ? Someone shared Christ with you. How did that person become a Christian? Someone shared with them, and back it goes to the early Christians. Spiritual multiplication involves leading a person to Christ and then helping that person grow to spiritual maturity so that he or she can then in turn lead others to Christ who can grow and reproduce their lives. Spiritual multiplication is a strategy that is not content with merely adding people to the kingdom; it also seeks to help them become workers in the kingdom.

Imagine that your Sunday school class has a lesson on outreach, and members of the class begin to capture a vision for witnessing. One man, Fred, who is an attorney, begins to share his faith and leads one person to faith in Christ each week. Every Sunday he pulls up in his BMW with a new believer in the passenger seat. Mary, a real estate agent, sees God using Fred in evangelism and thinks, *If God can use a lawyer, I know he can use me! I'm a real estate agent, and people actually like me!* She begins witnessing regularly and leads one person to faith in Christ every single day. Each Sunday morning Mary pulls up to the church in her van, and seven new believers get out.

There is a third member of your Sunday school class, John, who is a plumber. John is introverted, and it takes a huge step of faith for him to begin witnessing. But he does. And very soon he leads a fellow plumber named Bill to Christ. But unlike Fred and Mary, John does not simply bring Bill to church and drop him off for the church to disciple him. John begins to meet each week with Bill to encourage him in his walk with Christ. John teaches Bill how to have a morning devotional time, how to pray, and the basics of how he can testify of his newfound faith to others.

What would we see after six months of labor by these three class members? Fred would have brought twenty-six people to faith; Mary would have seen 183 people converted; John would have only seen one—his friend Bill. But John has discipled Bill to walk with Christ and to share him with others. What if they continued that pattern for sixteen years? Fred would have seen 832 people put their trust in Christ for salvation. Mary would have witnessed 5,840 people converted (you are going to need a bigger room for your Sunday school class). John, if he followed the pattern of leading someone to Christ and then discipling that person for six months, would multiply his influence. If that pattern of multiplication continued for sixteen years (two becoming four; four becoming eight; eight becoming sixteen; etc.), how many people would be reached? The answer is astounding: 4,294,967,296. More than four billion people—more than the number of unreached people in the world today![6]

We immediately want to protest—there must be something wrong with those numbers! There is nothing wrong with the math—what is wrong is that the church has largely been following an approach of addition versus multiplication. Consider these words of wisdom from Billy Graham:

> One of the first verses of Scripture that Dawson Trotman, founder of the Navigators, made me memorize was, "The things that thou hast heard of me among many witnesses, the same commit thou to faithful men, who shall be able to teach others also" (2 Tim. 2:2, KJV). This is a little like a mathematical formula for spreading the gospel and enlarging the Church. Paul taught Timothy; Timothy shared what he knew with faithful men; these faithful men would then teach others also. And so the process goes on and on. If every believer followed this pattern, the Church could reach the entire world with the gospel in one generation! Mass crusades, in which I believe and to which I have committed my life, will never finish the Great Commission; but a "one-by-one" ministry will.[7]

Why haven't we seen it happen? It is not because the strategy is not sound. The breakdown occurs with people. The strategy of multiplication is the best way to reach the world for Christ.

---

6. The Joshua Project has estimated that there are 3,230,000,000 in unreached people groups around the world as of January 2021: "Status of World Evangelization 2021," *Joshua Project*, https://joshuaproject.net/assets/media/handouts/status-of-world-evangelization.pdf.
7. Billy Graham, *The Holy Spirit: Activating God's Power in Your Life* (London: William Collins Sons, 1979), 147.

THE PROCESS OF MAKING DISCIPLES

The Great Commission is not about making decisions but about making disciples. So how do we make disciples? What are some practical steps we can follow? Christ is at the center of this process. We are not discipling people to be carbon copies of us; we want to see them become more faithful followers of Christ. Both the discipler and the church are involved in this process. The church provides the element of family, while the discipler is available to answer specific questions and speak to specific situations.

The process of evangelizing results in a new believer—a convert, a new follower of Christ. The bulk of this book has focused on this first phase of making disciples. The second phase of disciple-making is that of establishing. The process of establishing results in a growing disciple. Colossians 2:6–7 explains this process: "Therefore as you have received Christ Jesus the Lord, so walk in Him, having been firmly rooted and now being built up in Him and established in your faith, just as you were instructed, and overflowing with gratitude."

The third phase of disciple-making is equipping. Equipping is where the growing disciple is trained to become a reproducing disciple. Ephesians 4:11–13 speaks of this equipping process: "And He gave some as apostles, and some as prophets, and some as evangelists, and some as pastor and teachers, for the equipping of the saints for the work of service, to the building up of the body of Christ; until we all attain to the unity of the faith, and of the knowledge of the Son of God, to a mature man, to the measure of the stature which belongs to the fullness of Christ."

While there is a clear-cut line of demarcation between evangelizing (dealing with an unbeliever and seeing that person come to faith) and establishing (seeing a new convert become a growing disciple), that line of demarcation is not as clear between establishing and equipping. Even a new believer needs to begin serving Christ and others, and a more mature believer must never stop growing in Christ. But the emphasis in the establishing phase is spiritual growth, while in the equipping phase it is spiritual service.

THE PATTERN OF JESUS'S MINISTRY

In the next two sections I'll discussion two patterns for implementing a plan for making disciples. The first comes from the ministry of Jesus, and the second comes from the ministry of Paul. It is instructive to view Jesus's ministry through two lenses—what we could call his public ministry and what we could refer to as his private ministry. Jesus's public ministry included preaching and teaching to the masses, as well as performing healing and other miracles. Jesus's private ministry included both individual and group time with a small band of twelve disciples. When one studies the Scriptures to see how Jesus spent his time, it is readily apparent that he spent more time in his private ministry than his public ministry.

Most pastors have made a commitment to exemplify the public ministry of Jesus (preaching and teaching), but some have not made a similar commitment to exemplify Jesus's private ministry (personal evangelism and disciple-making). And while most laypersons will not be involved in ministries of preaching and teaching, they can all be involved in personal evangelism and disciplemaking.

Robert Coleman, in his classic work *The Master Plan of Evangelism*,[8] surveyed Jesus's ministry of disciple-making. I will summarize his key insights in the pages following, but readers should obtain a copy of Coleman's book and read it for themselves. One of the strengths of Coleman's work is that he focuses on principles, not methods. Years ago I learned this important distinction:

Methods are many,
Principles are few.
Methods often change,
Principles never do.

I will list the key points of how Jesus discipled his followers, and then suggest some points of application for us today.

---

8. Robert E. Coleman, *The Master Plan of Evangelism* (Old Tappan, NJ: Fleming H. Revell, 1963). Since its publication, more than three million copies have been sold. Coleman's book was selected by *Christianity Today* as one of the top fifty books that shaped evangelicalism.

Billy Graham, writing in the foreword for Coleman's book, notes:

The secret of this book's impact is not hard to discover. Instead of drawing on the latest popular fad or newest selling technique, Dr. Coleman has gone back to the Bible and has asked one critical question: what was Christ's strategy of evangelism? In so doing, he has pointed us to the unchanging, simple (and yet profound) biblical principles which must undergird any authentic evangelistic outreach.[9]

Coleman writes, "When his plan is reflected on, the basic philosophy is so different from that of the modern church that its implications are nothing less than revolutionary."[10]

At the heart of Jesus's ministry was the priority of people. Coleman shows how Jesus trained his disciples for the task before them. Coleman's book lists eight principles, but for the past several years when Coleman has taught this material, he has added a ninth principle: the principle of incarnation. So we will begin with that principle, even though Coleman does not cover it in his book.

Incarnation: He took the role of a servant and ministered to the needs of people (Mark 10:45).

He renounced His rights for our sakes. Paul highlights this truth in Philippians 2:2–11, and Mark 10:45 reminds us, "For even the Son of man did not come to be served, but to serve, and to give His life a ransom for many." He was not here to save himself, but to save the world. He went about meeting people's needs. The disciples witnessed how Jesus refused the things they cherished—physical satisfaction, popular acclaim, prestige—but willingly accepted the things they sought to escape—poverty, humiliation, sorrow, and even death.

Live the life of a servant. Servanthood is an attitude of the heart and mind that should impact our relationships with others. Serving people always brings opportunities to disciple them. Learn to be observant and recognize the needs of people. Servanthood is a challenge for Christian leaders, in part because they have responsibilities they alone can fulfill. Dawson

---

9. Billy Graham, foreword to Coleman, *The Master Plan of Evangelism*, 9.
10. Coleman, *The Master Plan of Evangelism*, 19.

Trotman, founder of the Navigators, argued that leaders should "Never do anything that someone else can do and will do, when there is so much of importance to be done which others cannot or will not do."[11] That principle of leadership must be kept in balance with the leader's need to model servanthood. Jesus had a unique ministry, but he made time to serve others.

Selection: He called out learners (Luke 6:12–13).

Coleman comments:

> It all started by Jesus calling a few men to follow him. This revealed immediately the direction his evangelistic strategy would take. His concern was not with programs to reach the multitudes, but with men whom the multitudes would follow. . . . Men were to be his method of winning the world to God. The initial objective of Jesus's plan was to enlist men who could bear witness to his life and carry on his work after he returned to the Father.[12]

This collection of disciples was not an impressive group. Most of them were common, ordinary laborers, without any type of professional religious training. Their critics referred to them as "uneducated and untrained men" (Acts 4:13). These were not the type of men who could be expected to win the world for Christ. Yet Jesus saw in these men great potential as kingdom workers. He selected them, not because of what they were at that time, but because of what they would become as they followed him. Thus his invitation, "Follow Me, and I will make you become fishers of men" (Mark 1:17). He saw teachable hearts in these men.

That immediately raises a question for many people: Why Judas? The immediate answer is "that the Scripture might be fulfilled" (John 17:12; Acts 1:12; cf. Ps. 41:9). But for believers today, it serves as a reminder that our Lord knows the pain of having a close friend turn against him. When we face pain and disappointment in ministry, our Lord understands. As we reflect on the principle of selection, we note only a few men were personally discipled by Jesus. Yet, as Coleman observes, "Though he did what

---

11. Betty Lee Skinner, *Daws: The Story of Dawson Trotman, Founder of the Navigators* (Grand Rapids: Zondervan, 1998), 82.
12. Coleman, *The Master Plan of Evangelism*, 21

he could to help the multitudes, he had to devote himself primarily to a few men, rather than to the masses, so that the masses could be saved."[13]

How can we employ the principle of selection? Like Jesus, it begins with prayer. Pray that God would lead you to the right persons to disciple. Be aware of those whom God has already placed within your sphere of influence—family members, coworkers, and friends. Pay attention to those persons who display spiritual hunger, a desire to grow deeper in the things of God.

The Navigators have long used the acrostic F-A-T as a basis of selection. As a disciple, you are looking for someone who is Faithful, Available, and Teachable. They need to be faithful (though do not equate faithfulness with perfection—we all fall short), available (willing to make time for training), and teachable (willing to learn—displaying a deep desire for spiritual things). Coleman comments, "Surely if the pattern of Jesus at this point means anything at all, it teaches that the first duty of a church leadership is to see to it that a foundation is laid in the beginning on which can be built an effective and continuing evangelistic ministry to the multitudes. . . . It will mean raising up trained disciplers 'for the work of service' along with the pastor and church staff."[14]

Association: He found ways to be together (Mark 3:14).

The starting point after selection was association. Jesus called these men that they might be "with him." As they spent time with him, they would learn what they needed to know for their future ministry involving the Great Commission. These twelve disciples were with him during a roughly three-year period. They travelled together, ate together, fished together, and ministered together. Coleman observes, "The time which Jesus invested in these few disciples was so much more by comparison to that given by others that it can only be regarded as a deliberate strategy. He actually spent more time with his disciples than with everybody else in the world put together."[15]

While Jesus ministered to people, his disciples were right there with him to observe and to learn. Jesus announced, "and you will bear witness also, because you have been with Me from the beginning" (John 15:27,

---

13. Coleman, *The Master Plan of Evangelism*, 33.
14. Coleman, *The Master Plan of Evangelism*, 33.
15. Coleman, *The Master Plan of Evangelism*, 42–43

my translation). Jesus put the disciples on notice that his practice of them being "with him" was to train them to serve as his witnesses after he was gone. How can we apply the principle of association today? Seek opportunities to be together: eat together, run errands together, spend time together out in the real world as much as possible. A good discipleship principle is, "Never go anywhere alone." While that principle obviously could be applied in an unhealthy way, it is a reminder of the principle of association. If you are going out to do ministry, take someone along with you! Let them observe and ask questions later. Utilize the travel time to discuss real life issues. Coleman concludes: "We must decide where we want our ministry to count—in the momentary applause of popular recognition or in the reproduction of our lives in a few chosen people who will carry on our work after we have gone."[16]

But notice as well that Jesus also spent time away from his disciples. Scripture points to times when he was not with other people but alone (Matt. 14:14; Mark 1:35; Luke 5:16; Matt. 10:1–14). Jesus not only modelled spending quality time with others (association) but also taking time apart for prayer.

Consecration: Jesus expected his disciples to obey him (Luke 9:23–24).

Jesus's disciples were expected to obey him and follow him wholeheartedly. The very term "disciple" meant they had become "learners" or "followers" of Christ. Not until much later were the disciples called by the name "Christian" (Acts 11:26). At first, following Jesus seemed easy for the disciples, but as time went on, they discovered more of the cost of consecration. They had to forsake their sin. Their old pattern of thinking primarily about themselves and their needs had to be replaced with a concern for others. When the realization of the cost grew greater, some of Jesus's "followers" left him (John 6:60–66).

Reflect on the patience Jesus exercised with his disciples as they were often slow to learn lessons of consecration. They balked at Jesus's teaching about serving others (John 13:1–10). They harshly judged those who did not agree with them (Luke 9:51–54), even wanting to call down fire from heaven upon them. They argued as to who would have the prominent

---

16. Coleman, *The Master Plan of Evangelism*, 32.

places in the kingdom of God (Mark 10:35–41). They displayed indignation at parents who wanted Jesus to bless their children (Mark 10:13).

Jesus taught the disciples that the proof of their love for him was their obedience to him: "If you love Me, you will keep My commandments" (John 14:15); "If anyone loves Me, he will keep My word; and My Father will love him, and We will come to him, and make Our abode with him" (John 14:23); and "If you keep My commandments, you will abide in My love; just as I have kept My Father's commandments, and abide in His love" (John 15:10).

Jesus modeled consecration to the disciples as he obeyed the will of the Father: "I do not seek My own will, but the will of Him who sent Me" (John 5:30); "I have kept my Father's commandments and abide in his love" (John 15:10); and "Not My will, but Yours be done" (Luke 22:42). Jesus not only taught about consecration and obedience; he modeled it before the disciples as well. His teaching was not "Do as I say, but not as I do," but "Follow my example."

An important clarification must be made at this point in applying this principle today. Jesus could demand that his disciples obey him because he is Lord! We do not insist that our disciples obey us, but that they obey the Lord Jesus Christ. Jesus could command obedience because he is Lord; as his followers we do not command obedience to ourselves, but to Christ as Lord.

We do not hear as much about consecration in our churches today as we used to hear. Have we subtly replaced living a consecrated life to Christ with a pursuit of other things? The teachings of Christ regarding self-denial and dedication seem to have been replaced with looking out for number one. We see much selfishness in our churches. Where is our spirit of consecration, of obedience to Christ no matter the cost? When we have the privilege of discipling others, we should challenge their faith. We should commit to practice spiritual disciplines together. We must always point them to obeying the Lord.

Impartation: All must be done in the power of the indwelling Spirit (John 6:63).

Jesus made clear that the Christian life must be lived through the power of the Holy Spirit: "It is the Spirit who gives life; the flesh profits nothing." That is why the beginning of spiritual life involves being "born again" (John 3:3–8). Not only the beginning, but the continuation of living as a disciple must be fueled by the Spirit (John 7:37–39).

Jesus taught the disciples that the Spirit would prepare the way for their ministry. He would give them utterance to speak when they were delivered up to the authorities (Matt. 10:16–20). He would convict the world "concerning sin and righteousness and judgment" (John 16:8). He would empower them for gospel witness (Acts 1:8). Jesus taught the disciples to rely on the Holy Spirit's power for their lives and ministries. Supernatural work can only be done with supernatural power. Coleman remarks, "In this light, evangelism was not interpreted as a human undertaking, but as a divine project which had been going on from the beginning and would continue until God's purpose was fulfilled. It was altogether the Spirit's work. All the disciples were asked to do was to let the Spirit have complete charge of their lives."[17]

We must constantly set before our disciples the reality of the Spirit-filled life. We must teach them—and model for them—what is means to be Spirit-led and Spirit-empowered. A. W. Tozer once maintained, "If the Holy Spirit was withdrawn from the church today, 95 percent of what we do would go on and no one would know the difference."[18] While it is possible that Tozer overstated the case, it is also possible that he put his finger on a major weakness of much of the evangelical church's practice.

Demonstration: He showed them how to minister (John 13:15).

Jesus washed the disciples' feet, and then taught, "For I gave you an example that you also should do as I did to you" (John 13:15). Jesus provided an example for his disciples in other ways besides humble service. Consider, for example, Jesus's prayer life. His disciples observed him making time for prayer even in the midst of hectic ministry. The disciples could see firsthand the perspective and strength that prayer brought to Jesus. More than twenty times the Gospels make note of Jesus praying. He prayed at key moments in his life: at his baptism (Luke 3:21); during the selection of the twelve apostles (Luke 5:12); while on the Mount of Transfiguration

---

17. Coleman, *The Master Plan of Evangelism*, 67.
18. Cited in R. T. Kendall, *Holy Fire: A Balanced Look at the Holy Spirit's Work in Our Lives* (Lake Mary, FL: Charisma House, 2014), 9.

(Luke 9:29); at the Last Supper (Matt. 26:27); in Gethsemane (Luke 22:39–46); and on the cross (Luke 23:46).

Jesus did not sit the disciples down one day and say, "Okay, today is lesson #27 in my curriculum for you all. Today I am going to teach you how to pray." No, Jesus modeled prayer for the disciples until the day came that they asked him to teach them how to pray. He explained to them some basic principles of prayer, and then illustrated those principles by giving the disciples a "model prayer" (Matt. 6:9–13; Luke 11:1–4). As Jesus continued to minister, he constantly reminded the disciples where their spiritual power would be found.

Jesus also modeled before his disciples the importance of and proper use of the Scriptures. He upheld the divine origin of the Scriptures, testifying that Scripture cannot be broken. Jesus correctly interpreted passages of Scripture that others were misinterpreting. Jesus quoted directly from the Old Testament over sixty times, with even more allusions to the Scripture that were not direct quotations. The disciples heard Jesus's Sermon on the Mount, where he emphasized the importance of not only hearing God's Word but also applying it (Matt. 7:24–27). They listened as Jesus described a disciple as one who would "abide in My Word" (John 8:31). He never once questioned the truthfulness of Scripture, but constantly affirmed its authority.

The disciples were not asked to do anything which he himself had not done. This demonstration meant when Jesus finally commanded his followers to "go and make disciples of all nations," they knew what he meant. He was instructing them to follow the pattern he had set before them. We must seek to model the Christian life and ministry before those we are discipling. As disciplers, we are to function as "player-coaches." Even though we are coaching and encouraging others, we cannot do that properly unless we are in the game ourselves! This reality certainly puts pressure on those who would disciple others. Paul described it in this way: "Follow me, as I follow Christ" (1 Cor. 11:1, my translation).

As you allow others to get close to you, they will see your strengths but also your weaknesses. In fact, I believe this reality is a key reason why some leaders do not disciple others. The closer we let someone get to us, the more they will see our weaknesses and failings. And yet showing others how we respond to our own wrongdoing provides a powerful example to them.

Delegation: Jesus involved them in his work (Matt. 4:19).

Matthew 4:19 says, "Follow Me, and I will make you fishers of men." Jesus involved his disciples in his ministry from the very beginning. Initially, he assigned them responsibilities such as baptizing his converts (John 4:1–2) and distributing food to the hungry (John 6:3–14). Jesus then sent them out on an evangelistic mission (Luke 10:1–16). As they went out, he challenged them to exercise wisdom: "be as wise as serpents, and innocent as doves" (Matt. 10:16, my translation). He challenged them to prepare for persecution, telling them he was sending them out "as sheep in the midst of wolves" (Matt. 10:16) and that they would be arrested and brought before governing authorities (Matt. 10:17–18). He then assured them with these words of encouragement: "But when they deliver you up, do not become anxious about how or what you will speak: for it shall be given you in that hour what you are to speak" (Matt. 10:19, my translation).[19]

Jesus sent out the disciples "two by two." (Luke 10:1). Why? Having another person with them would provide accountability, fellowship, and encouragement. As they went, they were going as Christ's representatives (Matt. 10:40). Jesus warned the disciples that their mission would not be easy; while there would be some who would accept their message, there would be others who would reject them and their message (Matt. 10:34–42).

As we are training growing disciples, we should challenge them to serve through ministry. Initially, they can participate in basic tasks, and as they grow in knowledge and skill, more difficult assignments can be encouraged. Churches and leaders can err on both sides of this issue. While we must not "lay hands upon anyone too hastily" (1 Tim. 5:22), we are called to "equip the saints for the work of ministry" (Eph. 4:12, ESV).

Supervision: Faithfulness in completing tasks was expected (Mark 6:30).

Mark 6:30 says, "And the apostles gathered together with Jesus; and they reported to Him all that they had done and taught." Jesus provided accountability to the disciples as they were learning to minister. For

---

19. This verse has been used by some to suggest that preachers do not need to prepare their messages, but instead should trust the Holy Spirit to give them what to say when they step into the pulpit. We must note the context of Jesus's promise here is not the "hour of proclamation" but the "hour of persecution."

example, after the seventy went out on their evangelistic mission, Jesus had them report on their efforts. They eagerly reported, "Lord, even the demons are subject to us in Your name" (Luke 10:17). Jesus rejoiced in their ministry success but then used this occasion to teach them an additional important principle: not to take pride in their accomplishments (Luke 10:20).

Reproduction: Reproduction was expected (John 15:16).

As Jesus was preparing the disciples for his leaving them, he testified, "You did not choose Me, but I chose you, and appointed you that you would go and bear fruit, and that your fruit would remain, so that whatever you ask of the Father in My name He may give to you" (John 15:16). Coleman observes:

> Jesus intended for the disciples to produce His likeness in and through the church being gathered out of the world. Thus his ministry in the Spirit would be duplicated manifold by His ministry in the lives of his disciples. Through them and others like them it would continue to expand in an ever-enlarging circumference until the multitudes might know in a similar way the opportunity which they had known with the Master. By this strategy the conquest of the world was only a matter of time and their faithfulness to his plan.[20]

Jesus entrusted his disciples to carry on his mission of reaching the entire world with the good news of the gospel of the kingdom (Matt. 24:14). He emphasized that the goal is not production but reproduction. Jesus shows that he expected others to believe in him because of the disciples' ministry (John 17:20). The book of Acts shows the disciples putting into practice the lessons they had learned from their Lord. As a believer becomes a growing disciple, set before him or her the challenge to become a reproducing disciple. Whom can they reach out to with the gospel message? Whom can they begin to encourage in their walk with Christ? How can they keep the multiplication process going forward?

What we are discussing here has no relation to personality. Each of us must learn to minister out of our own personality and gifts. Look at the

---

20. Coleman, *The Master Plan of Evangelism*, 99.

twelve disciples! You see a belligerent Peter and a quiet, unassuming Andrew. Some people will feel more comfortable with a behind-the-scenes, Andrew-type ministry. They will be able to minister to people that the aggressive Peter might intimidate or ignore.

Also, these principles are foundational regardless of one's occupation. Noted historian Kenneth Scott Latourette makes this observation about the spread of the gospel in the early church: "*The chief agents in the expansion of Christianity appear not to have been those who made it a profession or a major part of their occupation, but men and women who earned their livelihood in some purely secular manner and spoke of their faith to those whom they met in this natural fashion.*"[21]

Finally, you do not have to have it all together in your own life before you can begin to help someone else! If Tiger Woods were practicing on a driving range alongside me, he would be foolish to accept any golfing tips from me. But if I see a brand-new golfer on the range, holding the club at the wrong end, flailing helplessly at the golf ball, it would not be arrogant of me to walk over and help him learn to hold the club properly. We only need a short head start to be able to encourage others spiritually!

FOUR MEANS OF DISCIPLING USED BY THE APOSTLE PAUL[22]

Personal Contact (1 Thess. 2:8)

When possible, Paul followed up with new believers personally. His moving words to the church at Thessalonica show his pastoral heart: "Having thus a fond affection for you, we were well-pleased to impart to you not only the gospel of God but also our own lives, because you had become very dear to us" (1 Thess. 2:8, NASB 1977). In describing his personal ministry among them, Paul uses the images of a "nursing mother" (1 Thess. 2:7) and an encouraging father (1 Thess. 2:11). Personal contact allows the discipler to be able to see the new believer's situation first-hand and provide timely counsel and wisdom in living the Christian life.

---

21. Kenneth Scott Latourette, *A History of the Expansion of Christianity* (New York: Harper & Brothers, 1937), 1:116.
22. I was first introduced to these concepts by Moore, *Multiplying Disciples*, 42–47.

Follow-Up Materials (1 Thess. 1:1; 5:27)

Paul also used personal letters to follow up with new believers. Much of the New Testament is composed of follow-up letters Paul wrote to new churches. Paul could not be with them in person, so he shared his instructions to them in written form. He was discipling them through written material. With the available technology today, follow-up materials can be provided for new believers almost anywhere in the world![23] We can still write personal letters, but even emails and text messages can carry a personal touch as we reach out to new believers to challenge and encourage them.

Trained Representatives (1 Thess. 3:1–6)

When Paul was unable to visit new believers in person, he sometimes sent a representative in his place. Notice how Paul describes Timothy: "our brother and God's fellow worker in the gospel of Christ" (1 Thess. 3:2). Paul had trained Timothy, and now he was sending Timothy to the Thessalonians "to strengthen and encourage" them as to their faith (1 Thess. 3:2). On different occasions Paul sent Epaphroditus (Phil. 2:25) and Titus (2 Cor. 7:13–16) when he was unable to travel himself.

Prayer (1 Thess. 1:2; 3:9–10)

Paul's letters display the significance he placed on praying for others. For example, as he writes to the fledgling church at Thessalonica, he states, "We give thanks to God always for all of you, making mention of you in our prayers" (1 Thess. 1:2). He reinforces his commitment to pray for them later in the letter: "For what thanks can we render to God for you in return for all the joy with which we rejoice before our God on your account, as we night and day keep praying most earnestly that we may see your face, and may complete what is lacking in your faith?" (1 Thess. 3:9–10). With Paul's converts it was not "out of sight, out of mind." If he could not be with them personally, he was constantly praying for them. The prayers of Paul provide wonderful examples of how we can pray for new believers and well as maturing believers.[24]

---

23. Visit disciple-maker.org for helpful resources.
24. See D. A. Carson, *Praying with Paul: A Call to Spiritual Reformation* (Grand Rapids: Baker Academic, 2015) for a helpful overview and exegetical study on Paul's prayers.

Follow Key Principles

Focus on the basics.

I like to consider four key areas of training when discipling new believers or growing believers: doctrine, devotion, ministry, and character. Doctrine is important to help the new believer become theologically grounded and scripturally oriented. Devotion helps the new believer learn to walk with God on a daily basis. Topics such as prayer, a daily quiet time, and Christian fellowship help fuel a devotional life. Ministry is helping them learn to serve others, whereas character is helping the disciple display the spirit of Christ. There is overlap between these four areas in the establishing and equipping phases. While doctrine and devotion predominate in the establishing phase, new believers should also be encouraged to witness and to serve others and to grow in Christian character. And while ministry and character predominate in the equipping phase, a growing disciple must never abandon doctrine and devotion in order to keep growing and to maintain a healthy foundation from which to minister to others.

Tell them why.

Help new believers to develop their own convictions. While initially they might be having a daily quiet time because the discipler told them it is important, if they are going to maintain that practice over the long haul, it must become their own conviction. When I started growing as a new believer in college, I got up early each morning to meet with God because the man who was discipling me encouraged me to do so. But I still remember the day that practice became my own conviction. I realized one morning that even if my discipler came to me and told me he no longer thought it was important to have a daily quiet time, I would continue to maintain that spiritual discipline. Why? Because it was no longer his conviction that I was borrowing—it had become my conviction. We need to help disciples develop their own convictions about spiritual realities because that is what will keep them going when others are not around: "You, however, continue in the things you have learned and *become convinced of*" (2 Tim. 3:14, emphasis added).

Show them how.

Jesus told the disciples to follow him, not simply to listen to him.[25] The apostle Paul modeled this truth as well: "Follow me, as I follow Christ" (1 Cor. 11:1. my translation). Most people learn better by seeing an example than simply hearing an instruction. Robert Coleman argues, "One living sermon is worth one hundred explanations."[26]

Keep them going.

Hebrews 3:13 reminds us of the importance of encouragement: "But encourage one another day after day, as long as it is still called 'Today,' so that none of you will be hardened by the deceitfulness of sin." All believers need encouragement, and we need it daily! How much more the new believer who is just learning how to walk spiritually! Years ago I heard someone suggest that with new believers we should use 90 percent encouragement and 10 percent correction.

Point them to Christ.

Our objective is to help a person become a disciple of Jesus Christ, not of you or me. Point others to Christ. He is the only one who will never disappoint or fail us. He is the one who always remains faithful.

A BALANCED CHURCH PROGRAM OF DISCIPLESHIP

In Matthew 14 we see Jesus discipling others in three different contexts: large group (vv. 13–21), small group (vv. 22–27) and individually (vv. 28–33). Each of these approaches has strengths and weaknesses. One-on-one or one-on-two discipling provides individual instruction and allows the discipler to deal with individual needs. It is also strategic because anyone can do it—you do not need to have attended Bible college or seminary to disciple someone else. Individual discipling also allows for greater flexibility in meetings and provides for a greater ability to observe each person's life.

Small-group discipling provides a wonderful context for accountability and encouragement. It allows people to participate without always being put on the spot, and individuals can move in and out of the group without damaging the group dynamic. Different spiritual gifts among the different members of the group can bring balance, and different life experiences can help group members to see truths in new ways. Large-group discipling allows a master teacher to provide solid content to large numbers of people at one time. The larger group also creates a dynamic for new believers that they really are a part of a genuine spiritual family.

Follow basic guidelines.

These ten basic guidelines provide helpful direction for the establishing phase of disciple-making.

1. *God wants every believer to grow toward maturity (Col. 1:28).* We know that when we are discipling others toward spiritual maturity, we are following God's revealed will.

2. *God is the source for spiritual growth (1 Cor. 3:6; John 15).* While we plant and others water, only God can bring spiritual growth. We grow and bear much fruit as we are connected to Christ.

3. *There is a danger of a Christian falling away (Heb. 2:1).* While I do not believe a genuine believer will ever lose his or her salvation, believers can fall away from Christian fellowship.

4. *Growth occurs within the context of Christian relationships (Heb. 3:12–13; 10:23–25; Gal. 6:1-2; Prov. 27:17).* God designed us to function as a family of Christians, not as individual, "lone ranger" Christians.

5. *Establishing must be person-centered, rather than material-centered.* While follow-up materials are helpful, they are not "one size fits all." An individual's pressing need one week may be something that the follow-up material does not address until several weeks later, if at all. Tailor-make the material to fit the person, not vice versa.

6. *Spiritual growth is a lifelong process—no one has "arrived" (Phil. 3:12–14).* If the apostle Paul testified that he had not arrived, who are any of

us to think that we have arrived spiritually? This reality should keep all of us humble—the disciple and the discipler both.

7. *The first week of a new Christian's life in Christ is crucial to his or her ongoing spiritual growth.* Old patterns are being abandoned; new patterns are being established. Help the new believer to get off to a good start.

8. *In every ministry situation, certain problems will arise (Prov. 14:4).* One of the most helpful verses I learned as a growing Christian was Proverbs 14:4 (NASB 1977): "Where there are no oxen, the manger is clean; but much increase comes by the strength of the ox." That verse can be summarized by the acrostic N.M.N.M., meaning "No Mess, No Ministry." If we want to have a nice, clean life, then we need to stay away from other people. Then we will only have to clean up our own messes! But as believers, we are not afforded that option! We must be involved in other people's lives, and that means we will need to deal with messes. And before we get too sanctimonious and judgmental toward other people's messes, let's pause and thank God for the people who have helped us in our life when we were messy and those who will help us in the future.

9. *There is a distinction between helping and training.* Understanding this principle will help you avoid much heartache and disappointment. A person might approach you and ask, "Will you disciple me?" I have found it helpful to try to clarify exactly what they are asking. Many times they are asking for assistance in one particular area of struggle (helping) versus wanting you to help them grow into Christlikeness in every single area of their life (training). Helping is done on a short-term basis with a limited agenda on someone else's terms; training is done on an ongoing basis with a comprehensive agenda that both parties agree on. Understanding this distinction is crucial, because if you are trying to "train" someone who only wants to be "helped" in a specific area, you will both wind up frustrated. Helping is a legitimate ministry! We will help hundreds of people in our lifetimes, just as scores of people have helped us when we hit a rough patch in our lives. Training is much more comprehensive than helping someone with a particular issue or problem.

10. *Not everyone will grow (John 17:12; 2 Tim. 4:10).* Jesus experienced abandonment and betrayal by one of his close followers, Judas: "While I was with them, I was keeping them in Thy name which Thou hast given Me; and I guarded them, and not one of them perished but the son of perdition, that the Scripture might be fulfilled" (John 17:12, NASB 1977). The apostle Paul knew the heartbreak of a colleague abandoning him: "for Demas, having loved this present world, has deserted me" (2 Tim 4:10). You can pour your heart and soul into discipling another believer only to have him or her walk away from you and the church. When that happens, remember you are in good company.

IMPLEMENTATION OF ESTABLISHING

Initial follow-up

Edward Watke maintains, "Prayer by the discipler for the disciple must precede and pervade the entire disciple making process."[27] Meet with a new believer as soon as possible. Briefly explain the role of prayer and the reading of the Bible for spiritual intake. Explain the nature and importance of baptism (depending on your tradition) and the priority of identification with a local church. Make yourself available by email, phone, and text, and in person. Prepare the new believer to share his or her faith. Calendar future meeting times to provide encouragement and accountability. Arrange for other believers to contact the new believer for fellowship and support.

Ongoing follow-up

Arrange to get together regularly for a period of several weeks. Have a game plan to follow, utilizing structured materials but remembering the principle of relational intentionality. Deviate from the structured materials, both in time frame and in content, as necessary. Continue to pray for the person on a daily basis, and encourage the new believer day after day (Heb. 3:13).

---

27. Edward Watke and Joy Watke, "Establishing the New Convert through a Discipling Ministry," Revival in the Home Ministries, accessed October 15, 2020, https://watke.org/resources/Establishing_Convert.htm.

CHAPTER 29

Assurance of Salvation

D. JAMES KENNEDY POSES THE FOLLOWING hypothetical question in *Evangelism Explosion*: "Have you come to the place in your life where you know that if you died, you would go to heaven?"[1] Some will say you can't know for sure whether or not you will go to heaven when you die. Or they might respond, "Nobody can know that—only God knows. You won't know until you stand before him and he tells you." But is that really the case? What does the Bible teach?

How Can I Know I Am Forgiven by God?

The Bible does not leave us in the dark on this question. First John 5:13 reminds believers, "These things I have written to you who believe in the name of the Son of God, so that you may know that you have eternal life." This verse teaches that we can *know* we have been forgiven by God. Assurance of salvation is possible. The Scriptures not only tell the way to know but also warn us about some wrong things people trust in that will mislead them. How can we know who/what we are trusting to get us to heaven?

---

1. D. James Kennedy, *Evangelism Explosion: Equipping Churches for Friendship, Evangelism, Discipleship, and Healthy Growth*, 4th ed. (Carol Stream, IL: Tyndale House Publishers), 39

A second hypothetical question, again popularized by D. James Kennedy, serves as a diagnostic question: "If you were to stand before God and he were to ask you, 'Why should I let you into my heaven?' What would you say?"[2] This question is a legitimate hypothetical question because every person will die someday and will stand before their creator as judge. As physicians of the soul, it is the kind of question that we can ask of people to diagnose where their trust is placed. A person's answer to that question will tell you who/what they are trusting in for salvation.

On an airline flight one day I sat down next to a woman and noticed she was reading a book titled *History of the Bible.* I commented to her, "That looks like a fascinating book!" and she replied, "Oh, it is!" I asked her if she knew a lot about the Bible, and she responded, "I don't know *anything* about the Bible. That's why I bought the book. I thought it would be good to learn about the Bible." When I shared with her I was a minister and had studied the Bible for decades, her face lit up, and she began to ask me questions about the history of the Bible.

During a lull in our conversation, I asked her D. James Kennedy's second diagnostic question in this way: "If you were to die today and were to stand before God and he were to say, 'Susan, why should I let you into my heaven?' what would you tell him?" A look of panic crossed her face. She had never been asked that question before, but the weightiness of it captured her. She pondered the question for several seconds before she finally said, "I know what I'd say. I would say, 'My mom used to be a Sunday school teacher.'" She obviously had no good answer for that question, and deep down she realized that. I was able to share with her the hope we have in Christ's sinless life, substitutionary death, and victorious resurrection.

Illegitimate Foundations for Assurance

What are some things people are trusting in to take them to heaven that the Bible says will not work? There are two illegitimate foundations for assurance upon which some people are building their eternal hope.

---

2. Kennedy, *Evangelism Explosion*, 40.

Trusting in What I Have Done

Many persons maintain that they have been a good person or have done a lot of good works, and that will punch their ticket to heaven. They say things like:

- I've been baptized
- I've been through confirmation classes at my church
- I give to the United Way every year
- I'm a kind person
- I've done the best I can do
- I go to church

Jesus says no matter what you put in the blank, it is not enough. Doing good things cannot earn your way into heaven. Matthew 7:22–23 dispels that mistaken thought. Jesus is talking about the day of judgment and says, "Many will say to Me on that day, 'Lord, Lord, did we not prophesy in Your name, and in Your name cast out demons, and in Your name perform many miracles?' And then I will declare to them, 'I never knew you; depart from Me, you who practice lawlessness.'"

The Bible is very clear that God wants us to do good works. But it is also very clear that our good works cannot earn our salvation. Salvation is God's free gift to us because of his grace and love, not because we can possibly earn it. Ephesians 2:8–9 (NIV) says, "For it is by grace you have been saved, through faith—and this is not from yourselves, it is the gift of God—not by works, so that no one can boast." Trusting in what *we* have done leads to a false assurance. But there will be no bragging in heaven. Jesus gets all the glory. Jesus gets all the credit. The symbol of Christianity is not a ladder but a cross. Those who have repented and put their faith in Christ are undeserving sinners who have been saved by his grace.

Trusting in What I Haven't Done

Jesus told a parable about a Pharisee and a publican (tax collector) in Luke 18. The Pharisee prayed and said, "God, I thank You that I am not like other men" (Luke 18:11, ESV). This man was bragging on all of his accomplishments and the "big" sins that he had avoided. He had not swindled people, committed adultery, or extorted people's money. The tax collector, on the other hand, beat his breast and cried out to God for mercy:

"God be merciful to me a sinner." Jesus tells us the tax collector went home justified, not the Pharisee.

The Pharisee thought God would accept him because he had avoided the really bad sins. But in Matthew 23, Jesus called the Pharisees "white-washed tombs"—pretty on the outside but dead on the inside. Focusing on what we *haven't* done brings false assurance just like focusing on what we *have* done. Doing a lot of "good things" will not earn us salvation, but neither will trying to avoid doing really "bad things." We *should* do good, and we *should* avoid the bad! But the Bible is very clear—trusting in these things leads to false assurance. The only answer to the question of why God should let us into heaven is that we have been forgiven by God's grace, and we have received the free gift of salvation in our empty, outstretched hands by faith.

Proper Foundations for Assurance

The Bible points us to three foundations we must examine to have a proper assurance of salvation. It is important that we take all three of these together.

Promises of God

The ultimate foundation for our assurance is what God has done for us in Christ. Assurance of salvation rests on the character of God, the work of Jesus Christ, and the truth of God's promises. Reflect on the words of Jesus: "Truly, truly, I say to you, he who hears My word, and believes Him who sent Me, has eternal life, and does not come into judgment, but has passed out of death into life" (John 5:24); and "I give them eternal life, and they shall never perish; no one will snatch them out of my hand" (John 10:28, NIV).

Jesus promises that whoever believes in him will not be condemned but has crossed over from death to life. The ultimate foundation of our assurance is that we have a God who keeps his Word. He promises, "If anyone is in Christ, [s]he is a new creature; the old things passed away; behold, new things have come" (2 Cor. 5:17). The work of Christ, combined with the promises of God, provide the ultimate grounds of our assurance. When God makes a promise, he keeps it! Numbers 23:19 reminds us, "God is not a man, that He should lie; nor a son of man, that He should repent; has He said, and will He not do it? Or has He spoken, and will He not make it good?"

Some people trust in *themselves* (either *what they have done* or *what they haven't done*) to earn their way to heaven. But the Bible tells us in no uncertain terms that the only way to heaven is to trust Jesus Christ and his atoning sacrifice on the cross, to receive the salvation he freely offers. Jesus died on the cross to pay the penalty of sins for all who believe in him—he gives them eternal life. And he tells us that those who receive the salvation he offers can never lose that salvation: "no one will snatch them out of my hand" (John 10:28, NIV). God promises that all who trust in Jesus Christ will be saved and will receive eternal life. But the Bible doesn't stop there—it gives us guidance in how we can discern whether or not we have truly trusted in Christ to save us. A person can pray a prayer and say certain words but not really understand them or truly mean them. God knows our heart, and he tells us there are evidences we can examine to see whether or not we have really trusted in Christ.

Inner Witness of the Holy Spirit

Assurance can be confirmed through the inner witness of the Holy Spirit: "The Spirit himself testifies with our spirit that we are God's children" (Rom. 8:16, NIV). The inner witness of the Holy Spirit gives a confirming presence and confirming assurance that we belong to God, that he is in us and we are in him. The inner witness of the Spirit is the overwhelming sense of God's presence in your life. It is God confirming in the very core of your being that you are his child. This is a subjective reality, but genuine believers all experience this inner witness. The Spirit himself testifies, or bears witness with our spirit, that we are truly one of God's children and that we have been forgiven.

Evidence of a Changing Life

In addition to the promises of God and the inner witness of the Spirit, a third component is the evidence of a changing life. If someone says, "I believed in Christ thirty years ago," but then there has been no evidence of that belief over those thirty years, the Bible would raise questions about the legitimacy of that experience. Years ago, a popular question to ask was, "If you were arrested for being a Christian, would there be enough evidence to convict you?"

In the book of 1 John, John gives us several marks of true believers. When John writes, "These things have I written to you who believe in the name of the Son of God, so that you may know that you have eternal life" (1 John 5:13), what "things" is John talking about? The book of 1 John was written in part to help believers understand genuine assurance. Before we look at these evidences, it is important to understand two cautions. First, Scripture mandates the *presence* of these marks in our lives, not the *perfection* of them. That disclaimer is essential because if the perfection of these things is mandated, there is no hope for any of us! Spiritual perfection awaits us in a future life. However, the *presence* of these things must be there versus the complete *absence* of them.

Second, these marks of a genuine believer are the *fruit* of faith, not the *root* of faith. In other words, these things flow *out* of our relationship with God, they are not the means we can use to try and earn God's forgiveness. Jesus referred to the Pharisees as whitewashed tombs. It is possible to be all pretty on the outside but inside be spiritually dead. Some people may try to use "exterior decorating" to plaster these marks on their lives, but these characteristics are to be the fruit of faith, not the root of faith. We have these marks because we are in Christ rather than manufacturing these things in order to be accepted by Christ. So, keep in mind these two very important cautions: these outward evidences must be present, not perfect, and these evidences are the fruit of faith, not the root of faith.

EVIDENCES IN LIVES OF THOSE
WHO HAVE TRULY TRUSTED CHRIST

The Bible says that certain attitudes and actions will *accompany* salvation. There will be an *outward* manifestation of God's *inward* working. John gives certain marks or signs throughout the book of 1 John that can help us to know that there has been a change in our life. These "tests" from 1 John are more objective and can help us balance the "inner witness of the Holy Spirit," which is more subjective. Both components are important, and taken in tandem they provide a powerful basis for assurance. What are these objective evidences?

Do you enjoy worshiping God?

"Our fellowship is with the Father, and with His Son Jesus Christ" (1 John 1:3). Do you *enjoy* spending time with God in prayer? Do you desire fellowship with the Father, Son, and Spirit? Do you find delight in worshiping God and going to church to praise his name? Now, let me remind you of the caution that the evidence needs to be present in a person's life, but it does not have to be perfect. If you wake up one Sunday morning feeling very ill, you do not assume you must not be a true Christian because you did not feel like going to church that Sunday morning. Even as a pastor there have been a handful of Sunday mornings when I did not overflow with eagerness to head to the worship service. But what is the overall pattern of a person's life?

Delighting in private and corporate worship was one of the marks that clicked with me as a brand-new believer. I used to hate going to church. I viewed it as boring and a colossal waste of time. Why? Because I had no heart for it! However, once I met Christ I wanted to go to church, worship my Savior, sing his praises, and learn more about him. A desire to worship God is one of the marks of a heart that has been changed.

In one of my churches, as I was systematically contacting people whose names were on the church roll but who were never in church, I visited a man in his home. I introduced myself as the new pastor. He mentioned he had not attended church in a while. When I asked him what "a while" meant, he replied it had been eighteen years. Then he said to me, "But, pastor, don't worry about me. I'm good. God and I are close."

Seeking to speak the truth in love (Eph. 4:15), I said, "Sir, you said not to worry about you, but I am worried. I don't know how someone could have a genuine relationship with Christ and for eighteen years have no desire to worship or fellowship with him, or sing his praises." When our heart has been changed, we will have a desire for fellowship with the Father, Son, and Spirit. You want to spend time with people you love! We are not simply talking about *feelings*, but about where our *heart* is. If your heart does not look forward to worship and fellowship with God, then it may have never been changed in the first place.

Do you have an awareness of your sin?

First John 1:8 (NIV) says, "If we claim to be without sin, we deceive ourselves and the truth is not in us." This could appear to be counterintuitive because we understand, as Christians, our sins have been forgiven. Yet the closer we get to the Holy One, the greater awareness we have of our sin. What do unbelievers do with their sin? They rationalize it and seek to justify it: "It's not my fault"; "I was born into a dysfunctional family"; "Don't blame me." Unbelievers never seem to think sin is their fault. Christians see their sin and identify it for what it is.

When I first trusted Christ as my Lord and Savior, I knew I was a sinner. But I had no idea just how much of a sinner I was! The more that we learn about God, the more we study and understand his Word, the greater awareness we have of our sin. C. H. Spurgeon made this observation about the life of the apostle Paul. He pointed out that Paul said in Galatians, "I'm the least of the apostles." In other epistles Paul referred to himself as "the least of the saints." In his last epistle to Timothy, he describes himself as "the chief of sinners." Spurgeon maintained that progression ought to be true in every Christian's life. When we first come to Christ, we know that we are a sinner but as we get closer to the Holy One, we begin to discover attitudes and heart issues that we were completely clueless about before we knew Christ. Being aware of our sin and realizing our continual need to have our hearts set right is one of the marks of being a child of God. Believers do not live *perfect* lives, but they are aware of their sin and their need to confess that sin to God.

Do you seek to be obedient to the Word of God?

"We know that we have come to know Him, if we keep His commands" (1 John 2:3). One of the most powerful baptism testimonies I have ever heard came from a college student. When the pastor asked her to talk about her newfound faith in Christ, she replied, "I don't know much theology, but I know this much—I used to run after sin, and now I run away from it." That morning we witnessed a clear evidence of new life in Christ. She was not claiming to have achieved sinless perfection, but her heart had been changed, and her desires were different. One of the marks of a believer is we have a desire to obey God. We do not always do it perfectly, but the direction of our heart has been changed. We desire to obey because we want to please and honor him.

Do you love other Christians and want to be with them?

"We know that we have passed out of death into life, because we love the brethren" (1 John 3:14). Notice the introductory phrase in this verse: "we know that we have passed from death to life." *How* can we know that reality? How can we have confident assurance that we have transitioned from spiritual death to spiritual life? John tells us: because we love our brothers and sisters in Christ. Again, the reality of having this mark of a true believer in our life does not mean we love others with perfection.

All believers have rough edges—we can all irritate other people at times. And yet one of the marks that our heart has been changed is that we now no longer just look out for ourselves but also want to serve others. We desire to be with the people of God. Jesus instructs us in John 13:34–35, "A new commandment I give you, that you love one another, even as I have loved you. By this all men will know that you are My disciples, if you have love one for another." Do you love other Christians and want to be with them? Scripture makes clear that love for brothers and sisters in Christ marks those with genuine faith in Christ.

Do you display the fruit of the Spirit?

"We know that we live in him and he in us: He has given us of his Spirit" (1 John 4:13, NIV). The Spirit produces fruit in our lives. Assurance of salvation comes as we see the Holy Spirit producing his fruit in our life. Paul reminds us, "the fruit of the Spirit is love, joy, peace, patience, kindness, goodness, faithfulness, gentleness, and self-control" (Gal. 5:22–23). These are the evidences that 1 John says we are to examine to see if we have a basis for assurance of salvation.

DIRECTION, NOT PERFECTION

Again, I must reiterate an important caution. Scripture does not mandate the perfection of these marks in our life, but the presence of them. What is the overall direction of a person's life? If someone asked you which direction the Ohio River flows, a correct answer would be generally from northeast to southwest. But there is a bend in the river near downtown Louisville where the Ohio River actually flows back to the north! The overall direction of the river, however, is from northeast to southwest. Similarly, we can ask of a person, "What is the overall direction of your life?" Is it toward God, acknowledging your sin, obeying God, loving fellow believers, and displaying the fruit of the Spirit, or is it headed in the opposite direction? We are not talking about snapshots here (where the river may curve a different way at a moment in time) but a videotape— what is the overall direction?

In Matthew 7:16, Jesus taught we will know people "by their fruits." Just as different plants produce different amounts of fruit, so Christians grow at different paces. Believers do not grow at the same rate or display fruit to the same degree. Progress might not always be evident. But throughout a genuine believer's life, there will be growth in Christlikeness and fruitfulness. There are some people who are confident that the gospel seed was planted in their life years ago. Maybe it was; maybe it wasn't. How can we know? A person will not have the perfection of fruit in his or her life, but if there seems to be the complete *absence* of fruit, that person should seriously consider whether or not he or she is a genuine believer. Jesus's words in Matthew 7:22–23 haunt me, and should haunt you as well: "Many will say to me on that day, 'Lord, Lord, did we not prophecy in your name and in your name cast out demons, and in your name perform many miracles? And then I will declare to them, 'I never knew you; depart from me, you who practice lawlessness.'"

How do we go about sharing the gospel with people who "assume" they are believers, but who show no spiritual fruit in their lives? In such instances, I share with the person Jesus's word in Matthew 7:22–23, highlighting the word "many." Jesus did not say in the day of judgment there would be a few people who got it wrong, or some who misunderstood—he says there will be "many." I tell the person I care about them enough I do not want them to be among that "many."

CONCLUSION

With the subject of assurance of salvation, we need to be aware of three dangers. First is the danger of presumption. This danger is where we refuse to take an honest look at our heart and at our life; we just assume everything is okay. The second danger is the opposite of the first danger—unreasonable self-condemnation. This is where every time we sin, we automatically question whether or not we are a Christian. Remember the Bible requires the *presence* of evidences, not the *perfection* of them. What is the overall direction of my life? The third danger is when someone knows they are not converted but assume they have all the time in the world to repent of their sin and put their faith in Christ. Scripture admonishes us, "Today if you hear his voice, do not harden your hearts" (Heb. 3:15).

AFTERWORD

PEOPLE MATTER TO GOD. It has been said that the church is the only institution in the world that exists primarily for the people who are not yet a part of it. Jesus asked, "For what does it profit a man to gain the whole world, and forfeit his soul? For what will a man give in exchange for his soul?" (Mark 8:36). It is as if Jesus is challenging his listeners to put everything in the world on one side of a balance scale and put a human soul on the other side. The weight of that soul would throw all the items on the other side up in the air as if they were lighter than feathers.

When we reflect deeply about the gospel, we realize we cannot remain silent. We must speak about what we have seen and heard. Good news is for sharing! In Romans 1 the apostle Paul begins with a brief introduction of a personal nature and then reflects on the gospel. In Romans 1:14–16, Paul points us to three key attitudes that formed the basis for his evangelistic zeal. Paul writes: "I am under obligation both to Greeks and to barbarians, both to the wise and to the foolish. So, for my part, I am eager to preach the gospel to you also who are in Rome. For I am not ashamed of the gospel, for it is the power of God for salvation to everyone who believes, to the Jew first and also to the Greek." "I am under obligation" is a strong phrase, indicating a profound sense of indebtedness. We have become experts at rationalizing away our obligation. We say things like "It's not my gift," or "I'm not very good with people." But Jesus didn't say "Go into all the world, all you *extroverts*." Don't rationalize, *evangelize*!

Notice to whom Paul says he is under obligation: to the Greeks and to the barbarians (the non-Greeks), and to the wise and to the foolish. Taken together they encompass all humankind. Because of the salvation he had received and his calling by the Lord Jesus, he was a debtor to *all* people. We have a tendency to categorize people into different groups. Don't categorize, *evangelize*! Good news is for sharing! Possessing good news obligates us to share it! Have you come to grips with your obligation to share the gospel with others? To have good news *obligates* us to share it! To have the medicine of life *obligates* us to share it with the sick and dying! Have you come to grips with your *obligation* to share the gospel with others?

Paul makes it clear that he intends to fulfill his obligation. He is saying that regardless of what others may or may not do, he will do his part. He does not consider his obligation a burden he must bear. Paul did not need to be coerced or have his arm twisted to get him to share his faith. He was not only willing; he was eager! How eager are you to share the gospel with others? Are you not simply willing, but eager to share his love with others? If you cannot honestly answer yes, how can you get this eagerness? It comes back to the need for a daily time alone with God. Matthew 12:34 says "the mouth speaks out of that which fills the heart." The gospel is good news!

Do we really believe the gospel is the power of God for salvation? We give up on some people and think, "There is no way that person's life could change—they are too far gone." But we must remember Paul, the chief persecutor of the Christian church, became one of the greatest Christians to ever live. John Newton, a slave trader and alcoholic, wrote the hymn "Amazing Grace." Chuck Colson, part of the Nixon administration, was powerfully converted and wrote the bestselling books *Born Again* and *Loving God*. Nowhere in the Bible does it say, "Go into all the world and share the gospel with everyone who looks like they are a good candidate to become a Christian." We are to share with all!

Possessing good news obligates us to share it. Understanding just how good the good news is causes us to share it eagerly. Realizing the power of the good news motivates us to share it boldly. Recall the statement at the beginning of the chapter: "The church exists primarily for those who are not yet in it." Will you accept that challenge? Will you live your life to keep the main thing the main thing?

Examine your heart. You cannot effectively share the good news with others until you have embraced it yourself! Commit yourself to follow the Lord. God never commands us to do anything without giving us the necessary resources to do it. And commit to become a sower of the gospel seed. We are going to receive different responses to the message, but the response is not our responsibility. Our task is to sow the seed. May we be found to be faithful sowers!

BIBLIOGRAPHY

Abraham, William J. *The Logic of Evangelism*. Grand Rapids: Eerdmans, 1989.

Adams, Isaac. *What If I'm Discouraged in My Evangelism?* Wheaton, IL: Crossway, 2020.

Adams, James R. *So You Can't Stand Evangelism? A Thinking Person's Guide to Church Growth*. Cambridge, MA: Cowley, 1994.

Adeney, Frances S. *Graceful Evangelism: Christian Witness in a Complex World*. Grand Rapids: Baker, 2010.

Ahn, Che. *Spirit-Led Evangelism: Reaching the Lost through Love and Power*. Grand Rapids: Chosen Books, 2008.

Akin, Daniel L., Benjamin L. Merkle, and George G. Robinson. *40 Questions about the Great Commission*. Grand Rapids: Kregel, 2020.

Aldrich, Joseph C. *Gentle Persuasion: Creative Ways to Introduce Your Friends to Christ*. Portland, OR: Multnomah, 1988.

_____. *Life-Style Evangelism: Crossing Traditional Boundaries to Reach the Un-believing World*. Portland, OR: Multnomah Press, 1981.

Allen, Roland. *Missionary Methods: St. Paul's or Ours?* Grand Rapids: Eerdmans, 1962.

_____. *The Spontaneous Expansion of the Church*. London: World Dominion Press, 1927.

Allison, Lon and Mark Anderson. *Going Public with the Gospel: Reviving Evange-listic Proclamation*. Downers Grove: IVP, 2003.

Amberson, Talmadge. *Reaching Out to People*. Nashville: Broadman, 1980.

Anderson, Ken. *A Coward's Guide to Witnessing*. Carol Stream, IL: Creation House, 1972.

Anyabwile, Thabiti. *The Gospel for Muslims: An Encouragement to Share Christ with Confidence*. Chicago: Moody, 2010.

Archibald, Arthur C. *Man to Man*. Nashville: Broadman Press, 1955.

_____. *New Testament Evangelism: How It Works Today*. Philadelphia: Judson Press, 1952.

Arias, Mortimer, and Alan Johnson. *The Great Commission: Biblical Models for Evangelism*. Nashville: Abingdon, 1992.

Armstrong, D. Wade. *Evangelistic Growth in Acts 1 & 2*. Nashville: Broadman, 1983.

Armstrong, Richard. *Service Evangelism*. Philadelphia: Westminster, 1979.

_____. *The Pastor-Evangelist in the Parish*. Louisville: Westminster John Knox, 1990.

Arn, Win, and Charles Arn. *The Master's Plan for Making Disciples*. 2nd ed. Grand Rapids: Baker, 1998.

Arthurs, Sara T. *Bring Them Home: Preparing Hearts to Rescue Troubled Youth*. Arthurs Publishing, 2018.

Augsburger, Myron. *Evangelism as Discipling*. Scottsdale, PA: Herald, 1983.

_____. *Invitation to Discipleship: The Message of Evangelism*. Scottsdale, PA: 1964, n.d.

Autrey, C. E. *Basic Evangelism*. Grand Rapids: Zondervan, 1959.

_____. *Evangelism in the Acts*. Grand Rapids: Zondervan, n.d.

_____. *The Theology of Evangelism*. Nashville: Broadman, 1966.

_____. *You Can Win Souls: A Practical Guide for the Christian in Meeting His Major Responsibility*. Nashville: Broadman & Holman, 1961.

Bader, Jesse Moren. *Evangelism in a Changing America*. St. Louis: Bethany Press, 1957.

_____. *The Message and Method of the New Testament Evangelism*. New York: Round Table Press, 1937.

Bailey, Ambrose M. *Evangelism in a Changing World*. New York: Round Table Press, 1936.

Baker, Gordon Pratt. *A Practical Theory for Christian Evangelism*. Nashville: Abingdon, 1965.

Baker, Tim. *Witnessing 101*. Nashville: W Publishing Group, 2003.

Banks, Louis Albert. *Soul Winning Stories*. New York: American Tract Society, 1902.

Banks, William L. *In Search of the Great Commission: What Did Jesus Really Say?* Chicago: Moody, 1991.

Barclay, William T. *Fishers of Men*. Philadelphia: Westminster Press, 1966.

Barna, George. *Absolute Confusion: The Barna Report*. Ventura, CA: Regal Books, 1994.

_____. *Evangelism That Works*. Ventura, CA: Regal Books, 1997.

_____. *Reviving Evangelism: Current Realities That Demand a New Vision for Sharing Faith*. Ventura, CA: Barna Group, 2019.

Barnette, Jasper Newton. *The Place of the Sunday School in Evangelism*. Nashville: Sunday School Board of the Southern Baptist Convention, 1945.

Barrett, David B. *Evangelize: A Historical Survey of the Concept*. Birmingham, AL: New Hope, 1987.

Barrs, Jerram. *Learning Evangelism from Jesus*. Wheaton, IL: Crossway, 2009.

_____. *The Heart of Evangelism*. Wheaton, IL: Crossway, 2001.

Barton, Levi Elder. *Helps for the Soul Winner*. Montgomery, AL: Paragon, 1945.

Baugh, Ken. *Getting Real: An Interactive Guide to Relational Ministry*. Colorado Springs: NavPress, 2000.

Baxter, Richard. *The Autobiography of Richard Baxter*, ed. by N.H. Keeble. London: J. M. Dent & Sons, 1974.

_____. *The Reformed Pastor*. Edinburgh: Banner of Truth Trust, 1974.

Bayly, Joseph. *The Gospel Blimp*. Grand Rapids: Zondervan, 1960.

Beardsley, Frank G. *Religious Progress through Revivals*. New York: American Tract Society, 1943.

Beasley, Gary M., and Francis Anfuso. *Complete Evangelism: Fitting the Pieces Together*. South Lake Tahoe, CA: Christian Equippers, 1991.

Beasley-Murray, George R. *Evangelizing the Post-Christian Man*. London: Baptist Preacher's Association, 1969.

Bechtle, Mike. *Evangelism for the Rest of Us: Sharing Christ within Your Personality Style*. Grand Rapids: Baker Books, 2006.

Beeke, Joel R. *Puritan Evangelism: A Biblical Approach*. Grand Rapids: Reformation Heritage Books, 2007.

Beisner, E. Calvin. *Answers for Atheists, Agnostics, and Other Thoughtful Skeptics: Dialogs about Christian Faith and Life*. Wheaton, IL: Crossway, 1993.

Belcher, Richard P. *Preaching the Gospel: A Theological and a Personal Method*. Columbia, SC: Richbarry Press, 1986.

Belew, M. Wendell. *Churches and How They Grow*. Nashville: Broadman Press, 1971.

Bender, Urie A. *The Witness: Message, Method, Motivation*. Scottsdale, PA: Herald Press, 1970.

Benson, Dennis. *Electric Evangelism*. Nashville: Abingdon, 1973.

Beougher, Sharon, and Mary Dorsett. *Women and Evangelism: An Evangelistic Lifestyle from a Woman's Perspective*. Wheaton, IL: Billy Graham Center, Institute of Evangelism, 1994.

Beougher, Timothy K. *Overcoming Walls to Witnessing*. Charlotte, NC: Billy Graham Evangelistic Association, 1993.

_____. *Overcoming Walls to Witnessing*. Revised and Updated edition. Leyland, England: 10Publishing, 2021.

_____. *Richard Baxter and Conversion: A Study of the Puritan Concept of Becoming a Christian*. Fearn, Ross-shire, Scotland, UK: Mentor, 2007.

Berge, Selmer Alonzo. *Evangelism in the Congregation*. Minneapolis: Faith Action Movement, 1944.

Bettis, Chap. *Evangelism for the Tongue-Tied: How Anyone Can Tell Others about Jesus*. Trusted Books, 2014.

Biederwolf, William E. *Evangelism: Its Justification, Its Operation and Its Value.* New York: Revell, 1921.

Bill, Ingram Ebenezer. *Constructive Evangelism.* Philadelphia: Judson Press, 1921.

Bisagno, John R. *How to Build an Evangelistic Church.* Nashville: Broadman Press, 1971.

_____. *The Power of Positive Evangelism.* Nashville: Broadman Press, 1968.

_____. *The Power of Positive Preaching to the Lost.* Nashville: Broadman Press, 1973.

Bisagno, John R., Kenneth L. Chafin, and C. Wade Freeman, eds. *How to Win Them.* Nashville: Broadman, 1970.

Blackwood, Andrew W. *Evangelism in the Home Church.* New York: Abingdon-Cokesbury, 1942.

Blauw, Johannes. *The Missionary Nature of the Church.* New York: McGraw-Hill, 1962.

Blessitt, Arthur. *Tell the World: A Jesus People Manual.* Old Tappan, NJ: Revell, 1972.

Blue, Ron. *Evangelism and Missions: Strategies for Outreach in the 21st Century.* Nashville: Word Publishing, 2001.

Boda, Mark J. *Return to Me: A Biblical Theology of Repentance.* Downers Grove, IL: IVP, 2015.

Bonar, Horatius. *Words to Winners of Souls.* Phillipsburg, NJ: P & R, 1995.

Bonnke, Reinhard. *Evangelism by Fire.* Lake Mary, FL: Charisma House, 2011.

Booker, Mike, and Mark Ireland. *Evangelism—Which Way Now.* London: Church House, 2003.

Borchert, Gerald L. *Dynamics of Evangelism.* Dallas: Word, 1976.

Borthwick, Paul. *Stop Witnessing . . . and Start Loving.* Colorado Springs: NavPress, 2003.

Boston, Thomas. *The Art of Man-Fishing: How to Reach the Lost.* Ross-shire, Scotland: Christian Focus, 2012.

Bounds, E. M. *Power through Prayer.* Grand Rapids: Baker, 1972.

Bowen, John. *Evangelism for Normal People.* Minneapolis: Augsburg, 2002.

Breen, A. C. *Evangelism.* Armadale, Western Australia: The Reformed Guardian, 2008.

Brestin, Dee. *Finders Keepers: Personal & Small Group Evangelism.* Wheaton, IL: Harold Shaw, 1983.

Bright, Bill. *Come Help Change the World.* Old Tappan, NJ: Revell, 1970.

_____. *Have You Heard of the Four Spiritual Laws?* San Bernardino, CA: New Life, 1965.

_____. *Witnessing without Fear: How to Share Your Faith with Confidence.* San Bernardino, CA: Here's Life, 1987.

Briner, Bob. *Roaring Lambs.* Grand Rapids: Zondervan, 1993.

Brock, Charles. *Let This Mind Be in You.* Kansas City, MO: Church Growth, 1990.

Brooks, Phillips. *Lectures on Preaching.* New York: E.P. Dutton and Company, 1877.

Brooks, W. Hal. *Follow-Up Evangelism.* Nashville: Broadman, 1972.

Brown, Fred. *Secular Evangelism.* London: SCM, 1970.

Brown, Stanley C. *Evangelism in the Early Church.* Grand Rapids: Eerdmans, 1963.

Brueggemann, Walter. *Biblical Perspectives on Evangelism: Living in a Three-Storied Universe.* Nashville: Abingdon, 1993.

Bryan, Dawson Charles. *A Workable Plan of Evangelism.* New York: Abingdon-Cokesbury, 1945.

_____. *Building Church Membership through Evangelism.* New York: Abingdon-Cokesbury, 1952.

_____. *Handbook on Evangelism for Laymen.* New York: Abingdon-Cokesbury, 1948.

Bryan, O. E. *The Ethics of Evangelism.* Louisville: The Southern Baptist Theological Seminary, 1920.

Burroughs, P. E. *How to Win to Christ.* Nashville: Sunday School Board of the Southern Baptist Convention, 1934.

_____. *Winning to Christ: A Study in Evangelism.* Nashville: Sunday School Board of the Southern Baptist Convention, 1923.

Cahill, Mark. *One Thing You Can't Do in Heaven.* Rockwall, TX: Biblical Discipleship Publishers, 2007.

Cairns, Earle E. *An Endless Line of Splendor: Revivals and Their Leaders from the Great Awakening to the Present.* Wheaton, IL: Tyndale, 1986.

Caldwell, Max. L., ed. *Witness to Win: Positive Evangelism through the Sunday School.* Nashville: Convention Press, 1978.

Callahan, Kennon L. *Visiting in an Age of Mission: A Handbook for Person-to-Person Ministry.* San Francisco: Harper, 1994.

Callen, Barry. *Where Life Begins.* Anderson, IN: Warner Press, 1973.

Calver, Clive. *Sold Out: Taking the Lid Off Evangelism.* London: Lakeland, Marshall, Morgan and Scott, 1980.

Calver, Clive, ed. *A Guide to Evangelism.* Basingstoke: Marshall, Morgan & Scott, 1984.

Cameron, Kirk, and Ray Comfort. *The School of Biblical Evangelism.* Gainesville, FL: Bridge-Logos, 2004.

Campbell, Johnson Ben. *Speaking of God: Evangelism as Initial Spiritual Guidance.* Atlanta: Westminster John Knox, 1991.

Campbell, Robert C. *The Coming Revival.* Nashville: Broadman, 1939.

Cannon, W. R. *Evangelism in a Contemporary Context.* Nashville: Tidings Press, 1974.

Careaga, Andrew. *E-Vangelism: Sharing the Gospel in Cyberspace.* Lafayette, LA: Vital Issues, 1999.

Carson, D. A. *God's Love Compels Us: Taking the Gospel to the World*. Wheaton, IL: Crossway, 2015.

———. *Praying with Paul: A Call to Spiritual Reformation*. Grand Rapids: Baker Academic, 2015.

———, ed. *Telling the Truth: Evangelizing Postmoderns*. Grand Rapids: Zondervan, 2000.

Carswell, Roger. *And Some Evangelists*. Ross-shire, Great Britain: Christian Focus, 2014.

———. *Before You Say, "I Don't Believe."* Leyland, England: 10Publishing, 2017.

———. *Evangelistic Living: Sharing the Gospel Day by Day*. Leyland, England: 10Publishing, 2020.

———. *Facing a Task Unfinished: Cultivating Personal Evangelism Week by Week*. Ross-shire, Scotland: Christian Focus, 2015.

———. *Why I Believe*. Leyland, England: 10Publishing, 2018.

Cartwright, Lin D. *Evangelism for Today*. St. Louis: Bethany, 1943.

Cartwright, Peter. *Autobiography of Peter Cartwright*, ed. W.P. Strickland. New York: The Methodist Book Concern, n.d.

Cavey, Bruxy. *(Re)Union: The Good News of Jesus for Seekers, Saints, and Sinners*. Harrisonburg, VA: Herald Press, 2017.

Cecil, Douglas M. *The 7 Principles of an Evangelistic Life*. Chicago: Moody, 2003.

Chafer, Lewis Sperry. *True Evangelism: Winning Souls by Prayer*. Grand Rapids: Dunham Publishing Company, 1967.

Chafin, Kenneth L. *The Reluctant Witness*. Nashville: Broadman, 1974.

Chambers, Oswald. *Workmen of God*. New York: Grosset and Dunlap, 1938.

Chan, Sam. *Evangelism in a Skeptical World: How to Make the Unbelievable News about Jesus More Believable*. Grand Rapids: Zondervan, 2018.

Chandler, Matt. *The Explicit Gospel*. Wheaton, IL: Crossway, 2012.

Chaney, Charles L. and Granville Watson. *Evangelism: Today and Tomorrow*. Nashville: Broadman Press, 1993.

Chapman, J. Wilbur. *Fishing For Men*. Chicago: Winona Pub. Co., 1904.

———. *Present-Day Evangelism*. New York: Baker & Taylor Co, 1903.

Chapman, John C. *Know & Tell the Gospel: The Why and How of Evangelism*. London: Hodder and Stoughton, 1981.

———. *Setting Hearts on Fire: A Guide to Giving Evangelistic Talks*. Kingsford, UK: Matthias, 1999.

Chappell, E. B. *Evangelism in the Sunday School*. Nashville: Methodist Episcopal Church, South, 1925.

Chastain, Theron. *We Can Win Others*. Valley Forge, PA: Judson Press, 1953.

Chilcote, Paul W., and Laceye C. Warner, eds. *The Study of Evangelism: Exploring a Missional Practice of the Church*. Grand Rapids: Eerdmans, 2008.

Chirgwin, Arthur Mitchell. *The Bible in World Evangelism*. New York: Friendship Press, 1954.

Christenson, Evelyn. *Battling the Prince of Darkness*. Wheaton, IL: Victor, 1990.

Chitwood, Paul. "The Sinner's Prayer: An Historical and Theological Analysis." Ph.D. dissertation, Southern Baptist Theological Seminary, 2001.

Clark, Elliott. *Evangelism as Exiles: Life on Mission as Strangers in Our Own Land*. The Gospel Coalition, 2019.

Clark, Glenn. *Fishers of Men*. Boston: Little, Brown, 1928.

Clark, Gordon H. *Today's Evangelism: Counterfeit or Genuine?* Jefferson, MD: The Trinity Foundation, 1990.

Clark, Randy. *Power/Holiness/Evangelism: Rediscovering God's Purity, Power, and Passion for the Lost*. Shippensburg, PA: Destiny Image, 1999.

Coalter, Milton J, and Virgil Cruz, eds. *How Shall We Witness?: Faithful Evangelism in a Reformed Tradition*. Louisville: Westminster John Knox Press, 1995.

Cocoris, G. Michael. *Evangelism: A Biblical Approach*. Chicago: Moody, 1984.

Coggin, James E. *You Can Reach People Now*. Nashville: Broadman, 1971.

Coleman, Robert E., ed. *Evangelism on the Cutting Edge*. Old Tappan, NJ: Fleming H. Revell Company, 1986.

_____. *Nothing to Do But Save Souls: John Wesley's Charge to His Preachers*. Wilmore, KY: Wesley Heritage, 1990.

_____. *The Heart of the Gospel: The Theology behind the Master Plan of Evangelism*. Grand Rapids: Baker, 2011.

_____. *The Master Plan of Discipleship*. Old Tappan, NJ: Fleming H. Revell Company, 1987.

_____. *The Master Plan of Evangelism*. Old Tappan, NJ: Fleming H. Revell Company, 1963.

_____. *The Master's Way of Personal Evangelism*. Wheaton, IL: Crossway Books, 1997.

_____. *They Met the Master: A Study on the Personal Evangelism of Jesus*. Old Tappan, NJ: Revell, 1973.

Collier, Jarvis L. *Whatever Happened to Christian Evangelism?* Nashville: Sunday School Publishing Board, 2014.

Colson, Chuck, and Nancy Pearcey. *How Now Shall We Live?* Wheaton, IL: Tyndale House, 1999.

Come, Arnold B. *Agents of Reconciliation*. Philadelphia: Westminster Press, 1960.

Comer, Gary. *Soul Whisperer: Why the Church Must Change the Way It Views Evangelism*. Eugene, OR: Resource Publications, 2013.

Conant, J. E. *Every Member Evangelism*. New York: Harper & Brothers, 1922.

Conn, Harvie. *Evangelism: Doing Justice and Preaching Grace*. Phillipsburg, NJ: P & R Publishing, 1992.

Cook, Henry. *The Theology of Evangelism: The Gospel in the World of To-Day*. London: Carey Kingsgate Press Ltd, 1951.

Cooper, Clay. *Nothing to Win but the World*. Grand Rapids: Zondervan, 1965.

Coppenger, Mark. *Moral Apologetics for Contemporary Christians: Pushing Back against Cultural and Religious Critics.* B&H Studies in Christian Ethics. Nashville: B & H Academic, 2011.

Costas, Orlando. *Christ Outside the Gate.* Maryknoll, NY: Orbis, 1982.

Crandall, Ron. *The Contagious Witness: Exploring Christian Conversion.* Nashville: Abingdon Press, 1999.

Crawford, Percy B. *The Art of Fishing for Men.* Chicago: Moody Press, 1950.

Crosby, John F. *Witnesses for Christ.* Philadelphia: Westminster Press, 1965.

Crosetto, Beau. *Beyond Awkward: When Talking with Jesus Is Outside Your Comfort Zone.* Downers Grove, IL: InterVarsity, 2014.

Crouch, Austin. *The Plan of Salvation and How to Teach It.* Nashville: Sunday School Board of the Southern Baptist Convention, 1924.

Davis, Diana. *Fresh Ideas: 1,000 Ways to Grow a Thriving and Energetic Church.* Nashville: LifeWay, 2007.

Davis, Ozora S. *Evangelistic Preaching.* New York: Fleming H. Revell, 1921.

Dawson, David Miles. *More Power in Soul-Winning; How to Win Souls.* Grand Rapids: Zondervan, 1947.

Dawson, Scott. *Evangelism Today: Effectively Sharing the Gospel in a Rapidly Changing World.* Grand Rapids: Baker, 2009.

———. *The Complete Evangelism Guidebook: Expert Advice on Reaching Others for Christ.* Grand Rapids: Baker Books, 2006.

Dayton, Edward R., and David A. Fraser. *Planning Strategies for World Evangelization.* Grand Rapids: Eerdmans, 1990.

Dehoney, Wayne. *Set the Church Afire! How Churches Can Make the Gospel Work through Renewed Conviction and Enthusiasm.* Nashville: Broadman, 1971.

DeMoss, Nancy Leigh, and Tim Grissom. *Seeking Him: Experiencing the Joy of Personal Revival.* Chicago: Moody Publishers, 2004.

Denney, James. *The Death of Christ.* New Canaan, CT: Keats Publishing, Inc., 1981.

Denton, Ryan. *Even If None: Reclaiming Biblical Evangelism.* Dublin, CA: First-Love Publications, 2019.

———. and Scott Smith. *A Certain Sound: A Primer on Open Air Preaching.* Grand Rapids: Reformation Heritage Books, 2019.

Dever, Mark. *The Gospel and Personal Evangelism.* Wheaton, IL: Crossway, 2007.

DeWitt, Dan, ed. *A Guide to Evangelism: Guide Book No. 004.* Louisville: SBTS Press, 2013.

Dickerson, John S. *The Great Evangelical Recession: 6 Factors That Will Crash the American Church . . . and How to Prepare.* Grand Rapids: Baker Books, 2013.

Dickinson, Travis. *Everyday Apologetics.* Fort Worth, TX: Seminary Hill Press, 2015.

Dietrich, Suzanne de. *The Witnessing Community.* Philadelphia: Westminster, 1958.

Dobbins, Gaines S. *A Winning Witness*. Nashville: Sunday School Board of the Southern Baptist Convention, 1938.

_____. *Evangelism according to Christ*. Nashville: Broadman & Holman, 1949.

Dodd, C.H. *The Apostolic Preaching and Its Developments*. London: Hodder and Stoughton, 1936.

Dodson, Jonathan. *Gospel-Centered Discipleship*. Wheaton, IL: Crossway, 2012.

Dorsett, Lyle W. *A Passion for Souls: The Life of D. L. Moody*. Chicago: Moody, 1997.

Dorsett, Lyle W., and Ajith Fernando, eds. *Fulfilling the Great Commission in the Twenty-First Century: Essays on Revival, Evangelism, and Discipleship in Honor of Dr. Robert E. Coleman*. Franklin, TN: Seedbed, 2015.

Douglas, J.D., ed. *Let the Earth Hear His Voice*. Minneapolis: World Wide Publishers, 1975.

Downey, Murray W. *The Art of Soul-Winning*. Grand Rapids: Baker, 1989.

Downs, Tim. *Finding Common Ground*. Chicago: Moody Press, 1999.

Drummond, Lewis A. *Evangelism: The Counter-Revolution*. London: Marshall, Morgan and Scott, 1972.

_____. *Leading Your Church in Evangelism*. Nashville: Broadman, 1975.

_____. *Reaching Generation Next: Effective Evangelism in Today's Culture*. Grand Rapids: Baker, 2002.

_____. *The Word of the Cross: A Contemporary Theology of Evangelism*. Nashville: Broadman, 2000.

Drummond, Lewis A., and Paul R Baxter. *How to Respond to a Skeptic*. Chicago: Moody, 1986.

Durnbaugh, Donald F. *The Believers' Church: The History and Character of Radical Protestantism*. New York: Macmillan, 1968.

Earley, Dave, and Rod Dempsey. *Disciple-Making Is . . . How to Live the Great Commission with Passion and Confidence*. Nashville: B & H Publishing Group, 2013.

Earley, Dave, and David Wheeler. *Evangelism Is . . . How to Share Jesus with Passion and Confidence*. Nashville: B & H Academic, 2010.

Easley, Jordan, and Ernest Easley. *Resuscitating Evangelism*. Nashville: B & H, 2020.

Eastman, A. Theodore. *Chosen and Sent: Calling the Church to Mission*. Grand Rapids: Eerdmans, 1971.

Eastman, Dick. *Love on Its Knees*. Old Tappan, NJ: Chosen, 1989.

_____. *The Jericho Hour: The Church's Final Offensive*. Lake Mary, FL: Creation House.

Edge, Findley B. *The Greening of the Church*. Waco, TX: Word Books, 1971.

Eims, LeRoy. *One-to-One Evangelism: Winning Ways in Personal Witnessing*. Wheaton, IL: Victor, 1990.

Eisenman, Tom L. *Everyday Evangelism: Making the Most of Life's Common Moments*. Downers Grove, IL: InterVarsity Press, 1987.

Ellis, H. W. *Fishing for Men*. Grand Rapids: Zondervan, 1955.

Engel, James F., and Wilbert Norton. *What's Gone Wrong With the Harvest: A Communication Strategy for the Church and World Evangelism*. Grand Rapids: Zondervan, 1975.

Enroth, Ronald, ed. *Evangelizing the Cults: How to Share Jesus with Children, Parents, Neighbors, and Friends Who Are Involved in a Cult*. Ann Arbor, MI: Servant Publications, 1990.

Erickson, Millard J. *How Shall They Be Saved? The Destiny of Those Who Do Not Hear of Jesus*. Grand Rapids: Baker Books, 1996.

Estep, William R. *The Anabaptist Story*. Grand Rapids: Eerdmans, 1963.

Everts, Don. *The Reluctant Witness: Discovering the Delight of Spiritual Conversations*. Grand Rapids: IVP Books, 2019.

Fackre, Gabriel. *Word in Deed: Theological Themes in Evangelism*. Grand Rapids: Eerdmans, 1975.

Fackre, Gabriel, Ronald H. Nash, and John Sanders. *What about Those Who Have Never Heard? Three Views on the Destiny of the Unevangelized*. Edited by John Sanders. Downers Grove, IL: InterVarsity Press, 1995.

Fay, William. *Share Jesus without Fear*. Nashville: Broadman & Holman, 1999.

Feather, R. Othal. *A Manual for Promoting Personal Evangelism through the Sunday School*. Nashville: Convention Press, 1959.

_____. *Outreach Evangelism through the Sunday School*. Nashville: Convention Press, 1972.

Ferm, Robert O. *Billy Graham: Do the Conversions Last?* Minneapolis: World Wide Publications, 1988.

_____. *Cooperative Evangelism: Is Billy Graham Right or Wrong? Are His Policies Supported by Scripture and the Great Evangelists of History?* Grand Rapids: Zondervan Publishing House, 1958.

Fernando, Ajith. *Discipling in a Multicultural World*. Wheaton, IL: Crossway, 2019.

Ferrell, Daniel M. *The Unfolding Drama of Evangelism*. West Chester, OH: Morning Star Baptist Church, 2004.

Finley, Mark. *Padded Pews or Open Doors*. Nampa, ID: Pacific Press, 1988.

Finney, Charles G. *Lectures on Revival of Religion*. Old Tappan, NJ: Fleming H. Revell, n.d.

Finney, John. *Emerging Evangelism*. London: Darton, Longman & Todd, 2004.

Fish, Henry Clay. *Handbook of Revivals: For the Use of Winners of Souls*. Boston: J. H. Earle, 1874.

Fish, Roy. *Giving a Good Invitation*. Nashville: Broadman, 1974.

Fish, Roy, Al Fasol, Steve Gaines, and Ralph Douglas West. *Preaching Evangelistically: Proclaiming the Saving Message of Jesus*. Nashville: Broadman & Holman, 2006.

Flake, Arthur. *Building a Standard School*. Nashville: Sunday School Board of the Southern Baptist Convention, 1934.

Fletcher, Joseph. *Mission to Main Street: Five Study Units on the Work of the Church, the Function of the Lay Members, and the Place Where Witness Is Made*. Greenwich, CT: Seabury, 1962.

Fletcher, Lionel B. *The Effective Witness*. New York: George H. Doran, 1923.

Ford, Kevin. *Jesus for a New Generation*. Downers Grove, IL: InterVarsity, 1995.

Ford, Leighton. *Good New Is for Sharing: A Guide to Making Friends for Christ*. Elgin, IL: David C. Cook, 1977.

_____. *The Christian Persuader: A New Look at Evangelism Today*. New York: Harper & Row, 1966.

_____. *The Power of Story: Recovering the Oldest, Most Natural Way to Reach People for Christ*. Colorado Springs: NavPress, 1994.

Fordham, Keith. *"The Evangelist"—The Heart of God*. Del City, OK: Spirit, 2002.

Fordham, Keith, and Tom Johnston. *Worth and Work of the Evangelist: For Christ's Great Commission Church*. Liberty, MO: Evangelism Unlimited, 2013.

Forshee, Danny. *For the One*. Engedi Publishing LLC, 2019.

Forsyth, Peter Taylor. *The Soul of Prayer*. London: Independent Press, 1949.

Foster, Bill. *Meet the Skeptic: A Field Guide to Faith Conversations*. Green Forest, AR: Master Books, 2012.

Foust, Paul J. *Reborn to Multiply: Tested Techniques for Personal Evangelism*. St. Louis: Concordia, 1973.

Freeman, Clifford Wade, ed. *The Doctrine of Evangelism*. Nashville: Baptist General Conference of Texas, 1957.

Frost, Toby, Bill Sims, and Monty McWhorter. *The Evangelistic Block Party Manual*. Atlanta: NAMB, 2003.

Fuller, Andrew. *The Works of the Rev. Andrew Fuller*. New Haven, CT: S. Converse, 1824.

Gage, Albert H. *Evangelism of Youth*. Philadelphia: Judson, 1922.

Gager, Leroy. *Handbook for Soul Winners*. Grand Rapids: Zondervan, 1956.

Gallaty, Robby. *Firmly Planted: How to Cultivate a Faith Rooted in Christ*. Nashville: Cross Books, 2015.

Geisler, Norman, and David Geisler. *Conversational Evangelism: How to Listen and Speak So You Can Be Heard*. Eugene, OR: Harvest House, 2009.

Gerstner, John H. *Jonathan Edwards, Evangelist*. Morgan, PA: Soli Deo Gloria Publications, 1995.

Getz, Gene A. *Sharpening the Focus of the Church*. Chicago: Moody Press, 1974.

Gibbs, A. P. *Personal Evangelism*. Dubuque, IA: ECS Ministries, 2014.

Gilbert, Greg. *Assured*. Grand Rapids: Baker, 2019.

_____. *What Is the Gospel?* Wheaton, IL: Crossway, 2010.

Gilbert, Larry. *Team Evangelism—Giving New Meaning to Lay Evangelism*. Lynchburg, VA: Church Growth, 1991.

Gilbert, Mark. *Stepping Out in Faith: Former Catholics Tell Their Story*. Kingsford, NSW: Matthias Media, 2012.

Gilkey, Langdon Brown. *How the Church Can Minister to the World without Losing Itself.* New York: Harper & Row, 1964.

Gilroy, Mark, ed. *Sharing My Faith: A Teen's Guide to Evangelism.* Kansas City, MO: Beacon Hill Press, 1991.

Godfrey, George. *How to Win Souls and Influence People for Heaven.* Grand Rapids: Baker, 1973.

Gonzalez, Justo L. *The Story of Christianity: 2 vols.* San Franciso: HarperSanFrancisco, 1983.

Good, Kenneth H. *Christ's Teaching on the Theology of Evangelism.* Rochester, NY: Backus Book Publishers, 1988.

Goodell, Charles L. *Motives and Methods in Modern Evangelism.* New York: Revell, 1926.

_____. *Pastoral and Personal Evangelism.* New York: Revell, 1926.

Gordon, S. D. *Quiet Talks on Prayer.* Westwood, NJ: Fleming H. Revell, 1967.

Gortner, David. *Transforming Evangelism.* New York: Church Publishing, Inc., 2008.

Graf, Arthur E. *The Church in a Community: An Effective Evangelism Program for the Christian Congregation.* Grand Rapids: Eerdmans, 1965.

Graham, Billy. *A Biblical Standard for Evangelists: A Commentary on the Fifteen Affirmations Made by Participants at the International Conference for Itinerant Evangelists in Amsterdam, The Netherlands—July 1983.* Minneapolis: World Wide Publications, 1984.

_____. *Just As I Am.* San Francisco: HarperSanFrancisco, 1977.

_____. *Peace with God.* Nashville: Thomas Nelson, 2017.

_____. *The Holy Spirit: Activating God's Power in Your Life.* Waco, TX: Word Books, 1978.

_____. *The Journey: How to Live by Faith in an Uncertain World.* Nashville: Thomas Nelson, 2006.

_____. *World Aflame.* Old Tappan, NJ: Revell, 1964.

Greear, J. D. *Stop Asking Jesus into Your Heart: How to Know for Sure You Are Saved.* Nashville: Broadman & Holman, 2013.

Green, Bryan. *The Practice of Evangelism.* New York: Charles Scribner's Sons, 1951.

Green, Hollis L. *Why Churches Die: A Guide to Basic Evangelism and Church Growth.* Minneapolis: Bethany Fellowship, 1972.

_____. *Why Wait Till Sunday? An Action Approach to Local Evangelism.* Minneapolis: Bethany Fellowship, 1972.

Green, Michael. *Evangelism in the Early Church.* London: Hodder and Stoughton, 1970.

_____. *Evangelism Now and Then.* London: Daybreak, 1992.

_____. *Evangelism through the Local Church: A Comprehensive Guide to All Aspects of Evangelism.* London: Hodder and Stoughton, 1992.

_____. *One to One: How to Share Your Faith with a Friend*. Nashville: Moorings, 1995.

_____. *Who Is This Jesus?* Nashville: Thomas Nelson, 1992.

Green, Michael, and Alister McGrath. *How Shall We Reach Them?: Defending and Communicating the Christian Faith to Nonbelievers*. Nashville: Thomas Nelson, 1995.

Green, Oscar Olin. *Normal Evangelism*. New York: Revell, 1910.

Greenway, Roger S, ed. *The Pastor-Evangelist: Preacher, Model, and Mobilizer for Church Growth*. Phillipsburg, NJ: Presbyterian Reformed Pub. Co., 1987.

Greer, Sam. *The Gospel Conversational Church*. Bloomington, IN: WestBow Press, 2019.

Gresham, Charles, and Keith Keeran. *Evangelistic Preaching*. Joplin, MO: College Press, 1991.

Grindstaff, Wilmer E. *Ways to Win: Methods of Evangelism for the Local Church*. Nashville: Broadman, 1957.

Grubb, Norman. *Continuous Revival*. Fort Washington, PA: Christian Literature Crusade, 1971.

_____. *C. T. Studd: Cricketer and Pioneer*. Cambridge: Lutterworth, 2014.

Grudem, Wayne. *Bible Doctrine: Essential Teachings of the Christian Faith*. Grand Rapids: Zondervan, 1999.

Guinness, Os. *Fool's Talk: Recovering the Art of Christian Persuasion*. Downers Grove, IL: IVP, 2015.

Gumbel, Nicky. *Telling Others: The Alpha Initiative*. Eastbourne, Great Britain: Kingsway, 1994.

Gustafson, David M. *Gospel Witness: Evangelism in Word and Deed*. Grand Rapids: Eerdmans, 2019.

Hamilton, William Wistar. *Highways and Hedges*. Nashville: Broadman, 1938.

_____. *Sane Evangelism*. Philadelphia: American Baptist, 1909.

_____. *The Fine Art of Soul-Winning*. Nashville: Sunday School Board of the Southern Baptist Convention, 1935.

_____. *Wisdom in Soul Winning*. Nashville: Sunday School Board of the Southern Baptist Convention, 1929.

Haney, David P. *The Ministry Evangelism Weekend: Preparation Manual*. Atlanta: Renewal Evangelism, 1976.

Hanks, Billie, Jr. *Everyday Evangelism: How to Do It and How to Teach It*. Grand Rapids: Zondervan, 1983.

Hannan, F. Watson. *Evangelism*. New York: Methodist Book Concern, 1921.

Harney, Kevin G. *Organic Outreach for Ordinary People: Sharing Good News Naturally*. Grand Rapids: Zondervan, 2009.

Harrison, Eugene Myers. *How to Win Souls: A Manual of Personal Evangelism*. Wheaton, IL: Van Kampen, 1952.

Hartt, Julian N. *Toward a Theology of Evangelism*. New York: Abingdon Press, 1955.

Havlik, John F. *People-Centered Evangelism*. Nashville: Broadman, 1971.

_____. *The Evangelistic Church*. Nashville: Convention Press, 1976.

Hawkins, O. S. *Drawing the Net: 30 Practical Principles for Leading Others to Christ Publicly and Personally*. Nashville: Broadman Press, 1993.

Haykin, Michael A. G., and Jeff Robinson, *To the Ends of the Earth: Calvin's Missional Vision and Legacy*. Wheaton, IL: Crossway, 2014.

Haynes, Carlyle B. *Living Evangelism*. Takoma Park, WA: Review and Herald, 1937.

Head, Eldred Douglas. *Evangelism in Acts*. Fort Worth, TX: Southwestern Baptist Theological Seminary, 1950.

Hearn, Mark. *Discover the Witness Inside of You: A Witnessing Approach Accentuating Your Spiritual Gifts*. Columbus, GA: Brentwood Christian Press, 1993.

Heath, Elaine A. *The Mystic Way of Evangelism: A Contemplative Vision for Christian Outreach*. Grand Rapids: Baker, 2008.

Heck, Joel D., ed. *The Art of Sharing Your Faith*. Tarrytown, NY: Fleming H. Revell Company, 1991.

Hefner, Chris C. *Commissioned: Leading Our Neighbors and the Nations to Follow Jesus*. 2019.

Hemphill, Ken. *Empowering Kingdom Growth: The Heartbeat of God*. Nashville: Broadman & Holman, 2004.

_____. *Revitalizing the Sunday Morning Dinosaur: A Sunday School Growth Strategy for the 21st Century*. Nashville: Broadman & Holman Publishers, 1996.

_____. *The Antioch Effect: Eight Characteristics of Highly Effective Churches*. Nashville: Broadman, 1994.

Henard, Bill. *Can These Bones Live?: A Practical Guide to Church Revitalization*. Nashville: Broadman & Holman, 2015.

_____. *ReClaimed Church: How Churches Grow, Decline, and Experience Revitalization*. Nashville: Broadman & Holman, 2018.

Henard, William D., and Adam W. Greenway. *Evangelicals Engaging Emergent: A Discussion of the Emergent Church Movement*. Nashville: Broadman & Holman, 2009.

Henderson, Jim. *Evangelism without Additives*. Colorado Springs: WaterBrook Press, 2007.

Henderson, Robert T. *Joy to the World: An Introduction to Kingdom Evangelism*. Atlanta: John Knox Press, 1980.

Hendrick, John R. *Opening the Door of Faith: The Why, When, and Where of Evangelism*. Atlanta: John Knox Press, 1977.

Hendricks, Howard G. *Say It with Love: The Art and Joy of Telling the Good News*. Wheaton, IL: Victor, 1973.

Henrichsen, Walter A. *Disciples Are Made—Not Born*. Wheaton, IL: Victor, 1974.

Henry, Carl F. H. *A Plea for Evangelical Demonstration*. Grand Rapids: Baker Books, 1971.

_____. *The Uneasy Conscience of Modern Fundamentalism*. Grand Rapids: Eerdmans, 1947.

Henry, Carl F. H., and W. Stanley Mooneyham, eds. *One Race, One Gospel, One Task: World Congress on Evangelism,* 2 volumes. Minneapolis: World Wide Publications, 1967.

Herrick, Carl. *Modern Evangelism: A Practical Course in Effective Evangelistic Methods*. New York: Revell, 1929.

Hervey, George W. *Manual of Revivals*. New York: Funk & Wagnalls Company, 1884.

Hetherington, Andy. *Personal Evangelism: A Practical Guide to Sharing Your Faith*. Maitland, FL: Xulon, 2016.

Hicks, Joseph P. *Ten Lessons in Personal Evangelism*. New York: Doran, 1922.

Hildreth, D. Scott, and Steven A. McKinion. *Sharing Jesus without Freaking Out: Evangelism the Way You Were Born to Do It*. 2nd ed. Nashville: B & H Academic, 2020.

Hinkle, J. Herbert. *Soul Winning in Black Churches*. Grand Rapids: Baker, 1973.

Hinson, William H. *A Place to Dig In: Doing Evangelism in the Local Church*. Nashville: Abingdon, 1987.

Hobbs, Herschel H. *New Testament Evangelism: The Eternal Purpose*. Nashville: Convention Press, 1960.

Hogue, C. B. *I Want My Church to Grow*. Nashville: Broadman, 1977.

_____. *Lifestyle Evangelism*. Atlanta: Home Mission Board, SBC, 1973.

_____. *Love Leaves No Choice: Lifestyle Evangelism*. Waco, TX: Word Books, 1976.

Houghton, Will H. *Lessons in Soul-Winning*. Chicago: Moody Bible Institute of Chicago, 1936.

House, Paul R., and Gregory A. Thornbury, eds. *Who Will Be Saved? Defending the Biblical Understanding of God, Salvation, and Evangelism*. Wheaton, IL: Crossway, 2000.

Hull, Bill. *The Disciple Making Pastor*. Old Tappan, NJ: Revell, 1988.

Hulse, Erroll. *The Great Invitation*. Welwyn: Evangelical, 1986.

Humphreys, Kent and Davidene. *Show and Then Tell: Presenting the Gospel through Daily Encounters*. Chicago: Moody Press, 2000.

Hunter, George. *Church for the Unchurched*. Nashville: Abingdon, 1996.

_____. *How to Reach Secular People*. Nashville: Abingdon, 1992.

_____. *The Celtic Way of Evangelism: How Christianity Can Reach the West . . . Again*. Nashville: Abingdon Press, 2000.

Huston, Sterling. *Crusade Evangelism and the Local Church*. Minneapolis: World Wide, 1996.

Ingle, Clifford, ed. *Children and Conversion*. Nashville: Broadman, 1970.

Inserra, Dean. *The Unsaved Christian: Reaching Cultural Christianity with the Gospel*. Chicago: Moody, 2019.

Iorg, Jeff. *Unscripted: Sharing the Gospel as Life Happens*. Birmingham, AL: New Hope, 2014.

Isais, Juan M. *The Other Evangelism: One Man's View of Evangelism in Depth's Revolutionary Results*. Winona Lake, IN: Brethren Evangelistic Ministries, 1989.

Jacks, Bob and Betty Jacks. *Your Home a Lighthouse*. Colorado Springs: NavPress, 1989.

Jackson, Jack. *Offering Christ: John Wesley's Evangelistic Vision*. Nashville: Kingswood Books, 2017.

Johnson, Ben. *An Evangelism Primer: Practical Principles for Congregations*. Atlanta: John Knox, 1983.

Johnson, Ben Campbell. *Rethinking Evangelism: A Theological Approach*. Philadelphia: Westminster, 1987.

Johnson, Ronald W. *How Will They Hear If We Don't Listen: The Vital Role of Listening in Preaching and Personal Evangelism*. Nashville: Broadman & Holman Publishers, 1994.

Johnson, Torrey and Robert Cook. *Reaching Youth for Christ*. Chicago: Moody Press, 1944.

Johnston, Arthur P. *The Battle for World Evangelism*. Wheaton, IL: Tyndale House Publishers, 1978.

Johnston, Howard A. *Enlisting for Christ and the Church*. New York: Association, 1919.

Johnston, Thomas P. *Charts for a Theology of Evangelism*. Nashville: Broadman & Holman, 2007.

_____. *Examining Billy Graham's Theology of Evangelism*. Eugene, OR: Wipf & Stock, 2003.

_____. *Evangelizology*. 2 volumes. Liberty, MO: Evangelism Unlimited, 2011.

_____. *The Mindset of Eternity*. Deerfield, IL: Evangelism Unlimited, 1994.

_____. *Toward a Biblical-Historical Theology of Evangelism*. Liberty, MO: Evangelism Unlimited, 2006.

Johnston, Thomas P., ed. *A History of Evangelism in North America*. Grand Rapids: Kregel, 2021.

_____. *Mobilizing a Great Commission Church for Harvest: Voices and Views from the Southern Baptist Professors of Evangelism Fellowship*. Eugene, OR: Wipf & Stock, 2011.

Johnstone, Patrick. *Pray for the World*. Downers Grove, IL: InterVarsity, 2015.

Jones, Bob, Sr. *Evangelism Today: Where Is It Headed?* Greenville, SC: Bob Jones University Press, 1955.

Jones, E. Stanley. *Conversion*. New York: Abingdon, 1959.

Jones, Scott J. *The Evangelistic Love of God & Neighbor: A Theology of Witness and Discipleship*. Nashville: Abingdon, 2003.

Josling, Craig. *40 Rockets: Encouragement and Tips for Turbocharging Your Evangelism at Work*. Sydney, Australia: Matthias Media, 2017.

Jowett, John Henry. *The Passion for Souls*. New York: Revell, 1905.

June, Lee N., and Matthew Parker. *Evangelism & Discipleship in African-American Churches*. Grand Rapids: Zondervan, 1999.

Kallenberg, Brad J. *Live to Tell: Evangelism in a Postmodern Age*. Grand Rapids: Brazos Press, 2002.

Kantonen, T. A. *Theology of Evangelism*. Philadelphia: Muhlenberg, 1954.

Keller, Timothy. *Center Church: Doing Balanced, Gospel-Centered Ministry in Your City*. Grand Rapids: Zondervan, 2012.

_____. *The Reason for God: Belief in an Age of Skepticism*. New York: Dutton, 2008.

Kelley, Charles S., Jr. *Fuel the Fire: Lessons from the History of Southern Baptist Evangelism*. Nashville: Broadman & Holman, 2018.

_____. *How Did They Do It? The Story of Southern Baptist Evangelism*. New Orleans: Insight Press, 1993.

Kendall, R. T. *Holy Fire: A Balanced Look at the Holy Spirit's Work in Our Lives*. Lake Mary, FL: Charisma House, 2014.

_____. *Stand Up and Be Counted: Calling for Public Confession of Faith*. Grand Rapids: Zondervan Publishing House, 1984.

Kennedy, D. James. *Evangelism Explosion*. Carol Stream, IL: Tyndale House, 1976.

_____. *Skeptics Answered: Handling Tough Questions about the Christian Faith*. Sisters, OR: Multnomah, 1997.

_____. *Why I Believe*. Nashville: Word Publishing, 1999.

Kenyon, E. W. *Personal Evangelism*. Lynwood, WA: Kenyon Gospel Publishing, 2002.

Kernahan, A. Earl. *Adventures in Visitation Evangelism*. New York: Revell, 1928.

_____. *Christian Citizenship and Visitation Evangelism*. New York: Revell, 1929.

_____. *Visitation Evangelism: Its Methods and Results*. New York: Revell, 1935.

Kettner, Elmer A. *Adventures in Evangelism*. St. Louis: Concordia, 1964.

Kiker, Tommy. *Everyday Ministry*. Fort Worth, TX: Seminary Hill Press, 2017.

Kilbourn, William. *The Restless Church*. Philadelphia: J. B. Lippincott Co., 1966.

Klaiber, Walter. *Call and Response: Biblical Foundations of a Theology of Evangelism*. Nashville: Abingdon Press, 1997.

Klaassen, John. *Engaging with Muslims: Understand Their World through Sharing Good News*. London: The Good Book Company, 2015.

Knight, Henry H., III, and F. Douglas Powe Jr. *Tranforming Evangelism: The Wesleyan Way of Sharing Faith*. Nashville: Discipleship Resources, 2006.

Kolb, Robert. *Speaking the Gospel Today*. St. Louis: Concordia, 1995.

Korthals, Richard G. *Agape Evangelism: Roots That Reach Out*. Wheaton, IL: Tyndale, 1980.

Kostenberger, Andreas J. and Peter Thomas O'Brien. *Salvation to the Ends of the Earth: A Biblical Theology of Mission.* Downers Grove: IVP Academic, 2001.

Koukl, Gregory. *Tactics, 10th Anniversary Edition: A Game Plan for Discussing Your Christian Convictions.* Grand Rapids: Zondervan, 2019.

_____. *The Story of Reality: How the World Began, How It Ends, and Everything Important That Happens in Between.* Grand Rapids: Zondervan, 2017.

Kraft, Charles H. *Communicating the Gospel God's Way.* Pasadena, CA: William Carey, 1979.

Kramp, John. *Out of Their Faces and Into Their Shoes: How to Understand Spiritually Lost People and Give Them Directions to Find God.* Nashville: Broadman & Holman, 1995.

Krass, Alfred C. *Evangelizing Neopagan North America.* Scottsdale, PA: Herald Press, 1982.

Krupp, Nate. *A World to Win: Secrets of New Testament Evangelism.* Minneapolis: Bethany Fellowship, 1966.

Kuhne, Gary. *The Dynamics of Personal Follow-Up.* Grand Rapids: Zondervan, 1976.

Kuiper, R. B. *God-Centered Evangelism: A Presentation of the Scriptural Theology of Evangelism.* Carlisle, PA: Banner of Truth, 1978.

Laney, James T. *Evangelism: Mandates for Action.* New York: Hawthorn, 1975.

Larsen, David L. *The Evangelism Mandate: Recovering the Centrality of Gospel Preaching.* Wheaton, IL: Crossway, 1992.

Larson, Bruce. *Setting Men Free.* Grand Rapids: Zondervan, 1967.

Latourette, Kenneth Scott. *A History of the Expansion of Christianity.* 7 vols. New York: Harper & Brothers, 1937.

Laubach, Frank Charles. *How to Teach One and Win One for Christ.* Grand Rapids: Zondervan, 1964.

Laurie, Greg. *Making God Known: How to Bring Others to Faith.* Dana Point, CA: Allen David, 2007.

_____. *Tell Someone: You Can Share the Good News.* Nashville: B & H, 2016.

Lavin, Ronald J., ed. *The Human Chain for Divine Grace: Lutheran Sermons for Evangelical Outreach.* Philadelphia: Fortress, 1978.

Lawless, Chuck. *Discipled Warriors: Growing Healthy Churches That Are Equipped for Spiritual Warfare.* Grand Rapids: Kregel Publications, 2002.

Lawless, Chuck, and Adam W. Greenway, eds. *The Great Commission Resurgence: Fulfilling God's Mandate in Our Time.* Nashville: B & H Academic, 2010.

Lawless, Chuck, and Thom S. Rainer, eds. *The Challenge of the Great Commission: Essays on God's Mandate for the Local Church.* Pinnacle Publishers, 2005.

Lawrence, J. B. *The Holy Spirit in Evangelism.* Grand Rapids: Zondervan, 1954.

Lawrence, Michael. *Conversion: How God Creates a People.* Wheaton, IL: Crossway, 2017.

Leavell, Frank H. *Christian Witnessing.* Nashville: Broadman Press, 1942.

Leavell, Roland Q. *Evangelism: Christ's Imperative Commission*. Nashville: Broadman, 1951.

_____. *Helping Others to Become Christian*. Atlanta: Home Mission Board, SBC, 1939.

_____. *The Christian's Business: Being a Witness*. Nashville: Broadman, 1964.

_____. *Winning Others to Christ*. Nashville: Sunday School Board of the Southern Baptist Convention, 1936.

Lee, Robert G. *How to Lead a Soul to Christ*. Grand Rapids: Zondervan, 1955.

Legg, Steve. *A–Z Evangelism: The Ultimate Guide to Evangelism*. London: Hodder and Stoughton, 2002.

Lennox, John C. *Have No Fear: Being Salt and Light Even When It's Costly*. Leyland, England: 10Publishing, 2019.

Levicoff, Steve. *Street Smarts: A Survival Guide to Personal Evangelism and the Law*. Grand Rapids: Baker, 1994.

Lewis, Edwin. *Theology and Evangelism*. Nashville: Tidings, 1952.

Lewis, Robert. *The Church of Irresistable Influence: Bridge-Building Stories to Help Reach Your Community*. Grand Rapids: Zondervan, 2001.

Litfin, Duane. *Word versus Deed: Resetting the Scales to a Biblical Balance*. Wheaton: Crossway Books, 2012.

Little, Paul E. *His Guide to Evangelism*. Downers Grove, IL: InterVarsity, 1977.

_____. *How to Give Away Your Faith*. Downers Grove, IL: InterVarsity Press, 1966.

Little, Paul E, and Marie Little. *Know Why You Believe*. Colorado Springs: Victor, 1999.

Lorick, Nathan. *Dying to Grow: Reclaiming the Heart for Evangelism in the Church*. Abbotsford, WI: ANEKO Press, 2014.

Loscalzo, Craig A. *Evangelistic Preaching That Connects: Guidance in Shaping Fresh & Appealing Sermons*. Downers Grove, IL: InterVarsity, 1995.

Loud, Grover Cleveland. *Evangelized America*. Freeport, NY: Books for Libraries Press, 1971.

Lovett, C. S. *Soul-Winning Is Easy*. Baldwin Park, CA: Personal Christianity, 1964.

_____. *Visitation Made Easy*. Baldwin Park, CA: Personal Christianity, 1959.

Lowry, Oscar. *Scripture Memory for Successful Soul-Winning*. New York: Revell, 1934.

Lum, Ada. *How to Begin an Evangelistic Bible Study*. Downers Grove, IL: InterVarsity, 1971.

Lutzer, Erwin W. *How You Can Be Sure That You Will Spend Eternity with God*. Chicago: Moody Press, 1996.

Lyons, Gabe. *The Next Christians: The Good News about the End of Christian America*. New York: Doubleday & Company, 2010.

Mabie, Henry C. *Method in Soul-Winning: On Home and Foreign Fields*. New York: Revell, 1906.

MacArthur, John. *Evangelism: How to Share the Gospel Faithfully*. Nashville: Thomas Nelson, 2011.

Macaulay, J. C., and Robert H. Belton. *Personal Evangelism*. Chicago: Moody Press, 1956.

MacDonald, William C. *Modern Evangelism*. London: James Clarke, 1937.

Macleod, Donald. *Compel Them to Come In: Calvinism and the Free Offer of the Gospel*. Ross-shire, Scotland: Christian Focus, 2020.

MacMullen, Ramsay. *Christianizing the Roman Empire (A.D. 100-400)*. New Haven, CT: Yale University Press, 1984.

Mallalieu, W. F. *The Why, When and How of Revivals*. New York: Eaton and Mains, 1901.

Mallough, Don. *Grassroots Evangelism*. Grand Rapids: Baker, 1971.

Martin, George H. *Understanding Your New Life in Jesus Christ: Letters to a New Believer*. Rainer Publishing, 2014.

Martin, Gerald E. *The Future of Evangelism*. Grand Rapids: Zondervan, 1969.

Martin, Glen, and Gary L. McIntosh. *Finding Them, Keeping Them: Effective Strategies for Evangelism and Assimilation in the Local Church*. Nashville: Broadman & Holman, 1991.

Martin, O. Dean. *Invite: What Do You Do after the Sermon?* Nashville: Tidings, 1973.

Martin, William. *A Prophet with Honor: The Billy Graham Story*. Grand Rapids: Zondervan, 2018.

Marty, Martin E., and Frederick E. Greenspahn, eds. *Pushing the Faith: Proselytism and Civility in a Pluralistic World*. New York: Crossroad, 1988.

Massee, Jasper Cortenus. *Evangelism in the Pew*. Chicago: The Winona Publishing Company, 1907.

Matthews, C. E. *Every Christian's Job*. Nashville: Broadman, 1951.

_____. *The Southern Baptist Program of Evangelism*. Atlanta: Home Mission Board, SBC, 1949.

Mayfield, William H. *Restoring First-Century Evangelism*. Cincinnati: New Life, 1974.

McCauley, Paul, and David Williamson. *Everyday Evangelism: Sharing the Gospel in Conversation*. Kilmarnock, Scotland: John Ritchie Ltd, 2018.

McCloskey, Mark. *Tell It Often—Tell It Well: Making the Most of Witnessing Opportunities*. San Bernardino, CA: Here's Life Publishers, 1989.

McCullough, William James. *Home Visitation Evangelism for Laymen: A Manual*. New York: American Baptist Home Mission Society, 1946.

McDill, Wayne. *Evangelism in a Tangled World*. Nashville: Broadman, 1976.

_____. *Making Friends for Christ—A Practical Approach to Relational Evangelism*. Nashville: Broadman, 1979.

McDowell, Sean, and J. Warner Wallace. *So the Next Generation Will Know: Preparing Young Christians for a Challenging World*. Colorado Springs: David C. Cook, 2019.

McDowell, William Fraser. *That I May Save Some*. New York: Abingdon, 1928.

McGavran, Donald. *Understanding Church Growth*. Grand Rapids: Eerdmans, 1976.

_____. *Effective Evangelism: A Theological Mandate*. Phillipsburg, NJ: P & R Publishing, 1988.

McIntosh, Gary L. *Biblical Church Growth: How You Can Work with God to Build a Faithful Church*. Grand Rapids: Baker Books, 2003.

McKay, Charles L. *The Call of the Harvest*. Nashville: Convention Press, 1976.

McKinley, Mike. *Am I Really a Christian?* Wheaton, IL: Crossway, 2011.

McLaren, Brian D. *More Ready Than You Realize: Evangelism as Dance in the Postmodern Matrix*. Grand Rapids: Zondervan, 2002.

McLarry, Newman R., ed. *Handbook on Evangelism: A Program of Evangelism for Southern Baptists*. Nashville: Convention Press, 1965.

McLoughlin, William Gerald, Jr. *Modern Revivalism: Charles G. Finney to Billy Graham*. New York: Ronald Press Co., 1959.

McPhee, Arthur G. *Friendship Evangelism: The Caring Way to Share Your Faith*. Grand Rapids: Zondervan, 1978.

McRaney, Will, Jr. *The Art of Personal Evangelism: Sharing Jesus in a Changing Culture*. Nashville: Broadman & Holman, 2003.

Medearis, Carl. *Speaking of Jesus: The Art of Not-Evangelism*. Colorado Springs: David C. Cook, 2011.

Menzies, Robert. *Preaching and Pastoral Evangelism*. Edinburgh, Scotland: Saint Andrew Press, 1962.

Metcalf, Harold E. *The Magic of Telephone Evangelism*. Atlanta: Southern Union Conference, 1967.

Metzger, Will. *Tell the Truth: The Whole Gospel Wholly by Grace Communicated Truthfully and Lovingly*. Downers Grove, IL: InterVarsity Press, 2012.

Meyer, Daniel. *Witness Essentials: Evangelism That Makes Disciples*. Grand Rapids: IVP, 2012.

Mikalatos, Matt. *Good News for a Change: How to Talk to Anyone about Jesus*. Colorado Springs: NavPress, 2018.

Miles, Delos. *Evangelism and Social Involvement*. Nashville: Broadman Press, 1986.

_____. *Introduction to Evangelism*. Nashville: Broadman Press, 1983.

_____. *Master Principles of Evangelism: Examples from Jesus's Personal Witnessing*. Nashville: Broadman, 1982.

_____. *Overcoming Barriers to Witnessing*. Nashville: Broadman, 1984.

Miller, C. John. *Evangelism and Your Church*. Phillipsburg, NJ: P & R Publishing, 1980.

_____. *A Faith Worth Sharing*. Phillipsburg, NJ: P & R Publishing, 1999.

_____. *Powerful Evangelism for the Powerless*. Phillipsburg, NJ: P & R Publishing, 1997.

Miller, Calvin. *A View from the Fields*. Nashville: Broadman, 1978.

Miller, Herb. *Evangelism's Open Secret*. St. Louis: Bethany, 1977.

_____. *Fishing on the Asphalt: Effective Evangelism in Mainline Denominations*. St. Louis: Bethany, 1983.

Miller, Paul M. *Group Dynamics in Evangelism: The Potential of Christian Fellowship*. Scottsdale, PA: Herald Press, 1958.

Mims, Gene. *Kingdom Principles for Church Growth*. Revised. Nashville: LifeWay, 2001.

Misselbrook, Lawrence Richard. *Winning the People for Christ: An Experiment in Evangelism*. London: Carey Kingsgate Press Ltd, 1957.

Misselbrook, Lewis. *Sharing the Faith with Others: A Program for Training in Evangelism*. Valley Forge, PA: American Baptist, 1979.

Mittelberg, Mark. *Building a Contagious Church: Revolutionizing the Way We View and Do Evangelism*. Grand Rapids: Zondervan, 2000.

Moberg, David O. *The Great Personal Evangelism versus Social Concern*. Philadelphia, PA: Lippincott, 1972.

Mohler, R. Albert, Jr., ed. *Essential Reading on Evangelism*. Louisville, KY: The Southern Baptist Theological Seminary, 2019.

Monroe, Clayton, and William S. Taegel. *Witnessing Laymen Make Living Churches*. Waco, TX: Word Books, 1963.

Moody, D. L. *Sowing and Reaping*. Colportage Library. Chicago: Moody, n.d.

_____. *Prevailing Prayer: What Hinders It?* New York: Fleming H. Revell, 1885.

Moore, Waylon B. *Multiplying Disciples: The New Testament Method for Church Growth*. Tampa, FL: Missions Unlimited, 1981.

_____. *New Testament Follow-Up*. Grand Rapids: Eerdmans, 1963.

Morgan, G. Campbell. *Evangelism*. Chicago: Revell, 1904.

Morgenthaler, Sally. *Worship Evangelism: Inviting Believers into the Presence of God*. Grand Rapids: Zondervan, 1999.

Moseley, J. Edward, ed. *Evangelism—Commitment and Involvement*. St. Louis: Bethany, 1965.

Mott, John R. *Cooperation and the World Mission*. New York: International Missionary Council, 1935.

Mounce, R.H. *The Essential Nature of New Testament Preaching*. Grand Rapids: Eerdmans, 1960.

Moyer, R. Larry. *21 Things God Never Said: Correcting Our Misconceptions about Evangelism*. Grand Rapids: Kregel, 2004.

_____. *101 Tips for Evangelism: Practical Ways to Enhance Your Witness*. Peabody, MA: Hendrickson, 2017.

_____. *Free and Clear: Understanding and Communicating God's Offer of Eternal Life*. Grand Rapids: Kregel, 1997.

_____. *How-To Book on Personal Evangelism*. Grand Rapids: Kregel, 1998.

_____. *Show Me How to Answer Tough Questions*. Grand Rapids: Kregel, 1999.

Mueller, Charles S. *The Strategy of Evangelism: A Primer for Congregational Evangelism Committees*. St. Louis: Concordia, 1965.

Mumma, Howard E. *Take It to the People: New Ways in Soul-Winningc—Unconventional Evangelism*. New York: World, 1969.

Muncy, W. L., Jr. *A History of Evangelism in the United States*. Kansas City, KS: Central Seminary, 1945.

_____. *New Testament Evangelism*. Kansas City, KS: Central Seminary Press, 1937.

_____. *New Testament Evangelism for Today*. Kansas City, KS: Central Seminary Press, 1941.

Munro, Harry C. *Fellowship Evangelism through Church Groups*. St. Louis: Bethany, 1951.

Murphee, Jon Tal. *Responsible Evangelism: Relating Theory to Practice*. Toccoa Falls, GA: Toccoa Falls College, 1994.

Murray, Arthur L. *Reaching the Unchurched*. New York: Round Table, 1940.

Murray, Iain H. *The Invitation System*. Reprint. Edinburgh: The Banner of Truth Trust, 2002.

Nash, Ronald H. *Worldviews in Conflict: Choosing Christianity in a World of Ideas*. Grand Rapids: Zondervan, 1992.

Neighbour, Ralph W. *The Journey into Discipleship: The Journey into Lifestyle Evangelism and Ministry*. Memphis: Brotherhood Commission of the SBC, 1987.

_____. *Target-Group Evangelism*. Nashville: Broadman, 1975.

_____. *The Touch of the Spirit*. Nashville: Broadman, 1972.

Neil, Samuel Graham. *A Great Evangelism*. Philadelphia: Judson, 1929.

Neuenschwander, Mark, and Betsy Neuenschwander. *Crisis Evangelism: Preparing to Be Salt and Light When the World Needs Us Most*. Ventura, CA: Regal Books, 1999.

Neville, Joyce. *How to Share Your Faith without Being Offensive*. New York: Seabury, 1981.

Newbigin, Leslie. *The Gospel in a Pluralistic Society*. Grand Rapids: Eerdmans, 1989.

Newman, Bill. *Called to Proclaim: Keys for Evangelistic Preaching*. Carindale, Australia: Bill Newman Ministries, 1996.

Newman, Randy. *Bringing the Gospel Home: Witnessing to Family Members, Close Friends, and Others Who Know You Well*. Wheaton, IL: Crossway, 2011.

_____. *Questioning Evangelism: Engaging People's Hearts the Way Jesus Did*. 2nd ed. Grand Rapids: Kregel, 2017.

Nicholls, Bruce. *In Word and Deed: Evangelism and Social Responsibility*. Grand Rapids: Eerdmans, 1986.

Niebuhr, H. Richard. *Christ and Culture*. New York: Harper, 1951.

Niles, D. T. *The Message and Its Messengers*. New York: Abingdon, 1966.

_____. *That They May Have Life*. New York: Harper, 1951.

Noebel, David A. *The Battle for Truth: Defending the Christian Worldview in the Marketplace of Ideas*. Eugene, OR: Harvest House Publishers, 2001.

Noffsinger, Jack Ricks. *Heralds of Christ*. Nashville: Convention Press, 1966.

Noll, Mark A. *A History of Christianity in the United States and Canada*. Grand Rapids: Eerdmans, 1992.

Northey, James. *Outreach: Toward Effective Open-Air Evangelism*. London: Salvationist, 1976.

Nouwen, Henri. *Reaching Out*. Garden City, NY: Doubleday, 1975.

Nyquist, James F. and Jack Kuhatschek, *Leading Bible Discussions*. Downers Grove, IL: InterVarsity, 1985.

O'Brien, John A. *Bringing Souls to Christ: Methods of Sharing the Faith with Others*. Garden City, NY: Hanover House, 1955.

Ogden, Dave. *Transforming Discipleship: Making Disciples a Few at a Time*. Downers Grove, IL: InterVarsity, 2019.

Olford, Stephen. *The Secret of Soul-Winning*. Chicago: Moody, 1963.

Orr, J. Edwin. *Campus Aflame: A History of Evangelical Awakenings in Campus Communities,* ed. Richard Owen Roberts. Wheaton, IL: International Awakening, 1994.

Osborn, Lucy Drake. *Light on Soul-Winning*. New York: Fleming H. Revell, 1911.

Ott, Craig. *The Church on Mission: A Biblical Vision for Transformation among All People*. Grand Rapids: Baker Academic, 2019.

Outler, Albert C. *Evangelism in the Wesleyan Spirit*. Nashville: Tidings, 1971.

Overholtzer, J. Irvin. *Handbook on Evangelism*. Grand Rapids: Child Evangelism Fellowship, 1955.

Overstreet, Chris. *A Practical Guide to Evangelism—Supernaturally*. Shippensburg, PA: Destiny Image, 2011.

Owens, Daniel. *Sharing Christ When You Feel You Can't: Making It Easier to Tell Your Friends and Family about Your Faith in Christ*. Wheaton, IL: Crossway, 1997.

Ownbey, Richard L. *Evangelism in Christian Education*. Nashville: Abingdon, 1941.

Packer, J. I. *Evangelism and the Sovereignty of God*. Downers Grove, IL: InterVarsity Press, 1961.

Palau, Luis, and Timothy Robnett. *Telling the Story: Evangelism for the Next Generation*. Ventura, CA: Regal, 2006.

Palmer, Roland F. *Evangelism*. Toronto: The Canadian Churchman, 1940.

Pannell, William E. *Evangelism from the Bottom Up*. Grand Rapids: Zondervan, 1992.

Parker, J. Stephen. *Strategic Evangelism: Theory and Practice of Personal Evangelism*. Maitland, FL: Xulon Press, 2017.

Parrott, Leslie. *Building Today's Church*. Grand Rapids: Baker Books, 1973.

Parshall, Phil. *Muslim Evangelism: Contemporary Approaches to Contextualization*. Colorado Springs: Biblica, 2003.

Patterson, Robert James. *Happy Art of Catching Men*. New York: George H. Doran, 1914.

Payne, J. D. *Evangelism: A Biblical Response to Today's Questions*. Colorado Springs: Biblica, 2011.

Peace, Richard. *Witness*. Grand Rapids: Zondervan, 1971.

Peck, Jonas O. *The Revival and the Pastor*. New York: Eaton and Mains, 1894.

Perry, Lloyd Merle and John R. Strubbar, *Evangelistic Preaching*. Chicago: Moody, 1979.

Peters, George W. *A Biblical Theology of Missions*. Chicago: Moody, 1972.

_____. *Saturation Evangelism*. Grand Rapids: Zondervan, 1970.

Peters, Rob. *Evangel-Lies: Lies Christians Believe about Evangelism*. Maitland, FL: Xulon Press, 2007.

Petersen, Jim. *Evangelism as a Lifestyle: Reaching into Your World with the Gospel*. Colorado Springs: NavPress, 1980.

_____. *Evangelism for Our Generation*. Colorado Springs: NavPress, 1985.

_____. *Living Proof*. Colorado Springs: NavPress, 1989.

Peterson, Robert A. *Hell on Trial*. Phillipsburg, NJ: P & R Publishing, 1995.

Phillips, Richard D. *Jesus the Evangelist: Learning to Share the Gospel from the Book of John*. Lake Mary, FL: Reformation Trust Pub., 2007.

Phillips, Tom, and Bob Norsworthy. *The World at Your Door: Reaching International Students in Your Home, Church, and School*. Minneapolis: Bethany House, 1997.

Pickard, Stephen K. *Liberating Evangelism: Gospel, Theology & the Dynamics of Communication*. Harrisburg, PA: Trinity Press International, 1999.

Pickering, Ernest. *The Theology of Evangelism*. Clarks Summit, PA: Baptist Bible College Press, 1974.

Pierson, A. T. *Evangelistic Work in Principles and Practice*. New York: Baker and Taylor, 1887.

Piper, John. *Let the Nations Be Glad!: The Supremacy of God in Missions*. Grand Rapids: Baker, 1993.

Pippert, Rebecca Manley. *Evangelism: A Way of Life*. Downers Grove, IL: IVP Connect, 2000.

_____. *Out of the Salt Shaker and Into the World: Evangelism as a Way of Life*. Downers Grove, IL: InterVarsity, 1999.

_____. *Stay Salt: The World Has Changed: Our Message Must Not*. London: The Good Book Company, 2020.

Poe, Harry L. *The Gospel and Its Meaning: A Theology for Evangelism and Church Growth*. Grand Rapids: Zondervan Publishing House, 1996.

Pollack, John. *Billy Graham: Evangelist to the World*. Minneapolis: World Wide, 1979.

Pollard, Nick. *Evangelism Made Slightly Less Difficult: How to Interest People Who Aren't Interested*. Downers Grove: InterVarsity Press, 1997.

Porter, Douglas. *How to Develop and Use the Gift of Evangelism*. Lynchburg, VA: Church Growth, 1992.

Posterski, Don. *Why I Am Afraid to Tell You I'm a Christian: Witnessing Jesus's Way*. Downers Grove, IL: InterVarsity, 1983.

Price, Wm. Craig. *Engage: Tools for Contemporary Evangelism*. New Orleans: New Orleans Baptist Theological Seminary, 2019.

Prime, Derek. *Active Evangelism: Putting the Evangelism of Acts into Practice*. Fearn, Scotland: Christian Focus, 2003.

Prince, Matthew. *Winning through Caring: Handbook on Friendship Evangelism*. Grand Rapids: Baker, 1981.

Prior, Kenneth Francis William. *The Gospel in a Pagan Society: A Book for Modern Evangelists*. Downers Grove, IL: InterVarsity, 1975.

Pruitt, Shane, ed. *Evangelism Takes Heart*. Grapevine, TX: Southern Baptists of Texas Convention, 2017.

Queen, Matt. *Everyday Evangelism*. Fort Worth, TX: Seminary Hill Press, 2015.

_____. *Handbook for Internet Evangelism*. Alpharetta, GA: North American Mission Board, n.d.

_____. *Mobilize to Evangelize: The Pastor and Effective Congregational Evangelism*. Fort Worth, TX: Seminary Hill Press, 2018.

Queen, Matt, and Alex Sibley. *And You Will Be My Witnesses*. Fort Worth, TX: Seminary Hill Press, 2019.

Quere, Ralph W. *Evangelical Witness: The Message, Medium, Mission, and Method of Evangelism*. Minneapolis: Augsburg, 1975.

Rahn, Dave and Terry Linhart. *Evangelism Remixed: Empowering Students for Courageous and Contagious Faith*. Grand Rapids: Zondervan, 2009.

Rainer, Thom S. *Effective Evangelistic Churches: Successful Churches Reveal What Works and What Doesn't*. Nashville: Broadman & Holman Publishers, 1996.

_____. *The Unchurched Next Door: Understanding Faith Stages as Keys to Sharing Your Faith*. Grand Rapids: Zondervan, 2003.

Rainer, Thom S, ed. *Evangelism in the Twenty-First Century: The Critical Issues*. Wheaton, IL: Harold Shaw Publishers, 1989.

_____. *Surprising Insights from the Unchurched and Proven Ways to Reach Them*. Grand Rapids: Zondervan, 2001.

_____. *The Book of Church Growth: History, Theology, and Principles*. Nashville: Broadman, 1993.

Rainer, Thom S., and Chuck Lawless. *Eating the Elephant: Leading the Established Church to Growth*. New York: Pinnacle Publishers, 2003.

Rand, Ronald. *Won by One*. Ventura, CA: Regal, 1988.

Rausch, Thomas P. *Evangelizing America*. Mahwah, NJ: Paulist, 2004.

Rees, Paul S. *Evangelism and Mission*. Chicago: North Park Theological Seminary, 1966.

Reese, Martha Grace. *Unbinding the Gospel: Real Life Evangelism*. St. Louis: Chalice, 2006.

Reisinger, Ernest C. *God's Will, Man's Will, and Free Will*. Pensacola, FL: Mt. Zion Publications, n.d.

_____. *Today's Evangelism: Its Message and Methods*. Phillipsburg, NJ: P & R Publishing, 1982.

Rice, John R. *The Evangelist: His God-Given Place, Work, Importance; His Critics, His Defense, His Rewards, His Dangers*. Murfreesboro, TN: Sword of the Lord, 1968.

_____. *The Golden Path to Successful Soul Winning*. Wheaton, IL: Sword of the Lord, 1961.

Richard, Ramesh. *Preparing Evangelistic Sermons*. Grand Rapids: Baker, 2005.

Richardson, Rick. *Evangelism Outside the Box: New Ways to Help People Experience the Good News*. Downers Grove, IL: InterVarsity, 2000.

_____. *Reimagining Evangelism: Inviting Friends on a Spiritual Journey*. Downers Grove, IL: InterVarsity Press, 2006.

Riley, W. B. *The Crisis of the Church*. New York: Cooks, 1914.

_____. *The Perennial Revival: A Plea for Evangelism*. Chicago: The Winona Publishing Company, 1904.

Rinker, Rosalind. *You Can Witness with Confidence*. Grand Rapids: Zondervan, 1976.

Robertson, George W. *What Is Evangelism?* Phillipsburg, NJ: P & R, 2013.

Robinson, Bill D. *Getting beyond the Small Talk: A Step-by-Step Approach to Conversational Witnessing*. Minneapolis: World Wide, 1989.

Robinson, Darrell W. *People Sharing Jesus*. Nashville: Nelson, 1995.

_____. *Synergistic Evangelism*. Nashville: Cross Books, 2009.

_____. *Total Church Life*. Rev. Nashville: Broadman & Holman, 1993.

Rockey, Carroll J. *Fishing for Fishers of Men*. Philadelphia: United Lutheran, 1924.

Rockwell, Margaret. *Stepping Out: Sharing Christ in Everyday Circumstances*. Arrowhead Springs, CA: Here's Life, 1984.

Roesel, Charles L. *It's a God Thing: The Powerful Results of Ministry Evangelism*. Abbotsford, WI: ANEKO Press, 2014.

Root, Jerry, and Stan Guthrie. *The Sacrament of Evangelism*. Chicago: Moody Press, 2011.

Roozen, David A., and C. Kirk Hadaway, eds. *Church and Denominational Growth: What Does (and Does Not) Cause Growth or Decline*. Nashville: Abingdon Press, 1993.

Rosen, Moishe, and Ceil Rosen. *Witnessing to Jews: Practical Ways to Relate the Love of Jesus*. San Francisco: Purple Pomegranate Productions, 1998.

Rudnick, Milton L. *Speaking the Gospel through the Ages: A History of Evangelism*. St. Louis: Concordia, 1984.

Rueter, Alvin C. *Organizing for Evangelism: Planning an Effective Program for Witnessing*. Minneapolis: Augsburg, 1983.

Ruffcorn, Kevin E. *Rural Evangelism: Catching the Vision*. Minneapolis: Augsburg, 1994.

Rust, Charles Herbert. *Practical Ideas in Evangelism*. Philadelphia: Griffitt and Rowland Press, 1906.

Rutenber, Culbert C. *The Reconciling Gospel*. Nashville: Broadman Press, 1969.

Salter, Darius. *American Evangelism: Its Theology and Practice*. Grand Rapids: Baker, 1996.

Samuel, Leith. *Share Your Faith*. Grand Rapids: Baker, 1981.

Sanders, J. Oswald. *Effective Evangelism: The Divine Art of Soul-Winning*. Waynesboro, GA: STL Books, 1937.

Sanderson, Leonard. *Personal Soul-Winning*. Nashville: Convention Press, 1958.

_____. *Revival Plan Book*. Dallas: Division of Evangelism, Home Mission Board, SBC, 1960.

Sanderson, Leonard, and Ron Johnson. *Evangelism for All God's People: Approaches to Lay Ministries in the Marketplace*. Nashville: Broadman, 1990.

Sanny, Lorne. *The Art of Personal Witnessing*. Chicago: Moody, 1957.

Savelle, Jerry. *Sharing Jesus Effectively: A Handbook on Successful Soul-Winning*. Tulsa, OK: Harrison House, 1982.

Scarborough, L. R. *A Search for Souls: A Study in the Finest of the Arts—Winning the Lost to Christ*. Nashville: Sunday School Board of the Southern Baptist Convention, 1925.

_____. *Endued to Win*. Nashville: Sunday School Board of the Southern Baptist Convention, 1922.

_____. *How Jesus Won Men*. Minister's Paperback Library. Grand Rapids: Baker Book House, 1972.

_____. *With Christ after the Lost*. Edited by E. D. Head. Revised. Nashville: Broadman, 1952.

Scazzero, Peter. *The Emotionally Healthy Church: A Strategy for Discipleship That Actually Changes Lives*. Grand Rapids: Zondervan, 2003.

Schaeffer, Francis. *He Is There and He Is Not Silent*. Wheaton, IL: Tyndale House, 1972.

_____. *The God Who Is There: Speaking Historic Christianity into the Twentieth Century*. Downers Grove, IL: InterVarsity, 1968.

_____. *True Spirituality: How to Live for Jesus Moment by Moment*. Carol Stream, IL: Tyndale, 2001.

Scharpff, Paulus. *History of Evangelism*. Grand Rapids: Eerdmans, 1966.

Schmidt, Joseph. *Gospel-Centered Evangelism: A Theology and Practice of Intentional Evangelism*. Owosso, MI: One Million Tracts, 2017.

Schofield, J. Chris, ed. *The Gospel for the New Millennium*. Nashville: B & H, 2001.

Schweer, G. William. *Personal Evangelism for Today*. Nashville: Broadman Press, 1984.

Scroggins, Jimmy, and Steve Wright. *Turning Everyday Conversations into Gospel Conversations*. Nashville: Broadman & Holman, 2016.

Seiver, Randy. *Authentic Evangelism and Its Counterfeit*. Enumclaw, WA: New Wine Press, 2016.

Sellers, Ernest O. *Personal Evangelism: Studies in Individual Efforts to Lead Souls into Right Relations to Christ*. Nashville: Sunday School Board of the Southern Baptist Convention, 1923.

Sellers, James Earl. *The Outsider and the Word of God: A Study in Christian Communication*. New York: Abingdon, 1961.

Shadrach, Steve. *The Fuel and the Flame: 10 Keys to Ignite Your College Campus for Jesus Christ*. Conway, AR: The BodyBuilders, 2003.

Sheridan, Wilbur Fletcher. *The Sunday-Night Service: A Study in Continuous Evangelism*. Cincinnati, OH: Jennings and Graham, 1908.

Sherrod, Paul. *Successful Soul Winning: Proven Ideas to Challenge Every Christian to Be a Personal Worker*. Lubbock, TX: P. Sherrod, 1974.

Shibley, David. *A Force in the Earth: The Charismatic Renewal and World Evangelism*. Altamonte Springs, FL: Creation House, 1989.

Shipman, Mike. *Any 3: Anyone, Anywhere, Any Time*. Monument, CO: WIGTake Resources, 2013.

Shoemaker, Helen Smith. *Prayer and Evangelism*. Waco, TX: Word Books, 1974.

Shoemaker, Samuel. *The Conversion of the Church*. New York: Revell, 1932.

————. *With the Holy Spirit and with Fire*. New York: Harper & Brothers, 1960.

Short, Roy H. *Evangelism through the Local Church: Its Motivation and Practice*. Nashville: Abingdon, 1956.

Sibley, Alex, ed. *In Praise of a God Who Saves: 110 Stories of Everyday Evangelism*. Fort Worth, TX: Seminary Hill Press, 2018.

Sider, Ronald J. *Evangelism, Salvation and Social Justice*. Bramcote, UK: Grove, 1977.

Silvoso, Ed. *Prayer Evangelism*. Ventura, CA: Regal, 2000.

Simpson, Michael L. *Permission Evangelism: When to Talk, When to Walk*. Colorado Springs: NexGen, 2003.

Sisemore, Timothy A. *Finding God While Facing Death*. Ross-shire, Scotland: Christian Focus, 2017.

Sisson, Richard. *Evangelism Encounter*. Wheaton, IL: Victor Books, 1988.

————. *Training for Evangelism*. Chicago: Moody, 1979.

Sjogren, Steve. *Conspiracy of Kindness: A Refreshing New Approach to Sharing the Love of Jesus with Others*. Ann Arbor, MI: Servant Publications, 1993.

————. *Servant Warfare: How Kindness Conquers Spiritual Darkness*. Ann Arbor, MI: Servant, 1996.

Sjogren, Steve, Dave Ping, and Doug Pollock. *Irresistible Evangelism: Natural Ways to Open Others to Jesus*. Loveland, CO: Group, 2004.

Smallman, Stephen E. *Spiritual Birthline: Understanding How We Experience the New Birth*. Wheaton, IL: Crossway, 2006.

Smith, Bailey E. *Real Evangelism*. Nashville: Word Publishing, 1999.

Smith, Glenn C., ed. *Evangelizing Adults*. Washington, DC: Paulist National Catholic Evangelization Association, 1985.

Smith, Oswald J. *The New Evangelism*. Toronto: The People's Church, 1932.

_____. *The Passion for Souls*. London: Marshall, Morgan and Scott, 1965.

_____. *The Revival We Need*. London: Marshall, Morgan and Scott, 1940.

Smith, Ron. *Everyday Evangelism*. Bromley, England: Send the Light Trust, n.d.

Smith, Sean. *Prophetic Evangelism: Empowering a Generation to Seize Their Day*. Shippensburg, PA: Destiny Image, 2005.

Snook, Susan Brown. *Acts to Action: The New Testament's Guide to Evangelism and Mission*. Cincinnati: Forward Movement, 2018.

Southard, Samuel. *Pastoral Evangelism*. Nashville: Broadman, 1962.

Speed, Jon. *Evangelism in the New Testament: A Plea for Biblically Relevant Evangelism*. Owosso, MI: One Million Tracts, 2009.

Speer, Robert E. *The Church and Missions*. New York: George H. Doran, 1926.

Speidel, Royal. *Evangelism in the Small Membership Church*. Nashville: Abingdon, 2007.

Spencer, Ichabod S. *A Pastor's Sketches—Two Volumes in One: Conversations with Anxious Inquirers Respecting the Way of Salvation*. Scotts Valley, CA: CreateSpace Independent Publishing Platform, 2010.

Spencer, James R. *Hard Case Witnessing*. Tarrytown, NY: Chosen Books, 1991.

Spurgeon, C. H. *Advice for Seekers*. Edinburgh: Banner of Truth Trust, 2016.

_____. *The Soul Winner: How to Lead Sinners to the Savior*. Grand Rapids: William B. Eerdmans Publishing Company, 1963.

Stanfield, Vernon L. *Effective Evangelistic Preaching*. Grand Rapids: Baker Book House, 1968.

Starkes, M. Thomas. *Interfaith Witness*. Memphis: Brotherhood Commission of the SBC, 1971.

Stebbins, Tom. *Evangelism by the Book*. Camp Hill, PA: Christian, 1991.

Steitz, Walter. "The Proper Use of Revelation 3:20 in Evangelism." ThM thesis, Dallas Theological Seminary, 1983.

Steward, George, and Henry B. Wright. *Personal Evangelism among Students*. New York: Association Press, 1920.

Stewart, Donald Gordon. *Christian Education and Evangelism*. Philadelphia: Westminster Press, 1963.

Stewart, James A. *Evangelism*. Salem, OH: Schmul, 1981.

Stewart, James S. *A Faith to Proclaim*. New York: Scribner, 1953.

Stier, Greg. *Dare 2 Share: A Field Guide to Sharing Your Faith*. Colorado Springs: Focus on the Family, 2006.

_____. *Outbreak! Creating a Contagious Youth Ministry through Viral Evangelism*. Chicago: Moody, 2002.

Stiles, J. Mack. *Evangelism: How the Whole Church Speaks of Jesus*. Wheaton, IL: Crossway, 2014.

_____. *Marks of the Messenger: Knowing, Living and Speaking the Gospel*. Downers Grove, IL: IVP, 2010.

_____. *Speaking of Jesus: How to Tell Your Friends the Best News Ever*. Downers Grove, IL: IVP, 1995.

Stone, Bryan. *Evangelism after Christendom: The Theology and Practice of Christian Witness*. Grand Rapids: Brazos Press, 2007.

_____. *Evangelism after Pluralism: The Ethics of Christian Witness*. Grand Rapids: Baker, 2018.

Stone, John Timothy. *Recruiting for Christ: Hand to Hand Methods with Men*. New York: Revell, 1910.

_____. *Winning Men: Studies in Soul-Winning*. New York: Revell, 1946.

Stott, John R. W. *Between Two Worlds*. Grand Rapids: Eerdmans, 2017.

_____. *Evangelism: Why and How*. London: InterVarsity, 1962.

_____. *Fundamentalism and Evangelism*. Grand Rapids: Eerdmans, 1959.

_____. *Motives and Methods in Evangelism*. London: InterVarsity, 1963.

_____. *Our Guilty Silence: The Church, the Gospel and the World*. London: Hodder and Stoughton, 1967.

Stott, John R. W., ed. *Christian Mission in the Modern World*. Downers Grove, IL: InterVarsity, 1975.

Strachan, R. Kenneth. *The Inescapable Calling*. Grand Rapids: Eerdmans, 1968.

Streett, R. Alan. *The Effective Invitation: A Practical Guide for the Pastor*. Grand Rapids: Kregel, 1995.

Strobel, Lee. *Inside the Mind of the Unchurched Harry & Mary*. Grand Rapids: Zondervan, 1993.

_____. *The Case for Christ*. Grand Rapids: Zondervan, 2016.

_____. *The Case for Faith*. Grand Rapids: Zondervan, 2000.

_____. and Mark Mittelberg. *The Unexpected Adventure: Taking Everyday Risks to Talk with People about Jesus*. Grand Rapids: Zondervan, 2009.

Swearingen, Thomas E., and Mary G. Swearingen. *Heeding the Spirit in Evangelism*. Birmingham, AL: Keystone, 1965.

Sweazey, George E. *Effective Evangelism: The Greatest Work in the World*. New York: Harper & Brothers, 1953.

_____. *The Church as Evangelist*. New York: Harper & Row, 1978.

Sweet, William Warren. *Revivalism in America: Its Origin, Growth, and Decline*. Nashville: Abingdon, 1944.

Sweeting, George. *The No-Guilt Guide to Witnessing: How to Be Faithful in Sharing Christ*. Wheaton, IL: Victor Books, 1991.

Tabb, Mark. *Mission to Oz: Reaching Postmoderns without Losing Your Way*. Chicago: Moody, 2004.

Target, George W. *Tell It the Way It Is: A Primer for Christian Communicators*. London: Lutterworth, 1970.

Taylor, Frederick Eugene. *The Evangelistic Church*. Philadelphia: Judson, 1927.

Taylor, Mendell. *Exploring Evangelism: History, Methods, Theology*. Kansas City, MO: Beacon Hill, 1964.

Taylor, Vincent. *Doctrine and Evangelism*. London: Epworth Press, 1953.

Teasdale, Mark R. *Evangelism for Non-Evangelists: Sharing the Gospel Authentically*. Downers Grove, IL: IVP Academic, 2016.

Templeton, Charles B. *Evangelism for Tomorrow*. New York: Harper, 1957.

Terry, John Mark. *Church Evangelism: Creating a Culture for Growth in Your Congregation*. Nashville: Broadman & Holman, 1997.

———. *Evangelism: A Concise History*. Nashville: Broadman & Holman Publishers, 1994.

Thiessen, Elmer John. *The Ethics of Evangelism: A Philosophical Defense of Proselytizing and Persuasion*. Downers Grove, IL: IVP Academic, 2011.

Thomas, Lee E. *Praying Effectively for the Lost*. Milford, OH: John the Baptist Printing Ministry, 2003.

Thompson, W. Oscar. *Concentric Circles of Concern: From Self to Others through Lifestyle Evangelism*. Nashville: Broadman & Holman Publishers, 1981.

Thwing, Charles Franklin. *The Working Church*. New York: Baker and Taylor, 1888.

Tice, Rico. *Honest Evangelism: How to Talk about Jesus Even When It's Tough*. Croydon: The Good Book Company, 2015.

Tippett, Alan Richard. *Church Growth and the Word of God*. Grand Rapids: Eerdmans, 1970.

Torrey, Reuben A. *How to Bring Men to Christ*. Minneapolis: Bethany, 1977.

———. *Individual Soulwinning*. Los Angeles: Biola, 1917.

———. *The Wondrous Joy of Soul Winning*. Los Angeles: Biola, n.d.

———. *How to Work for Christ: A Compendium of Effective Methods*. New York: Revell, 1901.

Torrey, Reuben A., ed. *How to Promote and Conduct a Successful Revival*. Chicago: Revell, 1901.

Towns, Elmer L. *Evangelism and Church Growth*. Ventura, CA: Regal Books, 1995.

———. *Your Ministry of Evangelism: A Guide for Church Volunteers*. Calumet City, IL: Evangelical Training Association, 2014.

Traeger, Sebastian, and Greg Gilbert. *The Gospel at Work: How Working for King Jesus Gives Purpose and Meaning to Our Jobs*. Grand Rapids: Zondervan, 2013.

Trimble, Henry Burton. *To Every Creature*. Nashville: Cokesbury, 1939.

Trotman, Dawson. *Born to Reproduce*. Colorado Springs: NavPress, 1984.

Truett, George W. *A Quest for Souls*. New York: Doran, 1917.

Trumbull, Charles Gallaudet. *What Is the Gospel? Straightforward Talks on Evangelism*. Minneapolis: The Harrison Service, 1944.

———. *Taking Men Alive: Studies in the Principles and Practise of Individual Soul-Winning*. New York: Association Press, 1907.

Trumbull, Henry Clay. *Individual Work for Individuals: A Record of Personal Experiences and Convictions*. New York: The International Committee of the Young Men's Christian Association, 1901.

Tull, Nelson F. *Effective Christian Witnessing*. Memphis: Brotherhood Commission of the SBC, 1971.

Turnbull, Michael. *Parish Evangelism: A Practical Resource Book for the Local Church.* London: Mowbrays, 1980.

Turnbull, Ralph G., ed. *Evangelism Now.* Grand Rapids: Baker, 1972.

Turner, Harvey. *Friend of Sinners: An Approach to Evangelism.* Houston: Lucid Books, 2016.

Tuttle, Robert, Jr. *Someone Out There Needs Me: A Practical Guide to Relational Evangelism.* Grand Rapids: Zondervan, 1983.

_____. *The Story of Evangelism: A History of the Witness to the Gospel.* Nashville: Abingdon, 2006.

Vanderstelt, Jeff. *Gospel Fluency: Speaking the Truths of Jesus into the Everyday Stuff of Life.* Wheaton: Crossway, 2017.

Van Houten, Mark. *Profane Evangelism: Taking the Gospel into the "Unholy Places."* Grand Rapids: Zondervan, 1989.

Wagner, C. Peter. *Church Growth and the Whole Gospel: A Biblical Mandate.* San Francisco: Harper & Row, Publishers, 1981.

_____. *Church Planting for a Greater Harvest.* Ventura, CA: Regal, 1990.

Walker, Alan. *The New Evangelism.* Nashville: Abingdon, 1975.

_____. *The Whole Gospel for the Whole World.* New York: Abingdon, 1957.

Wallis, Jim. *The Call to Conversion: Why Faith Is Always Personal but Never Private.* San Francisco: HarperCollins Publishers, 2005.

Ward, Mark, Sr. *The Word Works: 151 Amazing Stories of Men and Women Saved through Gospel Literature.* Greenville, SC: Ambassador Emerald Int'l, 2002.

Warneck, Gustav. *Outline of the History of Protestant Missions.* Edinburgh: James Gernmell, 1994).

Warren, Max. *I Believe in the Great Commission.* Grand Rapids: Eerdmans, 1976.

_____. *Interpreters: A Study in Contemporary Evangelism.* London: Highway Press, 1936.

Warren, Rick. *The Purpose Driven Church: Growing without Compromising Your Message and Mission.* Grand Rapids: Zondervan Publishing House, 1995.

Washburn, A. V. *Outreach for the Unreached.* Nashville: Convention Press, 1960.

Washburn, Alphonson. *Reach Out to People: A People-to-People Emphasis.* Nashville: Convention Press, 1974.

Washer, Paul. *The Gospel Call and True Conversion.* Grand Rapids: Reformation Heritage Books, 2013.

_____. *The Gospel's Power and Message.* Recovering the Gospel. Grand Rapids: Reformation Heritage Books, 2012.

Water, Mark. *Sharing Your Faith Made Easy.* Grand Rapids: Hendricksen, 2000.

Watson, David. *I Believe in Evangelism.* Grand Rapids: Eerdmans, 1977.

Webber, Robert. *Ancient-Future Church: Making Your Church a Faith-Forming Community.* Grand Rapids: Baker, 2003.

_____. *Liturgical Evangelism.* Harrisburg, PA: Morehouse Publishing, 1992.

Weber, Jaroy. *Winning America to Christ.* Nashville: Broadman, 1975.

Webster, Douglas. *What Is Evangelism?* London: Highway Press, 1961.

Weisberger, Bernard A. *They Gathered at the River: The Story of the Great Revivalists and Their Impact upon Religion in America*. Boston: Little, Brown, 1958.

Welch, Bobby. *Evangelism through Sunday School: A Journey of Faith*. Nashville: LifeWay, 1997.

Wells, David F. *God the Evangelist: How the Holy Spirit Works to Bring Men to Christ*. Grand Rapids: Eerdmans, 1987.

_____. *Turning to God: Reclaiming Christian Conversion as Unique, Necessary, and Supernatural*. Grand Rapids: Baker Books, 2012.

Wesley, John. *The Journal of the Rev. John Wesley, A.M.*, ed. Percy Livingstone Parker, 4 vols. London: J. Kershaw, 1827.

White, F. C. *Evangelism Today*. London: Marshall, Morgan and Scott, 1939.

White, James E. *Opening the Front Door*. Nashville: Convention Press, 1992.

White, Robert A. *How to Win a Soul*. Nashville: Southern Publication Association, 1971.

Whitefield, George. *The Journal of George Whitefield*. London: W. Strahan, 1740.

Whitesell, Faris D. *Basic New Testament Evangelism*. Grand Rapids: Zondervan, 1949.

_____. *Evangelistic Preaching and the Old Testament*. Chicago: Moody Press, 1947.

_____. *Sixty-Five Ways to Give Evangelistic Invitations*. Grand Rapids: Zondervan, 1945.

Whitney, Donald S. *How Can I Be Sure I'm a Christian?* Colorado Springs: NavPress, 1994.

_____. *Spiritual Disciplines for the Christian Life*. Colorado Springs: NavPress, 1991.

Wilder, Jack B. *Biblical Blueprints for Building Witnessing Churches*. Tigerville, SC: Jewel, 1969.

Wiles, Jerry. *How to Win Others to Christ: Your Personal, Practical Guide to Evangelism*. Nashville: Thomas Nelson, 1992.

Wilkins, Scott G. *REACH: A Team Approach to Evangelism and Assimilation*. Grand Rapids: Baker, 2005.

Williams, Ethel Hudson. *Witnessing for Christ*. Nashville: Sunday School Board of the Southern Baptist Convention, 1936.

Wilson, Jim. *Weapons and Tactics: A Handbook on Personal Evangelism*. Moscow, ID: Canon Press, 2012.

Wimber, John. *Power Evangelism*. San Francisco: Harper & Row, 1986.

Winter, Ralph D., and Steven C. Hawthorne, eds. *Perspectives on the World Christian Movement: A Reader*. Pasadena, CA: William Carey Library, 1981.

Wirt, Sherwood, ed. *Evangelism: The Next Ten Years*. Waco, TX: Word, 1978.

Wood, A. Skevington. *Evangelism: Its Theology and Practice*. Grand Rapids: Zondervan, 1966.

Wood, Eernest J. *A Church Fulfilling Its Mission through Proclamation and Witness*. Nashville: SBC, 1964.

Wood, Frederick P. *Studies in Soul-Winning*. London: Marshall Brothers, National Young Life Campaign, 1934.

Wood, H. Wellington. *Winning Men One By One*. Philadelphia: S. S. Times Co., 1908.

Wood, Verda. *Ringing Door Bells: The Art of Visiting*. Nashville: Baptist Sunday School Board, 1946.

Woodson, Leslie. *Evangelism for Today's Church*. Grand Rapids: Zondervan, 1973.

Woolsey, Raymond H. *Evangelism Handbook*. Washington, DC: Review and Herald, 1972.

Workman, Herbert Brook. *Persecution in the Early Church*. London: Oxford University Press, 1980.

Wright, Linda Raney. *Christianity's Crisis in Evangelism: Going Where the People Are*. Portland, OR: Multnomah, 2000.

Yamamori, Tetsuanao. *God's New Envoys: A Bold Strategy for Penetrating "Closed Countries."* Portland, OR: Multnomah, 1987.

Yang, Laura. *Everyday Evangelism: Practical Tips to Use Today*. Bloomington, IN: WestBow Press, 2016.

Yoder, Gideon. *The Nurture and Evangelism of Children*. Scottdale, PA: Herald Press, 1959.

Zahniser, Charles Reed. *Case Work Evangelism: Studies in the Art of Christian Personal Work*. New York: Revell, 1927.

Zwemer, Samuel. *Evangelism Today: Message Not Method*. London: Revell, 1944.

INDEX